an odd boy

Doc Togden

Aro Books WORLDWIDE

2012

Aro Books WORLDWIDE
PO Box 111, Aro Khalding Tsang,
5 Court Close, Cardiff,
CF14 1JR, Wales, UK

First Edition 2012

ISBN: 978-1-898185-24-6 (paperback)

ISBN: 978-1-898185-25-3 (hardback)

ISBN: 978-1-898185-26-0 (ePub)

http://aro-books-worldwide.org/

odd dedications

*To my wife Caroline Togden; to my son Robert E Lee Togden and my
daughter Ræchel Renate Tresise Togden;
to my mother Renate, father Jesse, and brother Græham.*

To the lads: Steve Bruce; Ron Larkin; Jack Hackman.

*Also to John and Pauline Trevelyan; Rodney Stillwell Love;
Clive and Betty Bruce; Ernest Preece; Michael and Sandra Blenkinsopp;
John Morris; Dereck and Susan Crowe; and all my marvellous mentors.*

*To all my comrades-in-arms and guitars; to the heroines of Art who have
flittered—like fairies or valkyries—through my life, to show me the shine
on the passing moment.*

Contents

odd acknowledgements

Everlasting thanks to my dear and wonderful wife Caroline for unending patience with an *odd husband* who lived in a parallel reality whilst writing *an odd boy*. She joined me on *planet odd boy* on many evenings – reading chapters, in order that I could hear *the voice* in which the book was speaking. I needed to make sure *the voice* was congruous with the *texture of memory*. She let me know when I'd given *too much information* about guitar technicalities and Blues history.

The accuracy of date references vis-à-vis music in *an odd boy* are all due to gZa'tsal – the incomparable cowgirl and heroine who researched them. She ironed out many anomalies with regard to where I was and when. This was not easy – because I had contradictory memories of where and when I might have been. That however, was her smallest contribution. The major work she undertook was an exceptional feat of architectural editing. She took a morass of riotously random information and turned it inside out. The original 170,000 word essay on the Arts—on which this book was based—was an idiosyncratic stream-of-consciousness informational harangue. It was peppered with hilarity, bizarre incidents, haphazard anecdotes, and whimsical personal accounts – and few would have had the patience to read it. gZa'tsal took this misbegotten mangrove of miscellanies and defined its narrative skeleton. She connected dem bones, dem dry bones and provided copious advice as to how the viscera could be appended.

The 'Lady of Literary Creation' prompted her ersatz Ezekiel as to where the various vital organs should be placed – and ensured that veins and arteries of dialogue connected them. Finally she made sure that the nervous system—my ideas about Art—developed in such a way as to enable the *corpus literati* to move as a living entity. The result is far more handsome than Frankenstein's monster – and far more affable. A person could well be delighted to meet this unlikely assemblage on a dark night, or in a Blues Club in Montana . . . . Thanks also to Missin' Dixie Dé-zér—the other incomparable cowgirl and heroine—who contributed vastly to the musical references – as well as teaching me some mighty fine bass riffs. She and gZa'tsal are now majorly involved in producing the Savage Cabbage album that never was.

Without gZa'tsal's assistance *an odd boy* would have been a less frequented ward of Bedlam. She persistently questioned my extravagantly oblique references and interminable asides. She thus enabled me to breathe life into the vague personalities who populate my tale. She encouraged me to increase the dialogue and to deepen its resonance with those I remembered. My keyboard thus became a Ouija board – summoning up a gaggle of apparitions, all talking turkey. Streams of conversation re-emerged—out of nowhere—and for a while I lived partially within *that other time*.

Thanks to Big Mamma Métsal for her assiduous proofreading—many valuable suggestions—and for being an exemplary Blues vocal student. One day she's likely to be second only to Bessie Smith. Thanks also to Nor'dzin and 'ö-Dzin for final proofing of the text and for pushing this extravaganza forward into the domain of published reality.

Thanks to Don Young of NATIONAL RESOPHONIC Guitars for friendship, enthusiasm, lively correspondence concerning subjects too wide to enumerate, wonderful instruments, and for building me the 12 string resophonic guitars about which I previously only dreamt.

Thanks to Lindsay Berry née Goolding—my old school friend— who graciously provided suggestions, valuable insights into the historical *odd boy*, and information on events and dates pertaining to Netherfield School. She pressed me for the further chapters and provided frequent encouragement. To Elaine Pierce for kindly availing me of thirty odd songs I'd written between 1966 and 1972. I'd not seen these songs since October 1972 – when I discarded my own copies.

Lastly—and by no means *leastly*—thanks to: Græham and Jill Smith for hospitality, humanity and hilarity in times of adversity; Melissa Troupe for accomplishing the almost impossible task of teaching me to canter; Linda Donegan for antiquarian Western-wear; Craig Donegan for profound TELECASTER advice and many a jam session; Richard—Mad Dog—Simon for backing harp on many past and future vocals; Mad Og—*the Trappist*—Sinister Minister of Tympani, for percussion, and introducing me to the wonders of wah-wah bagpipes; Bronco Sally Yon supreme couturier and tailor-in-chief of my burgeoning personal wardrobe; Big Mamma Yeshé for unwithheld enthusiasm for my 'Speaking with Ravens' paintings; Small Mamma A'dze for her sheer vocal flair on many a night at the Blues Barn; Shoe-Shine Shardröl for tinkling the ivories; to Rig'dzin Dorje and David Chapman for reading the entire text of *an odd boy* aloud on several occasions; to 'Killer' Carl Grundberg and Ngakma Zér-mé, and finally to Seng-gé Dorje 'the Cholesterol Kid' for guitar enthusiasm.

I've been a poet and text writer – so narrative and dialogue were previously not my forté. I've come to love the métier however – and can only wonder what I shall do once *an odd boy* has been put to bed. I can hardly write another such book – unless I tackle some other part of my life. My Life as a Camel Driver in the Gobi Desert? A Street Sweeper in Ely Tells All? Fear and Loathing in Littlehampton? Maybe not. Maybe I might venture into the Himalayas . . . who can tell.

expressionism: *another odd preface*

The preface to *volume one* of *an odd boy* opened thus 'These are the facts: there *are* no facts.' The only certainty we have, is in the moment.

Yes . . . we all have memories. Some even have plans. Sometimes plans have wonderful fins, like those 1950s Chevrolet Impalas that were rare and wonderful sightings in 1960s England. But then . . . you drive your Chevy to the levy and the levy's dry. That's always on the cards. It's happened to me from time to time – but in general I've fired up the engine again and taken off for another levy – or another crossroads to wait for whatever . . . And now I'm one of those *good old boys* – but I rarely touch whiskey or rye. Calvados and Armagnac are the preference of my delighted dotage.

When I say that *all we have is the moment,* I'm no nihilist. I'm no rosy-spectacled buffoon either. There are certainly lessons to be learnt from life – but no one put them there, either for our convenience or inconvenience. Life happens and we happen into it like the whale that's randomly called into being above planet Magrathea.[1] Life has always suggested hope to me – because I've been lucky. I'm still lucky. I've always been lucky – but as Thomas Jefferson said '*I've always found that the harder I work – the more luck I have.*' I had all the hope there ever was at the age of 16—where this volume begins—and a healthy measure of luck. The coital union of hope and luck was a mighty leviathan shining like the Mississippi in full spate.

---

1 ' . . . *against all probability a sperm whale had suddenly been called into existence several miles above the surface of an alien planet.*' Douglas Adams—The Hitchhiker's Guide to the Galaxy—1978

Volume one of *an odd boy* contains *part one—the crossroads—*which is the first part of a six part mémoire. The *crossroads* is a recurring theme in my life – and at any given moment, I still find myself standing there. I'd stood at the crossroads when I was 12 – waiting for Papa Legba [2] with a plastic guitar under my arm. A lunatic idea for a 12 year old English lad – especially as I'd ridden there naked on a rather nasty bicycle with gears that slipped. Mr Love however, had told me about Legba and that meeting him would ensure you'd be as good a Bluesman as Robert Johnson. There was no choice as far as I could see. I met Mr Love when I was 7—shortly after losing Alice, the young love of my life—and he'd introduced me to Blues: real Black, American, Blues. Mr Love was a fine gentleman—while he lasted—but shell-shock took him to the lunatic asylum for his final days. Our continued association was deemed 'out of the question.' In any case Blues was a 'depraved row' in my father's view – he would have said 'the devil's music' but he didn't know that term. My father had all kinds of ideas that were extremely unwelcome to *an odd boy*.

School rolled by and at the age of 8 I met the lad who'd be on the brink of rivalling Jack Bruce by the end of Volume Two. At 14 I met Anelie Mandelbaum a 22 year old Swiss au pair girl who precipitated me into the adult world in a way that changed my life entirely – and in a mere 2 years, parental authority could no longer contain me.

---

2 Papa Legba is the name of *the one who comes to the crossroads* and who will accept your 'soul' in payment for unprecedented skills on the musical instrument of your choice. Legba is identified in societal Christian terms as 'the Devil' – but Legba actually emanates from West Africa. Legba is a contraction of Alegbara. Legba is both a trickster and an inspiration of music and language. He makes claims on the aspirant other than the Christian sense of the 'soul'.

At the same time, I met Ron Larkin. As far as I'm concerned—albeit tongue-in-cheek—he was the incarnation of Bach, Boccherini, Buddy Guy, and BB King; all rolled into one. We formed a Blues band with Jack Hackman – a drummer who started out as our weak point. He worked like the devil however —as anyone can—and started to look as if he had real potential.

After *a* 16 *year life time* I finally faced it out with my overbearing father – and was suddenly free to grow my hair, wear what I liked, and keep what hours I pleased. In the final chapter of *volume one* our Blues band is named *Savage Cabbage*, I'm named *Farquhar Arbuthnot*, and we play our first gig. Blues is our religion – and we're set to scale the heights.

An odd boy is a collage of recollections – an assemblage of images woven from memories of a time when the Arts permeated society and ran amok as street-culture. It *could* be called a *roman à thèse* [3] because I have an idea to present. *Everyone is an innate Artist.* It *could* also be called a *roman à clef* [4] although there's no scandal to obfuscate. Maybe it *should* be called a *roman à bass clef* as I played 2nd bass [5] for Savage Cabbage.

Like any story – this narrative is populated by personalities: the good, the bad, and the ugly – the wonderful, woesome, and weird. To be real, I have to *tell it as it was* – but I can't *tell it as it was for others*. We're all alternately heroes and villains for each other in any case – and what *I* was is anyone's guess.

---

3 Literally 'novel with a thesis' – a novel expounding a solution to a political, moral, or philosophical problem.
4 Literally 'novel with a key' – a biography or autobiography disguised as a novel, i.e. in which actual people or events appear under disguise.
5 Savage Cabbage was a two bass band. Steve Bruce on lead bass and the author on rhythm or backing bass.

' . . . for what do we live but to make sport for our neighbours and laugh at them in our turn.'
Jane Austen—Pride and Prejudice—1813

I don't choose to mock or vilify others. I'd rather limit myself to eulogies – but that would fail even as a fairy tale. My take on the past is romantic and highly subjective – because I believe that history is a story that can serve a noble purpose. My hope is that this account of my life—between August '68 and September '70—will inspire the idea that the Arts are open to everyone. The villains I describe are therefore necessary in terms of providing the friction which is essential for a creative life. There's always blood, sweat, and tears—in one way or another—and it's all the better if you can find humour in it. Faced with my villains, I've chosen to change personal names in order to protect the innocent and guilty alike. Where relentlessly damning statements couldn't be avoided, settings and events have been obfuscated.

Volume two of *an odd boy* contains *part two* and *part three* of the six part mémoire. *Part two—hellhound on my trail*—is the story of a romance with a ginger-haired heroine of the Arts – and, the story of the Blues band Savage Cabbage. *Part three—living on solid air*—is the story of one Summer out-of-time – a period of charismatic chaos in which the future persistently changes shape. The only constant feature is music and the quest to become what I thought I might be. The climax was the ovation I received at the Farnham Blues Festival. The zenith was meeting with the musical genius John Martyn.

an odd boy

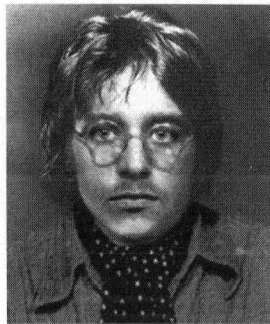

part two

september 1968 – may 1970

chapters one – ten: hellhound on my trail

"*Blues . . . John Mayall . . . he was about the first that I can think that really brought it out. But then I started hearing many others. When—*Cream—*came, that was—it.*"
BB King on the British Blues Boom, from an interview in 'Red, White and Blues'
a film by Mike Figgis in the Martin Scorsese series on Blues, 2003

"*There's something utterly primal and at the same time modern about what he did . . . He's playing Blues without counting to four. I think Wolf was counting to two . . . It's African. It's two beats; it's not four . . . A lot of people who belittle Wolf and other people who play extended bar patterns really are less sophisticated than the people they're putting down. What Wolf was doing is what Ornette Coleman spent his life looking for: freedom, erasing the bar lines.*"
Quote from Jim Dickinson concerning Howlin' Wolf, from Moanin' at Midnight—The Life and
Times of Howlin' Wolf—James Segrest and Mark Hoffman—chapter 6—I'm the Wolf—
page 97—2004

"Howlin' Wolf's 'Smokestack Lightin' is an amazing performance, a piece of pure Jazz Gothic, creating with no more properties than an echo chamber and his own remarkable voice an impression of Coleridge's demon lover wailing for his woman."

Philip Arthur Larkin [1922 – 1985], English poet—All What Jazz, a Record Diary—
Faber & Faber—1985

*"Ain't got no chance Blind Dog. You done—sold—your—soul.
You goin'—down—all—the way—down.
Hell hound's on your trail—boy—hell hound's on your trail."*

Scratch's henchman to the character Willie Brown in Crossroads—1986 [1]

---

1 In the movie 'Crossroads,' Legba's new name is 'Scratch.' The Willie Browne in the movie—although a wonderful character—bears little resemblance to the real Willie Browne who died many years earlier and was not a harp player. Blues players call a harmonica a harp.

1

september 1968 – november 1968

easy rider

Said James "In my opinion, there's nothing in this world, beats a '52 Vincent and a red-headed girl."
Richard Thompson—1952 Vincent Black Lightning—Rumour and Sigh—1996

It was no real answer to my situation – but my decision to buy a 500cc fixed-frame BSA motorcycle took my mind off the apparent dearth of artistically orientated romantic possibilities in Farnham. Those young ladies who could discuss the Arts had parents who hated me on sight. Those whose parents didn't want to call the police as soon as they saw me seemed to think that culture was the province of the elderly and that Frank Zappa and Captain Beefheart were deranged monsters whose criminally insane music was likely to give them nightmares.

So . . . the romance of the open road   and transforming my newly acquired BSA into a chopper—absorbed most of my attention; when I wasn't immersed in practice sessions with Savage Cabbage.[1] I'd passed my motorcycle test—back in July —on a 200cc Triumph and now, the sky was the limit.

---

1 The Savage Cabbage Blues Band was composed of Ron Larkin *(lead guitar)*; Steve Bruce *(bass)*; Jack Hackman *(percussion)* and Vic Simmerson aka Farquhar Arbuthnot *(vocals and harp)*. The formation of the band is described in *Volume I* of '*an odd boy*'.

Ape-hangers [2] and swept up exhausts gleamed at me. I'd struck lucky. I'd found a motorcycle on which someone had already begun the chopping process. The extended forks and Frisco pegs were already in place. Soon I'd be riding motorised Art into the sunset. I'd be free to arrive in grand style—anywhere—and see what happened.

Steve, Ron, and Jack all stared with undisguised envy when I rolled up. *"Thor just arrived"* Steve quipped as I strode into Weyflood village hall.

"Yeah – but—you—*got the hammer"* I replied. Steve grinned. He'd been playing the bass line to Cream's 'Sunshine of Your Love' as a warm-up exercise and I'd heard him even over the dull thunder of the engine as I pulled up. The next gig was on the horizon and there'd be more space in the transit without me. I'd be riding my chopper unless it was raining. The session went well. Ron was as brilliant as ever – and even had a kind word to offer about Jack's drumming. We worked hard and took the afternoon out – planning to meet up again in the evening.

Free for the afternoon, I sat in the garden removing the last traces of dirt from the front wheel. My mother sought my attention. She'd been sitting quietly with her cup of tea observing me at my obsessive toil. *"Veector . . . "* she enquired, quite out of the blue *" . . . I have been vondering . . . vott . . . attracts you to your girl-friends? I have met wiz fat vons, sin vons, short vons, tall vons—every shape—and every colour of hair . . . "* She'd seen a string of girlfriends after Anelie [3] left for Switzerland. They'd come and gone rapidly.

---

2 High-rise handlebars.
3 Anelie Mandelbaum was the 22 year old Swiss au pair girl with whom the author has a relationship at the age of 14 to 15. See chapter 9 of *Volume I* of '*an odd boy*'.

My mother was curious as to the briefness of my romantic associations.

"*They do all have—something—in common . . .* " I replied after a deliberate pause " *. . . they're all . . . female.*"

My mother laughed and shook her head in mock exasperation.

"*And . . .* " I continued "*I'd hoped to talk with each of them . . . in turn . . . about Art . . . about music, poetry, and painting.*"

"*Ja . . .* " my mother sighed " *. . . and did zey like ziss?*"

"*Well . . . they'd talk about it a little in the beginning – but then . . . in the end they seemed to lose interest. I suppose . . . I lost interest as well when they had nothing to say about anything.*"

I've never understood what attracted *anyone* to *anyone* – unless it was *the minds* of those to whom they were attracted. It was the *ideas of which ladies were possessed* that intrigued me – rather than what was fashionably alluring about them. There's always a *certain look* that's fashionable in any given period of time – and a *certain body type*. If you happen to be Rubenesque in a society that's decided emaciation is *the ideal* – you might perceive yourself as romantically doomed. The situation would be equally as ridiculous if it were reversed. Slaves of fashion like the style of romantic partner demanded by the legislature of the current trend. There are therefore relatively few people who admire who *they* admire – because *they* themselves admire them.

I didn't say any of this to my mother—I was weird enough as it was—but I went on to tell her "*I need to be able to talk with ladies . . . they need to be able to be subtle, witty, and ironic. I like to talk about . . . the nature of reality . . . and perception.*"

My mother nodded knowingly "*I hope you vill find such a girlfriend. I sink you have too high expectations. Maybe—Veector—some-von kind and generous vould develop such interests.*"

I thought that was a good point *"Anyone can become anything – and everyone is naturally creative – if you give them a chance."*

My mother smiled *"I am happy—and . . . a little relieved—zat you have ziss view of sings. I voss a little vorried for you . . . "*

"No need to worry" I smiled *"Life is fine . . . and . . . I'm off to a new school soon – so who knows what will happen."* What my mother didn't know was that I'd already had *exactly* the kind of relationship I'd described. It had been with Anelie – but there was no way I could discuss that at the time. I told my mother many years later – and she laughed 'til there were tears in her eyes *"You alvays verr incorrigible. It iss vell zat your farzher never knew of ziss. Vott else do I not know?"* she asked, wide eyed with anticipation.

I was sure that there were other girls like Anelie in the world. I was saddened by the loss of her – but not as traumatised as I'd been about Alice. The loss of Alice was utterly needless and tragic – but the loss of Anelie had been built into our arrangement from the outset. There was no sense in mourning something that had been wonderful by virtue of the fact that its wonderfulness was irredeemably locked into its temporariness. I'd had a few attempted relationships – but school girls all seemed a little 'adolescent' after Anelie.

Then—suddenly and entirely unexpectedly—Lindie Dale happened. Lindie Dale had extremely long ginger hair – and phosphorescent eyes. I never knew such beings existed. Well . . . yes—*I did*—but, suddenly, it was as if I'd never seen a lady before. Lindie was entirely magical. Unearthly – yet tantalisingly tangible. When she was there, nothing else seemed to exist – or if it did it was out of focus, sub-audible, and indistinct.

It was as if Alice—my first love—had returned as a fiery valkyrie. We met at a party – and it was broad grins at first sight. I was immediately and utterly overwhelmed. I'd not seen a grin like that since Anelie – but this was the grin that made all other grins pale into insignificance. This was the grin that kick-started a thousand motorcycles.

There's something about an unwithheld grin that stimulates hair growth, obliterates dandruff, and nourishes every major organ. I was simultaneously awestruck and invigorated – simultaneously besotted and clear headed. I exploded into the present moment knowing exactly where I was and with whom.

I came to learn that Virginia Water School was an epicentre from which parties erupted like seismic assaults on everyday normality. There were parties almost every weekend – *if* you were accepted by the Blues illuminati. It didn't take them long to find out that I was on stage with Savage Cabbage – and what with the mighty Greg Ford and Pete Bridgewater liking me, I was *there*—with—a tailor made swagger, *if* I'd wanted it. I was just happy to be kosher. I was going to enjoy this school.

I met Lindie at the beginning of the first term. I was walking toward the kitchen in the house where the party was being held – and *there she was*, backlit by a torrent of light from the upstairs landing. We both stopped in our tracks. After grinning at each other for an impossible duration I asked her *"D'you like motorcycles?"*

Lindie just kept grinning – but nodded in the affirmative.

"It's a nice evening for a ride – we could skip out and come back later?"

Yes. But then a cloud passed across her face *"I . . . wouldn't have a crash helmet . . ."*

Certainly she would. I always had one strapped to the sissy bars [4] – for *just* such eventualities. *"I only wear it when it's cold – and . . . it'll probably fit snugly with . . . all your . . . lovely long hair."* The words were out of my mouth before I could check them.

Lovely long hair. I was not used to gushing compliments quite so immediately. I feared I'd blown it by sounding like a gawky gigolo or something – but Lindie's grin widened even further.

And he pulled her on behind and down to Box Hill they did ride.
Richard Thompson—1952 Vincent Black Lightning—Rumour and Sigh—1996

Box Hill wasn't far off – but we didn't ride there *that* evening. We'd have our Emma and Mr Knightley [5] picnic on another occasion *(replete with picnic hamper)*. Lindie grasped my midriff in a manner that indicated that she had a clear message to convey. We rode 'round country lanes quite sedately enjoying the view in the last hours of daylight. I would have ridden all night had I not been aware that I'd eventually run out of petrol. We found a petrol station and tanked up. I went in to pay and when I came out Lindie was standing in the unreal glare of the sodium lighting – staring in rapt wonder. *"I've always wanted to have a ride on one of these."* She pronounced 'one of these' as if she were speaking of an object of extreme desire.

I replied *"It's entirely at your service—any time at all—anywhere you want to go."*

Lindie burst out laughing *"You are—very—romantic, or is it just me?"*

---

4 Back-bars at the rear of the saddle which prevents the pillion passenger succumbing to rapid acceleration.
5 Emma—by Jane Austen—describes a picnic at Box Hill, attended by Emma and Mr Knightley.

I deliberately misunderstood and replied *"It's just you – for me . . . at least."* I'd done it again – I had no control of my mouth—*at all*—but, at least I didn't stammer. Lindie just grinned at me as if to say I was immune from faux pas.

"I love choppers.[6] *I've only seen them in photos. Did you build it?"*

No. I hadn't built it. I'd just bought a half chopped fixed frame BSA and added to it. *"It already had the extended forks and frisco pegs. I fixed the ape-hangers and sissy bars"* Pause *"Oh, and the swept up exhausts. They're the newest adjunct."*

Lindie raised her eyebrows *"They're fun."* She pointed to the handle bars *"And . . . the dental mirrors? Can you see anything in them?"*

"I can see enough" I smiled *"I can see you at the moment – and . . . that's all I need to see."*

Lindie simply continued to grin. After some moments—staring at each other in unabashed fascination—it seemed as if we were due back at the party. There'd be friends wondering where she was. One friend had an elder sister who'd drive them all home. When we walked back into the house—where the party was in full swing—we were an established couple, without a word being spoken to confirm it.

We met frequently after that night – because we saw each other at school every day. We had a self-evident long-term amorous direction – laced with Art and non-stop conversation. Lindie was extraordinarily intelligent which was a *slight* problem, inasmuch as she had far fewer free periods than I did.

---

6 A chopper—or chopped motorcycle—is probably best exemplified by those ridden in the film *Easy Rider*—1969.

She took more subjects at examination level than seemed possible for a human being. She took Art, History, English, Latin, Italian, and French at 'A' Level. The thought of it almost made me cross-eyed. It didn't seem too much for her though – and she appeared to rattle through books at an alarming rate.

We talked about poetry: Byron, Keats, and Shelley. We were in the same English class. We both enjoyed Shakespeare and both felt the same about *Othello*. We ranted about it on the way to the sixth form common room.

"That is the only Shakespeare I'll not see again once the 'A' level exams are over" Lindie muttered in slight vexation.

"Yes . . . " I sighed *"It drives me*—insane—*the way that Othello lets Iago drive him to kill Desdemona. She's the love of his life – and he doesn't want to hear her explanation. She's guilty – merely because that— psychopath—Iago wants to ruin Othello's life. I know these things— happen—but . . . I still hate it. If I went to see that play, I'd have to stand up and shout 'Stop this right now! I demand a different outcome! Let's have Desdemona whack him on the head with a skillet!' Anything! Please!"* Pause *"Still . . . there's some fabulous language in it. So . . . I suppose we'll have to enjoy that and try to forget the conclusion."*

That had Lindie almost crying with laughter *"I hope I don't get a sudden image of you saying that when we're next reading it with Mr Havilland."*

"Mr Havilland" I groaned *"He could do with hearing you laugh – I think he lives in a lump of hardened ear wax. He's obsessed with school uniform – I mean he acts as if he gets something out of it. He's been at me about wearing a 'proper blazer' all term and I—refuse—to submit to that. My black Edwardian double-breasted suit is as close as I need to get to school uniform. The other teachers have no problem with it and the headmaster saw it at my interview and said nothing about it."*

Lindie said "*I like your clothes and the way you push the boundaries. Someone needs to make a stand and I'm glad it's you. I don't know what his problem is with wearing a suit with a waistcoat anyway.*"

I thought about that for a moment and replied "*I think he wants the uniform to be uniform. I think there are just people who don't like individuality and see it as insurrection or whatever. I'm not interested in being rebellious though. I just like what I like and don't like what I don't like.*"

Lindie wondered how my clothing ideas arose and so I explained that my sartorial sense was kick-started when I inherited my Uncle Charles' clothes "*. . . this is his suit. I wanted more clothes of the 1920s style my uncle wore – so I hit the charity shops and bought anything antiquarian I could find – the older the better. My father told me—in 1966—that unless I was prepared to dress conventionally, I'd have to buy my own clothes. So that's what I did. I got a weekend job at Farnham Hospital – and now . . . I wear exactly what I want to wear.*"

We sat smiling at each other—as we always did, sometimes silently—and I stretched my legs out to place my feet on the log that lay in front of the bench where we were sitting in the school grounds.

"*Where—did—you find those polo boots?*" Lindie asked.

My US Air Force polo boots were my pride and joy. "*That's no mystery*" I replied "*from the American Airbase. It's near Reading – and things occasionally turn up. You could get real Levi Strauss 501 shrink-to-fits there – years before they were generally available. My half sister—Monica from Santa Monica—is married to an American airman. She occasionally takes the family to the Airbase for dinner when she visits. Monica bought me my first three pairs of Levi 501s at the age of 8 – and I've been wearing 501s ever since. You know . . . Levi Strauss should give me a medal for long service or something.*" She found me to be a mine of unlikely information.

Sitting under the trees one lunch break, Lindie mused *"Clothing's some kind of Art for you isn't it."*

"Yes . . . I've always had a keen interest in apparel and what becomes apparent through appearance that has aplomb." I was on a run of 'app' words – and she giggled at my deliberately ludicrous alliteration.

"I don't believe you just—said—that. Can you just invent things like that out of nowhere?" she asked.

I thought about it *"Sometimes . . . but it's easier when I know it's going to amuse you."*

Lindie returned to the previous subject *"So the Art then – the Art of clothes?"*

"Yes . . . " I responded *" . . . it's a message . . . like painting . . . like poetry . . . like music"* I told Lindie *"Although I didn't emulate him—I admire Hendrix's sense of style. He's obviously thought a lot about his stage appearance. When his first royalties arrived he went straight to 'I Was Lord Kitchener's Valet' and bought his antique British military jacket."*

"The one with all the frogging and gold braid?" Lindie smiled *"I can see —you—in something like that."*

Yes indeed. *"I'd enjoy wearing something like that – but I think Jimi Hendrix makes it work better than I would. I need a more sedate stage image – something more like Mike Cooper's."* Lindie tilted her head – but I mistook her question *"Mike Cooper's a Country Blues musician. Plays the fiercest lap-slide outside the Delta."*

No, that wasn't what she meant to ask *"You're on stage?"*

I hadn't told her about Savage Cabbage. *"Yes . . . I'm a vocalist . . . for a Blues band. We've only played a few gigs so far – but we've been playing together for two years or so."*

Lindie seemed amazed that I'd not mentioned it before *"That's a very exciting thing to keep quiet about. What are you called?"*

"Don't laugh" I said – encouraging her to do just that *" . . . but we're called Savage Cabbage."*

Lindie doubled up in mirth *"What sort of name is that? It's . . . really . . . wild . . . and sort of—perplexingly—out of the ordinary. It's almost a joke – but then it has some after-taste that . . . well I don't know what to say."*

I grinned broadly and replied *"You've defined it perfectly. That's just what it is. It's all about the sound – rather than the literal sense of it."*

"Can I come and hear you play?" she asked.

Certainly she could. *"We've got a gig coming up at the Compton Bells in a fortnight – but if you want to hear us sooner . . . you could come to our rehearsal on Friday."*

She thought that would be great fun. *"The band won't mind?"*

What a thought. *"No indeed – they'd be . . . highly honoured."*

Lindie giggled *"You're the strangest—I mean loveliest—mixture of old world and avant-garde – but . . . what I wanted to ask was, why you don't go in for the Hendrix image – even though you like it?"*

"There's a difference I suppose . . . " I mused *" . . . between the ways different people develop an appearance. Jimi Hendrix has a clear idea of what he's presenting and he does it well. I never go in for anything exotic on stage – even though I appreciate those who do – but then . . . I can be more flamboyant off stage than on."*

Lindie grinned broadly *"I've seen that—it's brilliant—I wish I had the nerve to dress like . . . but my parents are funny about clothes . . . sometimes."*

I didn't quite know what to say about that.

"It's not always been easy for me to dress the way I want . . . but . . . I tend not to let go of ideas – if they're important to me."

Lindie wondered *"Doesn't not compromising get you into trouble."*

"Yes . . . " I said *"it's always got me into trouble – but . . . I don't see any alternative. I don't think I'd want to be alive if I had to compromise."*

Lindie looked quizzical *"How does that work with relationships?"*

That took me aback a bit because I'd never considered *not compromising* in terms of relationship.

"Refusing to compromise—as I mean it—has nothing to do with wanting my own way all the time. It's got more to do with things that affect me purely personally."

Lindie asked for some examples.

"My hair's probably got me into more trouble than anything else – but as it grows out of my head I consider it no one else's business what length it is. Then there are my clothes and the music I like."

Lindie looked relieved. *"That's it?"* she asked.

"Yes – it's not a long list. My appearance is an expression of Art to me but, it's all personal – all . . . things that should really—only—effect me. It's really just being sincere about my own æsthetics and having the courage of my convictions."

Lindie wanted to hear about the hair débâcle and so I told her about it.

"Your father sounds very much like mine – but . . . I can't imagine—my —father backing down. He just wouldn't do that—ever—and my mother never disagrees with him."

Lindie said she felt she was lucky to be a girl as she'd hate to have a military haircut if she were a boy. I told her I felt lucky she was a girl too – and she collapsed laughing.

It was a funny moment but it made me apprehensive. Her home situation sounded like a prison and I wondered what they'd make of me – if I ever had the misfortune to meet them.

"It'll all change . . ." I opined *"I think—in a couple of years—no one will get worked up by appearances any more. Even my father's come to accept the way I dress."*

Lindie had been pondering the idea of not compromising *"So what would 'not compromising' mean about how you'd live your life?"* She was evidently fascinated with the concept.

I thought for a moment *"I don't settle for 'near enough.' 'Near enough' kills Art – you can't live like that."*

Lindie looked a little surprised *"You're saying you're going to live life as Art? How's—that—possible?"*

I considered for a brief moment *"Well . . . Art simply happens by itself – unless you stop it happening. If you don't stop it happening—by worshipping conventionalism—then appreciation bursts into flames. I mean—you—looked like a conflagration when I first saw you."*

Lindie was convulsed with laughter. *"So I'm Art too."*
Indeed she was.

We talked about my ideas – about the synapse between the senses and the sense fields. *"Everyone has senses – and so everyone can dance with the sense fields."* Lindie had her quizzical expression and so I explained *"I mean 'sense organs' and how we understand 'the world they sense.'"*

Lindie nodded slowly *"So . . . what about . . . this 'dance' thing then? I mean . . . it sounds as if you think 'the world' and 'how we sense it' . . . are . . . sort of . . . the same?"*

That's exactly what I thought.

"*Yes . . . you can't really take them apart. I think . . . we—try—to live as if there was 'a world out there' that is separate . . . but it's not really like that – well . . . not for an Artist at least.*"

Lindie threw her hair back over her shoulders. It caught the light and shimmered in a way that I never failed to find entrancing.

"*How d'you think it is for other people?*" she asked "*I mean – people who aren't artistic?*"

"*It's the same*" I replied "*they just see less or hear less – but everyone's an Artist. Everyone has senses – so they can experience . . . creative embrace with the sense fields.*"

"*That sounds like a definition of inspiration.*"

"*Right*" I grinned.

Lindie pondered for a moment "*So . . . Art can be . . . anything for anyone? Like beauty being in the eye of the beholder.*"

"*Absolutely*" I beamed "*In the ear, finger, tongue, nose . . . and mind.*"

"*That sounds like paradise.*"

I concurred. "*Especially when we're together.*"

We'd once passed a row of 'bazaar paintings' hung on railings. We both found them ghastly. They were daubings of boats reflected in water and pine trees decked with snow. Lindie recalled them with revulsion.

"*Does that make those cheap method paintings Art?*"

This was an uncomfortable question. I would have liked to have said 'no' – but that wasn't possible. "*I'm afraid so . . . for those who like them . . . that's what they are.*"

"No, *even*—you—*can't say that*" Lindie spluttered.

I'd backed myself into a philosophical corner and there was only one way out. *"Art's a question of perception and appreciation. So what —to us—is a tragic waste of paint and canvas, could be Art to someone else."*

Lindie considered this for a moment. *"But surely . . . people—can —educate themselves."*

I thought that was true. *"Yeah . . . I'm all for championing—that— cause . . . but Art can only be 'what it is' for anyone, at any one time. As soon as you make laws about what can be called Art"* I continued *"you stifle Art and stifle the individual. So, although I hate those paintings . . . I'd never be able to tell a person who loved them that they weren't Art."*

Lindie saw the point and although it didn't sit easily she saw there was no way round the problem. Lindie loved painting – but she doubted she'd ever become an Artist. *"My parents are dead against me going to Art School."*

I thought that was a pity – because she had an amazing sense of colour and texture. She said she'd accepted the alternative. *"I'm going to study French literature at University – and although it's not my first choice I do enjoy it. My parents think there are far more career opportunities with foreign languages than Art . . . and they're probably right."*

I had to admit that they *were* probably right. I thought that French literature was a fine choice apart from the fact that we wouldn't be together. There were holidays and so forth, so I was sure we'd work something out. Lindie toyed with a tussock of grass before turning to look at me rather wanly *"I hope so."*

She thought my knowledge of the Arts and being so widely read would impress her parents. *"I hope you're right . . . "* I ventured with some internal trepidation.

I had the feeling that she might be wrong. I certainly *was* well spoken. I could also be as polite and courteous as even Lindie's parents might require – but most other social credentials were missing. I was a working class lad with a quasi-middle class cultural mien.

Lindie interrupted my uneasy reverie *"If more people appreciated Art there'd be fewer problems in the world."*

Fewer problems. Yes . . . the world could do with fewer problems.

Lindie's parents weren't that happy with her riding on a motorcycle – but as long as she always wore a helmet they accepted the horror on the basis that it was a short distance from the school to the bottom of their road. Her parents didn't want the neighbours seeing their daughter dismount from a motorcycle so I always dropped her off at the end of the prestigious avenue in which she lived. We'd usually chat for a while in the school car park before setting off. There was a bench there and I'd always make sure I parked next to it. We talked often about Art linking the senses with the sense fields – and how appreciation and communication couldn't be divided.

"That's a natural conversation which informs the day" Lindie beamed.

"I like the way you phrased that."

She smiled. I'd never met a person who took such pleasure in the smallest compliment.

At the end of one school day we met in the car park as usual and Lindie said she'd have to take me home to meet her parents at some point. She'd have to get them used to the idea first – as she'd never taken a boyfriend home.

I got an uneasy feeling about this meeting with her parents – but said nothing. I had no desire to alarm her – but I'd met parents before and apart from the Bruces, they were generally like something out of Madam Tussauds. I wondered how Lindie was going to get them used to the idea – but felt it insensitive to ask. When the awful day arrived I'd have to wear my school uniform and make my hair as unobtrusive as possible.

"Maybe in a few weeks?" Lindie suggested.

"Yes – whenever you feel . . . they've got used to the idea. There's no hurry though – let's make sure that they're as used to it as they can be."

Lindie laughed *"You sound nervous—you're not usually nervous—and they're not—that—bad. They're just a little conventional and proper. It's probably my father being a Brigadier and all that British Army thing – but your father was a Major wasn't he?"*

I replied that he was. I was nervous – but not for myself. *"It's more the fact that I'd hate there to be any problem about us. What if they really—did—take objection to me?"*

Lindie thought about the question for a moment before replying *"Well . . . I think they will find your hair a bit of a shock – but I think they'll like the way you speak. My father's a stickler for correct enunciation and good grammar – and . . . "* she laughed *" . . . you sound—almost —like him sometimes. That's why I sometimes giggle at your expressions."*

That sounded more hopeful – but her father far outranked mine. A war-time Major [7] would not impress a Brigadier [8] – especially a Brigadier with gallantry medals.

---

[7] Officers who came up through the ranks during periods of war when casualties were high were not regarded as the social equivalents of commissioned officers who began their military careers as officers.

[8] Brigadier is both the highest field rank and the first General appointment – ranking above a full Colonel and below a Major General.

Lindie swung up behind me—fastened on the helmet—and we purred off toward the traditional dropping-off point – just out of sight of her home. I pondered our sartorial-appearance conversation as I rode away—with a final look back over my shoulder at Lindie—and it occurred to me that if I was to typify the clothing I enjoyed most – it could best be portrayed by the candid photographs of the Beatles and Cream that came to mind. I never wore a caftan or Nehru jacket. I never wore an Afghani coat – although I would not have objected to one. I never wore beads, headbands, or tied a silk scarf around my left knee – well . . . actually, I did once wear a headband and tie a silk scarf around my left knee. I was going to a concert with a fellow called Medicineman – and he'd felt I needed to 'flow' a little more. However – it didn't last longer than the train ride to Twickenham.

Medicineman worked as a tea-boy on the road-works that were running through Frimley and Camberley in 1968. He'd greet me with "*Not seen you in many moons*" – even though I'd seen him the day before. I liked Medicineman. He was a genuinely gentle fellow. Always good-humoured – always slightly dazed.
He knew I was no weekend hippie because I knew—and performed—the music. We'd talk music and my credentials were accepted – my freshly-laundered ironed Levis overlooked.

They spent time every day trying to find me – in the birch groves under the hill / So I sit wearing nothing but random time while they're all dressed to kill. / The witches of jazz are laughing – they're cutting capers across the saloon / Feeding coins to the hydrogen jukebox so it'll sing them the cracks of doom / There are rockers in circumspection dialling up their identical twins / And the witches are flying down so low tonight – you can easily see them grin.
Larkin/Bruce/Schubert—Savage Cabbage—Witches of Jazz—Savoy Green—1970

The music was Blues. The music was Jimi Hendrix –
psychedelic Blues. The music was almost *any* band outside the
Pop music category. Pop music was the pabulum of cretins.
We had pretty catholic tastes in *the lost time* – and no one would
deride you for liking the occasional Pop song. We had room for
everyone. We had room for weekend hippies too. We even had
room for the Aldershot squaddies [9] – or at least I did.
I remember a group of young soldiers who approached me one
day – hair all brushed forward to look long and headbands in
place to keep it that way.

They were pretty floral too. Wide—wide—flared jeans,
expansive with 'sails' – brocade furnishing fabric inserts sewn
into the outside seams.

They said *"Don't judge us 'cause we're in the Army. Yer gotta do
somethin' f 'ra living—but we're hip, same as you."*

"Don't want to judge you." I smiled *"There's too much judging going on.
I'm glad you're hip – and . . . I'm happy you're friendly. I wish everyone
could be friendly with everyone."* I wasn't out to be elitist. I hated
elitism. I had no desire to tell anyone that they couldn't be hip –
or whatever they said they were. Anyone could be anything as
far as I was concerned. If soldiers wanted to be hippies – that
was all to the good. They might start changing the system and
embroidering their uniforms with orchids and poppies.
*"Guns are fun if you don't fire them at people. There's room for everyone.
I'd like to fire a gun if I could get my hands on one"* I said, and meant
it. We talked about music – and it was true, they were as hip as
anyone could wish. They seemed happy I'd talked with them
and I said I'd be happy to see them again any time.

---

9 1960's British slang for soldiers.

I didn't realise—back then—that I was living in *a pool of appreciative time* that was soon to be baked dry by the relentless sun of commercialist fashion. In the early years of *the lost time* – people made their own clothes or adapted their clothes to give them whatever æsthetic style they desired. Once, we bought 'granddad vests' from gentleman's outfitters and hand-dyed them – but it wasn't long before that image had been appropriated and marketed. The vests were shoddy in comparison and short-sleeved – but people bought them nonetheless. That happened to everything – and as each image was commercially appropriated I waved it goodbye for the last time. I never tie-dyed my granddad vests – I either dyed them indigo or left them as they were: I was a Bluesman.

I'd often reflect on the fact that fashion appropriated everything. In *the lost time* people were able to express their individuality. People appreciated each other's individuality – and rejoiced in each other's creativity. There was an atmosphere of freedom and experimentation. Then the malefactor of mercenary mercantile materialism ate it.

With the absolute heart of the poem of life butchered out of their own bodies good to eat a thousand years. / What sphinx of cement and aluminum bashed open their skulls and ate up their brains and imagination? / Moloch! . . . Ash cans and unobtainable dollars! . . . / Moloch the heavy judger of men! Moloch the incomprehensible prison! / Moloch the crossbone soulless jailhouse and Congress of sorrows! / Moloch whose buildings are judgment! Moloch the vast stone of war! Moloch the stunned governments! / Moloch whose mind is pure machinery! Moloch whose blood is running money! / Moloch whose fingers are ten armies! Moloch whose breast is a cannibal dynamo! / Moloch whose ear is a smoking tomb! Moloch whose eyes are a thousand blind windows! /

Moloch whose skyscrapers stand in the long streets like endless Jehovahs!
Moloch whose factories dream and croak in the fog! / . . . Moloch whose
love is endless oil and stone! Moloch whose soul is electricity and banks! /
. . . Moloch whose fate is a cloud of sexless hydrogen!
Allen Ginsberg—Howl—1956

Allen Ginsberg's rage at Moloch makes mine look insipid.
I accept that. I think I'd manage a degree of rage if I thought
that Moloch ate *the lost time* on purpose. I'd be angry if I thought
that Moloch acted in full knowledge of the consequences – but
Moloch's merely a misguided mutant miscreant. I feel sorry for
Moloch. His bedroom window is made out of bricks – and that
can't be conducive to a good night's sleep. I always sleep with
the window open – even in the depths of Winter.

Well he puts his cigar out in your face just for kicks / His bedroom
window, it is made out of bricks / The National Guard stands around his
door / No I ain't gonna work for Maggie's Pa no more.
Bob Dylan—Maggie's Farm—1965

Who'd want to be Moloch or Maggie's Pa? Who'd want Allen
Ginsberg and Bob Dylan vituperating about them in verse?
On hearing such tirades poor old Moloch must be weeping in
some forsaken corner somewhere. Makes me feel like calling
'Hey—*Moloch—come outta that corner and sing some songs with me!*
I'll be your friend – just quit eating everyone and everything everywhere.'

I mentioned the way that fashion was encroaching on our
clothing to Medicineman "*Fashion's a vile voracious vampire that*
sucks the individuality out of life. The fashion industry's a pack of jackals.
They tear the living flesh from people – and convert it into jackal meat."
Medicineman nodded his agreement – and that encouraged me
to venture further. "*I don't know whether jackals are cannibalistic . . .*"

Medicineman shrugged to indicate that he had no answer to that
question but suggested "*Dingoes are cannibals . . . I think . . .*"

I was glad my thesis wasn't entirely awry. "*Right—and I've got a certain antipathy toward cannibalism. Anything that eats its own kind is deranged.*"

Medicineman still nodding approval said "*Yeah man – fashion does that! It takes freak threads and turns 'em into straight jackets.*"

We'd almost reached the Queen's Oak pub when I decided to sum up the conversation "*Fashion eats individual culture to fatten consumerist conformity. It turns human beings into nonentities by making them afraid to make individual choices.*"

Medicineman nodded furiously—he'd got the drift—but as usual I sounded as if I were performing Shakespeare.

"*Yeah . . . it's too bad—but they'll lose in the end man—there's just too many freaks now. The times they are a-changin'.*"

Well yes . . . I could see that to a certain extent. I hoped he was right. "*Everyone could wear what they choose to wear—but they allow themselves to be regimented—even freaks.*"

"*Freaks?*" he enquired with some surprise.

"*Well . . . y'know . . . I've had comments on my ever-clean Levis.*"

Medicineman looked confused "*Up to you man—up to you what you wear—it's your thing. Ain't cool to judge people—you wash 'em much as y'like man. Freaks can wear anything—shouldn't list'n to'em—they're just longhaired straights.*"

That's what I'd concluded – but that's what made me slightly dubious about all these freaks who were going to overturn society. I decided to keep my feelings of pessimism to myself, as I knew Medicineman majored in positive thinking.

"*We sh'd 'ave freak tailors man*" he ventured "*Y'know, like dudes who c'ld make what—we—wanna wear.*"

I thought that was a fine notion. "*Yes. Sure. If we—really— wanted what we wanted, enough to pay the price, we could do that. It's just believing in what you want. It's not being sucked into fashion and thinking you don't like the clothes you had made last year. I still like my indigo satin shirt – but most people think it's funny now, y'know 'Carnaby Street's dead' and all that.*"

Medicineman nodded his disapproval of the closed-mindedness to which I'd alluded. I'd detected he'd started to glaze over a little so I told him I was looking forward to having him in the audience when Savage Cabbage played. "*Fierce, man!*" he grinned "*Not heard the—Cabbage—in many moons.*"

I'm not a social historian – I was just alive in the '60s at near enough the right age. I have an abundance of vivid impressions and flamboyant recollections. I was carried by a sense of something momentous happening in the world and felt privileged to be part of it. There were so many avenues of interest throughout the Arts – and these enabled those who rose to the occasion, to break free of the conservatism and ossified conventionality of the time. Then in 1972 the oppressive regime of fashionable banality began to contract the creative environment. It did nothing to dampen my enthusiasm for the beauty of the world – but I became aware that I was increasingly isolated in that enthusiasm. The experience of sensory beauty has remained with me. It's remained as the texture of my life in the present – and as the vibrant memory of those who pioneered *the lost time*.

In *the lost time* Rock and Blues musicians *were* Artists – or rather, the best were Artists. Being Artists, they naturally interested themselves in all the Arts. They were not simply people who produced music in the Rock idiom.

They were not slaves of fashion or commercial 'tunesters' – they were exploring the field of what was possible. Bob Dylan's statement *'A new world of art was opening up my mind'* rang a vast bell. That *is* how it was. That's how I hoped it would continue. An Artist cannot help being influenced by *all* the Arts. This was why bands such as the Beatles became involved in the appearance of their album sleeves. Why leave your album sleeve to someone else? The album sleeve is part of the album. The book cover is part of the book.

If you want to time travel to 1967 – you just need to open your eyes and allow your senses to function ever-so-slightly outside conventional parameters. You don't have to ingest psychoactive substances. You don't even have to don a set of headphones and close your eyes. You merely need to let your senses *do what they do* rather than following the dictates of codified societal legislation. You have to look at *what is there*

One lunch time Lindie and I sat under the oak trees at the end of the playing fields eating fish and chips from the Friar Tuck. Lindie relished fish and chips – but her parents disapproved of such food as 'vulgar', especially eating it out of newspapers.

Lindie laughed. *"Is this also Art?"* she said holding up the fish and chips.

"It's Art" I replied *"Art's pleasure, enjoyment, and the essential love of existence."*

Lindie grinned at me *"Living as an Artist would be endlessly delightful."*

I asked Lindie *"What would that sound like in French"* and she set about translating it on the newspaper which constrained her lunch. She read it out to me and I was amazed at how poetic it sounded.

"It's a shame you didn't take French. You'd have liked it and it would have been fun to have worked together on things."

"There's some French Surrealist poetry I'd like to translate" I replied *"It would be fantastic if you had time to help me with it. Working with a dictionary's all very well – but I'm never sure whether I'm just making a word-salad out of it."*

She was happy to help me and said that she'd be able to dovetail it into her course work. Perfect. The lunch break was over – so we stood up and walked off toward a litter bin where we could deposit our fish and chip papers. I could have stayed at school with Lindie for the rest of my life.

Lindie thought Art should bring out our finer qualities and that Art which portrayed hopelessness lacked humanity. One day after English class she caught my attention *"Art should provide hope. It should give us determination to overcome difficulties."*

I could see that Lindie was her father's daughter in many ways – and I liked the strength of her emphasis on commitment and honour. I'd also inherited that from my parents. I believed in hope. I also believed in hard work. Thomas Jefferson said *'I am a great believer in luck – and I find the harder I work, the more I have of it.'* Hope on its own could be futile or desperate but together with hard work and enthusiasm – there's no stopping people from winning through to a better world.

I told Lindie that I was never a great fan of 'realism' in terms of Art – if realism meant the depiction of misery. Modern Literature is particularly bad in this regard.

"If I want to see realism . . . " I told Lindie *"I'll go sit on a park bench or walk through town or something – and there it'll be."*

Lindie chuckled about the way I expressed that idea.

"Human beings do come to sad ends – but I don't want to be entertained by that. Reality's joy as well as misery." Lindie lay back on the grass to enjoy the flickering shadows cast by the leaves above us as they dappled her face. *"The problem is"* she said *"that if serious authors are to win literary prizes, they have to write about misery. A 'happy ending' would be a real literary novelty."*

That was true – then *and* now. *"If any serious talented writer were to write a fine work of literature with a 'happy ending' it would be the most revolutionary achievement in the better part of a century"* I sighed.

I loved these conversations with Lindie. They were like and unlike my conversations with Anelie.

They were *unlike* because Lindie was English, and *like* because she was highly intelligent – and I was enraptured by her. The enrapturement had no major carnal consequences – but somehow that posed no problems. Unlike the other lads I knew – I had no pressing incentive to prove anything to myself. I'd be content for Lindie to lead the way when the time came.

Ain't got no window—I ain't got no door. / But I can feel the sun shining where it's never shined before. Keb Mo—Everything I Need—1998

One morning I took the DEBIL to school to show it to Lindie and to play it in the school assembly. Every 6th year pupil had to *present* at least once in the morning school religious assembly. The contribution didn't have to be religious but it had to be some kind of meaningful statement about life. I sang *'John the Revelator'* by Son House.

Now Christ had 12 apostles, and three he laid away / He said "Watch for me one hour, while I go yonder and pray." / And tell me who's that writing, John the Revelator, / Tell me who's that writing, John the Revelator / Who's that writing, John the Revelator – wrote the book of the seven seals. Son House—John the Revelator—1937

That presentation caused a quandary. *'John the Revelator'* was appropriate for a school religious assembly—in being religious— but inappropriate in being as far from religion as the average English citizen could comprehend. I was extremely loud and more than a little ferocious. There was a storm of applause at the end of the song—a thing unheard of in a school assembly— and a hail of whistles. When I heard those whistles I *knew* there'd be trouble.

'John the Revelator' was irreverent from the point of view of most of the teachers present. Their faces displayed the most immoderate displeasure.

I'd belted out that song as if Son House was my ol' Pa and we'd been singing it together at every juke joint down the length of Highway 61. I waited for the heavy hand of authority to descend – but, surprisingly, all turned out well. It was deemed—after due consideration—that I was to be praised for my performance. I was, however, never required to present at an assembly again.

I learned—just before I left Virginia Water—that Mr Blenkinsopp was responsible for having assuaged the headmaster's concern with regard to my Son House rendition. There were a few teachers apparently who'd suspected me of blasphemy.

"I told Mr Ironsides" he said *"that you seemed to have made a study of American Negro music—and that you gave a most creditable performance —being as I have a copy of that particular song"* Mr Blenkinsopp smiled *"I also praised your 'unusual guitar.' I was astonished to hear that you fabricated it yourself. It is very much—like—an authentic instrument of the period, although the sound is . . . unusual."*

It would have been a pleasure to have talked with him about music sooner – but I suppose it required the more informal circumstances of my being on the cusp of departure. Teachers at that time were extremely cautious of boundaries and remained teachers 'til such time as their charges were no longer their charges.

Lindie was amazed. *"You can sing really loudly! And that—*accent *—is quite something. You'd never think to hear you that you were brought up in Surrey."*

"I wasn't" I laughed *"I was born a po' black boy in Mississippi."* Lindie chuckled and I recited her *the gospel of Blues* as it had been for me since the age of eight in Mr Love's Garden.

She was intrigued by it all and wondered where on earth I came from. *"You're like something from a film. I never know what amazing thing you're going to do next"* Lindie giggled.

"I hope . . . " I replied, alluding to my future meeting with Brigadier and Mrs Dale *"that the film will have a happy ending. That's a message I'd like to give to the whole world."*

The message in *the lost time* was:

ART AND KNOWLEDGE MAKE LIFE WORTHWHILE.

It was written—or woven—into the molecular structure of everyday life. It was obvious. I was lucky. I came across wonderful teachers: Alice and her parents who gave me a love of nature and collage; Mr Love who introduced me to Blues; Steve Bruce and his parents who'd inspired me to play guitar and read literature; Anelie who opened my mind to Surrealism and other wonders; Mr Preece who enabled me to write poetry – and Lindie Dale who seemed to connect every teacher I'd ever had.

I'd spent time with a few ladies who let me jabber on – but after a while they'd say they had no idea what I was talking about. Not only did Lindie know what I was talking about – she had a whole bunch of things to say herself. Her parents may have been military but they had a great belief in a classical education. A girl had to be accomplished and cultured. This was right out of Jane Austen – but it suited me just fine.

So I'll ride my road to the distance – I'll lose track of my eyes in the view / There's a scrapbook of musical virtues that I've stitched to the soles of my shoes / And you won't find me lost in conjecture – I'll be thundering out on the bass / In a room full of maniac music where everyone sees through my face / So goodbye to morbid mathematics it's a vile demented disease / It'll never tie me down—I won't stick around—I'm just a thread in the breeze.
Larkin/Bruce/Schubert—Savage Cabbage— Just a Thread in the Breeze—Savoy Green—1970

I rode my motorcycle like Art—through landscapes of Art—in the weather of Art. I wore a leather RAF flying cap – that looked rather like a balaclava with straps, brass press-studs, and earflaps for headphones. The open road was an Art Gallery of vignettes with a cast of Artists who wouldn't have considered themselves to be Artists. Their Art lay entirely within their lifestyles and their appearances.

Life-style Art is an arena in which anyone can perform. You simply have to invest in your own sensory enthusiasm. You simply take an idea and develop it. The zeitgeist of *the lost time* contained many creative threads whose creativity lay in their emotive colour. Whether the people I remember saw themselves as *actors on the living stage* or not, is not possible to say – but I remember them as part of a glorious epic.

I occasionally frequented 'The Old Manor Cafe' [10] – when Lindie was out of circulation and the lads were bogged down in homework. It took chutzpah to go to this Biker's Den – but if it was known that you'd had a cup of coffee there, the prestige allocated was significant. I wasn't eager for peer prestige at any cost – but it seemed it was one of those things I needed to do. Pete Bridgewater warned me "*You*—can't—*go there looking like that, they'll*—mangle—*you.*"

It was the brown RAF Flying jacket, brown Polo boots, and the forest-green German despatch-rider trousers. It was not the regulation black. Pete thought I was insane – but I was not keen on sartorial laws – whether issued by my father or the local Rockers. I went to 'The Old Manor Cafe' just as I was. Strangely enough, it was those very items of clothing that caused the much-feared Rocker Ron to approach me. He leaned over me menacingly, breathing the ominous words "*So . . . y'like*— brown—*do yer?*"

This was Ronald Bigsleigh – the one who'd served time in prison for assault. He'd torn a hand-wash basin from a wall and thrown it at a fellow who'd made a remark about his girlfriend. He broke most of the fellow's ribs.

I looked at Rocker Ron with all the confidence I could muster— in what appeared to be the last moments of my life—and replied "*Yes . . . I like brown . . . I like my flying jacket.*"

I wanted to say I liked everything I wore—and that the trousers were green, in any case—but thought I'd quit while I was ahead. Ron was silent. The whole place was silent.

---

10 Pronounced Kaff – as in Kafka, but with a hard British 'a'.

Then Ron smiled and said, in a huge voice *"Well—gooooooooood—f'you"* Pregnant pause *"I—like—originality."* He grinned and slapped me on the back hard enough to crack a barn door and rejoined his associates laughing *"Likes brown—'e says—'e's a—real—card."*

I was still alive. I could hardly believe it. I greeted Rocker Ron thereafter—extremely politely—whenever I entered the premises. He'd just nod. One time, however, he said *"See that Pixie Chariot of yours is still shiny-clean."*

I smiled and replied, quoting Penny Lane *"I like to keep my fire engine clean – it's a clean machine."*

That got a laugh from Rocker Ron – preceded by nervy expressions from Rocker Ron's associates. When they heard Rocker Ron laugh however, they chimed in *"Goo-goo goo-joob!"*

Right band, wrong song – but I thought it wisest not to comment. Rocker Ron called my motorcycle the 'Pixie Chariot'. He was an old-fashioned Rocker who didn't hold with choppers. A chopper wasn't his idea of a motorbike.

My father, however—who knew nothing at all about Hell's Angels—decided that chopping my BSA was a move in the right direction. It looked nothing like the bikes that the motorcycle gangs rode. My BSA soon had a lustrously dark pink metal flake petrol tank with the words 'Pixie Chariot' emblazoned in dusky maroon psychedelic lettering. Rocker Ron was touched by the fact that I'd run with his teasing remark. Then he died. Ronald Bigsleigh—the man who rode a Vincent 1000 'widow maker' [11]—killed in a car crash.

---

11 The Vincent 1000—nicknamed the 'widow maker'—had a flawed design, which made it perilous to decelerate on a bend over 70 miles an hour. The frame would whip – and the motorcycle would invariably spin out of control.

There's a rumour, that Richard Thompson based his song '1952 Vincent Black Lightning' on Rocker Ron – but the facts of his death are different. James was 21 when he died and Rocker Ron was in his mid 30s. Rocker Ron didn't have a ginger-haired fiancé called Molly – but the song brings Rocker Ron vividly to mind. James has Rocker Ron's speech patterns – and Richard Thompson makes James the hero that Rocker Ron was for many. He was a modern-day Dick Turpin.

Ronald Bigsleigh was interred at Aldershot Crematorium. The funeral was arranged and Rocker Ron's mates told me *"Y'll be goin' t' Ron's funeral. 'e'd've—wanted—y'there. 'e liked you. Dunno why – but 'e did."*

It would be an honour of course. Both my father and mother thought it was not a good idea. My father cautioned *"It might be dangerous. What if violence breaks out? People have been killed."*

They didn't quite grasp the fact that if I did *not* go to Rocker Ron's funeral – they'd most likely soon be going to mine.

Something beyond mere self-preservation however, inspired my need to attend. Rocker Ron had accepted me *as I was*. It was an act of kindness and generosity that lay outside the realm of what was ordinarily possible. His acceptance had given me some weird special status at the Old Manor Cafe – with everyone who knew Rocker Ron, and with those who had even heard of him. Eyebrows would invariably be raised when it was understood that I was on speaking terms with him. It was a little like being noticed by the King or Queen – or by some man-eating tiger . . . My father no longer attempted to control me, so the choice was obvious. I hit the road to pay my last respects.

"There were close to a thousand motorcycles" I confided to Lindie afterward *"They came from all across Britain – there were people who'd come down from Scotland."*

Lindie looked surprised *"Scotland?"*

"Yes – somehow, word got round that the 'King of the Open Road' died. People who'd never met Rocker Ron took to the road to be there at the last" I explained.

Lindie was still puzzled *"So . . . did they all know him?"*

"No . . . I don't think so" I replied *"I think . . . it was as if—just being there—marked a person out in some way – almost like the scene in Spartacus where all the slaves start shouting 'I am Spartacus!' . . . "*

"And then the Romans . . . " Lindie nodded *" . . . crucify them all."*

"Yes . . . " I smiled very slightly *" . . . there—was—some sense of that."*

The Mod and Rocker battles that took place in the seaside towns of the South of England in the early 60s had created a fear of desperadoes on two wheels. Vandalism and violence had been expected. The town was a fortress under siege. The police force, were there *in* force to *en*force whatever – but . . . no force was needed. They were simply a uniformed segment of the cavalcade – a guard of honour. Suburban faces peered out through curtained windows at the Vandals, Goths, and Visigoths who rode by at 15 mph in the incongruent cortège. The contingent was in mourning. Nothing was damaged. No laws were contravened. The service was quiet. No one said anything. Had I been older I might have organised a recital of 'Leader of the Pack'.

At school they all stop and stare – I can't hide my tears but I don't care – I'll never forget him the leader of the pack.
Morton/Barry/Greenwich—The Shangri-las—Leader of the Pack—1964

The motorcycles and their hirsute, black-apparelled, gauntleted riders vanished into the anonymous history of *a day that never was.*

The funeral hit the newspapers the day before – but the day itself hardly received a mention. The press were eager to be aghast and righteously indignant but the press were disappointed – no one wanted to hear anything good of motorcycles or those who rode them. I planned to create a Rocker Ron memorial jacket – a black leather motorcycle jacket like the one worn by the young Marlon Brando. It was to be brown with brass zippers in memory of Rocker Ron who said "*Well— goooooooooood—f'you. I—like—originality.*" It'd bear a red and blue embroidered label inside with the words 'THE ROCKER RON MEMORIAL JACKET: RONALD BIGSLEIGH—KING OF THE OPEN ROAD—ROAR IN PEACE'.[12]

Lindie said she was relieved that her parents had not enquired whether I'd been at the funeral – as "*That would have been a little . . . difficult.*"

"*Yes . . .*" I replied "*it wasn't easy for my parents to understand that I was obliged to go. It was . . . a question of honour, I suppose. Rocker Ron liked me – and . . . I felt I owed it to him – even though we didn't really know each other.*"

Lindie laughed "*You're like something out of Robert Louis Stevenson.*"[13]

Some make their choices as they run – some try to bide their time / Some take their logic seriously and think they're doing fine, / But you know it's all for nothing if you've never been awake / 'cause you'll never make it to the hills before the floodgates break.
Larkin/Bruce/Schubert—Savage Cabbage—Before the Floodgates Break—Savoy Green—1970

---

12 Created in 2011 by seamstress Sally Yon. Label embroidered in Thamel, Kathmandu, Nepal.

13 Robert Louis Stevenson [1850 – 1894]. Scottish poet, essayist, novelist, and travel writer best known for his adventure and horror stories which include: Treasure Island, The Strange Case of Dr Jekyll and Mr Hyde, and The Master of Ballantræ.

2

j s bach

*I took a ride along the day to watch the night come through / There were
seven strands of shining sands that felt more than I knew / There were
seven shoals on seven shores like sapphires in the dew / And I knew the
time was coming when I'd fall right in with you.*

Larkin/Bruce/Schubert—Savage Cabbage—Unless You Shed Your Skin—Savoy Green—1970

Virginia Water School had been a gear shift. People liked me.
Greg Ford and Pete Bridgewater—two prime movers—accepted
that I was a bona fide player on the scene. I had opinions to
offer. I was the vocalist and harp player with Savage Cabbage.
The Virginia Water lads talked Hendrix and Cream. I talked
Muddy Waters, Son House, Robert Johnson – the Mississippi
Delta origins of Blues. I talked in a way that obviously
interested them – and I was careful not to hold forth for too
long or too often. I usually waited for the questions. I told
them about the original artists who performed the numbers
Cream had brought to public attention in Britain – and so I
came to be regarded as an unquestioned authority on Blues.
I admitted my ignorance on the subject of Rock and that gave
others a chance to supply me with information.

Cream—Jack Bruce, Ginger Baker and Eric Clapton—were an
enormous influence on Savage Cabbage. Even Ron with his
love of Chicago Blues had to admit that Cream were *the way to go.*

Cream seemed to answer something for Ron in terms of his classical training and his love of Bach – and his major enthusiasm was to play counterpoint with Steve in alarmingly long improvisations. It was Blues as seen through the lens of Jazz – and Johann Sebastian Bach. That's the closest stab I can make at describing Savage Cabbage musically. Cream playing 'Spoonful' on 'Wheels of Fire' comes close – apart from minimalist partially-pianissimo percussion that favoured cymbals above all else. The main difference of course was Ron. He was the wild card. He was also the trump and the royal flush. He played a hand of electric poker. He'd lay down 3 Kings: BB King, Albert King, and Freddie King – but there'd always be a couple of aces up his sleeve that he'd throw down when least expected. Sometimes he'd throw in a mutant Hendrix phrase interspersed with hybrid Baroque motifs that moved in ways that defied description. Steve used to marvel at Ron's latest tour de force with great excitement – and wonder how long it would take him, even to start approaching that standard.

We played Weyflood Village Hall again just before the Autumn term commenced. We saw it as the grand finale – before the real shows began. Even Ron felt it was time to put out feelers in the direction of pub venues – where we'd be spared the toil of advertising ourselves. The hall was packed almost from the start – and we all felt relaxed and mischievous. Jack performed a 30 *second Toad* – before we'd positioned ourselves. Ron laughed and turned to give Jack a grin of encouragement. I was glad that Jack had the confidence to do that kind of thing and glad that Ron didn't take it amiss.

I was delighted as ever to be on stage singing and playing harp –
but I was becoming aware of *an issue*. It had been all very well in
rehearsal to stand or sit listening to long improvisations – in fact
it had been wonderful. With no one looking at me but the band
—who weren't looking at me anyway—during the instrumental
breaks, I felt quite natural. I was just listening to the music I
loved. The first few gigs were also wonderful – but now I had
50 or 60 people in front of me and it wasn't clear to me what I
should be doing. I thought of retiring to the back to sit on a
chair – but that seemed as awkward as standing there like a
zombie. I put the idea to one side. I'd just have to get used to
the situation in a professional manner – beside which, listening
to Ron was a delight that never palled.

Ron may not have been any faster than Eric Clapton or Jimi
Hendrix – but he certainly wasn't slower. I never cared either
way. Jack was thrilled by speed – but Ron and Steve didn't look
at music as some kind of race. The speed thing was obsessing
everyone at the time – but although we enjoyed fast licks, we
never considered them to be the heart of Blues. I called him
Lightning Ron Larkin – but that was because of his sheer
fluency. He went to earth like lightning – right down to the
open bass string. In that sense—although we emulated Cream
—we sounded different. Ron also played more slide guitar. Ron
wasn't an aficionado of high-speed-beyond-the-12th-fret riffs.
He was imaginatively rich and subtle – playing riffs that ran the
entire length of the fretboard.

Ron never mentioned speed. Never talked about it or admired
it. He *did* admire other players – but what he admired was
phrasing and emotional nuances perfectly executed. The speed
of a riff was the speed it needed to be in order to play good
Blues – no more, no less.

The duration of the riff was the same. It only lasted as long as it needed to last, in order to fulfil emotional requirements. Ron could play some mind-bogglingly long riffs – but he didn't make a habit of it unless we'd taken off into a 20 minute improvisation. In that way Ron was truer to the Black musicians. I'd mentioned Frank Zappa as a fine guitarist and Ron added "*Yeah he's an innovator—and—he plays riffs two octaves lower than most 'guitar legends'. There's far more clout in that register. That's the difference between the Black greats and most White players. A lot of White guitarists mainly end their riffs high up the neck – and . . . there's never any real—guts—in that.*" I listened to a few albums after that and saw exactly what Ron meant. Blues doesn't scream – it moans and growls.

The ladies standing wreathed in dusk had scored the symphony / Arranged the scales and tempo and set them rolling free / The strings were singing nebulae and distant galaxies / And woodwinds murmured backwards through my earthquake reverie.
Larkin/Bruce/Schubert—Savage Cabbage— Ladies Wreathed in Dusk—Savoy Green—1970

The lads were always keen to read reviews in the music magazines – yet it was sometimes a frustrating experience. We were all after serious musical information – but it was often a question of reading between the lines. The music critics were slightly too enamoured of their subjectivity and made statements that we found irrelevant. We weren't interested in other people's opinions about music. We had enough opinions ourselves – and some were better informed, especially with regard to Blues. One critic—in praise of Cream—had described another Blues band as 'the stale smell of yesterday'. Although we loved Cream and had no great enthusiasm for the other band – we found such statements juvenile.

"*I suppose that puts Bach in the stale smell category?*" I commented – which made the lads laugh.

"*All this 'latest thing' business* . . . " Steve sighed "*is* . . . *such*—sad
—*commercial rubbish. It's useful to break into charts with*—good—
music . . . *but it's still a trap if it makes you change what you play to
satisfy popular demand.*"

The lads nodded approval. It occurred to me that music critics
were responsible—in part—for driving the machine of
mediocrity. There were ideas about what was popular and what
people would like – but the main drive, was toward what would
sell. Some bands got rich but the money mainly seemed to go to
the music industry.

Steve commented "*The more I look at the music industry the more it
looks like some huge leech. Everyone needs to make a living* – *but why
does it have to be so cut throat?*"

Ron waved his hand dismissively in portrayal of his distaste.
"*Yeah* . . . *music journals, record companies*—and—*the wankers who
allocate TV and radio airtime* . . . "

Ron ran out of words at that point and I finished his sentence.

"*I guess they'll always dictate public taste. It's the death of creativity* – *but
that needn't worry us. Good music will always win out. There's a lot of
useless twaddle on the radio especially now the Pirate Stations* [1] *are gone* –
but there's also plenty of experimental music out there."

The lads seemed encouraged by that comment – and Ron went
in search of an apple.

---

1 The Pirate Stations—Radio Caroline and Radio London—were radio stations that
operated from ships in the English Channel during the '60s. When they were finally forced
to close down they were replaced by BBC Radio 1 which—apart from the John Peel
programme—has been the bastion of mediocrity ever since.

There's stifling heat beneath my feet and a storm is running high / Critics calculate like lemmings as they watch the brooding sky, / They move too slow to take the leap – as they fail they hesitate / And manicure their futures before the floodgates break.

Larkin/Bruce/Schubert—Savage Cabbage—Before the Floodgates Break—Savoy Green—1970

"*Some—fucking—critic*" Jack almost yelled "*. . . describes—*Eric Clapton—*as* '*. . . a master of blues clichés . . . a virtuoso at performing other peoples' ideas.*' *What a load of bollocks!*"

I felt this was a mean-minded thing for a critic to write. I wasn't the greatest Eric Clapton enthusiast because I couldn't help comparing him with Ron – but I thought that he was an extremely fine musician. I also felt the criticism was based on a grave misconception and opined "*Blues players have been influenced by each other since Blues began as far as I'm aware.*"

Steve nodded in agreement and said "*Ron—you can play any riff that Clapton plays—so, what's your take on that?*"

Ron replied "*It's a piece of stupid journalism. If Eric Clapton is clichéd —then so am I—and so are a lot of other people. Who's this idiot critic anyway? Can he play guitar?*"

Jack laughed and took off where Ron had left off. "*He probably just plays with himself. I mean – can he even use the lavatory on his own?*" Jack laughed hysterically at his own ribaldry. Ron and I shook our heads and grinned at Jack. We could always rely upon Jack to get carried away.

I reflected for a moment and replied "*Anyone—who knows anything about Blues—knows it's not about innovation – even though innovation happens. Blues could be described as clichéd – if you were looking for something completely new. There—is—originality in lyrics or phrasing – but you have to be completely immersed in it to see that.*"

"The beauty of Blues isn't in originality" I continued *"it's in the passion and humour. The lyrics and instrumental phrasing of Blues are simply a conduit for emotion. Anyone can get up and sing 'I went down to the station – looked up at the board—I couldn't see no train I couldn't hear no whistle blow . . .' and make it as real as they have the power to make it."*

Ron wore an expression I was seeing ever more frequently when I held forth. I was aware that I was no longer the over-enthusiastic maniac he first took me to be. It was ever-so-slightly eerie to witness Ron's obvious respect and approval of my statements.

"Thing is" said Ron *" . . . if these people could play it, they'd be playing it – not criticising those who can."* Ron knew exactly who Eric Clapton imitated – because he'd been influenced by the same Blues marvels. *"And who did—they—imitate?"* Ron asked rhetorically
" . . . they imitated the Blues greats before them. Changes occur down the line—sure—and sometimes someone stands out like a giant – but they owe that as much to their background as to themselves. It's a tradition – and it grows like any tradition grows."

That statement struck me as profound. Blues was a tradition. We'd become part of the tradition – by playing Blues. I had no idea whether I'd ever write a Blues classic – but that was less important than the fact that I was becoming part of something. I'd become a point in time – a point between the past and future of a musical tradition. It wasn't about going down in history. We'd all go down in history whatever happened – but we might not be remembered. I thought Ron and Steve would be remembered – and maybe someone might think I had a voice. That was enough for me.

Ron played some riffs for us – so that we could 'compare and contrast'. First he played an extended riff from 'Spoonful' exactly as Eric Clapton played it. Then he showed us its provenance. He showed me similarities between Eric Clapton's phrasing and that of BB King and Albert King – but he also showed me how he'd made the riffs his own.

"So it's not even true" I said *"He wasn't lifting riffs from Albert King."*

Ron nodded *"It wouldn't make much sense to say Eric Clapton lifted those riffs . . . because he gives them a different feel and dynamic. He's exceptionally smooth in his approach—maybe too smooth for my liking— but he does what everyone does. He takes phrases—rephrases them—and plays them in his own style."* Ron then played the Eric Clapton riffs again – throwing his own changes on them. From there he showed me where BB King and Albert King found their influences. They went right back to the Delta. Ron reproduced every riff with graceful ease and fidelity – but also with raging verve. He showed me what it was like to play with technical perfection – but without heart. I recognised the difference immediately – as passion was my forte.

I learnt a great deal from Ron – and so did Steve. Ron would show us the technicalities of what Jack Bruce was playing. *"I sometimes get the feeling"* said Ron *"that Jack Bruce listens to Bach. I sometimes—*feel*—as if I'm hearing fragments of counterpoint melody I recognise. I'm sure he sneaks Baroque arpeggios into his Jazz-Blues bass riffs."*

Steve and I were mystified and so Ron had to pull a record out of its sleeve to show us what he meant. He selected the '**D** minor Sarabande'.[2]

---

2 A sarabande is a slow stately Spanish dance in triple time; a piece of music for this dance, or in its rhythm, often has a lengthened note on the second beat of the bar.

Steve was never that interested in this kind of music but I could listen to it for hours and was glad that Ron felt the same way.

We listened in silence for a few minutes and then Ron yelled *"That's it! That there! I'm bloody—*sure*—he does that on Spoonful! I'll play it 'gain."*

Ron played it again. Then he played the section of Spoonful where he'd remembered it—which took a while to find—then he played the Sarabande again. Steve shook his head to imply he was lost – but I caught what Ron meant. We played the two records over and over and hummed the line for Steve 'til he finally got it.

"But it's only half a dozen notes at the most" Steve groaned, a little exasperated by our enthusiasm. *"What's so fascinating about that? Apart from the fact that it sounds . . . well it sounds slightly out of place if you know what I mean."*

Ron shook his head. *"Yeah—*in one way*—but you have to look at —how—he leads into it and out of it and how it works as counterpoint to what Clapton's doing on lead."* Ron played it again, and again, and again – and finally Steve grinned.

*"Yeah Ron . . . but—*bloody hell*—that takes—*some*—furious listening."*

Ron nodded *"Yeah . . . well – that's the game isn't it – and old Frank Schubert here picked it up pretty fast."* I was feeling a little uncomfortable at this point because I'd known Steve for what seemed to be my entire life – and Ron had only become a friend recently.

"Yeah Ron – but I can't play anything can I? I may have ears like a bat – but they're not much use if I can't wrap my fingers 'round a barré chord."

Steve detected that I was standing up for him. I noticed the nearly imperceptible smile, the movement of eyebrows, and the gaze that flitted in my direction for a split second.

Ron recognised he'd been heavy handed and said " . . . *'course . . . Baroque contrapuntal Jazz isn't really your thing – so it'll not be as easy for you as it is for the*—great—*grand nephew*—*of Schubert.*" Ron cackled – and Steve burst out laughing. "*That's just such a wild idea. Makes me laugh every time I think about it.*" Ron was becoming quite skilled at changing the subject and I was glad that he'd taken the spotlight off Steve.

I nodded my head in mock weariness at the Schubert reference and said "*Yeah Ron*—really—*creases me up* [3] *completely.*"

Ron went to find another apple from the dining room and when he came back he said "*Anyway . . . I reckon we could do something like this.*" He indicated the sheet music in his hand "*I've been listening to Bach's 'Well Tempered Clavier' and . . . looking through my sister's sheet music. There are some phrases there that would sound wild on lead*—if—*I could find the right moment to throw 'em in.*"

Steve chortled "*That'd turn it into Bach's 'Bad Tempered Clavier'.*"
I froze for a moment, wondering what Ron would make of that comment. The vaguest flicker crossed his eyes – but he recognised Steve's remark as a humorous compliment rather than sarcasm.

"*Right*" I followed on "*should've heard Ron playing Otis Spann piano riffs on guitar.*" That seemed to interest Steve and he asked Ron if he'd play something from Bach's 'Well Tempered Clavier'. Ron obliged on piano and I was awestruck. Then he translated it on TELECASTER – which had Steve and me grinning like fiends.

---

3 'Creases me up' is 1960s British vernacular meaning 'has me laughing uproariously'.

Jack wasn't too interested but Steve nodded furiously in token of some massive new understanding.

"*You're right Ron. I'm really going to*—have—*to look into this. After all – Music College is going to take me in this direction – so I really do need to start exploring it. I think I could get seriously enthusiastic about this. I'd just never thought of this kind of music as being so . . . well . . . it's amazing. It's as if that was written this morning.*"

The next day Steve and I were rehashing the startling revelations that had occurred in conversation with Ron and I said
"*Y'know . . . I've been thinking about counterpoint and how two melody lines play in and out of each other and I've been wondering about using that idea in lyrics. I could weave themes in and out of each other – and that could end up sounding quite interesting. I'd just have to settle on themes that weren't discordant – or not so discordant that it sounded like a word stew.*"

Steve thought that sounded intriguing "*I'd like to see the outcome – it sounds as if it's got real possibilities.*"

We'd been writing songs together since 1964. Most had been discarded on the basis that they looked as if they'd been written by early adolescents – but we'd kept a record of the odd lines we thought worth preserving. There was always the tantalising notion of making an album and how we'd construct it. 'Sgt. Pepper's Lonely Hearts Club Band' had fired our imaginations with the fact that you could develop a theme.

"*I think . . .*" Steve mused "*. . . it's time we started playing some of our own numbers.*"

"*Yes!*" I agreed with delight "*I think we could use at least one in every set – y'know to show people we've got variety and write our own material.*"

"*Yeah . . .*" Steve concluded "*No one gets*—anywhere—*without writing their own material.*"

Steve loved Blues – but was not quite as obsessed as Ron and I, so he was pleased that I still wanted to write songs in other genres. *"Well certainly Steve, I think Ron would agree entirely. The only thing we object to is watering down Blues – or speeding it up into dance music. I think our Blues covers should remain real Blues — then our Acid Rock*[4] *numbers would be the place we pull in threads from everywhere. I have a lot of ideas about certain songs and the way they sound, like 'Taxman'. Then there's 'I'm only Sleeping' and 'Tomorrow Never Knows'. They're brilliant songs – and I think that Ron would have some good ideas about how to write those kinds of melodies – but . . . in our own style."*

It had occurred to me that Jack Bruce and Pete Brown wrote some fine songs – which had the feeling of Blues numbers whilst being something else. Most British bands that called themselves 'Blues bands' were basically Rock'n'Roll bands who played Blues too fast – but we were a Blues band who played Acid Rock. We wanted our Rock numbers to be gritty – but highly polished, like 'White Room' and 'Sunshine of Your Love'. These were *serious songs* – and the band felt that I could write lyrics of that calibre. I didn't quite have their confidence – but I knew I could write poetry. I knew I had the vocabulary to be generous with verses. My main problem, was knowing the words to omit. I had to be on guard against proliferating a pyrotechnic profusion of perilously impertinent polysyllabics.

After my conversation with Steve I'd written some new lyrics that I'd entitled 'The Women and Their Ravens'. I'd had the idea some time back – after Jack's confusion about the ravens on the band poster.

---

4 Psychedelic Rock.

It occurred to me that I could make more of the theme – especially if I imagined myself explaining ravens to Jack. What more could I say to Jack that would bewilder him poetically? Or—maybe better—what could I write to show him that bewilderment was glorious?

I had a line in my head about '*the moonlight's shining upward from the planet's misty core*' and I was playing with ways of bringing ravens into that. I sat in my parents' garden watching the birds drinking water from the bird bath. They had a curious way of continually checking the situation, and the rhyme of another line sprang to mind:
'*Looking backward—looking forwards—three miles through the floor.*'

I pulled out my notebook and arranged the words. I decided to have all the lines rhyme so I penned some alternative rhymes for 'core' and 'floor'. I was watching the birds and waiting for an idea when that idea itself turned into a line:
'*While I'm watching and waiting – wondering what's the score.*'

Then I had to get some kind of direction and fix the order of the lines. I needed something to connect them. My mother was standing by the door and had just called me in to dinner when it became obvious:
'*The women with their ravens were standing by the door.*'

That line would have to come first. Then looking backwards and forwards. Then the moonlight. Then the watching and waiting. That was interesting – but there was something missing. I went in and took my place at the dinner table. My father seemed in a relatively jocular mood. He'd landed a contract for surveying work and he was pleased about it.

My brother Græham was receiving some admonition about the fact that time was moving fast and that he'd need to start thinking about whether he was going to go on to Grammar School or to one of the Technical Colleges.

The radio was burbling away. The radio announcer droned on " *. . . showers in Northern Ireland . . . winds light to moderate . . . Dogger, German Bight, Biscay . . . gale force eight . . . cold front approaching from South East Iceland . . . wind veering . . . visibility good.* " [5] I'd been in some distant reverie when the term 'cold front' intruded and merged with the idea of time moving. I peered into the evening sky beyond the French Windows. Suddenly I had another line:
'Looking out through walls of weather and time is moving fast.'

It wasn't the missing line – but I decided I'd use this somewhere else. The rest of the song came together quite quickly after that. I showed it to Steve who put his mind to it and after a few changes – it was complete. The lads thought it was 'a dynamite number'. Jack—being more fanciful than Steve and Ron— thought the song was Cream, Bob Dylan, and the Beatles rolled into one. A preposterous notion – but I was elated to have it so well received. I worked with Ron and Steve on the melody line and we came up with a mutant Blues-based foray in **E** minor. It had an atmosphere a little like Cream's 'White Room' – but the chorus was less wistful.

The chorus ran:
'I'm looking at the future – and I'm looking at the past, / Trying to get a fix on you through scales of frosted glass. / Looking out through walls of weather and time is moving fast, / But the women and their ravens have made me out at last.'

---

5 The BBC Radio 4 shipping forecast was broadcast four times a day.

Then there were five verses that were variations of the following:

The women with their ravens were standing by the door, / Looking backward—looking forwards—three miles through the floor, / And the moonlight's shining upward from the planet's misty core / While I'm watching and awaiting – wondering what's the score.

The women with their ravens – turned round to look at me, / They'd thrown their dresses at the sky – their hair flowed like the sea, / Behind the sun their voices shone like florid coquetry / And I caught that wildness just in time for incongruity. Larkin/Bruce/Schubert—Savage Cabbage—The Women and Their Ravens—Savoy Green—1970

We just had to have good original material. Ron thought *that* was what I wrote; even if it was highly Baroque. I was never entirely happy with my lyrics. I felt they wafted between pretentiousness on one hand and banality on the other. I was impatient to write the perfect song. There *were* perfect songs out there—mostly by Bob Dylan and the Beatles—but every once in a while I'd catch another perfect song like 'The Weight' by The Band.

I pulled into Nazareth, was feeling 'bout half past dead, / I just need to find some place where I can lay my head.
Robbie Robertson—The Band—The Weight—Music From Big Pink—1968

Or 'Waterloo Sunset' by the Kinks.

Dirty old river, must you keep rolling, flowing into the night – people so busy make me feel dizzy, taxi lights shine so bright.
Ray Davies—The Kinks—Waterloo Sunset—1967

Savage Cabbage could make songs like these harder edged – in a similar vein to Cream's 'White Room'. We didn't want to play covers of anything apart from traditional Blues – but before we built up our own repertoire – we accepted that we had to play a few Acid Rock covers.

We tried 'Itchycoo Park' one day as an experiment.

Over bridge of sighs to rest my eyes in shades of green / Under dreaming spires to Itchycoo Park, that's where I've been.
Steve Marriot—Small Faces—Itchycoo Park—1967

I put some snarl into those words; Jack surpassed himself on percussion; and, Steve welded frenzy and accuracy into a missile. Ron did what he always did – and group consensus held that it flew like a B52 bomber. If we could do that with 'Itchycoo Park' we could do it with any song *we* wrote. We just needed to be the band we were. We tried various covers and I found I could convert almost anything into Blues. I just needed to syncopate it heavily and add the characteristic unrestrained rubato. Ron, Steve and Jack just needed to play as they played with 'Spoonful' or 'Born Under a Bad Sign'.

Jack suggested we try 'Whiter Shade of Pale'. He loved that song – so we hit it with a sledge hammer and turned it into the meanest song any hippie ever sang.

And so it was that later as the miller told his tale, / That her face at first just ghostly – turned a whiter shade of pale.
Brooker/Fisher/Reid—Procol Harum—Whiter Shade of Pale—1967

Jack stared at me when we got finished with that number and said *"Fierce! You could make 'Feeling Groovy' sound like the bloody devil's national anthem!"*

So I did—so we did—and our versions of these songs were not entirely unlike Joe Cocker's 1969 version of 'With a Little Help From My Friends'. The similarities were: slower tempo; dropped key; the addition of $7^{th\text{-diminished}}$ chords; and long improvised instrumental sections. Joe Cocker's version of 'With a Little Help From My Friends' was a Rock-Soul fusion and ours were Rock-Blues fusions. We also remained a little closer to the original melody lines of the songs we revamped.

Acid Rock was a highly varied genre and included approaches that ranged between wistful dreams to rampant bedlam.[6] In '68 there was an explosion of Acid Rock which started to show teeth. We had: 'Evil', 'Death of an Electric Citizen', and the album 'Wasa Wasa' by the Edgar Broughton Band. There was a great deal more [7] – some that we liked a great deal and some that we considered decidedly appalling.

We decided we were good at this jet-propelled Acid Rock gear change. We lined up a few of these to add variety to our gigs 'til we had enough original material to drop everything else apart from Blues. It was just a question of composing melody lines for my lyrics and both Steve and Ron agreed that it shouldn't be rushed. We'd played a few shows and audiences seemed to like our covers so it was no big problem in the interim. It had been hard work organising and promoting gigs ourselves – but word had got round that we were good and more people turned up on each occasion. Then our first real gig crept up on us, at the speed of light. I'd talked about Savage Cabbage with Greg Ford at Virginia Water one day and he said *"Try the Compton Bells mate – bands play there every weekend. I'll be there tonight. I'll see what's coming up."*

I decided almost immediately that there was no point waiting for Greg to check it out for me. *"I'll see you up there – I may as well get the lay of the land."*

---

6 1966: *Rain, I'm Only Sleeping*, and *Tomorrow Never Knows* by the Beatles; *Eight Miles High* by the Byrds; and *Paint it Black* by the Stones. 1967: *White Rabbit* and *Spare Chaynge* by Jefferson Airplane; *Purple Haze* and *Third Stone From The Sun* by Jimi Hendrix; *Sing This Song All Together* by the Stones; *Blue Jay Way, Baby You're a Rich Man, Lucy in the Sky with Diamonds, I Am the Walrus,* and *Strawberry Fields Forever* by the Beatles.

7 *That's It for the Other One* by The Grateful Dead; *Voodoo Child (Slight Return), EXP, All Along the Watchtower, 1983 (A Merman I Should Turn To Be),* and *If 6 Was 9* by Jimi Hendrix; *White Room* and *Badge* by Cream; *Crown of Creation* by Jefferson Airplane; *Set the Controls for the Heart of the Sun* by Pink Floyd; *Dazed and Confused* by Led Zeppelin; and *Acid Queen* by the Who.

When I arrived Greg was sitting behind a pint with Pete.
I joined them with my usual ginger beer.

"Fella over there—name's Dave—I told him you'd be by" and then
conspiratorially *"Think you—might—be in with a chance. They've
had a cancellation – but . . . play it cool. Don't sound—too—eager . . .
if y'know what I mean."*

I strolled over in what I imagined to be the epitome of
nonchalance. I opened in the deepest tone I could manage
"Dave?"

It was too deep. He didn't hear me. I was drowned in the
background noise of the pub. Bad start. I swung into the seat
next to him and caught his eye.

*"Dave, m'name's Vic—friend of Greg—think he mentioned me. I'm the
vocalist with the Savage Cabbage Blues band."*

Dave looked slightly puzzled at first – but then remembered
someone had said something earlier that evening.

*"Heard you had a cancellation – thought you might want someone to fill
in."*

Dave nodded in a deliberately casual manner and said *"Yeah . . .
short notice—it'appens—can you fill next Saturday?"*

Sure we could. Although, I had no idea whether Steve, Ron, and
Jack would be up for it. *"I'll have to check it with the lads – but I see
no problem."*

Dave peered at me with what I took to be an enquiring
expression. *"Are you—good?"*

I shook my head slowly and replied *"No . . . "* Pause *"We're—
better."*

"You better be" Dave grinned *"or I'll 'ave yer guts for garters."*

56

"Don't think you'd cut a dash dress-wise, with our intestines round your legs" I grinned.

"Joker eh?" Dave responded with quite a chuckle *"Talk t'the crowd like that and y'll be*—well in—*mate, well in"* Pause *"Y're on then. 7:30 to 9:30 – but, be here at 6 sharp. Whaddya play by the way?"*

"Blues – Chicago Blues."

Dave shook his head. *"Yeah—yeah—yeah, y'told me*—that—*before mate. I mean, what*—equipment—*yer got?"*

This was my trump card. "Fenders . . . Telecaster, Precision bass, 6 *string* Hagstrom bass, Gibson EB3, EB0, Marshall *amps. Oh . . . and* Ludwig *drums."*

Dave winked in approval with a tilt of his head. *"Nice kit mate— niiiiice kit—wouldn't 'ave'em if yer couldn't play'em eh? 'nough said son – bring it on over."* And that was it. I shook hands on the deal and walked back to join Greg.

"You got the gig then" he said with a huge affable smirk.

"How d'you know?"

"Cool as an ice cube—you—*are. Y're grinning all over yer face"* Greg laughed *"Still you swung it. Good for you mate."*

I had to admit that pleasure had entirely overcome any sense of 'cool' I'd attempted to adopt. *"Still . . . "* I grinned, misquoting Son House *"Dontcha mind if I'm grinning in yo' face – just bear this in mind a true friend is hard to find."*

"Docile bugger . . . I'll stab you in the back next time" Greg shook his head laughing *"Just make sure you get front seats for me and the bird."*

I nodded and avoided saying 'The bird must be at least a pelican—or a pretty flamingo—to warrant its own seat.' Our first real gig – and all I had to do was tell the lads what I'd let them in for. As it happened – the lads were all free and unanimously delighted.

"Mister Arbuthnot nothing – he's Mister Fix-it" Jack almost yelled.

I made no comment about how gruesome that sounded to me. *"It was an accident Jack – and mainly due to Greg Ford being in the know."*

The gig came and went. It was no different from the gigs we'd arranged ourselves – but there was a sense that we were on new territory. We'd arrived. Dave the organiser wasn't cool at all after we came off at the end. There was no trace of his former superiority of tone.

"Stone the crows, when you said you were 'better than good', well—bloody *—hell—you were un—be—fucking—lievable. Want you back 'ere lads, when*—ever. *Crowd loved you. What y'doing next month? Know it's close – but hey . . . fantastic lads—bloody—fantastic."* He gave us a list of evenings.

"We'll call when we've sorted out the dates." That was Ron being 'Mister Nonchalant'. Ron could do that well. I could hardly do it at all.

On the way home we discussed the gig. It was good as far as Jack and I were concerned. Steve thought we could have played better – but Ron was a little annoyed. He felt we could have been a great deal better – especially Jack. He told Jack *"You've just gotta put in more practice Jack, or you won't be able to roll with the changes when we improvise. You can't just go crazy y'know. That's*—not *—the way to be like Ginger Baker."*

Jack was a little disgruntled. *"The man said we were fantastic! What more d'you want?"*

Ron shook his head *"I want you to be like Ginger Baker"* Pause *" . . . 'sides . . . that bloke said we were fantastic because he hasn't heard anything but Rock'n'Roll head bangers. We can't start thinking we're fantastic just because a bloody gig organiser liked us."*

Steve and I sat and listened to this in silence. We both knew Ron was right – but we both felt sorry for Jack.

"*What d'you think then Steve?*" Jack enquired. "*You're not saying anything.*"

"*Well . . .*" Steve pondered artificially to give the impression that he didn't know exactly what he was going to say. "*You're a lot more inventive now Jack . . . but . . . you could listen a little more to the direction we're taking when we improvise. You sometimes don't notice when we're slowing down – y'know, to come back into the main melody line.*" Steve—although not as critical as Ron—agreed that Jack needed to avoid losing it when he went wild.

Jack looked to me. "*Well Jack – you know how I am with rhythm . . . I can't really comment apart from the fact that I'd always listen to Ron and Steve. They passed grade eight music sometime in the early Jurassic period.*" The van was silent for a while as Jack brooded.

Ron eventually broke the silence. "*Sorry Jack . . . that was a bit heavy . . . I mean we—all—have to practise. Think you got it in yer though – or I wouldn't've said it.*" Steve and I concurred. Jack had it in him. Jack brightened – and then admitted that Ron was right.

"*It's just . . . well it was a bit of a come down after the gig – and after that bloke telling us the crowd loved us.*"

Ron acknowledged he should have let the evening roll. "*Sorry 'bout that . . . I could've waited for some other time. Didn't have to give you a bloody crit walking off stage. I s'pose I got used to it from music lessons and the piano and guitar recitals . . . I've had teachers chew me out for making the slightest slip. I should remember that if you're not used to it, it can be . . . well . . . bloody horrible I s'pose.*"

Jack said he'd practise. He'd get it down.

Jack could sometimes live in a fantasy world – but he recognised he had to make the grade with Ron and Steve. It had been hard for him to understand at first – because he'd have made an acceptable drummer in most local bands. When he recognised that Ron was a world class musician however, he must have decided to take advantage of that fact rather than being aggrieved by rightful criticism. He'd recognised that both Ron and Steve were giving him a chance. He was the new lad on the scene and he knew they weren't obliged to keep him if he didn't pull his weight. With me however, there was a sense of ambiguity. I was a vocalist, harp player, and amateur guitarist. I think that Jack saw me as being on a par with him – whatever Ron and Steve said about me. I had no interest in placing Jack in fourth position – even though Steve and I saw Ron as the main man.

I appreciated Jack's feelings – socially, in terms of receiving artistic criticism when Steve and I were present. I think that's why he always addressed me as 'Mr Arbuthnot' when he knew that Steve called me Vic and Ron called me Frank. It must have been his way of telling me that he'd flexed his muscles with regard to my name. Ron and Steve would have been happy to have gone with Frank Schubert as my band name – but Jack had prevailed. I didn't mind either way – but I did wish that Jack would relax about his status. I made sure I always complimented his drumming – but knew that compliments were only worth anything if they came from Ron or Steve.

Jack took a while to warm to me because I was almost *too* much of an odd ball for him. I was too weird on one side and too starchy on the other. I almost never swore and displayed a marked disinterest in scatological humour.

Jack however found fæcal references of almost unending
entertainment. His favourite expression of surprise concerned
mutilating his genitalia with the aid of a jubilee clip.[8] I tried my
best to find him amusing at such times – but there was a limit to
how often I could laugh about references to *grilled turds* or tales
of setting fire to flatulence.

Rumours that Cream were splitting up had begun circulating the
music scene. It seemed ominous somehow – with an impact
extending beyond the possible loss of the band. They'd been
riding a tide of brilliance – and their influence had been
profound. *Had been* . . . We talked about it as if we were at a
wake before the death knell had rung – but after a few such
discussions we started to see that it was a beginning as well as an
end. Savage Cabbage were going to take Blues forward. We had
an amazing future. All Savage Cabbage needed was to stay
together. Then we'd hone ourselves into the finest Blues band
there'd ever been. Ron was easily capable of the feat. Steve was
more than good enough. Jack would improve – and, even if he
never became another Ginger Baker, it was not crucial to our
sound that he be on a par with Ron and Steve. Then *the odd boy*.
What of him? He had a voice, played harp, and produced
surrealist lyrics. The lads were in awe of my lyrics – but I was
never content with them. I was driven to improve them. I
wanted to arrive at a point where they'd stand alongside Bob
Dylan and the Beatles. I felt I needed to offer more than my
voice and occasional harp.

A notion began to gnaw my neurons. It was a wild idea in a
world of wild ideas. It seemed within the bounds of normalcy
for me – and I *had* to take some kind of new initiative.

---

8 Hose clamp in the USA.

Steve would be with me. Jack wouldn't mind as long as he thought it would get him closer to a drum solo. I'd raised the subject a couple of times in the past with Ron – but he'd been distinctly unimpressed. What would he think now? It was the talk of solos that made me feel it was time to raise the question again. It was a question of my playing 'second bass'. If I could play rhythm bass Steve could go out there with Ron and we'd have two lead instruments. The more I thought about it the more convinced I became. I sat, walked, rode, and lay in bed staring at that idea. It was as perfect as any idea could be . . . if I could learn enough fast enough – and . . . if Ron could be convinced. A serious discussion was looking inevitable.

3

november 1968 – december 1968

basso continuo

A numinous notion had been nibbling at me for some years.
It began when I first touched a bass guitar. Somehow, although
Steve and I talked about it from time to time – the question was
never entirely resolved. What would I *do* with my birthday bass
—I wondered—when Steve was obviously going to be the bass
player of whatever band we formed? Well . . . Jimi Hendrix had
brought 'wild' into mainstream consciousness in '67 – and so the
path *should* have been clear to go to the limits of imagination.

It was however, not quite as simple as that – not where Ron and
Chicago Blues were concerned. Ron was a purist. I admired
and respected him for that – but it presented certain obstacles.
I'd mentioned my wild idea to him—briefly—in '66 not long
after we'd first met. *"So Ron . . . when I'm 18 I'll be getting the*
Gibson *EB0 and amp that used to belong to Steve's uncle Stan – and . . .*
that'll set me up really nicely. It's a beautiful guitar."

"Yeah—good—that'll be nice. Although . . . " Ron—with slightly
narrowed eyes—replied *" . . . what y'gonna do with it?"*

I put on a patient parental face – resigned to dealing with folly
"Well Ron, I—thought—*I'd learn to play some weighty Blues with it."*

"Well yeah. I worked—that—*out for myself."*

"Good" I replied ignoring Ron's antithetical position to my
enthusiasm. *"I've been working on the* **A** *pentatonic Blues scale round at*
Steve's and I'm starting to get a good feel for it."

Ron shook his head "*What I meant, was*—with—*the band. What y'gonna do with it*—with—*the band?*"

"*Well Ron, I*—thought—*that I'd play it*" I explained again with patient incomprehension. "*Isn't that how it usually goes? You*— learn—*the instrument, then you*—play—*the instrument.*"

Ron laughed rather quietly—and a little nervously—aware that he'd hit an unexpected fogbank of derangement. "*Right Vic*— *well yeah*—*so . . . you're thinking 'bout a two bass line up. Have you ever* —talked—*about this with Steve?*"

"*Yes, certainly*—*off and on*—*I've talked about it with Steve for the last four years.*"

"*And . . . Steve didn't ever*—mention—*that no one*—does—*that?*"

Steve *had* mentioned something along those lines "*Yes . . . so did his father . . . but they never said it was out of the question – just that it'd be unusual. Steve thought it was a wild idea – I mean people are doing*— all kinds of things—*now, aren't they?*"

Ron was obviously dumbfounded by my persistence – so I took a step back "*Still . . . I don't have the* EB0 *at the moment – so . . . it's not really in question right now. Thing is . . . I feel we ought to be open to being experimental. Just because no one does a thing doesn't mean it*— can't—*be done. It's just about finding a way that works.*"

Ron sighed as if he was involved in a discussion with the densest lump of matter in the known universe "*Don't you think . . . if there was*—any—*possibility of it working, that someone wouldn't have tried it by now?*"

That made no sense to me because surprising innovations were always possible.

"*Well . . . you could look at it like that – but . . . they thought the earth was flat once didn't they? And they avoided travelling too far west in order not to fall off the edge. And someone must have said 'Don't you think . . . if there was—any—possibility of the earth being round, that someone wouldn't have sailed round it by now?'.*"

"*Well . . . yeah*" Ron laughed "*You got me there.*" He rubbed his chin " *. . . you* could *look at it like that . . . but it's not that we don't—* know—*what a bass sounds like. Having two basses would be really . . . bloody . . . muddy.*"

"*Nice rhyme Ron – but I'm still not convinced it's—*not—*worth a try.*"

"*Right . . . well I can't say it wouldn't be an experiment*" Ron grinned "*So let's experiment – but . . . let's wait 'til you—*get—*that bloody bass —and—learn to play*" Pause "*And then . . . we'll see how it sounds.*"

"*You could see how it sounded . . . now. I've been playing around on it for a few years.*"

"*Well yeah . . .*" Ron groaned " *. . . but getting up to speed with the band'll take more than that*" Pause "*And—y'know Vic—once you get it down on bass . . . you just might change your mind about this whole thing. It's not that I don't think you've some really good ideas – but this one . . . well . . .* " Pause "*I think it sounds interesting—*as you imagine it— *but that might not turn out to be what it actually is. Some things sound great as ideas and then you find out that they don't work. But . . . I don't want to cramp your style or anything. I'll give it a go when the time comes.*"

"*Good on yer—cheers Ron—I'm not asking for any more than the chance to see how it sounds. You know I respect your pure approach with Chicago Blues. I'm really with you—*all—*the way . . . mainly I mean . . .* " Pause "*You know I don't want horns and keyboards or any of that lounge-lizard bilge – but . . . I think there—*are—*other things we can do that—*could—*grow into our individual style.*"

Ron had a real loathing of the horns and keyboards where Blues was concerned – so this was always the right thing to say. Ron pulled a dismissive expression. *"God yeah . . . bloody horns and keyboards – you're right there. If I want a sodding orchestra I'll listen to bloody Boccherini."*

Ron hadn't been sure about me back in '66 – but the longer we knew each other, the more he listened to my 'wild ideas'. He gradually came to respect the fact that my *craziness* was not silliness – and that I was, as he put it *'just kind of exceptionally and uncommonly unconventional'*. He read my poetry and—although it went beyond his ability to judge—he admitted to being mightily impressed by it. *"Your poetry's always unpredictable. You think you know where it's going and it goes somewhere else."* He liked my lyrics as well *"You know I can definitely see our set including your songs. I mentioned it to Steve and we'd like to get together with you on the melody lines."*

The idea of playing bass never left me – even when I'd constructed the DEBIL. The GIBSON EB0 simply hung suspended in the experiential distance – awaiting the 6th of June 1970. I had ideas about the bass spectrum that had been sparked off by the existence of Steve's 6 string HAGSTROM BASS. A bass could be tuned in a variety of ways – either an octave down from a lead guitar – or **B** to **B**. I liked the idea of having an even lower string. That low **B** sounded like something from the depths of the earth.

"Could you take it further I wonder?" I asked Steve in '67. He'd looked doubtful.

*"Some say . . . the low **B** is the lowest pitch the human ear can distinguish. That's why the classical double bass sometimes has one if it's a five string double bass – but I think it's—possible—to go lower by a few notes."*

That had me thinking. *"So . . . maybe . . . even if you couldn't distinguish a low* **A** *from a low* **B** *that easily . . . you'd still*—feel—*it."*

Steve made his side-to-side head movement indicating *'yes – but so?'* Then he seemed to understand what I meant. *"You're thinking about the two bass line-up again, aren't you?"*

"Aren't I, always?"

"Yes, you are" Steve laughed.

"Thing is . . . I know—Ron—*doesn't agree – but . . . I think it*—could—*work."*

"So what's your idea now, then?"

"Right—*here it goes*—*y'know that Ron tunes* **D G C F A D** *rather than standard* **E** *to* **E**."

"Yes . . ."

"Well . . . if I could drop a string lower: **A D G C** *rather than* **D G C F**."

"Ah . . . so that's why you were wondering about going lower than the low **B**."

"Yes . . ." Pause *" . . . and*—you said—*it was possible."*

"Yes . . . scientifically speaking . . . but it might be—really—*difficult to tune by ear unless you were a pachyderm or cetacean* [1] *or whatever hears frequencies like that."*

"Well y'know me Steve . . . I'm a third strain from a triceratops – but all you need to do is play the **A** *an octave above and I'll feel it in."*

"All right . . . I'm with you so far . . . "

---

1 Pachyderm or cetacean – elephant or whale. Steve Bruce has a fascination with zoology when young. See chapter 3, in Volume I of 'an odd boy'.

"*Good!*" I grinned "*Then—you—could tune your* HAGSTROM *from the* **G** *string up* **G C F A D G**. *That way . . . we wouldn't have that big sea of mud that Ron's so worried about. It'd be like some kind of earthquake.*"

"*Tempting . . . tempting . . .* " Steve chuckled " *. . . that would answer a lot of questions for me. I love bass but I've always missed playing standard guitar. It's where I started – and that's why I like the 6 string Hagstrom. So . . . this would let me well into Ron's range whilst still being bass*" Pause "*Mmmm . . . but . . . convincing Ron . . . that won't be easy. He told me you'd brought the idea up last year and he thought you were three sheets to the wind.*"

"*I don't think he thinks like—that—anymore.*"

"*No . . . but he's got pretty fixed ideas on how Chicago Blues should be played.*"

The 'second bass' idea was shelved again – but I'd earmarked it for another airing a few months on.

Once I'd got a taste of playing gigs – the idea returned with greater strength. Standing there looking around the hall doing nothing during the long instrumental improvisations was not ideal by any means. There were the times I played harp – but harp was not required on every number.

Steve had been making enormous strides with bass. He'd taken to flying all over the neck with his riffs. He was elaborating on the bass lines and throwing in alternative motifs – much to the approbation of Ron. I was also delighted – but vexed. This new development simply made it more obvious to me that there was a definite rôle for bass in our band – both a rhythm and melody instrument. With Steve on lead bass playing melody in counterpoint to Ron, the band would require the background wallop of a simple bass line.

The more I listened to Ron and Steve jamming the more excited I became about the real possibility of a *twin-bass line-up*. The time had come for me to make my case to Ron again.

"Ron . . . I've got to talk to you about something—we talked about it before—but this time it's different."

"What the hell are you talking about?" Ron almost cackled *"You sound . . . well, serious . . . what's this about?"*

"It's my idea about the two bass line-up" I launched in and started enthusing – but noticed that Ron had that *'not this again'* look on his face. *"No Ron. I'd like you to listen to this—with—an open mind. Way I see it . . . Steve's good enough now to play 'lead bass'—he's really taken off."*

"Yeah. He's good. He's actually very good" Ron nodded. *"He's really been working at it. I can hear it every time we rehearse — but what's this 'lead-bass' thing? D'you mean splitting bass like you split guitars? Like lead-bass and rhythm-bass?"*

"Exactly Ron!" I whooped exultantly. *"Steve wants to be another Jack Bruce – and he'll get there, the way he's working at it. Then there'll be a rôle for me playing a—very—very—very—simple rhythm-bass – y'know . . . in the background."* Ron looked as if I was talking about having been abducted by aliens – but I pressed on *"I've been practising at Steve's and he doesn't think it would take too much for me to be able to handle—extremely—simple lines."*

Ron skewed his nose and scratched his ear *"Right . . . Steve thinks that, does he?"* Pause *"I think . . . I'd still be a bit concerned about fuzz . . . y'know . . . dampening the attack"* Pause *"It might get in the way of your vocals too."*

I thought that over for a moment.

"Yes . . . that's something I'm willing to consider. I don't want to make a mess of the sound. What I'm thinking is that I could play—really—low-volume so I'm felt rather than heard . . . if you know what I mean."

Ron went in search of an apple and returned with two prodigious Russets. He threw one to me as he knew I liked them. *"Right . . . well . . . yeah . . . no harm in—trying—it"* Pause *"But . . . you won't be seriously pissed off with me if I think it sounds crap-awful?"*

"If you—really—think it sounds bad I'll go along with you" I assured Ron *"but I think this—is—going to work. I can hear it in my mind."*

Ron looked at me in partially doubtful curiosity *"In your mind?"*

"Yes Ron . . . " I beamed back *" . . . in my mind . . . I hear'n'see things there, y'know."*

Steve turned up later and Ron put the idea to him.

"Vic on 2nd bass! Yeah! I'm—all—for it" Steve cheered. *"He'll be getting my Uncle's* GIBSON EB0 *when he's 18 – so he may as well prepare – he could borrow the* DANELECTRO *. . . that way my parents won't think I said anything about the EB0."*

Ron screwed up his nose at the idea of the DANELECTRO. He hated it. *"If it's—gotta—be . . . there's my EB3 – but . . . y'know . . . I—really—don't know about this idea."*

"I've been listening a lot—to my mother's Classical pieces—and . . . I think I've learnt something interesting" Steve fixed Ron with a deadly gleam in his eye *"Bass and lead don't cover it, and—as we're all dead set against keyboards and horns—we need something to get a broader spectrum. An orchestra has cellos and violas as well as violins and basses – so . . . "*

"So yeah . . . " Ron stared into the distance – rapt in some kind of inner conjecture *"Right . . . "*

At length he grinned *"So . . . you'd be prepared to tune up then?"*
Steve nodded his agreement. *"Get more into the baritone register?"*
Ron enquired further *"That's . . . not exactly your preferred range
though . . . is it?"*

"Mmmm . . . I wouldn't want to tune—that—*high . . . "* Steve replied
" . . . but . . . what if Vic tuned—down—*maybe* **A D G C** *. . . and I
tuned up* **G C F A D G** *. . . we'd have a*—very—*interesting spread."*

"Yeah . . . " Ron pondered *" . . . that'd obscure bum notes."* Ron
caught my expression *"Not that Frank's gonna do that I mean – I'm
sure he could handle a simple bass line."*

"Absolutely – no doubt" Steve exclaimed. *"He's getting a real feel for
this thing. I think you'll be surprised at what he can do now. He's a
natural with bends and vibrato too."*

"Yeah Frank's—always—*surprising."* Ron devoured the core of
his apple. He liked the slightly bitter taste of the pips. *" . . .
y'know . . . maybe . . . it*—could—*work . . . "* Ron cackled. *"Hears
it in his mind*—y'know—*like bloody Mozart."* Ron sympathised with
my situation. He knew I was desperate to be holding any kind
of guitar on stage.

"You see Ron . . . apart from the fact that I love bass . . . I've—had it—
with standing there like 'Stammering Lemon Gauche' " Pause *"When the
three of you get into half hour improvisations – I'm just left standing there.
What am I supposed to do?"*

"Yeah . . . " Ron sighed *"Fair comment . . . "*

"Right" I stated, turned my palms upward *"I don't know*—what—
to do with my hands when I'm not singing – and" I laughed *"I'm*—not
—*repeat*—not—*going to shake a goddamn tambourine."*

"Too right Frank!" Ron laughed *"We don't want no bloody*—
green—*tambourine."*

71

There was a ring on the doorbell. It was Jack. Ron went to let him in saying *"Let's ask Jack what he thinks."* Jack threw himself into an armchair as if he'd had a hard day at work. We could all tell he'd had some sort of hard time with his parents. We observed him changing gear over a few moments – and suddenly he grinned.

"We've got a question for you" Steve began, when Jack was obviously in his usual 'being with my mates' mode.

Jack wiggled his eyebrows and said *"Hit me with it."*

"It's like this" Steve proceeded *"Vic's had it with standing around like a lemon when we're improvising – and he's had the idea of being 2nd bass – playing rhythm while I play a lead bass melody line. I really like the idea – but Ron's not sure about it. What do you think? Think it's worth a try?"*

Jack—always the joker—turned to me and suggested *"You could make moves like Mick Jagger."*

That was not the answer I wanted to hear. *"Jack . . . y'know . . . I may be a lover but I—ain't—no dancer."*

Well will you won't you want me to make you / I'm coming down fast but don't let me break you / Tell me tell me tell me the answer / You may be a lover but you ain't no dancer.

Lennon/McCartney—Helter Skelter—White Album—1968

I *was* something of a dancer – but flamboyant dancing on stage did not seem dignified when it came to Blues. It was all right for Rock'n'Roll – but I saw Blues as more akin to playing in a Baroque string quartet. It was important to be a little formal with Blues. Muddy Waters didn't gyrate – he just stood there like the king of the planet. Undaunted, I returned to the theme of 2nd bass.

"Thing is Jack . . . I've wanted to be a musician since early last century. I know I play harp – but harp isn't always needed. I won't go into the big long horrible story of it – but it's important to me. Steve and I have an idea about it that might work." Jack assumed a 'tell me all about it' face and I continued *"The idea's this. Steve'd be on 6 string* HAGSTROM *– tuning higher:* **G C F A D G**. *I'd tune down:* **A D G C**. *Then I'd play* —extremely—*simple patterns that . . . "*

"I still think this is seriously weird . . . " Ron interrupted laughing *" . . . but what's—your—verdict Mister Rhythm Man?"*

"Why not?" Jack shrugged *"Might be good"* Pause *"Might keep Mr Arbuthnot here from going off on his own with the bloody vocals; like he—* does—*sometimes."* Jack was never wildly keen on my rubato – especially because Ron and Steve found it easy to fall in with my shifts in tempo.

"Question is . . . " said Ron *"I just don't know how that'd sound . . . could be brilliant of course. Frank's enthusiastic about it . . . so maybe it —is—brilliant."* Jack looked baffled at that comment but said nothing.

Ron went into one of his pensive trances as we sat back and listened to Cream. 'I'm So Glad' was in its improvisation section. It filled the space of the living room. Silences were a common occurrence with the lads when music was playing – and it often provided a valuable counterbalance to the direction of conversations.

Ron had obviously been weighing the idea up *" . . . although . . . y'know . . . Frank on my* EB3 *. . . and Steve being free to phrase in more complex ways . . . I think I'm starting to like it. Y'know . . . listening to Cream just now, kind of opened it up . . . "*

"Yeah!" Jack exclaimed. *"Steve's really been letting rip!"*

"Yeah" Ron nodded *"And I—really—like the direction it's going."*

Steve smiled a highly gratified smile – and Ron turned to me "*But . . . you'd*—*have*—*to play low volume. I mean*—really low volume—*'til you learn*—*all*—*the basic riffs for the numbers in our set.*"

"*You just show me Ron. I'll start now.*"

"*No bloody stopping him is there?*" Ron fell back laughing. "*You'd better borrow my* EB3."

My eyes lit up. "*You'd*—*really*—*loan me your* EB3*?*"

Ron nodded. He walked off to the music room and came back with the fabulous black beast. He strapped it on unplugged. "*This is Spoonful.*" Then he handed it over to me and watched as I copied him. Ron showed me the fingering and I set to immediately. After a few confused attempts I caught on. The lads continued chatting whilst I burbled away in the background – at a suitable distance so that I'd not be too closely observed.

After twenty minutes I called over "*How's this?*" and played the bass line to Spoonful.

"*Well bugger me!*" Ron laughed "*Natural born*—bloody—*bass player!*" His remark was comical – but it was delivered with some kind of joy that was highly encouraging. Then he applied the brake "*Now you've just got to learn to sing at the same time – and that's going to be more difficult.*"

He was right of course and I could see that this was going to be more difficult than I'd imagined. Steve saw my expression as I tried to sing over the counterpoint melody of the bass and came to the rescue. "*I can't do it either – but then I can't sing, so it's not a problem. You'll get it in the end – you'll just have to keep at it.*"

Ron nodded and added "*Of course*—*at first*—*you can leave off playing when you sing. That'll get you used to playing with the band and playing on stage.*"

It was a relief to hear that – as I'd suddenly felt as if it would be years before I could stand on stage with that EB3. I tuned the EB3 down to **A D G C**. Steve tuned the Hagstrom up **G** to **G** – and we were a going concern.

I'd already found an old leather rifle sling in the Army Surplus shop and adapted it to use as a strap, for the day the much-dreamed-of EB0 would come my way. In the interim, I wondered whether Ron would sell me his EB3. Ron said he'd think about it.

"In the meanwhile" he laughed *"you're welcome to practise with it and use it on stage. Any serious musician has to have more than one instrument. I'm thinking of getting a* Gibson *ES355—y'know, like the one BB King plays—and . . . your buying my* EB3 *would make that a whole lot easier."*

I could see myself on stage with two Gibson bass guitars . . . I could try different tunings – and who knew where that might lead. Had anyone ever tried playing slide on bass? I was suddenly full of crazy ideas and started saving for a Marshall bass amplifier.

Once I'd got up to speed a little Ron announced *"I think we're ready to try this two bass line-up on stage."* And then there we were – at The Cordwainer's Arms. It was eerie walking on stage with a bass. There were one or two surprised expressions from those who knew their music – and of course Gazzer Mitchell was there with his well-trained pedigree sneer.

Gazzer . . . why did *he* have to be there. Still I couldn't allow myself to be affected by Gazzer. I'd done my ground work and I was going to play like a professional – even though I was a kindergarten professional.

The gig went well and I kept my bass lines under control – but it put a crimp in my stage personality to some extent. The concentration was far more exhausting than I imagined. I even wondered a few times whether it wasn't just a terrible idea. Ron had to be talked into it and I wondered if he'd regretted it. On the way home, Ron leant in my direction. *"Nice one."* I was a bass player.

The EB3 has a short scale length—30 inches—and has a fast action. The lighter string tension of the short scale length allows severe note bending – and that became my major stylistic: maliciously slow riffs with giant bends. I started out producing a dull thudding sound to cover any errors – but it became evident to Ron that I'd got the hang of the bass riffs in our repertoire – he whispered conspiratorially *"Time to wind the volume up a notch Frank."*

When I became more reliable on bass Ron started teaching Steve how to wield slide on his HAGSTROM. Another of my insane ideas that just happened to work out. This time however, Ron liked the idea immediately. He'd got used to my wild ideas having something in them. When Steve got the hang of slide, Savage Cabbage started sounding maniacally eerie.

Ron was evidently enjoying my simple bass behind Steve's increasingly elaborate riffs and slides, and I started feeling I was a real musician. As Savage Cabbage started to become known – a growing following evolved on the pub circuit. We saw familiar faces amongst the audience. There were people who were obviously enjoying our music and looking at us in some way that had a zing to it. We were starting to feel as if we were growing into our stage personas. We'd walk on stage with the natural right to be there.

It wasn't that we'd become blasé—or that we were no longer nervous—it was more that we were no longer taking a risk. We'd arrived at some kind of destination. We hadn't made it big time – but we weren't failing. We saw grins when we switched our amplifiers on and swung to face the audience. There'd once been a look in people's faces as if they were thinking: '. . . *wonder what this is going to be like?*' Now people knew exactly what this was going to be like. It was going to be Blues – and it wasn't going to be lounge lizard Blues. It was going to be unhurried thousand ton footsteps – with menacing riffs. There'd be the percussionist who—although not the greatest—looked suitably deranged. Jack was nothing if not frenzied. He gave *good value for money* purely as theatre – but he'd taken Ron's advice and listened to Ginger Baker almost in the style of daily devotions. He'd worked hard and his efforts were showing. There was the two-bass line-up: the increasingly amazing lead bass – and the rhythm bass of the maniacal vocalist. Then there was Ron. People noticed Ron even though he was the complete antithesis of Jack on stage. He just placed himself on stage and played. He played with fantastic emotion but without any facial movement. Ron might occasionally lean backward slightly during a particularly ecstatic riff. That was the sum-total of his movement other than his hands.

November arrived and the final news that Cream were no more. It was a tragedy. I had a vision of life in which Cream were pivotal – they were the cutting edge of Blues. There were Blues classics such as 'Born Under a Bad Sign', 'Spoonful', and 'Sitting On Top of the World' but, there were not many of these absolutely riveting numbers. Jack Bruce and Pete Brown had written one—'Politician'—and it stood alongside the best Blues ever performed. The bass line was magnificent. I'd hoped there'd be other numbers like 'Politician'.

"Y'know . . . Cream could have done—so—much more . . ." I sighed *"I think that bands owe a loyalty to those who appreciate them – to remain together."*

Jack was all for that. *"We'll not be splitting up – we've got our ticket!"* Steve thought that Jack was probably the most anxious about the possibility of a split. Jack knew he was the weakest member. I always tried to reassure him that we were a band of brothers— that we were all there to bring each other on—but somehow that reassurance could only come from Ron or Steve. I was just the vocalist and the low volume experimental rhythm bassist.

Later that week I met up with Steve in Farnham having sloped off early from Virginia Water. Lindie was off sick so there'd been no point in my hanging 'round at school longer than was necessary. It wasn't hard to disappear if you were discreet enough about making your exit from the car park.

I met Steve as he emerged from Farnham Grammar and gave him a lift into town where we had a cup of coffee in a place we called 'The Nostril'. It was made out to look like a cave with stalactites – but we thought it resembled the nose of an ogre with a heavy cold. The sad news about Cream was still on our minds . . .

"Jack was right when he said we had our ticket" I said. *"We really have. I really hope we'll be a band who stays together . . . and grows musically. The idea of musical friendship is really important to me."*

Steve agreed and said *"Yeah . . . Cream splitting up's such a terrible waste."*

"Right . . . " I replied stretching my legs under the table *" . . . they had it worked out—so—perfectly on 'Wheels of Fire'. The live Blues disc —and—the studio psychedelic disc. It was the perfect formula."*

Steve was of the same mind *"And the—way—they were working with Blues was unique! That blend of Blues and Avant-Guard Jazz was a whole new dimension."*

I regretted the albums that would never be: Wheels of Air, Wheels of Space . . .

They'll sell you tickets for the morning, when the system's wearing thin, / But they'll stop you getting through the door on the dusky outer rim, / They lie in wait in chains and drains snorting cans of Vim,[2] */ There's no final throw, no way to go, unless you shed your skin.*
Larkin/Bruce/Schubert—Savage Cabbage—Unless You Shed Your Skin—Savoy Green—1970

We gathered again on the Friday evening as we had a gig at The Queen's Oak. We unloaded the gear—set up—and sat 'round behind the stage chatting about our music. We were absorbed with the ins-and-outs of our new material. Ron pulled out a large Cox's Orange Pippin and sank his teeth into it. I pulled out my usual flask of elderflower cordial. My mother made it and it was fabulously refreshing. I passed the flask to Steve who took a healthy swig. Jack declined as usual. *"Smells like cat's piss – that stuff."* He hated it. His mother had impressed upon him the idea that parents who went in for *home-made products* were somehow to be pitied. Such parents did it because they couldn't afford to buy 'the real thing'.

"Way I see it . . . " I said *"It's important we don't wind the throttle. 'Rolling and Tumbling'—is—our fast number – but I wouldn't want it turning into Rock'n'Roll. It's exciting – but speed'll ruin it. I think we should slow it down just a little."*

"You're right Frank" Ron agreed and took another bite from the apple.

---

2 Vim was a white domestic cleaning powder in Britain.

He loved apples and ate them almost incessantly. *"That song's got a life of its own and almost everyone goes at it like a race."*

Steve had no problem with slowing it down.

Jack was especially delighted. *"Great"* Jack beamed *"That'll give me a chance to bring in the cymbals and hi-hat a bit more."*

I liked what Jack did on cymbals. The hissing and crackling of them was much more—*my*—idea of percussion than the insistent walloping of skins.

"Y'know . . . I think we need to play some solos. I've been working like hell on a solo. I think it'll be fierce. I'd like you lot to listen to it."

We all nodded – but Ron said *"Yeah sure Jack, in time, but—none —of us are soloing yet. It's certainly something we could—aim—for though. Steve's ready on bass and Frank could do it on harp – but . . . we'd have to rehearse it pretty seriously if we were all to take a turn."*

Jack shrugged *"Yeah – but I'd like you to listen though."*

Ron grinned *"We'll listen."*

And so we did – but Ron was not impressed.

"You've got about two minutes' worth there Jack" Ron opined *"Don't get me wrong, you're a lot better*—a lot better—*but . . . a drum solo's gotta be a story . . . it's gotta keep changing to keep the audience interested. You've got a few nice patterns there – just not enough for the length of time you want to use."*

Jack looked disappointed and I never liked to see that look on anyone's face. I must have had that look on my face at various points in my life and I knew it wasn't a wonderful feeling. It had occurred to me—with the mention of cymbals—that something *was* possible, so I stepped in with an idea.

"*I've been thinking . . .* " I almost whispered " *. . . y'know . . . 'bout solos . . .* " I turned to Ron "*You said I could take a solo on harp . . . well, what about my playing a Traintime?*" [3]

Ron nodded in nascent approval – so I continued "*Not exactly the way Jack Bruce plays it though—something more like you've heard me play on my own. Y'know . . . the train starts to move slowly—it picks up speed 'til it's hurtling—then it slows to a standstill and lets out a final howl.*"

"*Yeah . . . heard you do—that—at Steve's when we were in the 5ᵗʰ year*" Ron grinned "*That's a—niiiiice—piece! Bet you've got better at it too. What were you thinking? On your own? Or in the interval or something?*"

"*Could do either . . . but what—I—was thinking . . . was that it would be something I might do with Jack.*" I turned to Jack with a grin. "*It'd be a possibility for you to play more-or-less a drum solo.*" Jack didn't look too impressed – but I went on. "*What I mean is that —you—could set the rhythm – with the train speeding up and slowing down and all that—and I'd just wail along with you.*"

"*That could work . . .* " Jack nodded "*You mean you'd really follow— me? You wouldn't go out on a limb like you do with your vocals?*"

"*Jack . . . c'mon*" Ron chided.

"*Happy to follow you Jack – in fact it would be fun.*" I flew in quickly so Ron's irritation didn't throw Jack into a tail spin. "*It'd be simple to follow your rhythm if I wasn't singing. You see . . . my idea would be to play it purely as an instrumental.*"

"*I*—like—*it . . .* " Ron grinned – aware that Jack was having mixed feelings. He was getting his drum solo – but it wasn't *exactly* solo . . . I'd be playing harp.

---

3 'Traintime' refers to a Blues piece which is imitative of a train and is played on either harp or guitar, but mainly harp. It was named after Jack Bruce's piece that was named 'Traintime'.

"*Yeah . . . alright then Mister Arbuthnot. I'll work something out and let you know when I've built the train – but maybe I need to hear what you do on your own first just to get an idea.*" Jack seemed to have re-adjusted the idea in his mind. It would be his piece and I'd play along with him. I was glad to be able to work something out for Jack because I knew he had difficult feelings about being an add-on to the 'almighty trio'.

"*Right Jack, it goes like this. This'll be shorter than I'd usually play— and it can be as long as you like—but it'll give you an idea.*" I pulled out a **G** harp – but before I commenced to blow I added "*It starts extremely slow – as if you can't really play harp at all—kind of limp and useless—then it builds.*" I played a few almost folksy chords – then threw in a little vibrato. Then I hit a single note and sucked it down. "*That's when the audience knows it's—*Blues*—y'see. At first they don't know what in hell's going on – but then . . .*" I started feathering a slow rhythm with occasional brief trills. Then I built the rhythm up to a speed and started wailing and plunging —flapping out a wild vibrato—my shoulders pumping like forge bellows. Then slowly . . . I took the train to a stop – and howled a long——slow——howl.

"*Bloody . . . hell . . .*" Jack murmured. "*That was . . .*" Jack was lost for words.

"*Tell y'what—*that*—was Jack*" Ron grinned maniacally "*That was Frank Schubert! And he was playing the best bloody Traintime I've—*ever*—heard!*"

"*Alright—alright! I'm with—you—Mister Arbuthnot!*" yelled Jack. "*I can do something with—*that*—alright! That's a nuclear—bloody— train mate! We'll slay 'em dead!*"

"*I want to be alive at the end of it though Jack! So don't let it run on more than ten minutes or so – or you'll have to carry me off on a stretcher.*"

The lads burst out laughing. *"That'll be a useful break too"* Steve added enthusiastically when they recovered their composure *"because Ron and I can use that time to change tuning for the slide number we've been working on. That's a number we'd like to play without percussion – y'know a really slow howling slide instrumental. That way you'd be able to take a rest after blowing your lungs out on harp."*

"Y'know . . ." said Ron with a grin *" . . . it's bloody interesting to watch you with a harp. It's different from watching you with the* EB3. *I mean, when you're holding that* EB3 *you look as if you've got your arms 'round Lindie or something – but when you're blowing that bloody harp man!"* Ron never completed his line of reasoning – because Steve and Jack were practically choking with mirth and it was a while before I could get *any* sense out of *any* of them. Instead, I cast my eye over at the case where the EB3 sat waiting. It was almost time for us to mount the stage. There was something about the procedure of connecting the lead and switching on the bass amplifier that never failed to feel momentous. It was the magic wand I'd always wanted.

4

gazzer mitchell

Now there's a lot I could say about Gazzer Mitchell – but . . . I'd
rather leave it to Ron:

"Gazzer's a fat upper-class git [1] with a penis for a brain."

I wouldn't have called him 'fat' myself. He *was* stockily built—
true—but I considered that right and proper for a bassist.
Gazzer was bass player for a local R&B [2] band called Freighttrain.
He was a few years older than us – and had a dark blue beard
shadow due to his dark hair. I wondered why he hadn't
developed imaginative facial topiary. He had an exceptionally
fine head of hair. Mine was thin and mousy—even though it
streamed—but his was luxurious. It cascaded down his back in
natural ringlets that made him look like some sort of Aramis or
d'Artagnan – one of the Musketeers. I would have liked a head
of hair like that – but I'd have rather been free of my stammer.
Ron didn't give a damn about his hair *or* my stammer.

Steve mused on the Musketeer image and opined *"Porthos comes
more readily to mind."*

Ron shrugged *"Right*—as I said—*he's a fat git."*

---

1 British slang denoting contempt – common in the '60s.
2 Rhythm and Blues.

Gazzer had heard Ron play on a fair few occasions since September. On the first occasion he came wearing a self-satisfied expression that he must have imagined would be intimidating. He'd evidently been waiting to sneer at the upstart teenager with the TELECASTER. Gazzer considered the TELECASTER a relic of the past and had no idea why anyone would choose to play one rather than a STRATOCASTER.

"That's 'cause he's a wanker and always has been." When Ron took a dislike to someone you knew *all* about it. *"Don't know where he gets this 'Gazzer' from either – his name's Gerald. You've gotta be called Gareth to be Gazzer. It's like calling yourself Jack when your name's Giles. Gazzer's always trying to get one over on people – it's his pastime. He likes to think he rules the roost – the stupid tosser."*

Gazzer was expecting to leave our gig feeling good about himself and his band – but then he heard Ron. Then his eyes widened. Then his jaw dropped.

I knew Ron could play anything that any of the greats could play. Ron was not out to improve his speed as if he was some kind of Olympic athlete. He sought to improve in subtle ways. He wanted to speak through his guitar. He wanted his TELECASTER to enunciate in Delta dialects, Texas dialects, Chicago dialects, Hendrix dialect, and in as-yet-unknown dialects. He was after some sort of angelic or demonic purity – some kind of phrasing that couldn't be bettered through speed.

"A repeated note can be perfect" Ron had rhapsodised on a previous occasion *"if it speaks emotional volumes; if the pulse is true; if the way you picked that string came through the whole length of your arm."* I'd nodded enthusiastically. *"And . . . if . . . "* he added *" . . . it sounds like the last note before the world ends."*

I chuckled silently with delight at the notion *"Yes – that's what happens when you just become the music."*

We'd talked about it at great length – and I knew exactly what he meant. There was a way the notes could follow each other in such a stream of rapturous nuances that anyone with a heart and mind would hear – and say *'That stands alone as the moment the universe began.'*

As the term rolled on we got gigs at various pubs with small attached halls. We were liked immediately everywhere we played. We gave our last gig at Weyflood Village Hall but continued to have rehearsals there. Lindie came to a few rehearsals and enjoyed them. *"It's brilliant being behind the scenes and seeing how you put it all together – it's so interesting watching you work together."*

The lads grinned at her appreciatively each time as if she was visiting royalty. I noticed the way she moved and spoke. I noticed her innate savoir-faire and elegance. I saw her as some heroine from a great work of literature. It wasn't that I'd never seen it before – but somehow in relation to the lads a new impression of her had been unveiled. It was as if she hypnotised them slightly – especially Steve and Ron. Lindie found the lads highly personable and enjoyed talking with them. On her first visit Ron showed her how to play a few chords on his TELECASTER and she smiled at being behind a thing that was capable of so much power in terms of volume.

"It's a little like being on Vic's motorbike – except I'm driving" she said and played the two finger **E**7th Ron had showed her. She grinned broadly as the chord rang out across the room.

"See whatcher mean – maybe I'll put a kick start on the amp" Ron nodded with a big smile. Then Steve let her handle his bass.

"Oh—this—is very exciting too" Lindie responded, almost gushing. *"It goes right through you – doesn't it. I've only heard a sound like this before from a full orchestra when the double basses swell."*

"Looks like we might become a quintet" Steve laughed.

Lindie blushed—almost imperceptibly. *"You mustn't let me interrupt your practice. I'll go and sit by the window again and listen."*

The lads—as if released from some kind of enchantment—prepared to kick into the next rehearsal number. I noticed Jack's look of disappointment when he realised that Lindie wasn't going to take a turn behind his drums. It occurred to me that I'd probably have to tell him he hadn't been snubbed – and that it was Steve's gallant remark that had thrown Lindie. She would not have left him out on purpose.

After that rehearsal Lindie and I stopped off at the Queen's Oak to have a drink and chat about her experience. *"I like them"* Lindie said *"especially Steve and Ron – they're mature and intelligent. Jack seems a little . . . well . . . juvenile in some ways. Don't get me wrong, I like him – but he seems the odd one out."* Lindie had the thing wrapped up pretty well.

"Yes . . ." I replied *"I don't think he's had much experience of life."* It was out of my mouth before I could check myself. I knew Lindie was going to ask me what I meant by that – and she did. *"Well . . . I don't know him that well . . . but I think he's horribly dominated by his parents . . . He never takes holiday jobs – and so he doesn't have his own money. Steve and Ron do. I think it makes a big difference. I think that really affects Jack. He has no freedom. Jack's parents hold the purse strings and so they call all the shots."*

Lindie mused *"Well . . . that's how it is for me too."*

"It obviously depends on the parents" I answered quickly *" . . . but I don't think parental control or financial dependency affects girls in—quite the same way."*

Lindie asked – but not critically *"How did you arrive at that idea?"*

"Well . . . it's the girls I've known. They've all seemed . . . kind of . . . self contained. It's as if they had their own lives inside themselves somehow. They seem independent of the whole thing – although that's not exactly what I mean. I don't really know how to describe what I mean."

"Maybe young men have to prove themselves in ways that we don't."

That was about the way of it. *"Yes . . . I think that Ron's and Steve's parents have helped them to be what they are – whereas Jack's mother and father have him on a lead"* Pause *"Thing is . . . they don't like him being in the band and drumming's the one thing that gives him the possibility of being his own man. Without the drums Jack would be . . . well . . . he'd be a schoolboy."*

Lindie shifted slightly in her chair. She took a swift glance through the window *"You're . . . not a schoolboy are you."* It was a statement rather than a question.

"No . . . gave that up when I was 14.*"* Explaining how that came to be didn't seem appropriate. I'd probably tell her about Anelie some time later – when it seemed . . . fitting.

"I'm sorry that I didn't have a go on Jack's drums—I hope he wasn't offended—but it seemed I shouldn't be interrupting your rehearsal" Lindie said as if to change the subject.

"I don't think Jack was offended . . . I think he had other things on his mind. Jack's always got some sort of hassle going on at home and sometimes he can be a little distracted. He's happiest when he's playing y'know . . . He's really pleased now that there are a whole line of gigs to look forward to." I told Lindie that it was good of her to consider his feelings. *"I've—never—seen the lads so gracious or . . . well . . . so riveted."* Lindie thought they were just being friendly and welcoming. *"Well yes—they were—but they were also slightly in awe of you. I could see that."*

We got another gig at The Cordwainer's Arms and a return gig at The Compton Bells. Lindie attended both. The audience simply grew by themselves and home-made posters became a thing of the past. Almost everyone who came to our gigs had their eyes on Ron.

Ron was apologetic *"That's cause we're not playing to musicians are we . . . otherwise they'd be listening to the bass as much as the lead. Steve's out there playing some seriously wild phrases"* Pause *"I saw some girls out there with their eyes on—*you*—though Frank"* Ron grinned at me.

The only girl I wanted with her eyes on me was Lindie. *"Glad they like my voice."*

Ron shook his head. *"Total Romeo—*you are*—still . . . if it keeps y'mind on the vocals."* This was a reference to Lindie's attendance at our gigs and rehearsals – Ron noticed that I was inclined to grin at her a little too often. *"Can't say as I blame you – Lindie's quite a looker."*

Gazzer had become a regular. He'd been there at Weyflood Village Hall, The Cordwainer's Arms, The Queen's Oak, and The Compton Bells – and gradually I got used to his predatory observation. When he looked at Ron there was no sneer – just intense concentration as if he were trying to remember every note. Sometimes Gazzer would lose his cool and grin broadly when Ron had sent some startling flight-of-riffs into the night. It was good to be appreciated – but Gazzer made Jack edgy.

"That bloke's always there with his beady eye on you" said Jack after the gig was over.

Ron twisted his nose in distaste *"Yeah . . . Gazzer – the tosser can look at me as much as he likes – long as he pays to get in."*

Jack had a look of slight concern on his face *"He might have his eye on you Ron . . . y'know . . . for his band . . . "*

Ron laughed "*Yeah . . . well – maybe if I—wanted—to play Rock'n'Roll . . .* "

None of us wanted to play Rock'n'Roll. Not that we didn't enjoy it – but it wasn't what we wanted to play.

"*Most British Blues bands . . .*" Ron said " *. . . are really Rock'n'Roll bands. Even when they play Blues they play it too fast – and fast Blues is more-or-less Rock'n'Roll.*"

Jack chuckled "*Freighttrain play 'My Ding-a-Ling'* [3] *as a regular standard – and . . . that sums Gazzer up.*" We could always rely on Jack to lighten the atmosphere with humour – and sometimes, he was quite perceptive. "*Gazzer thinks the whole world revolves around his ding-a-ling.*"

Ron chuckled about that and said "*I don't think we've got anything to worry about from any direction—if—we practise.*"

Jack took the message and nodded "*I'm at those sodding skins— every—day Ron. And – I have to throw towels on 'em to keep my parents from going bloody bananas. I even play pillows 'cause they really— don't—like me practising as much as I do.*"

"*We'll get there*" I said and smiled at Jack to let him know his effort was alright with me.

"*Yeah it's possible*" said Ron "*especially with Frank's lyrics. Blues and Acid Rock – that's how Cream cut the cake. They played authentic Blues alongside their Acid Rock weirdo numbers.*" Ron took a bite of an apple. "*That's where—we're—going.*"

---

3 Dave Bartholomew released 'My Ding-a-Ling' in 1952. In 1954 The Bees released a version called 'Toy Bell' and Chuck Berry released it again as 'My Ding-a-Ling' in 1972.

I shook the floor with a minor tour of labyrinthine towers, / A major maze of blazing haze – the rooks laughed in their bowers, / I was feeling lost in permafrost and whirling cut glass flowers / When I came in view of your visual cues in a meteoric shower.

Larkin/Bruce/Schubert—Savage Cabbage—Unless You Shed Your Skin—Savoy Green—1970

We were all a little startled by Ron's comment – because we knew him to be strictly rational about plans. He wasn't given to flights of fancy – or if he was, he kept it to himself. Jack sat back to enjoy the direction Ron had taken and had that look of feeling vindicated on his face. Ron tended to write off Jack's boyish enthusiasm as if he were ten years his senior and sometimes Jack felt a little flattened.

Ron noticed our surprise and continued *"No—Jack's right—I've been thinking about it—a lot—and the more I think about it the more obvious it is. We—are—going to fill the vacuum left by Cream."*

I looked at Ron—vaguely stunned—and said *"Well yes . . . sure— that's certainly what I had in mind too – but . . . you know me, I can be unrealistic."*

Jack was almost bouncing in his chair at this point.

"I'm serious" Ron stated quite flatly *"There's a real gap – and . . . there's no one 'round who's looking like they want to fill it. Those bands who used to play Blues are all going Progressive Rock right? And the small Blues bands that are left are either playing Rock'n'Roll like Gazzer's band – or they're playing sort of . . . limited cabaret Blues. It's alright in its way – but it's the avant garde Jazz evolution that Jack Bruce and Ginger Baker throw into the mix that's exciting. And it's not even that we have to do it—their—way. We can explore the thing our— own—way now that Steve and I are playing counterpoint. No one is doing that. Probably no one's capable of doing that. So . . . the field's wide open."*

We almost had to scrape Jack off the wall he was so excited. Steve and I nodded slowly—taking it in—almost as if we'd just heard that aliens had landed in the back garden.

"Right . . . " I volunteered *"it's definitely possible . . . "*

*"We—*could*—do that, so we may as well aim for it"* Ron continued *"No point in setting our sights on anything less."*

Steve looked a little shocked and responded *"But what about Music College and Art School?"*

"I'm not talking about next year!" Ron laughed *"I'm talking about the future! I think we can take our time. I mean . . . Blues isn't going to disappear is it? It's been here since the end of the last century – so it's going to be able to wait three years – and I'd like us to come out all guns blazing."*

What a thought.

"I'm glad we're in agreement on that" Steve chimed in *"because I need to learn a lot more about music. I'm only just beginning with counterpoint and I need to get far more fluent with it. I'm just winging it at the moment."*

"You're winging it pretty well Steve" Ron responded *"I can hear that you've been working on Bach contrapuntal lines. You've got a real feel for it now."*

Steve looked pleased *"Thanks, I got the impression you'd noticed the difference."*

I'd noticed too. Steve was surpassing himself. The two basses were light years apart – but I was feeling my rôle in the band becoming increasingly purposeful. I was providing the structure along with Jack – and from that rhythmic platform Ron and Steve leapt into a fiery firmament in which Blues and Bach cavorted with each other.

"Looks as if the public won't have to do without Cream after all"
I chuckled

Jack naturally included himself in my eulogy *"Straight up,
Mr Arbuthnot. Cream—was—the only real British Blues band 'till—
we—came along."*

He was always one for premature glory. *"What about John
Mayall?"* Ron asked.

Jack grimaced *"Yeah—alright—but they're a bit docile . . . I mean
they're not on fire or anything are they?"*

"True . . . " Steve responded *" . . . but there are the Blues purists who
feel Cream's Blues numbers are too Rock influenced."*

"Yeah . . . well . . . " Ron scratched his head *" . . . people say all
kinds of stupid things. What they—did—was, take Blues in the direction
of Jazz. That's where the long improvisations come from. That's not Rock
originally – even though Rock's gone that way. Pretty tedious too – just
endless diddly-diddly-dees up and down pentatonic scales."*

"Far as I'm concerned . . . " I agreed *"Cream were the only band taking
Blues forward – and now . . . "*

Jack leapt up with his arms spread wide *"There's us!"* That had
us all in hysterics. We could always rely on Jack for enthusiasm.
This time Ron beamed at him.

The next time the lads got together Ron had a story to tell.
He'd been waiting for me to arrive before commencing. *"Right
then—now Frank's 'ere—I'll spill the beans"* Pause *"Met up with old
—Gazzer—didn't I . . . the tosser. Sidled up to me on Wednesday at
The Compton Bells—didn't he . . . steaming great pillock . . . "* Ron
cradled his chin and rocked his head from side to side.
"Started talking Blues" Pause *"That was alright . . . at first. I'll talk
Blues with him because he actually knows quite a lot about what's
happening in London."*

Jack nodded vigorously "*And—that's—always worth hearing even though he's a turd-burglar. He's up there a lot of the time – bumps into all kinds of people at clubs.*"

Ron jiggled his head idly as if to say that he agreed but would rather not be interrupted. "*Yeah—says—'e knows Chris Youlden – y'know, Savoy Brown Blues Band. How well, I don't know, but . . . anyhow – told me Chris Youlden thinks Jim's a fantastic drummer. Another bloody—Ginger Baker—no less. And . . . he thought Freighttrain were lucky to have him.*" Ron laughed as if it was the funniest thing he's ever heard – and repeated "*Another Ginger Baker . . . right . . . I was—so—impressed . . .*"

That had Jack guffawing – highly relieved that he wasn't being compared with Jim. "*Another Ginger Baker! My left testicle! He's got fresh fried turkey turds for brains*" Jack jeered.

"*They'd played Kooks Kleek in London, right . . .*" Ron continued as if Jack hadn't spoken " *. . . and Chris Youlden saw'em. Liked Jim's work on drums*" Pause "*I told Gazzer 'Jim Sutton's good – but he's a Rock'n'Roll drummer. Ginger Baker's a Jazz percussionist.' Jim's—*not *—in that league. Nowhere close. He'd have to learn a hell of a lot if he wanted to be recognised in—that—class.*" Ron elongated his legs – eyeing us all somewhat mischievously "*That . . . slowed Gazzer down. But then he comes back at me, doesn't he – with something about Jim being—so—much better than our Jack. Said it was hardly worth comparing 'em.*" Jack flushed red—turned white almost immediately after—but said nothing. "*Well*" continued Ron "*that got—right—up my nose 'cause Jack's worked hard and he's got a lot better than he was back in the Summer – but . . .* " Ron smiled ruefully at Jack "*I had to agree . . . Jim—is—better.*" Jack looked truculent – but knew that Ron was accurate in his appraisal.

Ron gave Jack an encouraging nod and returned to his story *"So . . . I said 'Yeah . . . Jim's better – but . . . Jim's a lot older isn't he? Said Jim must be 40 – and Jack's 16.' Told him you had a lot of time to improve – and that you'd been practising like a bastard."* Jack looked somewhat relieved at that point. *"Asked him 'Did you actually— hear—Jack at the last gig?' Gazzer admitted he hadn't. I said 'Jack's come on a—long—way. He's movin'—mate—he's movin'.' That threw Gazzer – no mistake."* Jack cheered up considerably – which was clearly what Ron had in mind. Ron was getting much better at human relations. *"So—then—I ask Gazzer 'How much better d'you think Jim's gonna get? I mean . . . realistically?' That threw him again – the bloody tosser."*

I could imagine this exchange – and was vaguely relieved I hadn't been there. I was surprised they'd not come to blows – because Gazzer was hardly less shy of a fist fight than Ron.

"Gazzer was losing ground and knew it – so . . . he starts coming nearer the point doesn't he" Ron cackled like a fiend. *"Tells me he wouldn't argue the toss about how good Jim was – but that Jim was 25! Said he had a lot of experience which was good for getting gigs and for dealing with the kind of people who'd push you around"* Pause *"I said I thought that was a good point."*

I was surprised Jim was as young as that. *"Mmmm . . . 25 . . . really?"* I questioned *"Hope I look better than that when I'm 25."*

"25 . . ." Steve concurred *"That—is—hard to believe."*

"Unless . . . " Jack said *"you remember that Jim's been mainlining*[4] *since he was in a pushchair. That stuff ages you something rotten – and he hits everything he can get hold of."*

---

4 Mainlining: heroin via hypodermic syringe.

Ron wagged his head *"Yeah—it's true—he's a bleeding walking chemistry lab. Got Christmas[5] up his bloody nose most of the time."*

"They're all the same as far as cocaine goes" Steve added *"Got some idea they're immortal – that you can do that stuff forever."*

"It's a severe downhill track" Ron shook his head *"Makes you crazy – that's no big secret."*

Jack chuckled *"Speed[6] to keep you flying and downers[7] to knock you out. Recipe for bloody disaster. I'm planning on getting old. Some people may think it's groovy to be as high as a kite every night – and blow your bloody brains out – but I'd rather survive."*

We were all in agreement on that. We needed to steer well clear of the narcotics scene.

"Anyhow . . . " Ron pressed on *"Gazzer thought he'd impressed me with the idea that Jim was 'in the know' – so he approached the real thing he had on his mind. Told me the—real—problem was Ed the lead player. Told me 'Ed ain't Clapton or Pete Green. Never would be.' Said Ed was feeble – completely docile."*

"That's an ugly thing to say about a band member and a supposed friend" I commented.

"Yeah . . . " said Ron *"but that's no surprise coming from Gazzer the fat git."*

The Ed in question was Edward Woodward. I'd heard him playing with Freighttrain at The Cordwainer's Arms and I didn't think he was *that* bad.

---

5 Cocaine.

6 Speed: Amphetamine Sulphate – a stimulant. Common substitutes are Benzedrine and Dexedrine. These drugs were used legally as performance enhancers and tended to be popular amongst late night musicians.

7 Barbiturates.

He was a little stiff and wooden – but he could wipe the floor with me as a guitarist any evening of the week.

Jack called him 'Ed wood-wood-wood' which amused Ron and Steve immensely. The predicament for Gazzer was that Ed wasn't Ron – and never would be. In fact, he wasn't a thousand miles near to Ron – from any direction. They lived on separate planets. Gazzer was bright enough to see that – horribly clearly. No one was going to dedicate graffiti to his name. No one was going to write 'Ed wood-wood-wood is God' on subway walls and tenement halls.

And the signs said, 'The words of the prophets are written on the subway walls / and tenement halls'.
Simon and Garfunkel—Sound of Silence—Sounds of Silence—1966

When Gazzer had said *'Ed ain't Clapton or Pete Green'* he was insinuating pretty directly that Ron *was* – and he wanted Ron in his band about as desperately as anyone could want anything. It took a lot to gain praise from Gazzer – but Gazzer gushed with flattery about Ron. That didn't work because Ron hated flattery. He liked appreciation—as we all did—but flattery nauseated him. Ron wasn't interested in the idea that he was 'as good as Eric Clapton'. He had no interest in being measured against others. He wasn't obsessed with being 'better than' anyone – apart from the Ron who played yesterday. It wasn't that he was humble—or anything of that nature—he just thought that it was immature to rank musicians as if there was some sort of credibility in being thought 'the best'. 'The best' was a meaningless concept as far as he was concerned.

"Real musicians—always—try to improve!" Ron almost snapped *"That's it. Finish. The—sodding—end"* Pause *"Anyhow Gazzer— the fat git—took a long guzzle of his beer at that point . . . y'know, leaving me to reckon the arithmetic."*

"Whaddya think he says—then?" Ron cackled *"He says 'Looks like we're both stuck with people who're letting us down.' What*—do you three—*reckon—to that?"*

Steve said *"Sounds pretty gross."*

"Sounds sleazy " said Jack – but he was obviously unsettled by the idea.

"So . . . " Ron continued *" . . . then . . . he tells me that what*—I needed—*was t'be in a 'power trio' like Cream – or Hendrix. He says quartets are 'slow' – and that you look like the Beatles or some Pop group if you're a quartet."*

"Big insult" Jack jeered *"Total loser if anyone saw us as the Beatles eh. Bloody turd-burglar."*

Ron chuckled and looked at me *"Then . . . Gazzer says I could get rid of you – and get Steve to sing. He thought that would be an improvement."* I froze for a moment because I thought this was not an impossible proposal. I was just a vocalist who bumbled on bass. *"Or . . . "* Ron continued with fiendish relish *" . . . get rid of Steve if—Frank here—could get up to speed on bass."* Ron was grinning like a wolf at this point. *"Then . . . he tells me—he's— better than both of you put together."* Steve thought that was hysterical. *"And now—here's the best part—Gazzer says there's nothing Jack Bruce can play that he can't play – so there's no point in me hanging round with losers like you three."* Ron keeled over backward laughing at this. *"How—d'you—three 'losers' like that eh? Didn't know whether to piss myself laughing or smack him in the head."* He announced this with a maniacal laugh that practically made the window rattle. He was proud of his achievement in not hitting Gazzer *"Two years ago I would have pummelled his nose into his face for insulting my friends. Must be getting mellow in my old age."*

We asked Ron about the quartet idea. We were all wondering about this notion of being 'over-staffed'. We all felt that the 'power trio' was ideal in many ways. Much as we were irked by Gazzer and his opinions, he was right about that. Ron deliberated for a moment in which he took another large bite out of yet another apple *"Yeah the power trio works extremely well and I wouldn't go with a quartet either . . . if it wasn't for the quartet we've got. I don't want to sing—I can't sing—and nor can you two."* Steve and Jack nodded. That was fair. They couldn't sing. Didn't want to try. *"So we're a quartet"* Ron continued *"The Stones are a quintet and they're a Rock-Blues band. Being a quintet didn't stop them getting where they are. We've got a vocalist—like the Stones—except Frank's got a deeper pitch than Mick Jagger and he doesn't have to swallow the mic to make himself heard."* It was good to hear this from Ron. *"We've also got this two-bass line-up now. No one else has that."* We shook our heads. We were unique. *"As far as I can see, we've got it made as a quartet. All we need to do is keep practising."*

This was *quite* a story. Jack—and even Steve—were obviously touched that Ron had no thought of leaving us – but I never doubted Ron would do other than he did.

"Gazzer's competent on bass—won't deny it—but he's nowhere— nowhere—*near Steve"* Ron stated mater-of-factly *"He can look pretty nifty in pentatonic—if you're not a player—but that's about all he knows."* Steve was moved by that – but said nothing.

Steve tended to be the quiet one – so, on his behalf I added *"To say what he said about Jack Bruce either makes him irredeemably dim – or he's never actually listened to him."*

Jack piped up characteristically *"Fuck him anyway . . . bone idle bastard. Can't see him getting any better. I mean – does he practise? Doubt it. Thinks too much of himself to get any better – and, he's as subtle as a shit sandwich."*

That was true – yet still, I thought Gazzer was pretty nimble.
I wished I was half as good – but this was no time for
moderating statements. *"The bollock-brain's just a showman"* Jack
sneered *"He swaggers 'round as if he was God's gift or something."*

Yes. That was also true. I could take showmanship from Jimi
Hendrix, because he was Jimi Hendrix – but Gazzer was Gazzer.
Gazzer also grimaced – and I admitted *"I wouldn't stand on stage
with anyone who grimaced quite that excessively."*

Jack nodded his agreement *"Ed's got that niiiiiiiiice* STRAT *though—I
know Ron doesn't agree but I love'em. However . . . that's not going to
make him any—*better*—either is it? I doubt it."*

I couldn't defend Ed – even with my love of effects pedals.

*"He's got enough effects to build his own chamber of horrors—frigging—
fairground ride"* Ron remarked – and that seemed to close the
subject.

We were all laughing about Ron's story by that time – which did
a lot to compensate for how unnerved we'd felt about it earlier
on in the evening. There was a sense in which we'd been
weighed up – even though Ron obviously never considered the
deal for one moment. Jack remained a little put out that Ron
had agreed he wasn't in Jim's league – but Ron told Jack that he
needed to be realistic. Jim had been playing for a decade longer
– and there was no reason why Jack couldn't overtake him in a
couple of years *if* he worked at it.

Ron had actually spared Jack the worst. Ron told me in private
later that Gazzer had said *'You've got a drummer with hair like a
poodle who sounds like a tea-chest full of door knobs.'*

This comment on Jack's percussion was merely derisory rather than an informed observation – but Jack did have a somewhat odd sense of coiffure. *"Still chaqu'on à son goût[8] we each have our peculiarities"* I'd confided later to Ron *"None of us are exactly Adoni of the male gender – but we are dedicated musicians."*

Turning his focus from Jack to me, Ron opined *"Frank . . . you need to keep working at bass too – but . . . you're our vocalist and harp player – so . . . bass is just what you're adding to the mix. Gazzer couldn't make any real comment about—you—anyhow 'cause he sings like a constipated chicken. The one big advantage that Freighttrain have . . . "* Ron pointed out *" . . . is that they—all—sing . . . "* Pause *" . . . just not very well."*

I met Steve the next day after school in the Nostril in Farnham – and it seemed as if he wanted to rehash the previous evening. *"The shocking thing about Gazzer attempting to poach Ron . . . is recognising that Ron's poachable. I mean . . . I've always known it – but we've never talked about it before."*

I found that a little flummoxing *"But . . . it was clear to me—as soon as Ron started talking—that he had no interest in joining Freighttrain."*

"Really?"

I was surprised by Steve's lack of confidence.

"I have no doubt of it. I know Ron well enough to rely on his friendship. I'm also confident that he respects me as a vocalist." Then I laughed *"He also respects me as a musician, if only as a budding musician – but he knows I'm deadly serious and that I'll practise. He said I'd wipe the floor with Gazzer way before I get the EB0. I can't see—that—but I think I'll catch up with him before I get through Art School."*

---

8 The correct French for 'to each his taste' is: *à chacun son goût*. The common English corruption *chaqu'on à son goût* is used in order to represent 1960's usage.

Steve said that he thought I was actually being a little pessimistic
"*You'll be there before that.*"

I laughed and reminded Steve how slow I was at learning music.
"*But Steve . . .*" I said, voicing a thought that had emerged "*Don't
you see—yourself—as poachable?*" Steve looked surprised.
"*You're damn good you know. Ron may be the mæstro – but you're not
really—that—far behind. Ron's said as much to me. You've really leapt
ahead since we started rehearsing and . . .*" I chuckled "*you've been
JS Bach-ing up the right tree.*"

Steve laughed at the pun and shook his head in bewilderment.
"*Well yeah . . . I know . . . things have changed. I'm . . . looking at Jack
Bruce now as . . . someone I—can—be, maybe even in the next few
years . . . maybe sooner. I don't know – but I can follow him and
reproduce his riffs much quicker. They make sense to me now and I catch
the pattern. I've even started improvising on his themes like Ron does with
the Chicago Blues guitarists.*"

I had a wide grin on my face and it took me a while to speak.
"*We're really there – aren't we.*"

Steve didn't even have to articulate an answer. We were there.

5

december 1968

les langoustines

Life was firing on all cylinders. Savage Cabbage was a known name – and people would sometimes call across the bar of whatever pub and say *"Nice set last night—liked—your 'Traintime' man."*

I was striding wherever I went. I was imbued with an amorphous sense of capability – and . . . something nameless that I *could* call destiny – but that word makes little sense to me. It was a sense of apertive aptness. There was no idea of being a big cheese. No notion that I was superior to anyone. I had no desire to be Mister Superior, Sister Superior, or even Mother Superior. I didn't even want to jump the gun. I was simply *Doctor Blues*. I'd spent so long being an inferior with my male peers at Netherfield, that peer approbation was almost overwhelming. The audiences seemed so generous. They felt like my family. I felt able to walk up to anyone – and talk to them with relaxed equality. I liked everyone, just for being who they were. This was how it—*ought*—to be. I was singing in the rain – *and* any kind of goddamn weather that came along.

Life felt *made-to-measure*, like a hand-tailored suit of clothes – like my uncle's three piece double breasted Edwardian suits.
They fitted me as they must have fitted him – and I felt natural being myself.

I'd found a tie that was almost the same as the Virginia Water School tie but it was wider with a richer, deeper navy and an almost metallic gold. It was the tie of some regiment or other – but I never found out which. I learnt to tie a *Double Windsor* knot and stuck it through with my uncle's ruby tie pin. It sat there below my chin like a statement of something majestic. I'd bought up a bunch of white satin Carnaby Street shirts – high collared with long points that disappeared into the waistcoat. It was as far from school uniform as it was possible to get whilst conforming sufficiently to evade scrutiny. Most teachers greeted the appearance with a smile apart from Mr Havilland – who knew me for a deviant and kept reminding me that I wasn't wearing the school uniform. Fortunately the Headmaster felt that my slightly askew imitation of uniform was not a serious infringement and that a modicum of latitude should be allowed in cases where dress was not slovenly. I was far from slovenly.

The only low spot left in my ecstatic existence was the fateful Friday afternoon that lowered on the horizon. The date had been set when I was to meet Lindie's mother and father – and finally, it hove into view. As the appointed time drew closer I started to hear snatches of Berlioz's *'March to the Scaffold'*. I heard it in the hum of traffic and in the drone of car tyres on the asphalt – each morning as I rode to school.

I was to have 'tea and cake' with Brigadier and Mrs Dale. Mrs Dale made wonderful caraway cake—according to Lindie—and I decided that I'd look forward to it rather than dreading her parents. *And the condemned man ate a hearty slice of caraway cake . . .* I knew how it was going to be – it was just the final outcome that was uncertain. Brigadier and Mrs Dale wanted to take a look at me. I was, after all, 'paying court to their daughter' – so it was only proper.

The Dickensian linguistics didn't bode well – but I was capable of Victorianisms myself. Far be it from me, not to be up for the challenge. I could *talk turkey* or *talk Tory* with the best—or worst—of them, unless my stammer tripped me. All I had to do was speak as my father spoke and I'd sound like some remnant of the British Raj.

"Cry, God for Harry, England, and Saint George!" I sighed as I turned into the familiar lane which led to Virginia Water – for the end of the school day would herald my meeting with Brigadier and Mrs Dale. The irony of it was too delicious to avoid. It would be the kind of response of which Lindie's parents would probably approve – but there'd be no opportunity to voice such a sentiment in their living room. The three flying ducks [1] might fall off the wall – anything could happen.

The school day ended too quickly for me – and at its closure, Lindie and I rode off to meet her parents together. We left the pixie chariot at a discreet distance and walked up the unmade road that led to her house. We reached the long gravel drive more quickly than I'd have liked. Lindie opened the impressive wrought iron gates. The hinges needed oiling. We made our way down the drive. The gravel crunched unnecessarily loudly. I attempted to amuse myself with what I definitely would *not* say to the Dales. *'Delightfully deafening drive you have—fine deterrent against intruders—I'll warrant it would terrify the blighters.'* The house was far larger than I'd anticipated. I'd never ridden up close enough to take a look at it. My family home resembled a modest rabbit hutch by comparison.

---

1 Many working class homes in 1950s / 1960s Britain had a set of 3 plaster ducks *(in diminishing size according to ascending order)* on the living room wall. The author was unaware—at the time—that there would be no flying ducks in Lindie's home.

Lindie and I avoided holding hands as we walked down the drive. It was not a prearranged precaution – simply something that appeared to be mutually understood. Lindie occasionally caught my eye. She grinned encouragingly – but with what I can only describe as a 'deer caught in the headlights' expression – which rather nullified her effort to put me at my ease.
The effect was eerie as it merely prompted me with ideas for humorous pronouncements that would be . . . impossible to utter.

Once more unto the breach, dear friends, once more / Or close the wall up with our English dead. / In peace there's nothing so becomes a man / As modest stillness and humility: / But when the blast of war blows in our ears . . .
William Shakespeare—Henry V—Act III—Scene I—Eve of the battle with the French—1600

I'd learnt a great deal of Shakespeare by heart – but quoting would have been insensitive. I could make fun of my own situation – but this was also Lindie's situation.

"I'm sure it'll be fine" I reassured her – as she couldn't reassure me.

Lindie nodded vigorously. *"Yes"* she replied – exhibiting slightly less trepidation *"Especially if you use some of your . . . Victorianisms . . . They'll like it that you're well spoken – and you sometimes sound quite like my father."*

I told Lindie *"I'll do my best – and . . . I'll try not to overdo it."*

As we got close I detected movement in the front room. I affected not to notice – and surveyed the rose beds as if I was monstrously interested in them. Suddenly the front door swung wide—and there they were—in all state, come to welcome their daughter and her abominable travesty of humanity to their home. Why was I having such thoughts? I'd do myself no good supposing the worst. Her parents *might* even be human.

"*Good afternoon Brigadier Dale—Mrs Dale—pleasure to meet you at last.*" There was a tickle of a stammer on the 'B' of 'Brigadier' and I was almost thrown into a state of panic. Down at the first fence. No – I'd charge into the fray regardless. It wasn't illegal to have a stammer after all.

Brigadier Dale seemed to be getting me into focus as I approached. He had a cheery, ruddy, expression – a face that had seen some weather. As his focus sharpened however, his countenance metamorphosed into something that resembled a mutant lobster. I decided to ignore the impression – and put it down to an overdose of Monty Python. Mrs Dale smiled a tense impression of serenity which I returned with as natural a smile as I could muster. We were ushered in, almost as if Lindie was also a visitor.

The hallway was impressive—there seemed to be a stuffed coelacanth mounted on a plaque on the left hand wall—but I had little opportunity to survey its imperial charm – we were all too soon in the front parlour.

"*So Victor, Victor—Simmerson—is that right?*" Brigadier Dale commenced. He sounded as if he was reading from a memorandum – addressing a private soldier up for disciplinary measures.

"*Yes sir – Victor Howard Simmerson.*" I thought I'd give him a full response to match his official enquiry.

Brigadier Dale nodded "*Yes – yes . . . Linda has been telling us about you.*"

Well yes . . . I could imagine that would have been the case – but I was not sure what I ought to say in response.

"*And your father*" he recommenced "*retired soldier, I believe?*"

"Yes sir. He was a major . . . in the Royal Engineers" I replied. He nodded—evidently as lost as I was for something to say—so I continued *"He retired with a heart condition in* 1954*"* Silence *"He now has a position with the Department of Works[2] in Aldershot as a quantity surveyor."*

Brigadier Dale nodded with what appeared to be approval. *"Army man all his life then?"*

"Yes sir" I replied *"He was in India . . . Rawalpindi –* 1927*."*

Brigadier Dale raised his eyebrows *"*1927*? Remarkably*—young. *What age would he have been in* 1927*– if you don't mind my asking?"*

"Certainly not sir" I replied *"He was* 19*. Born in* 1902*. He was in charge of the power station near the Khyber Pass in* 1927*."*

Brigadier Dale eyed me in a manner that betokened *nothing* I could fathom *"Well travelled man, by all accounts. Army life suited him then?"*

"Yes sir – I believe it did" I responded *"He was in Greece, Turkey, Egypt, Palestine, Lebanon, Syria, North Africa, and China . . . He was responsible for re-building sections of the Great Wall of China . . . It was damaged in the Boxer Rebellion."* Why was I telling him about the Boxer Rebellion and the Great Wall of China? I wondered if I had gone too far.

"Yes, yes – Germany too I believe" Pause *"Your mother's . . . a German – is she not?"*

'No' I thought '*My mother's German*' but said nothing to that effect. *"She's the grand niece of Franz Schubert"* Pause *"Her mother was Clara Schubert – but not*—the—*Clara Schubert"* I replied.

---

2 The author's father worked for the British Army as a civilian, liaising with military officials responsible for building and repairs to Army housing.

In for a penny in for a pound.

"Really . . . you don't say – you don't say " he responded with slight incredulity.

'*Yes*' I thought '*I*—did—*say*' but again – I said nothing.
I wanted to tell him that my mother's family had been anti-Hitler and that they suffered under his regime – but somehow the opportunity passed. I was torn between defending my mother and seeing no reason why I needed to defend her – especially to this offensive ignoramus. But then, how was he to know that my grandmother had to escape to Denmark for the aid she rendered to Jewish families?

"You like the German composers then?" he interjected – as if it was démodé to like 'the German composers'.

"Yes sir—particularly Bach—but I like many European composers: Debussy, Ravel, Chopin, Liszt, Saint-Saëns, Scarlatti, Boccherini, Vivaldi, Telemann . . . I very much enjoy Baroque chamber music."
My answer seemed to unsettle Brigadier Dale a little. Had he expected a moron for afternoon tea? Was he frustrated that it wasn't easy to intimidate me?

"You surprise me."

'*You surprise me?*' I thought '*You just don't know how*—much—*I'd surprise you.*' No. Maybe I'd just regale him with a few more composers.

"I like a wide variety of music. English composers as well – like Vaughan Williams, William Walton, Elgar, Holst, and Charles Wood . . ." I was wondering if I'd offered too much information but decided I may as well round the things off. *"I like Eric Satie too . . . "*

Lindie was looking pale and anxious – and I had the feeling that however eloquently I was responding to my interrogation – it was *not* going well.

"So—what—do you two find to talk about?" Mrs Dale almost snapped, frozen with restrained disapproval.

"Art" Lindie replied.

" . . . music, and poetry" I added.

"We've been translating French Surrealist poetry" Lindie continued. Mrs Dale looked as though she'd detected a prearranged answer.

"Yes . . . my daughter told me you were applying to Art School." She uttered the words 'Art School' as if they were utterly disgusting to her – and Brigadier Dale continued *"You know—of course—that there is little chance of employment if you take that route – do you not?"*

Damnation. I was cornered. This was his royal flush and I was holding the dead man's hand.[3] *"I have been told it could be difficult – but I was also told that there were always possibilities for those who worked hard – and were sufficiently determined. I am certainly sufficiently determined – and I work very hard."*

The Brigadier sprang to his feet and poked the fire as though he were bayoneting the Hun. *"You've been told—that—have you. Have-you-indeed. Have—you—indeed."*

It was the crispest most vitriolic mutter I'd ever heard. Yes—I thought—that is exactly what I'd been told. I decided that silence was the best response to belligerence and sunk my teeth into the cake – as delicately as I could.

"And" he continued *"you sing in a Pop group. What do you expect to come from—that—may I ask?"*

I was dead already. I knew there was no point in dissembling – Pop singer indeed! This was *too* much to be borne! *"It's a Blues band sir – and I am the vocalist, lyricist, and rhythm bass player."*

---

3 Aces and eights – the hand Wild Bill Hickok was holding when he was shot.

Mrs Dale swivelled slightly *"Music of the American negro . . . "* she commented with disdain *"That is a—far—cry from Classical music, is—it—not?"*

"In some ways" I explained *" . . . but I love music of all kinds and find it hard to segregate it."* Damn—why—did I have to be clever and use the word 'segregate'? *"The bass player of my favourite band was classically trained—for example—and he uses counterpoint, influenced by Bach, in his improvisations."* I wanted to say more but I dried up.

"So you are—serious—about making a living this way?" she asked.

That was a direct question and so I'd have to give an answer that Lindie would also accept as an honest answer *"I have no immediate plans apart from performing on occasional weekends – because whatever happens will have to wait until I finish Art School. The others in the band are going to Music College – so we're all in a similar situation."*

Unnatural silence. I heard later that her mother thought I was one of the Rolling Stones—she really did—but how she came to that conclusion I'd no idea. It could only have been her impression that one 'loud electric guitar band' was much like another. Lindie told them I was 'musical' and that I was the singer in a Blues band. They put two and two together – and made nineteen nervous breakdowns of it.

You better stop, look around, here it comes—here it comes—here it comes —here it comes – here comes your 19th nervous breakdown.

Jagger/Richards—The Rolling Stones—19th Nervous Breakdown—1966

"You are—proud—of your father I presume?" Brigadier Dale enquired in a slightly softer tone than he'd previously employed. I detected a trap of some sort – but couldn't second-guess him. Where could this be leading?

"Certainly sir" I replied *"He served his country in two World Wars."*

One war more than you, I insinuated *"He worked very hard to achieve what he achieved in his life. He's a self-made man. He worked his way up through the ranks."* I was stating the obvious. I wanted to let him know that I knew the score. For some reason I—*was*—feeling proud of my father, especially in relation to Brigadier Dale's hauteur. Brigadier Dale had not been made-up from the ranks,[4] and he knew it. He knew it as clearly as he knew my father—*had*—been made-up from the ranks. I wanted him to know that I was not concerned by his view of my father's inferior status. I wanted to say I was proud of my mother too – but I couldn't quite see how I'd approach that subject without sounding both defensive and belligerent.

Brigadier Dale held my gaze *"Having once been a . . . military man . . . "* he asked, failing to say 'officer' *"does he approve of the manner in which you keep your hair?"*

This was the exact moment in which old-fashioned phraseology would be perfectly employed. *"No sir . . . he does not. As one might expect . . . he views my hair as an Army officer naturally would. We—do —however have a mutual understanding."* I made my statement in as dignified a manner as I was capable – and made no move to avoid his gaze.

"And what—pray—might that be?" Mrs Dale interjected with evident consternation.

"I apologise for being opaque Mrs Dale – our understanding is that I should endeavour to be worthy of respect . . . " I took a deep breath *" . . . that I endeavour to be civil, polite, courteous . . . and above all – honourable."*

---

4 Being 'made-up from the ranks' is a British Army expression for 'promoted from the ranks'.

This was straight out of Jane Austen. They'd obviously not anticipated a foray into antebellum sentiments. The Dales—finally dumbfounded—fell silent.

Lindie looked across at me – but her expression betrayed heightened anxiety. I smiled as best I could – and she tried her best in return. Mrs Dale noticed our exchange and stiffened. I was dead meat.

What *could* they have expected of me? What chance were they giving me? If I'd been an upper-middle class young man I might have addressed the Dales with a modicum of indignation. I might have said '*You will excuse me – but I have not been accustomed to being interrogated with incivility when I have done nothing to warrant it. I have been courteous and affable – and you have treated me with contempt.*' As it was, I acted in keeping with my station in life. I accepted the indignity of their treatment – as if I could have expected no better. That had me pegged as working class without further reference. Even if I—had been—an upper-middle class young man, I could not have subjected Lindie to the results of 'elevated indignation'. I was fried both ways.

The silence continued. Mrs Dale twitched.

"*You have a very fine garden*" I offered – dissembling at the speed of light.

By this time the Brigadier was facing the window with his back to me. His hands were knotted into each other. He flexed his fingers slowly as if trying to control a surge of rage. Mrs Dale sat there rigidly—white-fingered as a porcelain streptocarpus—attempting to merge with the minimally upholstered chaise longue, as she assiduously avoided my gaze.

Lindie leant over and whispered – half choked "*There's something —really—wrong with my parents. I'm going to have to talk to them alone . . . so maybe you'd better leave now . . . I think . . .*" Lindie was silently weeping.

I said "*Whatever you think best—yes, certainly—I'll just say goodbye and . . . well . . .*" I stood up quickly "*Brigadier Dale, Mrs Dale, thank you very much for the tea and cake – but I think I should probably leave now. Goodbye and . . .*" I ran out of words again – but at least I'd not stammered once since my first trip on the 'B' of Brigadier Dale.

The Brigadier snorted something almost polite and his wife coughed stiffly in agreement. Their standards of enunciation had obviously deserted them – not to mention common courtesy. Lindie followed me out of the room and was about to accompany me up the drive when her mother called her inside.

"*You'd better go in . . .*" I whispered "*. . . we . . . we can talk at school on Monday . . . I hope it won't be bad for you because of me.*" I wanted more than anything to kiss her goodbye – but the impossibility of that gripped us both like steel manacles.

Lindie, still silently weeping, turned away with a small wave of her hand – one she obviously hoped her parents wouldn't detect. I walked slowly to the end of the drive. Why I walked so slowly – I have no idea. Maybe I had some idea of sparing Lindie for a while. As long as I still trod the gravel she'd be safe from her parents' inevitable discussion of the criminally insane creature she'd brought home. I could feel their eyes on me right to the end of the drive and realised that they had been able to take in the full horror of the length of my hair.

I mounted my motorcycle and slid silently down the road before starting the engine. I drove off as quietly as I was able – still hanging on to some desperate hope that *something* could be salvaged.

So let them say your hair's too long, / 'cause I don't care, with you I can't go wrong. Sonny and Cher—I Got You Babe—1965

Meeting Brigadier Dale had been like meeting my father before the hair débâcle – but this man was 20 years younger and somehow more intractable and severe. How—*could*—that be? I thought *my* father was the bastion of conservatism. If thoughts had muscles her parents would have physically hurled me through the front door. It was as if I'd personally invented heroin or something.

Lindie was not around on the following Monday—for reasons I can no longer remember—but when I next saw her she gave me the bad news.

"My father and mother . . . I've never seen them like this before. They're . . . well . . . it's as if they've lost all sense of reason. I just don't know what to do. They've forbidden me to have anything to do with you. I'm not even supposed to speak to you at school" she looked wretched *"I'll always speak to you, we'll always be friends but my parents are adamant that you can't be my boyfriend. I don't know if they'll ever change either – so . . . I'm going to have to go along with them until they calm down."*

I felt as if I was about to vaporise – it was the most shocking assault on my senses I'd received for as long as I could remember. I couldn't speak for a moment – but pulled myself together in order not to disturb her *"Maybe when you're 18 you could . . ."*

"*Yes . . .*" Lindie said – almost as if she were sleep walking "*That's when school is over . . . maybe they will change their minds in time – I don't know. I don't understand them – I don't know anything.*"

I should have known it. I might be able to stand up to one overbearing parent – but I couldn't really expect that of her. Lindie had two overbearing parents who were of one militaristic mind. We talked for a while – but it was clear that we had no alternative. Lindie apologised profusely – but her parents had apparently hated me with such ferocity that . . . well . . .
This was one of those occasions when it occurred to me that my father was not entirely wrong. His perception of the world was accurate with respect to a world that clung to an antebellum ethos.

"*I'm a hard core drug-fiend as far as the Dales are concerned*" I told my friend Pete that afternoon – because he was the first person to befriend me at Virginia Water.

"*Yeah mate—bloody criminally depraved pervert—but good for you.*"

Good for me? "*Right Pete . . .*" I replied "*rebel without a clause – without even an—*adjectival—*sub clause.*"

"*Well . . . I 'spose you—*do—*wear those blue tints . . . fierce glasses mate – but I bet they put a twist in the Brigadier's knickers eh?*"
Pete laughed.

Yes. I always wore those round National Health glasses.
My father gave me my first pair in all innocence of what they represented. They'd belonged to him in World War II. They were nickel plated and had quarter-inch wide arms with stout spring-backs.

I had the opticians put in lenses with the pale blue tint that I'd learnt was de rigueur in the 1880s. Blue-tinted spectacles were also de rigueur in the late 1960s amongst those who wanted you to know they had heads full of snow [5] – but I only found that out in 2007.

When the wind blows and the rain feels cold with a head full of snow – with a head full of snow.
Jagger/Richards—Rolling Stones—Moonlight Mile—Sticky Fingers—1971

Keith Richards said "*I don't remember anyone saying 'I'm going to get into drugs.' But then drugs are like that. They kind of slip up behind you. There was a certain amount of clubbishness about it, you know? 'Is he a head*[6] *or isn't he? Oh my God, poor chap.' And then you'd go round wearing blue tinted glasses, and all that crap.*" [7]

I *was* that 'poor chap'. I was also wearing those blue-tinted glasses – in complete ignorance of the statement they were making to the psychotropic cognoscenti. I just liked them. In many ways I was an innocent abroad – and always have been. I had no notion at the time what Brigadier Dale made of those spectacles. At that time I never imagined that—having reached the age of 50—I'd come to look more like Brigadier Dale—out of uniform—than most people I see from day to day. I'd imagine that even the 'young farmers' of 1968—who looked at me with faint horror in Farnham—must look less conservative than I do 40 years on. Those bucolic young farmers used to make me a little edgy as I drifted through the quaint villages of Surrey on my way to assignations with people who looked weirder than I did.

---

5 Snow – cocaine or heroine.
6 The term 'head' is an abbreviation of 'acid-head' *(lysergic acid diethylamide)* and pertains to persons who are *hallucinogenically-familiar.*
7 Interview by Kurt Loder in the 40th edition of Rolling Stone Magazine—17th May 2007

They weren't known for active belligerence – but there was a sense of animosity toward the weirdoes from the Art School – and anyone who looked as if they were destined to attend the Art School. There was a mainstream conservative fear of weirdoes at that time – which seemed to encourage some people to be categorised as such.

"*I never went*—out of my way—*to look weird y'know*" I told Pete.

"*Made a bloody good accident of it then*" Pete laughed.

"*No—really—Pete. I have—no—interest in cultivating a weird image. I just go for what I like – and if that makes me a weirdo, then I'm a weirdo by default.*"

Pete shook his head in disbelief "*Brigadier Dale has a pretty clear idea of what your image represents y'know.*"

"*Yes . . . I suppose he does*" I had to agree "*It means the ruination of his daughter.*"

"*More than—that—mate*" Pete added "*It's the ruination of the entire bloody country. That's how that pot-bellied sod and his fossilised wife see it.*"

Pete seemed to have a far clearer idea than I had of the facts of the matter. Pete always had something I lacked – common sense and a hard-edged sense of realism.

"*I suppose*" I commented naïvely "*I must have been labouring under the misconception that he'd see me as an individual.*"

Pete burst out laughing "*Sorry*" he said, controlling his reaction "*I don't mean to laugh – but you really are a loony sometimes. You've got this idealistic view of life – and it'll probably get you killed one day.*"

"*You're right Pete . . .* " I laughed "*Almost told the Brigadier he had a very fine moustache . . .* "

"*Well . . . maybe . . . you could've said that . . .* " Pete didn't laugh –
but stretched a slight sympathetic smile "*It would have shown you
had*—something—*in common.*" Then he burst out laughing again.
"*Her parents are fucking prehistoric reptiles . . . belong in a bloody
museum.*"

"*True enough . . .* " I sighed "*but that's*—most of the population
over 30—*isn't it.*"

"*Sure – but you're not wanted for bloody murder or anything*" Pete
replied angrily – on my behalf.

"*True – although Savage Cabbage play 'Bloody Murder'*—*you know that
Otis Spann number?*"

"*Yeah . . . very funny*" Pete chuckled "*But seriously mate, her parents
should be stuffed and mounted.*"

How could I disagree? "*They*—are—*deranged. I'm actually quite
pleasant from some parental points of view. But then . . . there's the long
list of evils isn't there: long hair, the moustache, and the motorbike*" Pause
"*Then*—*in addition*—*I'm a working class delinquent with a German
mother*" Pause "*My father's an upstart made-up-from-the-ranks major.
Then to cap it all I'm a prospective art student, and card-carrying weirdo
with penchant for antique clothes.*"

"*And vocalist for a 'shag-yer-daughter Blues band' . . .* " Pete shrugged
" *. . . that's either life-imprisonment or the death sentence as far as those
Tory lunatics are concerned. It'll change though mate – they're doomed to
extinction, those people. It's just a shame that they still have power over
Lindie . . .* "

"*It's a shame alright . . . heavy blow . . . but I*—am—*going to roll with it
. . . bide my time*" I said "*A year and a half'll see things change. Things
have already changed a lot since '67. She'll be 18 then. She'll be an
independent adult – and . . .* "

Pete—furrowing his brow—interrupted "*Yeah . . . that's the theory mate – that's the theory. I hope you're right*" Pause "*Still – look on the bright side eh? In the meantime . . .*" he winked " *. . . world's your oyster.*"

I thanked Pete for his sage counsel "*Right—exactly—I got rhythm, I got music . . . hey who could ask for anything more?*"

Pete laughed and shook his head "*Good luck mate – but I think she's gone.*"

No. I was *not* going to accept that. The world *didn't* look like *any* kind of oyster to me. It looked more like the fish guts and crab shells that sometimes littered the fishing cove in Cadgwith. I used to sit and watch the seagulls feasting on that morass of stinking detritus. I enjoyed the spectacle – but now . . . I was sitting in the emotional corollary of that avian restaurant—*that nauseating aquatic mortuary*—wondering if there were poisson on the menu that weren't poison. I'd eaten oysters with Lindie once in London on a school trip to the Tate Gallery. I found them to be cold salty samplings of nothing. I was otherwise fond of dainty fish hors d'œuvres – but oysters left me decidedly cold.

I left Pete to his painting and wandered off to the common room to listen to music or distract myself with whatever happened next. I shuffled along the corridor—the expectant stride of a brilliant destiny no longer possible—thinking ' *. . . after enough time has passed . . . Lindie and I can resume our romance . . . nothing obvious – we'll just see each other every day . . . although nothing'll occur outside school . . . it could look quite similar . . . then in time . . . it could just take off again from where it left off . . . nothing would have to be said . . . it would be better that way . . . we'll still feel what we felt for each other . . .* '

After ruminating for an hour in this convoluted manner I succeeded in making myself feel better. There—*was*—still hope.

Lindie and I had poetry to discuss. We did just that – almost as if nothing had changed. After a week the Dales had relented on their sanction against me as far as conversation went. They agreed that it was an extreme measure – but trusted that Lindie understood it was to go no further. She told them that although I was unhappy – that I was willing to refrain from encouraging anything further than conversation. After a few weeks Lindie took to staying on at school a little longer in order that we'd have time together. Her parents failed to take exception to her delayed arrival home and we meandered into some kind of twilight zone – hovering between cordiality and tentative affection. True to my word—even though I'd not given it—I did nothing to change the situation. I was continually viscerally impelled to change the situation – but knew it would be disastrous. The change would have to await her coming of age – the 8th of August 1970. So many things hung on this mysterious coming of age. The GIBSON EB0 also floated in the distance – the 6th of June 1970. As far as I could see the Summer of 1970 was going to be like the Boston Tea Party or something. I'd sing La Marseillaise.

Allons enfants de la Patrie, / Le jour de gloire est arrivé! / Contre nous de la tyrannie, / L'étendard sanglant est levé. / Arise, progeny of Mother Earth, Our day of glory is arriven! Though tyranny's bloodied banner is raised against us. Author's translation—with Lindie Dale—1968

In the meantime, I'd continue educating myself as I'd always done: the history of Art; the history of Music; the history of Blues; the history of costume, architecture, maritime adventure, or whatever. I'd immerse myself in the endless interconnecting streams of influence that ran through history.

It gave me ample avenues of discussion with Lindie – without having to dwell on the horror of what had happened to us at the hands of her inhuman parents. The subject matter of our discussions assumed the function of rose-tinted spectacles – and as long as I wore them I could forget that there was an enormous problem that was not likely to go away. 'Les Langoustines'[8]—as I privately termed the Dales—were still eyeing me from afar.

---

8 Langoustine is used as the author used the word at the time – to mean lobster. Homard is the correct French word for lobster. Langouste is crayfish, rock-lobster, or spiny lobster. Langoustine is French for scampi or Dublin Bay Prawn. Sailors in the 1700s and 1800s nicknamed soldiers 'lobsters' because of their red and white uniforms.

6

savoy green

We'd gone—looking suitably feral and feisty—to the Compton Bells, in order to hear Freighttrain. They were supposed to have some startling new song. It was one of their own – and composed by Gazzer. It had a refrain that people were humming and words that ran something to the effect of '. . . *only —yooooou—can—dooooo—me like yer do* . . . ' Lyrics like that did have some kind of whiz to them—with the right bass line—but they sounded 'done to death' as far as I was concerned. Ron, Steve, and I were interested to hear what all the fuss was about and Jack came too in order to be unimpressed.

While we waited for the set to begin we sat chatting about the inevitable. It was the subject that always put an end to girlfriends for Ron and Steve; as not—that—many girls could endure discussion of musical technicalities. We were obsessed with what other musicians played – and how they played it. We talked about it incessantly. We knew what everyone played – and even what they *used* to play. There were continual debates amongst our friends as to the best guitar for different styles of music.

The music journals such as 'New Musical Express' and 'Melody Maker' were full of it. They sometimes carried articles which would give rise to heated discussion.

'*This*—wilting—*pillock doesn't know what the hell he's talking about!*' was a phrase I heard quite often during break times at Virginia Waters. Such outbursts would usually be followed by lively debate amongst the Rock-Blues illuminati – that is to say, everyone in sight.

Everyone seemed to be some sort of expert on the most arcane aspects of instruments – right down to the electrical circuitry. You couldn't hold your head up in decent society unless you were outrageously well informed about every model of FENDER and GIBSON there'd ever been – and this occasionally gave me the edge because I also knew about NATIONAL and DOBRO guitars.

The place I *didn't* have an edge was with the actual playing. I was a primitive bass player and a self-taught Delta lap-slide player. Ron wasn't in favour of solos 'til such time as we'd individually be up to it. He and Steve were way-up-and-beyond it – but Jack needed a fair few years unless I was accompanying him on harp. He thought I was well up to it on harp without Jack – but that solo vocal didn't work that well with an electric set. He did however feel it was important for me to play solo for my own development. For that reason he suggested that I might like to play solo acoustic in the longer intermissions we had at the Colleges and Universities – so I'd occasionally play a solo piece as part of those gigs. I'd mic up the DEBIL for that.

"*I like it that you've got that extra string to your bow . . .* " Ron commented when Jack went to the bar for another pint ". . . *gives us breadth.*"

I never quite believed that we needed the extra breadth of acoustic Delta Blues – but was glad to take Ron's suggestion.

"*I thought you weren't in favour of us playing solo yet?* " I murmured.

"I'm not – but this way it gets 'round having to give in to Jack about his bloody tadpole [1] *. . . "* Ron whispered so that Jack wouldn't overhear his comment as he returned from the bar *"Anyway . . ."* he added *" . . . it's good for you to flex your muscles musically."*

"I wish I could get some tuition in lap-slide though – I mean beyond listening to records."

"Jimi Hendrix is self-taught" Steve observed.

"Yes . . . that's a fact which always gives me hope" I replied *"I've got stumpy little fingers though . . . "*

"Jack Bruce doesn't have much in the way of fingers . . . " Steve laughed *" . . . and that doesn't hold him back all that much."*

"Maybe there's hope for a vocalist with a speech impediment yet then" I said somewhat ironically.

"Bloody certain mate" Ron piped up – misunderstanding that I was merely jesting at my own expense *"Hendrix had a stammer when he was a child—and it never really left him—heard that somewhere . . . "*

That was most encouraging – I seemed to be in good company.

Jack weighed in enthusiastically *"He's left handed too – and plays a right-handed* STRAT *upside down and re-strung left-handed!"*

We all knew that but we nodded as if to suggest that Jack had told us something new.

"Y'know . . . " mused Ron *" . . .* FENDER *should make a right-handed Hendrix* STRAT.*"*

"Why's that Ron?" I asked.

---

1 Tadpole refers to Jack Hackman's attempts to emulate Ginger Baker's Toad drum solo.

"*Well . . . playing* STRAT *strung upside down affects the sound. The three bass strings get a bright sound and the three treble strings get a mellow sound.*" Ron noticed me looking quizzical – and continued "*That's owing to the bias of the pickups . . . The pickups are biased for bass and treble and reversing the strings reverses the bias.*"

I grinned from ear to ear. I loved this kind of information. "*That sounds ideal for Blues.*"

"*Yeah . . .*" Ron replied " *. . . in a lot of ways – but I'd rather have a system where I could flip the bias – or have two guitars . . . That'd be the thing to go for in the long term*" Pause "*And there's another thing too – turning a* STRAT *upside-down puts the tremolo arm above the strings*" Ron grinned. "*That arrangement lets you use tremolo far more easily when you're picking. I don't usually go for effects – but that's something even I'd consider – on a* TELECASTER *that is.*"

Jack—sensing the show was about to begin—emptied the remains of his beer in one gulp and nodded to the barman for a fresh supply. "*Did you—know*" he exclaimed in fevered glee "*that Hendrix can play right handed too—and—play a right handed guitar upside down—without—restringing it!*"

"*News to me*" Ron replied "*I'm impressed.*"

"*That—is—astonishing*" Steve chimed in "*I hadn't heard—that— before either.*"

"*Wild alright . . .*" I added " *. . . but, then Ron's not left handed – so he's never had to try that kind of thing*" I said turning to Ron. "*I can't see you—not—being able to do that . . . if you put your mind to it I mean. But . . . there's not a lot of point is there? I mean it's the sound isn't it. I'm not saying that Hendrix isn't a genius – but I'm not that interested in the showman side of his playing.*"

"Yeah – y'right Frank—I'd go along with that . . . " Ron said – evidently touched by my loyal support of his musicianship *"but being able to play reversed strings means you have a mind for music that's quite subtle and elaborate."*

"Yes . . . I suppose you'd have to know a guitar neck inside out to do that" I replied *"But what's there in that, that you can't do?"*

"Well I don't know yet, do I . . . haven't tried it . . . " Ron responded *" . . . but what impresses me about Hendrix, is that he speaks in different languages on guitar."*

"Right Mr Arbuthnot – that's far more than showmanship" Jack cut in *"Hendrix is a bloody genius."*

"Yeah Jack" I came back – to reassure Jack about my respect for Hendrix *"I'm not saying he's not. It's just that this playing-with-his-teeth number doesn't particularly impress me – but there's no showmanship in finding your way around a reversed set of strings. That—is—monstrously impressive."*

"Right Frank" Ron observed *"I'm not interested in playing left handed – but reversing the strings might be a—very—interesting experiment."*

If you can just get your mind together then come on across to me / We'll hold hands and then we'll watch the sunrise from the bottom of the sea / But first, are you experienced? Jimi Hendrix—The Jimi Hendrix Experience—Are You Experienced—Are You Experienced—1967

Jack grinned. *"Yeah I think it would give you another view of things."* Jack had obviously researched the matter. He read anything he could find on Jimi Hendrix and we always made a good audience. *"Hendrix says that he combines what he called the 'earth' of Blues with the 'space' of psychedelic – and that's what his style's based on."*

"Jack and Jimi have my vote" I replied *"I think that's where we're going with our Acid Rock numbers . . . "* I had other things to say – but suddenly Freighttrain pulled into the freightyard all whistles blowing – so we sat back to listen. Gazzer was slicked up in black leather trousers and singlet.[2] He had buccaneer boots and a broad flashing leer that he threw liberally at all the girls in the audience.

"You gotta hand it to him" said Jack *"He's got style."*

"Yes Jack . . . just not a great deal . . . " I replied.

"And what he has got" Ron continued *"would look better on a Turkish wrestler."*

We were then cut off in mid flow by 'Johnny B Goode' and a whole shoal of other such numbers. I watched Gazzer on bass and wondered how long it would take me to catch up. I thought he was better than Ron and Steve made him out to be – but then, that was maybe because they were observing from some lofty peak that I'd not ascended. He looked pretty nimble to me and he didn't look at the neck. They played six numbers before the interval and I spent most of my time watching Gazzer's fingers. I found myself flitting from *'I could play that'* to *'three years before I could get anywhere near that.'*

"Freighttrain certainly have their moments" Ron commented.

"Yeah . . . " Steve yawned *"They're a standard good-time Rock'n'Roll band –but their idea of Blues is Chuck Berry—not that I don't rate Chuck Berry—but 'Johnny B Goode' is not Blues."*

"True . . ." Ron said *" . . . although Johnny Winter plays a nice cover of it on 'Second Winter' – but . . . as you say, it's not Blues."*

---

2 A sleeveless vest or under-shirt with wide cutaway arm holes.

Jack nodded. *"Besides which Freighttrain just play everything as fast as they can"* he sneered *"to make it sound as if they're the major force in the universe or something"* he directed this at Ron *"and they have zero imagination – they never play anything original."*

"Well let's wait 'til we hear Gazzer's gargantuan jingle in the second half . . . " Steve suggested *" . . . he might have a surprise in store for us."*

We usually commandeered the settee and one of the armchairs at the Compton Bells – and somehow it was an unspoken law of nature that I got the armchair. Usually midway through his set Gazzer would stroll by—accompanied as ever by his sneer—and say *'check—the—neck.'* And this occasion was no different.

Gazzer rambled—guitar under his arm—trying to give the impression that he was on a stroll through his own personal living quarters. *"Check—the—neck."*

"Yeah Gazzer . . . " I yawned *" . . . amazing . . . your guitar has a neck."*

"Yeah man, not like that girlie-guitar of yours—hey."

He was trying to bait me—for reasons only known to himself— and consistently failing to understand that I couldn't be baited in that way.

"Yeah—I know Gazzer—that's the reason I like it—so—much. In fact . . . Jack Bruce entirely shares my view of the matter" I replied.

Gazzer gave me a quick thin shifty grin in response—a slightly vacant look in his eye—and languidly slipped round to the side of the bar out of range of my unconcerned gaze.

The Gibson Thunderbird IV had a long scale neck – and Gazzer made a point of gloating about it. The neck was four inches longer than the Gibson EB3 I played – and according to Gazzer, that was supposed to insinuate something about our respective physical dimensions. Ron had to explain this to me because I missed the joke. I looked at Ron with complete incredulity *"You mean he's really* that *stupid?"*

Ron laughed *"Yeah . . . Gazzer's really*—that—*stupid."*

Steve agreed *"And he's got that ugly*—*ugly*—ugly—Gibson Thunderbird IV *bass – you'd have to be retarded to buy a thing like that."*

"Right Steve" I concurred *"Looks like a fossilised amœba – like some sort of Henry Moore sculpture . . . a cross between a road-flattened dog and a transistor radio."*

"Yeah—*it's ugly*—*but looks aren't everything.* Thunderbird's *a fine instrument – but . . . "* Ron remarked turning to me *" . . . you can't bend notes on it like you can with an* EB3."

A peculiar moment had followed my off-the-wall comment about Jack Bruce liking the diminutive qualities of the Gibson EB3. I'd missed it entirely but it was apparent to Ron and Jack —who were watching Gazzer closely at the time—that I'd left him feeling unsure as to how I came to know what Jack Bruce felt about the Gibson EB3. They overheard Gazzer a few minutes later enquiring discreetly of someone he knew at the bar *"Y'know Fucker Arbuthnot?"* The other fellow had shrugged. *"Jesus man*—*'course y'know know him*—*him over there with the blue tints* —*Savage Cabbage singer."* The other fellow nodded that he knew me. *"D'yer know . . . if he*—*knows*—*Jack Bruce?"* The fellow shrugged again. No one there knew me that well. Gazzer was extremely wary of seeming to be interested in—or impressed by —anyone. Ron and Jack found this monumentally amusing.

Jack said *"I'd like to ring the pub tomorrow and tell the landlord I was Jack Bruce wanting a word with Mr Arbuthnot, if we could arrange some way for Gazzer to be in earshot."* Jack imagined how the conversation would go and gave us a rendition *'Yeah Jack—sure —that would be great, I'm sure that the lads would be really keen to jam. Right—yeah—right. That's perfect Jack—yeah—really good, I think that'd work well with wah-wah. Brilliant. Really? You don't say. He—is!? And—Jimi!? Shame though – we can't really make New York. Well that's amazing anyway. Yeah—sure—excellent. Right – thanks Jack. Are you sure we don't need to bring amps? We'll all be up on the weekend then. Bye Jack.'*

Jack was highly excited about pulling this hoax – but I turned out to be a wet blanket.

"The idea's a lot of fun Jack – without having to take it any further." I didn't say so – but I felt that pulling a stunt like that would put me in the same sleaze bracket as Gazzer. Jack was just about to argue the point when Gazzer strode back onto the stage, stuck his guitar between his legs and ran a finger high up the **G** string. Freighttrain burst into a breakneck version of 'Rolling and Tumbling'. They ran through their standard repertoire and ended on Gazzer's number. It had a nice rolling bass line and he played quite a fine introduction in unison with the lead player. For once Gazzer was concentrating on technique too much to flaunt his theatricals and I found myself enjoying his song. It was a good song – even though I could hear 'Sunshine of Your Love' as the inspiration.

I came away feeling that Gazzer's song was actually quite good. Ron agreed with me but Jack and Steve concurred that it was nothing to get excited about.

Steve wasn't keen on Gazzer. He saw him as something of a thug despite his wealth of extremely sharp clothing and his Public School[3] accent. I felt sorry for him in various ways though. I tended to see him as being trapped in a form of archetypal male primitivism—with *all* that this entailed.

"His racist humour and obnoxious views about women – are the main thing I find difficult about him" I threw in.

"That's the least of it" said Steve *"He's just a wheeler-dealer and treats people as objects to be moved and adjusted to suit his ambition. He's always got his eye on the main chance and I find that disgusting."* I couldn't argue with that – but I didn't like panning him too much.

There was—in early '69—a feeling that we could do anything and go anywhere with Savage Cabbage. We were a mutual admiration society – and we were *not* embarrassed by the fact that this was not a well kept secret. Friday and Saturday evenings were times we were always together as a band— whether playing gigs or not—and these were the times when we'd try out some unlikely number such as 'Suzanne' as slow Blues. The main criterion was that the lyrics were good.

. . . and just when you mean to tell her that you have no love to give her, / She gets you on her wave-length and lets the river answer that you've always been her lover. Leonard Cohen—Suzanne—Songs of Leonard Cohen—1967

---

3 In Britain Public Schools are not what they are in the USA. Public schools in the USA are called state schools in Britain. Public Schools in Britain are actually private, fee-paying schools such as Eton, Harrow, Rugby, Stoneyhurst, Downside, Roedean, Cheltenham Ladies College, and Westonbirt.

We'd occasionally try these numbers out in small gigs at pubs and village halls – and mainly got good responses to them. Leonard Cohen had a wealth of fine lyrics. He had a way with words that was not entirely unlike Bob Dylan – but his presentation was different. I heard lines like '*she feeds you tea and oranges that come all the way from China*' from 'Suzanne' and wondered why I couldn't write like that. It was mysterious. I talked about it with the band – but they couldn't see the problem. They couldn't see anything particularly special about lines like that – and I found myself stuck as to why these words had some special magic. It concerned ordinariness and extraordinariness and the way they flittered in and out of each other. Ron and Jack had no idea what I was talking about – but Steve, being far more literary, had some notion of what I meant.

"*I can write poetry – and I'm happy with what I write – but song lyrics are some other category*" I said.

He thought I should just keep writing and it would all start coming in time. He thought that we'd develop something together and that Ron and Jack could throw in ideas.

"*After all Eric Clapton and George Harrison wrote 'Badge' together with a line from Ringo. If you wanted to make your lyrics more ordinary we could bring you down*" he laughed "*What a bring down!*"

So you know what you know in your head, / Will you, won't you, do you, don't you know when a head's dead / What a bringdown!
Ginger Baker—Cream—What a Bringdown—Goodbye Cream—1969

That thought was encouraging. Then Steve pointed out that I might possibly be seeing more than there actually was – purely because of my unusual approach to language. He said "*Look at the words to 'Doing That Scrapyard Thing' – I mean, it's funny – but it's not exactly inspired.*"

135

I thought about it and replied "*Well – it looks like their version of Edward Lear. I like it for that reason – but those aren't the kind of words I'm trying to find.*"

When I was young they gave me a mongrel piano – spent all my time inventing the cup of tea. / Writing your name in the sea, banging my favourite head.
Jack Bruce/Pete Brown—Cream—Doing That Scrapyard Thing—Goodbye Cream—1969

Yes . . . I'd consider the notion that '*Aristotle's orchestra are living on the pill*' but how did Ginger Baker find words like that? And were these great words or not? Combining the ordinary and the extraordinary – could be both brilliant and banal – or it could be either. How was I to make the distinction? That was going to be a complex, subtle, and possibly endless endeavour – and school was not helping to that end. The English teacher at Virginia Water was not Mr Preece. He was alright in his own way – but he had no interest in my search for creative lyrics.

At that time no one seemed to know what I meant when I obsessed on the subject. The distinction between poetry and lyrics baffled me.

My songs read as rhyming poetry rather than lyrics [4] – but I thought there ought to have been a place for Rock poetry – after all Bob Dylan seemed to be able to straddle the divide. Steve liked my lyrics and was concerned that I never seemed content with what I'd written. He took me aside one day and said "*I hope you don't mind some personal comments?*"

I wondered what he was going to say. "*Fine*" I replied.

---

4 "*Pete [Brown]'s lyrics were very important*" *Jack says.* "*Very clever. Very poetic. Pete was always more of a poet than a lyricist; there's a very definite but very fine distinction between the two.*"
Jack—biography of Jack Bruce—Steven Myatt—chapter 11—page 144

"*It's this thing with your lyrics*" Steve launched in "*I think you're trying for the impossible.*"

"*Thanks Steve . . .*" I replied completely misunderstanding his intention.

"*No . . . that's not what I'm saying. What I want to say is that*—your lyrics—*may be different from the lyrics*—you—*like . . . but I think your lyrics are totally fierce. They're more poetic than most lyrics*—and *amazingly crammed with imagery*—but I don't see that as any kind of *problem apart from the fact that*—you—*think they should be something else. Thing is . . . when you look at the lyrics*—you—*really admire, you're looking at them with the melody-line in your mind. You're not reading the lyrics cold.*"

"*Yeah—true—can't argue with that*" I sighed.

"*So . . . if you were able to read the words of a Jack Bruce/Pete Brown song or a Lennon/McCartney song*—before—*you heard it played and sung – you might*—not—*think the lyrics were as brilliant.*"

"*Right . . . theoretically . . . that*—could—*happen – but I'm not going to find out unless I get to read the lyrics of the next Beatles album before it appears.*"

"*But if you did . . .*" Steve persisted "*. . . the lyrics*—might—*seem as if you could improve on them – and all of*—us—*think you could. You could lay down a lot more verses too – Beatles songs are*—always— *too short.*"

"*True . . .*" I agreed "*. . . I always wish they'd write longer songs . . . 'I'm Only Sleeping' deserves a few more verses. Cream too. 'White Room' should definitely be longer.*"

"*Maybe you should start by writing extra verses for tracks you like best – and maybe we could perform them.*"

It was good, naturally, to hear such sentiments *"I think I'll take a shot at that"* but it still left me a little baffled. *"Maybe when we get an album out . . . "* I said *" . . . and people start responding well to our songs, I'll start seeing them in a different light. At the moment it just seems tenuous that they're real songs. With Blues, I know where we are but with these things I compose I just have no way of being able to see them outside of being poetry."*

Steve shook his head *"You're obsessed Vic . . . You're just stuck with the idea that the Lennon/McCartney and Pete Brown lyrics are better than your lyrics and different and at some high level you can't reach. The only difference—really—is that—we—don't have an album – and half the world's not talking about—us."*

"Roll—on—the—adjectival—day . . . " I exhaled as a sigh mixed with a grin.

"But when that day—comes" Steve emphasised *"and it—will—you're going to have to settle for being who you are."*

"Right . . . well . . . that—is—an interesting angle . . . I'm going to have to think about that . . . but—of course—there's really no way I can make this idea part of how I look at my lyrics" I shrugged *"I suppose I'm just going to have to accept that you all like what I write and that I earn my keep in the band."*

Steve laughed and shook his head in an exaggerated gesture of disbelief. *"You do—far—more than earn your keep. We wouldn't get anywhere if we were simply a Blues band – even with Ron's genius lead playing. I know Blues is what we all love but we're going to—have—to be broader than that. We need to have other material to make people listen to Blues. Y'know a lot of people started out raving about 'Sunshine of Your Love' and ended up preferring 'Spoonful'."*

Steve had put his finger on something quite important – something I'd never considered.

He'd had conversations with Ron about presenting Blues and they'd concluded that a Blues band—in Britain at least—had a duty to introduce people to the genre.

"*Thing is . . .* " Steve concluded " *. . . to make the big time—and get people excited about Blues—we'll need to develop our Acid Rock material. That's—your—job and you do it really well – with me and Ron writing the melody line.*"

I nodded slowly and ponderously. I was slightly off-to-the-side, somewhere in my own dream world as Steve continued "*Not that you won't compose melody too—you'll definitely be up for that before too long—and we'll bring you on with that. We've already decided to set aside some time to give you music theory lessons during our time at Music College.*"

"*Really?*" I was touched by their concern and the degree of their involvement with my development as a musician.

"*Yeah—really—Ron's always said you've got the 'ear' and he's right – it's just that you don't have all the tools yet*" Pause "*But Ron believes . . . that when you've got some music theory under your belt – we'll be looking the big time square in the face – and when I say 'we' I mean you, me and Ron. Ron says that you're a force to be reckoned with – in your own right. He says it's amazing what you've done and where you've got on next to nothing and no help at all from your parents.*"

I was still sitting there with the words 'big time' hovering on the horizon of plausibility. What a thing that would be. That was the dream now – but it was a workable dream. The dream had overtaken Jack's wishful thinking—*and*—our overexcited imaginations, when Ron had decided that filling the vacuum left by Cream was actually realistic.

I didn't have to take Jack seriously on such subjects – but when Ron and Steve made such statements, I knew we—*were*—looking the big time square in the face. Having Steve in agreement with Ron on this point was ever-so-slightly terrifying. The reception we got at gigs in pubs—and in town and village halls—was not to be denied. We were definitely highly professional and unquestionably innovative.

"*And Jack?*" I asked "*You haven't mentioned him in the big line up.*"

Steve assumed a face of discomfiture "*Jack . . . well Jack's our drummer . . . I know you stand up for him – but he's not a*—musician's musician—*he's getting more competent as time goes by – but Ron and I don't think he'll ever be more than a working drummer. The closest he's likely to get to Ginger Baker is listening to him on 'Wheels of Fire'.*"

"*You and Ron are not open to being surprised . . . ?*"

Steve stared for a moment and shrugged "*Well . . . put it this way. You didn't take Music 'O' Level because it wasn't available as a subject. Jack went to Grammar School and he could have taken Music. I know a lot of bands can be described as 'three musicians and a drummer' but that's not what we want with Savage Cabbage.*"

"*Maybe Jack's parents laid down the law on what 'O' levels he took . . . ?*"

"*Maybe . . .*" Pause " *. . . maybe you're right. I don't know . . . maybe we'll be surprised. Jack could always catch up when we're at College. He'd have three years to develop . . . and if he really put heart and soul into it . . . he could surprise us.*"

"*I'd just feel happier if you and Ron would give him the benefit of the doubt . . . y'know . . . he needs encouragement . . .*"

I finally won Steve round – but felt that I'd done so on the basis of our friendship rather than his better judgement.

At least he agreed that we had to collaborate positively if our stage act was to succeed – even in the short term. Jack had to feel that he had a future.

It's not easy to describe being on stage with a Blues band – or with any kind of band. Maybe it is the same for actors, pugilists, or politicians.

I support the left, though I'm leaning to the right, / But I'm just not there when it's coming to a fight.
Jack Bruce/Pete Brown—Cream—Politician—Wheels of Fire—1968

I used to sing '*I support the left, but I'm leaning: leaning, leaning—*leaning—*to the right*' because . . . I enjoyed the irony too much. One night it irritated someone who shouted "*Cream don't sing it like that mate!*" So I threw in a new verse.

House of Commons—baby—I always sing it right, / House-a-Lords now —mamma—I always, always, always—always—sing it right / Left in my own constituency—yeah—I make my errors, just in spite.
The Author—parody of Politician—1969

Fortunately the man—somewhere in his mid 20s—laughed when I sang those lines.

Ron said "*Y'know Frank, I'd have whacked someone a couple of years back for throwing a trick like the one you pulled with switching the lyrics. He was a big bloke too y'know . . . could've hauled you down off the stage and pummelled the holy crap out of you.*"

I nodded to Ron with a sheepish grin in token of the fact that he was right.

"*Bloody funny though*" Ron responded.

"*Don't know how you get away with it – but it's*—hilarious—*when you do that*" Steve howled – unable to keep a straight face.

Jack was convulsed to the point of tears. He kept laughing about it all the way back in the van and setting us all off each time.

Usually the crowd was friendly and appreciative. Usually I was in some sort of altered state. There'd often be the light that made it a little hard to see what was beyond the stage or stage area – it wasn't always an elevated platform. It was like living outside the normal run of time. The time on stage would seem eternal and then—almost without warning—it would be over. Protracted and fleeting. A distended gestalt that collapsed inward on itself. It sometimes seemed like being on a ship – a contained environment that was regulated by an hour-glass. Songs ticked off the time like the watches: some lengthy; some like the dogwatch – swiftly curtailed. There was always the strange fluctuation between being alone on stage and being in precise collusion with each other. Ron would always cue me in with a nod or a gesture – because I'd sometimes lose track of what was going on. I'd follow the cues conveyed by his stance – and he'd watch and listen in order to follow my vocal line where necessary. In the improvisational sections I'd follow Steve in order to maintain a sense of where we were going. Ron would be unfathomable at those times and would almost recede in my hearing – so strong was my focus on Steve.

I could hear Jack improving as time went on. He became more confident too. It was heart-warming to hear his improvements and see his efforts to be what he needed to be. It also served to remind me that my work on bass needed to continue to improve – but although that was work it was also endless pleasure.

On the streaming grey Atlantic where the bass riffs never end / You can rhyme with nascent memories – you never need pretend / You can roll right down like roller blinds of subcutaneous surf / As random messages replay your attempts to leave the earth / Please never reconsider your possibility of flight / Or you won't go down in history as the queen who stole the night.
Larkin/Bruce/Schubert—Savage Cabbage—The Queen Who Stole The Night—Savoy Green—1970

"You know Steve . . . " I mused *"We're better than I ever thought we could be."* Steve was looking through me to some distant point on the horizon as his fingers flashed silently over the strings of his Precision bass. He now practised Bach and Bruce in every spare moment.

"No doubt about it. We've got Ron" Steve replied in a somewhat distracted tone.

*"Yes we have. And we've also got—*Steve*—the Bruce."* [5] That seemed to startle Steve out of his reverie – and even he, with his residual self-doubt, had to admit that there was nothing he couldn't play.

*"I'm not 'Jack the Bruce' yet y'know – but . . . I can see the future. I can see that it's just a matter of time. I've made some real breakthroughs after talking with Ron—*and*—you. It seemed—for a few years—I'd not been improving much . . . I felt cramped up—tight—but then something happened."*

"You and Ron aren't really—so—far apart any more as far as I can hear . . . " I insisted *" . . . and you know what Ron says about my 'having the ear'."*

---

5 A play is being made on Robert the 1st King of Scots [1274 – 1329] known as Robert the Bruce.

This was one of those momentous occasions and we both knew it. Steve decided not to disagree and settled into his new-found confidence – as if it had happened right there in that moment. We were silent as 'Born Under a Bad Sign' played out.

Steve turned to me *"I think it started when you picked up Ron's EB3. Something about watching you work at it flipped the switch . . . and then working on Bach's 'cello Suites – but mainly it was seeing how hard you were working and how happy you were. I've always been sort of . . . determined and serious but . . . I'd lost the pleasure somewhere."*

I interrupted *"And—now—it's back again!"*

Steve cackled wildly and uncharacteristically *"Right! It's like I lost the pleasure with all that practice – and now I'm having fun again. It's like . . . well I feel free . . . "*

That was too much of an opportunity to be lost so I quoted the song *"You mean you can walk down the street, and there's no one there – though the pavements are one huge crowd?"* [6]

Steve chuckled and he shook his head *"There's no curing you is there – but seriously something's really changed."*

It was obvious. I agreed enthusiastically *"That's the thing really – that's the important thing about a band staying together. We can encourage each other and bring each other on musically. You and Ron have been brilliant – and it makes me feel that I've not lost out as much as I thought through not having music lessons or taking Music at school. There's—*nothing—*we can't do if we help each other."*

---

6 Pete Brown/Jack Bruce—Cream—I Feel Free—Fresh Cream—1966

*Life is carefully adjusted in suburban sobriety / But the catalogue of
comfort is like a mortuary / They got perfect nests of tables and ducks on
every wall / That deliberate like herrings in a sea of rigmarole / If you've
not been hit by flying lead or drowned in chemistry / You can throw away
your insurance plan – it don't mean that much to me.*
Larkin/Bruce/Schubert—Savage Cabbage—It Don't Mean that Much To Me—Savoy Green—
1970

Amazing things were erupting with the band – but my lingering
school years kept a lid on things. I was ambivalent about school.
On the one hand it took time away from music – but on the
other it was where I met Lindie and translated French Surrealist
poetry. School was frustrating – even though Mathematics was
no longer on the curriculum. The school was not happy that I
wasn't taking more subjects for examination – but I had what I
needed for Art College and was not going to give way to
pressure. I wasn't keen on digesting facts for their own sake –
no matter how worthy it was made to appear. Geography *should*
have been interesting – but it wasn't. The examinations board
had seen to that. Glaciation was fascinating – but comparing
and contrasting major industries in Chicago and Baltimore was
mind-numbing. I did not want to know. It was useless
information. It wasn't that Chicago couldn't be fascinating.
Chicago Blues was the heart of the music we played – and that
seemed to make matters worse. It was like being a Wagner
enthusiast studying Bayreuth without reference to Wagner or the
amazing annual festival there. It was like studying Wien [7]
without a word being mentioned about Wolfgang Amadeus
Mozart. If I'd been able to study Chicago from the point of
view of Blues and the migration of Black Southern workers to
the Northern industrial cities – it would have been worthwhile.

---

7 Vienna

Compare and contrast Blues in the Mississippi Delta, Texas, and Chicago. Fascinating! That would have been the Geography class for me. It could also have included industry – what about the rise of NATIONAL RESOPHONIC, GIBSON, and FENDER as guitar manufacturers? The Geography class could have morphed into a history class, a music class, and a sociology class – but it didn't.

I put this point to the Headmaster Mr Ironsides – but his response was simply *"That is not what appears on the syllabus – and it isn't ever likely to. If you persist in wanting the world to be as you want it to be – you will find yourself unemployed and unemployable."* Fine by me – I had my future employment worked out. Four years at Art School – then directly into the life of a psychedelic Blues musician.

School *could have* helped with my future plans but it didn't. Schools were not primarily places of education – they were institutions that operated according to set criteria. You had to memorise information in order to regurgitate it – and it didn't really matter much what the information was. I'd asked about music as soon as I arrived at the school – but I was told that I had too little knowledge and experience to join an 'O' Level class let alone an 'A' level class. I offered to join the year below 'O' Level – but that was also not possible. I'd suggested attending the music class of each year and making up time that way – but that was not permitted. It would interfere with the way the classes were taught or whatever. Someone might have a hernia or World War III might break out. The rule book of Moloch denied access to education within a system that deemed education necessary. I'd let the Geography A level class drop after the first year – which left me with English and Art. That was all I needed from school to achieve the minimum requirement for Art School: 5 'O' levels and 2 'A' levels.

*The government's in crisis – appointing guarantees, / They're struggling for
the power to issue their decrees / But you don't have to listen much, to how
they want to win / 'cause the hour's nearing midnight and the owls are on
the wing. / There's a place I go where freedom is not an unknown word /
Where ideas fly like crystal feathers in a tapestry of birds / Won't you
come with me it's time to leave – the prison walls are thin / 'cause the
hour's nearing midnight and the owls are on the wing.*

Larkin/Bruce/Schubert—Savage Cabbage—The Owls Are On the Wing—Savoy Green—1970

I used the free periods to draw, paint, and write songs.
I delivered the song lyrics to Ron and Steve – a copy each.
Then I'd sit with them while they considered keys and chord
structures. I'd throw in my own ideas of where I wanted a
minor or major 7th. Every now and then when I wasn't quite
satisfied with a melody line Ron would ponder a while and say
"How about this?" He'd almost always surprise me.

*"Yes—that's it—what did you do to get that? It sounds like the same
notes but the feel is completely different."*

Ron grinned *"Good ear. I changed to a different mode in the same key."*

"Modes?"

"Yeah . . . " Ron replied with a mischievous grin *"they're also called
Church Scales. They're mediæval."* Ron was always delighted when
my ears pricked up at anything musical. *"Modes are important to
understand, for composition and improvisation. Each mode has a different
feel. This one always feels like Middle Eastern Blues – which is why I
thought you'd like it. I think that's what you're after sometimes when you
want a minor or major 7th chord."* I was wide-eyed with wonder.
*"Don't worry – it's not as difficult as you think. It's all about moving the
half tones."* Ron played a few examples. *"When you shift the
position of the half tones you get a whole other kind of music."*

"That's wild! It's like they're entirely different languages!"

"*Yeah – they are!*" Ron laughed "*That's what's so bloody amazing about music! Steve and I have decided we're going to teach you music theory. I think you'll enjoy it – you've got that kind of mind.*"

"*Glad you think so Ron – and yes, I would enjoy it – no matter how difficult it is. I'm slow – but I'll keep at it.*"

"*Yeah . . . it's a shame you couldn't have learnt it at school.*"

"*Yeah . . . when I think of all the dreary, dreary, dreary*—dreary—*drivel I had to plough my way through*" I responded in a somewhat dogged tone "*when I—could—have been learning music theory.*"

"*Well . . . doesn't matter . . .*" Ron replied cheerily "*. . . you'll just be getting it later.*"

"*I really am grateful that you both want to help me this way.*"

"*No need Frank – we need you in on melody composition. I know you're the lyricist – but if you had a grasp of music theory you wouldn't have to rewrite lyrics so much when we worked on the melody lines – you'd have the thing in shape already . . . and we'd all be talking the same language. You've definitely got the musical talent y'know. I mean, we already listen to anything you have to say about the melodies we come up with – so it's important to get you the right tools for the job*" Pause "*That's all you need – it's like you've got a lot of ideas that are well advanced of most people – but you lack the basics and that training. That means that when you get the basics down you'll fly!*" Ron laughed almost maniacally "*You'll leave me and Steve in the dust!*"

"*Alright Ron . . . big joke – but I'm glad you think I'll be able to join you.*"

"*I'm not joking Frank. I was completely wrong about having two basses in the band – and you were completely right. I learnt something from that – that you can imagine things in a different way. I can't do that. I can do all kinds of things but I can't . . . think sideways or whatever it is you do . . .*"

Ron continued " . . . *and . . . Steve agrees with me – you're a serious weirdo – but you can see things . . . like you said to me about rhythm bass. That's some kind of strange genius or something and Steve and I want to bring that on.*"

I was somehow always surprised that Ron and Steve were keen to have my musical input.

"*Y'know Ron – what you've said . . . it really makes me feel I've got a real future ahead of me in terms of song writing.*"

"*Bloody docile bugger . . .* " Ron laughed " *. . . you had it before I met you.*"

"*Yeah . . . well . . . maybe – but now I can see that there's a way lyrics work with melody that makes it difficult to write lyrics without having music in mind. The words have to hit the right stresses – and that's why I have to rewrite the lyrics as we hammer out the melody line.*"

"*Exactly*" Ron grinned "*and that'll be important when we're working on albums.*"

The idea of making an album was exhilarating. I met Steve later at The Nostril and we talked about it.

"*Maybe that's the route we should take rather than playing small clubs and Art Schools*" I proposed – rapt in a bubbling sense of wonder that welled up from somewhere "*After all we we're developing our own material – and there's no reason why we shouldn't try approaching record companies with tapes and transcripts of our own songs.*"

"*Simmerson, Larkin and Bruce – Song Writers!*" Steve exclaimed. "*What an idea. Somehow . . . those names together . . . has a ring to it – like Lennon/McCartney or Crosby, Stills and Nash.*"

"*I'd rather go with Schubert, Larkin and Bruce . . .* " I replied " *. . . or better still – Larkin, Bruce and Schubert.*"

"*Yes, really,* lbs!" [8] Steve laughed "*That has—weight—to it!*"

We talked for several hours about album sleeve designs and the ideas flew so profusely that Steve got out a note book to jot down the impressions we were generating. It was hard not to be derivative because album sleeves like 'Sgt. Pepper's Lonely Hearts Club Band' kept insinuating themselves into our thinking. I thought that costume was a powerful visual communication and pointed out that Cream's 'Fresh Cream' sleeve was '*extremely evocative of something inexplicable*' – I was always saying things like that. I liked Johnny Winter's 'Second Winter' sleeve too with its infra-red photography. I talked about the possibility of my painting a Savoy cabbage as the album sleeve – one of those convoluted intricate cabbages. Steve thought that was a possibility. "*We could call the album 'Savoy Green' – but . . . maybe it's not a good idea to make references to other bands.*"

Steve was thinking of the Savoy Brown Blues Band. I didn't think it was out of the question in view of our band name. I had the idea of drawing our faces into the folds of the cabbage. I would have to work large in order to make that work – but it was quite an exciting idea. "*Maybe the Savoy cabbage could be photographed in infra-red for the back – maybe cut in half like the apple on the Beatles albums*" I ventured "*I could write a song for the album that played on the idea of a Savoy cabbage.*"

Steve roared with laughter "*Write a song about a cabbage! Not even —you—could do that and pull it off.*" I was always up for that kind of challenge so I set to and wrote the song. Steve was almost shocked by what I'd written because I wrote it in twenty minutes whilst he sat there listening to Cream.

---

8 'lbs' is the British abbreviation for 'pounds' as a measure of weight.

You won't find it here tomorrow on your way from yesterday / You won't find it in the masquerades that tickle what you say, / It's not there in what you think you heard or what you haven't seen / In the emerald ricochet smoke trails as they spiral Savoy green.

You won't find the way birds fly South and bend toward the sun / You won't find the way the seconds tick when you think they're on the run, / It's not in the blur of motor wheels where you think you've never been / It's the emerald ricochet smoke trails as they spiral Savoy green.

You're looking for the sundials that catalogue how to be / And you're flipping through the register in case you might get free / But you can't find the clues to show there's something you've not seen / In the emerald ricochet smoke trails as they spiral Savoy green.

The fields of glass are splintering fast and the wolves begin to howl, / A drunken hare runs through the fair singing like an owl / You stand and stare into the air as if it was a dream / Of the emerald ricochet smoke trails as they spiral Savoy green.

There's an endless trail of hammered nails that hide inside your shoes / And you keep them sharp to make them bark any time you choose, / But you never see the sliding scree or find a way to dream / Of the emerald ricochet smoke trails as they spiral Savoy green.

You sowed your fields with memory to sit and watch it grow / And you chained my letters to the night so I would never know, / But you can't account for my whereabouts or why I seemed so keen / On the emerald ricochet smoke trails as they spiral Savoy green.

Your press release is riveted to the fuselage of a jet / And you try in vain to steal the rain but you ain't made it yet, / In a time of hide and seek you might have been a queen / Of the emerald ricochet smoke trails as they spiral Savoy green.

Larkin/Bruce/Schubert—Savage Cabbage—Savoy Green—Savoy Green—1970

It was just too easy to be influenced about ideas for album sleeves. Steve liked the idea of moving water taken at lengthy shutter speeds so that the water turned into a strange swirling haze. I thought it would be wild to situate the Eiffel Tower in the sea and give the album an oblique name like Eiffel Shower, Eiffel Towel, Eiffel Trowel. Steve suggested Eiffel Trapeze – and having a shimmering circus-clad lady flying across the image of the Eiffel Tower and sea. It occurred to me that I'd have to write a song that tied all those images together.

I rode on seas of plethory with phantoms of the dawn / As Gustave Eiffel called the shots behind his oaken doors, / The trapeze flying valkyrie was headed for the shore / And I couldn't blink—or stop to think—just what I'd come here for.
Larkin/Bruce/Schubert—Savage Cabbage—Unless You Shed Your Skin—Savoy Green—1970

We talked about putting lyrics to music, rehearsing, and building our repertoire. Then we met up with Jack and Ron and put it into practice. There was no stopping us. And then—almost as if it was sudden and unexpected—we'd move from rehearsals to the stage and there'd be people out there in the dark gazing expectantly at us. Jack would get anxious and crack his knuckles. Steve would shift his weight from one foot to the other as if he were a pugilist in a boxing ring. I'd tap the strings of the bass – almost silently whilst gazing into the sea of faces. Ron would stand motionless staring into space; until—suddenly —he'd pivot, catch my eye, and send out a stream of notes descending into a shuddering $B7^{\text{th-diminished}}$. Steve would begin the sombre yet deliciously fluent rolling riff – waiting for me to take over the simple line that allowed him to depart for other regions of the neck.

We'd never speak our way in. I'd always introduce the band at the end. The concept of saying anything at the start was anathema to us all. The crowd knew we were Savage Cabbage – and they knew that Farquhar Arbuthnot was the hoochie-coochie man.

*On the seventh hour, of the seventh day, / On the seventh month, the seven doctors say: / "He was born for good luck" and I know you see, / I got seven hundred—*million—*dollars, don't you mess with me. / Y'know I'm here—and I've really got my share / I'm the hoochie-coochie man – everybody knows I am.* Adapted from Hoochie-coochie Man—Willie Dixon—1954

7

folds of cloud in the face unknown

*On the coast there are nine circling ravens — and a windmill where I have
no ties / There's a stairway with eight different landings — and an oak tree
that reaches the sky / There's a palace born of the morning and it looms in
shimmering frost / But no one looks out of its windows or sends me their
words through the post / I might spend nearly every day grinning at the
glitter of frost on the trees / But they can't tie me down—I won't stick
around—I'm just a thread in the breeze.*

Larkin/Bruce/Schubert—Savage Cabbage—Just a Thread in the Breeze—Savoy Green—1970

By the end of the school year—July '69—metamorphosis had
occurred. Apart from Jack who maintained his mutant mullet –
we'd avoided the barber for a year. Ron's and Steve's parents
seemed to be of the opinion: *youth is a time for experimentation.*
They believed that their sons would conform to normal
standards in the fullness of time and that it would be both unfair
and unwise to rob them of their one chance to be a little wild.

My father had given up a year before and so I had a head start in
the puissant pursuit of hirsute heaven. Jack's parents had strict
limits as to how long his hair could grow. We all wished he'd
see sense and grow it out – but he was so proud of his coiffure
that we didn't comment. Some things are as they are – and we
regarded personal appearance as sacrosanct.

Steve's naturally dense frizzy blond hair had burgeoned, and he
started looking like some kind of transfigured troll – a Nordic
Jimi Hendrix. He abandoned his Roy Orbison spectacles in
favour of round, gold wire-framed National Health spectacles –
and would've graced the cover of OZ [1] magazine with his
unearthliness.

Ron's sideburns had reached his jaw line. He started looking
distinctly . . . feral. Feral is the wrong word – but . . . menacing
or sinister would be misleading. His sideburns seemed to reflect
the shape of his TELECASTER – the way the pick-guard cuts across
the body in a shockingly straight line. It gave him the air of
being beyond question as the monarch of the guitar universe.

Not only did my hair stream down my back – but my moustache
had crept down to my chin. I'd developed a lean and hungry
look. Ron told me I stared out at the audience like some lethal
feline held in check by flimsy bars. I felt nothing remotely like
that – but I had become utterly unafraid of going out on a limb
with the melody line. I was not another Robert Plant or
anything like that – but I was *something-or-other* that had become
increasingly dramatic. I'd evolved a touch of the Southern
Baptist in my vocals – along with my own variation of the
menace that I'd heard in Jack Bruce.

Savage Cabbage had a fair number of gigs under its collective
belt. We'd played Reading University for the Student Union
concert and dance. We'd also played Winchester, Reigate,
Guildford, Maidstone, and Epsom Schools of Art. August was
lined up for The Cordwainer's Arms, Queen's Oak, and
Compton Bells – and there were Art School, College, and
University gigs on the Autumn horizon.

---

1 OZ was a psychedelic magazine published in London from 1967 – 1973.

Being on stage was some kind of paradise as far as I was concerned. Somehow I never stammered when I yelled out *"Lightning Ron Larkin on lead guitar—give it Hell and sideways Ron! Big Steve Bruce on lead bass—hey splatter that thing all—*over—*the night! Little Jack Hackman on pneumatic percussion—jack-hammer ain't in it at all—hailstorm from far away as Jupiter's sulphur mines! And last . . . and certainly least . . . "* I'd give a final volley on harp before we quit the stage *"Yours truly on rhythm-bass—larynx—pharynx— œsophagus—harp! Goodnight Alton Town Hall . . . where—*ever— *you are!"*

Apart from the fact that I wouldn't be seeing Lindie 'til September I was excited about the Summer. The pub and local gigs were easy, close at hand, and the locals gave us a fanatic reception. Although we spent time aplenty together during school hours – Lindie didn't want to deceive her parents by seeing me during the holidays. I couldn't find it in myself to be persuasive on that score – because . . . well, I admired Lindie's integrity. To try to divide Lindie and her integrity was unthinkable. It would have meant not appreciating her as she was. If I'd been stupid enough to have tried it – I would merely have devalued myself in her eyes. There was also my own integrity to think about – and there were just some things that didn't feel right.

Jack thought I was an idiot to have such principles *"Why do her parents need to know about anything. Fuck'em, I say."*

Ron shook his head and said *"Up to you Frank . . . but . . . if it was me . . . I might say 'Bugger your parents. Tell'em and be damned' . . . She needs to stand up to 'em y'know. It's—*her—*life after all."*

Steve was more understanding of my position – but even he said *"Y'know . . . it—*is—*possible that you could be taking things a little too far with this 'being understanding' business."*

"Well . . . yes Steve—I always take everything too far—but then . . . that's me isn't it."

"That's true enough" Steve replied *"but I think she owes you something more than this. I like her – but . . . well – she's not a child is she."*

"No Steve—she's not—but . . . I wouldn't feel good about putting her under pressure to go against les langoustines. If I—did—that . . . I'd no longer be the person she knew . . . would I?"

The lads nodded in grim acceptance of the fact that I wouldn't be able to see Lindie for two months. I felt touched that they felt sorry for me.

"So, anyhow . . . " I said, changing the subject *"I'm not about to turn into some sort of sodden blanket. There's more to my life than suffering the military dictatorship of Brigadier Dale. Let's work through those numbers! I've got a bass to play and I'm—eager—to get going on your ideas about re-working our set. Turn those amps on – and let's give the thing hell."*

Jack gave a dramatic drum roll combined with unusually elaborate counter-clatter on the crash and ride.

"Niiiiice one Jack – nice one" I grinned – and the lads instantly understood my point of view. My two passions didn't conflict or undermine each other. We began throwing changes on numbers Ron and Steve thought could be improved. The fundamental bass line didn't change – so all I had to do was attempt to sing and play at the same time. It was slow progress for me and I had to simplify to single repeated notes when I sang. Jack worked hard and—to my ear—seemed to improve week by week. I liked his work on cymbals and made a point of letting him know. Jack—however—was never ecstatic about praise from me. I couldn't blame him. I understood that it was Ron's approbation he needed. Still, Jack was good enough to look pleased.

"*Your bass is coming on too—Mr Arbuthnot*" he replied. I grinned
back at him, acknowledging the delight of musical comradeship
– but understanding that far more was possible. I'd repeat bass
lines at Ron's home 'til my fingers would stand it no more.
I sometimes played with plasters on my fingers to stop them
from getting raw. I had a system. It seemed that if I played a
bass riff 100 times – I'd have it down reasonably well. If I
played it 300 times – I'd have the thing easily. If I played it 500
times – I'd be able to play it without keeping my eye on the
neck. If I played it 1,000 times I'd be branded with it like a steer.

I loved musical instruments – I just had no natural facility or
dexterity with them. I wanted to play bass – but had to work far
—far—harder than Jack. The hard work paid off however.
Both Ron and Steve started nodding in my direction more often
– as if to say 'well done'. By the Autumn term I'd got the segue
worked out with Steve in terms of the vocal line. I knew exactly
when to cut out – and Steve knew exactly where to cut in. We
dovetailed perfectly. In the lead up to the improvisation
sections Steve would wait for me to cut into the rhythm-bass
line—join me for a few bars—and then take off with Ron into
the madcap sonic landscape of unearthly improvisation. When it
worked well—which happened increasingly—it was seamless.
It was fabulously invigorating to maintain rhythm-bass behind
Steve and Ron. I became spellbound by it. Once my fingers felt
their ways into the pattern – they lived a life of their own.
I hovered there whilst it happened – or walked the stage like
a somnambulist lucidly dreaming a dream of being awake on
a stage.

Sometimes I made the egregious error of commenting internally
on my playing. Then I'd become self-conscious and lose the riff
for a moment.

No one ever seemed to notice. I'd flip back into rhythm – and find myself back on Bifröst[2] again.

We'd listened to Cream leading back into the final verse of Spoonful so many times that we all had a feel for it. Ron and Steve didn't emulate the phrasing of Jack Bruce and Eric Clapton – but they teased the melody line back into existence in increments with a similar mælstrom of maniac magic. They'd make three movements back toward the melody line but pull it back, before the melody line was fully formed. The fourth advance was the cue for me to be ready on the beat with *'Might be a spoonful . . .'* Ron and Steve choreographed the improvisation with increasing fluency. They created a perfectly implausible symbiosis of order and chaos – and I felt privileged to be an intimate although minor part of it.

I told Ron later *"I think it's good to be able to rely on Steve taking over rhythm bass when I sing – but . . . it's not*—the musician's choice—*is it? I mean, I've really*—got—*to get beyond that . . . and . . . I can't see* —any—*way round it apart from playing and singing as much as I can on my own."*

Ron grinned. It was one of his encouraging grins. *"You keep on this way*—you maniac—*and you'll be in danger of getting seriously good."*

In danger of getting good. That was music to my ears. *"That's where I want to go – and, slow as I am, I'm determined to get there."* I mused for a moment – and told him what was on my mind *"So . . . as soon as you're able to*—sell me—*that EB3 and amp – I'll work at it 'til I get it. I'll be able to play at home*—unamplified—*and that'll really bring me on."*

---

2 In Norse mythology Bifröst is 'the tremulous way' which boils with fire. It is the bridge from Midgaard *(the human realm)* to Asgaard *(the god realm)*.

Ron nodded *"Yeah—that'll do it—but . . . y'know . . . it—is—bloody hard singing and playing in counterpoint. There aren't that many bass-player vocalists"* Ron pondered a moment *"There's Willie Dixon, Jack Bruce, Paul McCartney . . . can't think of any others right now – but it's not the combination of choice, even for professional musicians. Mind you . . . if, or rather—when—you get it, you'll shoot ahead musically like a bloody asteroid."* Ron let out a peal of laughter at that point and it occurred to me that he really believed what he was saying. *"Then—you'll—start writing melody line—no—sweat. And you'll be bloody good. I can tell. You—got—the ear. Always said so. You'll get your answer with lyrics too – 'cause you'll be right there in the middle of it. You'll get clues from the rhythm and the accents'n'all."*

What a thought. I was staring directly into The Great Mystery. I felt I was on the verge of some kind of magic: the miraculous and marvellously mercurial dimension of music. The place where Johann Sebastian Bach lived – and where Jack Bruce sang impossible perfection in 'Spoonful'. The place where Muddy Waters electrified the Mississippi Delta and Jo Ann Kelly invented the Thames Delta.

"You're being . . . serious . . . are you Ron?" I asked *"because—this— is the most important thing in life to me. I—want—to be . . . a real musician – and to write the songs. I feel I've got it in me to write songs – but I always feel blocked by my lack of knowledge when it comes to creating melody."*

"I'm being absolutely serious" Ron replied *"It's just a matter of time. I didn't learn music in a year y'know. I've been playing . . . over twelve years—three quarters of my bloody life—and you've only just started. You've got to get things in perspective."*

"Well . . . yes . . . but I've played at Steve's since I was at junior school."

"*Leave it out you loony – that's bloody ridiculous. I'm talking about playing*—every day—*for sodding hours. If you added up all your playing since you were* 10 *it'd be 'bout a week – fortnight at the most. You've played more in the last year than you've played in y'bloody life – but y'not going to be like Steve in two months – or even two years. You*—will—*get there though. You just need time to practise.*"

"*Yes . . .* " I sighed " *. . . can't really argue too much with that. I just wish I*—had—*more time to practise . . . the Summer's taken up with the Army kitchens you know . . .* "

Ron considered for a moment "*D'you*—have—*to work all Summer?*"

"*No . . . and I don't. I cut it short so that we can have more practice sessions. That's why I'm so pushy about making sure we get together as often as possible. Thing is . . . I can't cut back any more . . . because I want to buy your* EB3. *I need to save for that. It's frustrating . . . but there's no choice. I also need to be independent when it comes to money. I can't ask my father for anything.*"

"*Stingy*—sodding—*bastard . . .* " Ron almost spat.

"*Well . . . maybe . . . but*—actually—*he really doesn't have the money for much. I'm sure my father'd try to buy me what I needed if it was something that would put me in the way of a conventional career or whatever – but he's not going to buy me an* EB3 *or a* 200 *watt* PA *system . . .* "

Ron shook his head wearily. He seemed to understand my situation. It was a combination of factors – working to buy the bass removed a great deal of the time I would have had to practise with it. It sometimes took steady thought and logical contemplation to avoid a sense of resentment stealing up on me in relation to money.

Steve had talked to his parents about loaning me the EB0 – but they'd said that they didn't want to go against my father's wishes 'til I was 18. I'd be an adult then and their relationship with me would be one that functioned on an adult-to-adult basis. Steve's father—as a Police Superintendent—had that way of thinking and there was no getting round it. Ron wanted to give me his EB3 and let me pay for it when I'd got the money together – but his parents were not keen on that idea. Still, I played it on stage – and that would have to be enough 'til I'd got the wherewithal.

Playing with good professional equipment was an immense pleasure. I could stand on stage and the relative poverty of my background meant less than nothing. I was as good as anyone else – on stage: I had equipment no one could deride—and I did not stammer. The only thing to hold me back was my painfully slow progress with bass – but I moved on like a 1,000 ton snail. There was no stopping me. I *would* improve. I *would* learn to sing and play at the same time.

Steve borrowed his father's Jazz band Transit [3] van for our gigs. It was perfect for our requirements. There were screw-fittings for the Jazz band name boards which emblazoned the side of the van – and I made up a set for the band. 'SAVAGE CABBAGE – *the* Blues Band' painted in emerald green on Prussian blue looked striking. If only we'd had roadies – the impression would've been stupendous. The Transit van was carpeted—bottom and sides—to protect instruments. It also worked well for passengers. Steve's father and friends had made a fine job of it – which put the onus on us to look after it.

---

3 The Ford Transit was a light commercial vehicle in Britain that became so popular that 'Transit van' became the generic term for any vehicle of that type. In terms of band-prestige, possession of a Transit van was a mark of success.

We took it in turns to ride shotgun, up front with Steve – but in fine weather I'd ride the pixie chariot. We talked about the time when we'd have roadies. We'd have an articulated lorry with armchairs in the back and a refrigerator for drinks. We were nothing if not optimistic.

We had a growing following and no qualms about our competence. We had no doubts about the fact that we were different – without *trying to be different*. Some bands we'd heard were good – but lacked power in the vocals and bass section. We had two basses – so we ended up ahead, quite by accident. I'd often get crazy with the vocals and make up lines as I went.

No ya can't stick a knife, in an outsized woman's shoe, / You should be staying at home stabbing your own, trying to make a sandal of it too.
Author's parody—Outsize Woman's Shoe—1969

The actual lines are:
You know you can't watch your wife and your outside women, too. / When you're out with your women, your wife will be at home, / Doing your dirt, cooking your food, buddy what you trying to do?
Arthur 'Blind Willie' Reynolds—Outside Women Blues—1929—covered by Cream—1967

Our first big time gig was Eel Pie Island. Dave from the Compton Bells arranged that. Dave turned out to be a good fellow. He wasn't quite the cut-throat wheeler-dealer he first appeared to be. He liked our music and felt he'd stumbled on an upcoming sensation. He was a Blues aficionado and put us in touch with the organiser at Eel Pie Island.

"Naaah mate—nothin' to it—'appy to 'elp" he said when I thanked him profusely *" . . . 'sides, it'll line my pockets too. Once you lads start playin' big venues I'll 'ave-t'-turn'em away at the door. Marquee Club London next eh?"*

My eyes widened *"You could—swing—that?"*

Dave grinned *"Can't—promise—to swing it mate – but I c'd get the —ball—rollin' y'know. Dave's the name and fame's the game – know the right people, I do. 'course . . . y'd 'ave-t'make a tape. They'd wanna —hear—something first – know what I mean? But you lads won't 'ave —any—trouble getting there. Y'll breeze it – no bloody competition."*

We played Eel Pie Island several times after that – twice as the main act. Dave had put us in contact with Kooks Kleek – and we were pretty much assured of gigs there in the Summer of 1970. He'd suggested there was a good possibility of a gig at the Marquee Club – so we were rolling! We had a fine set of numbers to which we were always adding: *Spoonful; Born Under a Bad Sign; Hoochie Coochie Man; Evil, Rolling and Tumbling; Crossroad Blues; Sugar Mamma; Death Letter Blues; and Politician.* We knew the possibly apocryphal fourth verse to 'Politician'. Ron had picked it up from Gazzer Mitchell and Freighttrain:

I run this country – and I run that country over there too, / You'd better watch me baby 'cause I'm gonna be running after you.

We never did discover whether that was an authentic verse by Jack Bruce and Pete Brown – but I sang it anyway along with a few other verses I composed to give more scope to my vocals.

I got seven departments – working seven days of the week, / I wanna hold you closer baby – when we're dancing cheek to cheek. / Got ministerial speeches – I got some brilliant things to say, / Gonna tell everyone around you – they're standing in my way. / Minister without portfolio – must've left it in my chair, / To get you behind closed doors baby – I'd go anywhere.
The Author—parody verses of Politician—1969

Composing extra verses for our Blues numbers—and parodies like 'Born Under a Glad Sign'—proved helpful to my lyric writing. I realised that songs could be inspired by almost anything. I was always working on a song wherever I was – and words would come to mind simply though life.

I always had a notebook with me in order to scribble down word sequences. I'd hear strange accounts on the radio. I'd hear about the historical origin of the Dracula story as having stemmed from Vlad the Impaler – and the words would roll around in my mind. How could I avoid writing a song about someone called Vlad the Impaler?

Through rolling coasters stacked in decks of helter-skelter rails / I turned my back on mental clamps: Vlad the Impaler's finger nails / Dracul means 'Son of the Dragon' – but he's dragging in my wake / He's doing Marie Antoinette's bidding and eating up his cake, / He's confiscated everything – he's fuming at his plough / But I've never shied from what I've dreamed – I'm headed right there now. Larkin/Bruce/Schubert—Savage Cabbage— I'm Headed Right There Now—Savoy Green—1970

"I'm not really satisfied with these lyrics" I told Steve.

"They're really interesting. What's wrong with them?"

"Well . . . they always seem as if—I—wrote them."

"That's because you did – you maniac!" Steve laughed.

"Yeah . . . and that drives me frantic sometimes. But, I—do—always come back to what you told me – and it does help. I think Ron's right too – about how bass playing will help. It's just . . . "

" . . . that it's not all happening immediately?" Steve interrupted cackling wildly.

"Precisely" I replied *"I suppose that's it really. I'm impatient"* Pause *"I suppose . . . if—you—were talking to—me—about this, I'd tell you to relax wouldn't I . . . "*

Steve laughed again *"Glad I didn't have to point that out – but, y'know, there's nothing wrong with impatience as long as you don't beat yourself up about it."*

"I know you want to write like the people you admire" Steve continued *"but . . . you can't do that without copying them – and you obviously don't want to do that. So . . . what you're trying to do isn't possible – trying to sound like John Lennon without copying John Lennon."*

Steve always made ruthless sense on this point and there was no way I could counter his argument.

"So . . . everything I write sounding hopelessly like me – is . . . "

Steve finished my sentence *"As good as it gets—and as good as it can get—'til other people start recording covers of your songs and you start seeing it from that point of view."*

I always ended up agreeing with Steve – but it didn't take more than a day or two before I started feeling trapped again in the strange semantic cage from which I could not escape. I had some idea that there was a 'secret' I could discover that would allow me to be *like* Lennon/McCartney – but *without* being derivative.

She was a Moldavian princess, daughter of the Moldavian King / She went to Transylvania to throw off her clothes and sing / She dreamed of magnetism and the Sultan's younger son / But no one understood that she was only out for fun / So she headed home last Friday night mounted on her sow / But I've never shied from what I've dreamed – I'm headed right there now. Larkin/Bruce/Schubert—Savage Cabbage—I'm Headed Right There Now—Savoy Green—1970

A Lennon/McCartney song would—*not*—rhyme 'now' with 'sow'. The fact that 'she headed home last Friday' was good—I liked that—but then I had to get fancy and have her 'mounted on her sow'. And it wasn't because I was stuck for a rhyme. I was pretty good at rhyming. I could usually conjure words pretty well – but I always seemed to miss something.

So she headed home last Friday she's missing him I'll trow / confusion knits her brow / her timing's off somehow / a figureheaded prow / slung beneath the bough / primed to take a bow / forsaking thee and thou / ready for a row / wading through a slough.

How would I change that line for the better without losing the first part? Steve and Ron thought it was a fine line and had no idea why I was discontented with it. To have used *she's missing him I'll trow* would have been delightful – but *trow* is archaic English for 'think' or 'believe' and I felt it was somehow illegal to slip Jane Austen phraseology into a Rock song.

After a period of absurd internal writhing I decided that Steve was right and I'd have to let the writing take care of itself. I'd just write and see what happened. We'd never know 'til we recorded an album anyway. Maybe it was true that the only difference between my lyrics and the lyrics I admired was that I wasn't looking at them from the outside. Maybe Bob Dylan felt something similar – but how was I ever to find out? Virginia Water School was not inclined to help me develop as an Artist in any way apart from painting and drawing. I was glad of Miss Rodham, the cigar-smoking Art teacher. She always looked as if she knew what was going on – but she had no idea about lyrics.

"Your lyrics—are—highly inventive . . ." she said *" . . . but I have no real experience with creative language – especially lyrics. I couldn't say whether one lyric was any better than another – other than saying that yours are nothing like the common Pop lyrics I hear."*

So I wrote down lyrics from various song writers I admired and asked Miss Rodham what she made of the difference between them.

"These lyrics of yours seem at least the equal of these others . . . " she offered *" . . . but beyond that, I have nothing useful to say. I'm not a writer, so I have nothing on which I can base a realistic opinion."*

There was no way that I could get a reality check no matter how hard I tried.

The English teacher—Mr Havilland—had no interest at all in the subject. *"Unless lyrics make sense I cannot comment on them."*

"Would the same apply—from your point of view—to Surrealist poetry?" I asked *"To poets such as Pierre Reverdy?"*

Mr Havilland seemed somewhat irritated that I'd found something within his realm that made no linear sense. *"I am not familiar with Surrealist poetry and therefore have no comment. In any case I would need to look at the poem in the original French. It is impossible to judge from a translation."*

I handed him a sheet of paper from my satchel.

Fire that dances / Bird that sings / Wind that dies / Icy waves and surges of rumour in the ear / Distant cries of days that pass all the weary flames / Voice of the voyager / Powder in the sky and heel on the earth / Eye fixed on the road where inscribed steps number what unrolls / Names that have left folds of cloud in the face unknown / The one you watch but which has not come. Pierre Reverdy—Traits—translated by the Author with Lindie Dale

He asked who translated it. *"Lindie Dale and I translated it, sir"* I ventured *"We translated this one as well – by Philippe Soupault."*

Courageous like a stamp he went his way / tapping hands softly to count steps / His heart red as a beat—beat—beating like a pink green butterfly / Now and then—when he'd walked a lot—he planted a minuscule satin flag and sat down to rest / He fell asleep – but since that day there have been numerous clouds in the sky and countless birds in the trees / There's a great quantity of salt in the sea / There are—also—lots of other things too.
Philippe Soupault—Sport Articles—translated by the Author with Lindie Dale

Mr Havilland was unimpressed *"You would be better served by studying Yeats – as you are to be examined on your understanding of that poet."*

Well yes, I—*was*—studying Yeats, I enjoyed Yeats. It was not so marvellous however, to have found myself with Mr Havilland after Mr Preece. I loved English – but the militaristic approach of Mr Havilland was not easy to appreciate.

"I wonder why he's an English teacher when he obviously takes no joy in literature" I told Steve *"He's determined that every phrase in a poem has a specific meaning. He has no interest whatsoever in the fact that language can speak outside the remit of conventional meaning."*

"It's more-or-less the same in my English literature class" Steve replied *"but I don't really expect it to be any different. I suppose I'm not as idealistic as you are. Maybe I should be . . . "*

"You're idealistic enough Steve – but you're also realistic . . . I just get bound up in how things could be and think that's how they ought to be. It would probably be better if it didn't vex me . . . but the heavy-handed Havilland wants us to learn the terminally tedious 'code book' for Yeats. They tell us what Yeats meant – and then we have to regurgitate it. It's diabolically dreary."

"Yeah . . . v" Steve replied. *"We have something similar – but it's just a means to an end and sometimes the code books are interesting in their own way."*

"Here and there—alright—maybe, but I don't enjoy my understanding of Yeats being tied to the dictatorship of someone else's subjective analysis. What's wrong with—my—subjective analysis?"

"Nothing!" Steve burst out laughing *"but it's not what the Associated Examination Board are going to mark you on."*

There was no getting round that.

Therefore—when it came to the examination—I wrote '*So-and-so explains Yeats thus . . . personally I see these lines as linguistic images – words that are sometimes deliberately ungainly in order to portray the feeling tone of creative anxiety. There is a sense of yearning that displays itself through disquieting semantic interactions.*'

This approach—surprisingly—had no ill effect on my final grade, so I was eventually left feeling that Mr Havilland was more out of step than I was. I got an A[4] in English. When the examination results came through Mr Havilland expressed surprise and congratulated me in an ever-so-slightly grudging manner. I told him "*I think I owe my success to my interest in nonlinear imagery.*" This was a habit of mine. I found it difficult not to take a stance – and it took me a fair few years before I managed to resist the temptation to say things I didn't have to say. At that time though – we all seemed to be engaged in a war of sorts. We were fighting against conservatism and the thick suffocating blanket of mainstream existence. We were the warriors in a psychedelic crusade against what we saw as a totalitarian regime. Most teachers were petty dictators as far as we were concerned—and this attitude tended to colour everything—even though I knew there were good teachers such as Mr Preece and Miss Rodham.

A soldier's hair's neither here nor there – but they try to make it reach / The eyebrows they've tattooed in place like frostbite on a peach / Where mystery's a treason and rancour is entrenched / They flee the rain in terror to sidestep getting drenched / They're running scared and ill-prepared to turn the tide just now / But I've never shied from what I've dreamed – I'm headed right there now. Larkin/Bruce/Schubert—Savage Cabbage—I'm Headed Right There Now—Savoy Green—1970

---

4 A was the highest level in the British school A level examinations.

Steve and I met up one afternoon when we'd both finished school early. We sat in 'The Nostril' talking about the usual ocean of musical and literary ideas.

"Where's the School of Blues when I need it?" I sighed *"I could be spending all this time learning what I—need—to learn. Instead . . . I have to listen to Havilland crucifying English Literature for the sins of the Associated Examination Board."*

Steve loved reading but agreed *"Studying literature at school does tend to destroy my enjoyment of reading . . . apart from Shakespeare, that is."*

I nodded *"Yes . . . that—needs—study. Somehow the turbid Havilland's not managed to mangle that too badly. I wish I could take English Language at A level.[5] I really miss creative writing – y'know, short stories and essays . . . There's no possibility of that with A level English. I want to develop creative language like I used to with Mr Preece. I wish there was some sort of cross over with the Arts . . . or anything that would move out of the academic rut that school makes of everything apart from oil painting."*

"Why worry?" Steve replied. *"You're doing fine – and you always have done as long as I've known you. And . . . as far as your lyrics go – there wouldn't be anyone qualified to help you anyway because teachers don't know about Jazz—let alone Acid Rock. There'll probably be opportunities at Art School."*

"You're right Steve . . . it just seems a long way off somehow – but, in the meantime, I've been working on that Pierre Reverdy piece I showed you: 'Traits'. That line 'Names that have left folds of cloud in the face unknown' has been sitting staring at me like some kind of couchant tiger."

---

5 English Language was available as an A level examination subject – but it was not on the curriculum of most schools in the Home Counties (counties contiguous to London).

Steve laughed "*Only—you—could come out with a line like that – I thought you weren't taking French?*"

"*I'm not*" I replied "*but I work on French Surrealist poetry with Lindie. She's practically bilingual.*"

Steve looked a little troubled by the mention of Lindie "*Y'know . . . you really—should—give up there . . . I know she's really—well I'd go for her too—but you're not going to get past her parents are you?*"

No I wasn't – not yet at any rate.

"*No harm in translating poetry with her though – is there?*"

"*No . . .*" Steve shrugged "*. . . but it's not—just—translation is it?*"

"*No . . . it's not . . .*" I had to admit that "*. . . but . . . 'til I go to Art School there's no point in cutting off, is there?*"

Steve looked as if he was weighing the idea up favourably – so I continued "*We actually really—like—spending time together. It's just a situation that'll . . . come to some sort of end – and I really still don't know for certain what's going to happen . . . do I? I mean . . . the future— could—still turn into anything couldn't it? Lindie gets a year older— year-by-year—and eventually . . . her parents will stop calling the shots.*"

Steve grudgingly agreed "*Yeah . . . but my parents—and they really care about you, y'know—think you'll make yourself miserable by living in hope this way . . . for so long.*"

I felt like replying '*Well—sod—your parents Steve*' but it was a moment of peevishness that passed quite quickly. It would be churlish to take offence. I also knew Steve's parents really—*did* —have my best interests at heart. They were kind, decent, open-minded people – and . . . their analysis was probably painfully correct.

"*Yes . . .*" I groaned "*they're probably right . . . it's just that I don't—want—them to be right. Not at this moment at any rate. Maybe they can be right later . . . when I leave Virginia Water. It's just – seeing her every day . . . makes it impossible to do anything else.*"

Steve looked sad. He didn't know what to say for a moment. "*Well yeah . . . I suppose . . . I can understand that. So . . . you're . . . just going to see it out to the end?*"

"*Yes . . . it doesn't feel as if there's a choice . . . and . . . the future—is—still unknown. I really don't go for that predestination stuff. You may as well say there'll never be another Cream.*"

Steve grinned "*I wouldn't have thought of looking at it like that – but I suppose you're right . . . it's just hard watching you go through it.*"

"*In that case Steve*" I laughed "*I'll wear a big 'happy hat'. I've got—no—intention of looking like a dead haddock.*"

Steve guffawed at that image "*I'll buy that, you certainly don't walk around looking—too—stricken or anything.*"

"*Right! I've got my stage persona to maintain . . . and I can't maintain that—on—stage, if I can't live it—off—stage. Besides which – I'm learning bass! That EB3 slaps a big smile all across my face every time I get hold of it! Just wait 'til I get that big amp!*"

"*Right! That—will—be brilliant! Jack won't need any amplification for his bass drum when you get that!*" Steve almost yelled.

"*So . . . let's take a look at this song then – this . . . translation you did with Lindie.*"

I passed Steve the song. "*It's not exactly a translation – it's something I worked on. I tried to turn it into lyrics – but . . .*"

There's a fire that dances – a bird that sings – a wind that dies on icy waves, / There's a surging rumour in my ears that rings – a distant cry of passing days. / Powder in the sky and heels on the earth – a voyager's voice fixed on the road, / Inscribes the steps where the numbers unroll – eyes fixed ready for the sky to show. / Names leave folds of cloud in the face unknown – the one you watch but never comes, / Singing in time to the birds all alone – fabric made from the dreams you've spun.
The Author—unfinished song—September 1969

"*Mmmm . . .* " Steve mused "*I can imagine it as a ballad of some kind . . . but you're right – it's not exactly Acid Rock.*"

"*Right. It's fluent enough – but it lacks any kind of punch*" I agreed.

Steve nodded introspectively " *. . . it rhymes well, though.*"

I burst out laughing "*Maybe that's*—all—*it does. But I can do*—much—*better than that. I've got some ideas now and I am going to try something more . . .* " Pause " *. . . or actually . . . maybe less.*"

Steve had tears in his eyes from laughter – but eventually he exclaimed "*You're really going to*—do—*this, aren't you – you're going to make that breakthrough!*"

I nodded emphatically "*I really am.*"

8

synthetic cynthia

They're counting pebbles in their driveways — throwing lies across the deck / Their persuasion is miscalculation — their speech is fecklessness / Don't you see the bullets flying — see the bankers taking toll / And the physicists are checking out the density of coal / I see the spores of night are spiralling — into a vast reality / But their spiral privet hedges — they don't mean that much to me. Larkin/Bruce/Schubert—Savage Cabbage—It Don't Mean that Much to Me—Savoy Green—1970

The Autumn term wore on – and at some point it hit me. Time was running out for the lads as sixth formers.[1] I didn't object to that—I was eager to get to Art School—but I was going to miss Steve and Ron when they went to Music College. They'd be leaving the area. I knew we'd meet up in the holidays – but we wouldn't play together as frequently as before. For a while I'd lived as if the *sixth years* were going to last for ever. Time seemed to stretch out – but as I stretched with it, I noticed it was flying by. The gigs telescoped into each other and I lost track of the where-and-when of it all.

School days—apart from time spent with Lindie—were a blur. English classes were interesting but dull. The books were fascinating—especially Shakespeare and Chaucer—but Mr Havilland was lugubrious and turgid.

---

1 The first year 6th and second year 6th ran from 16 to 18 years old – at the end of which the A Level examinations were taken.

The Art classes were *always* marvellous. Miss Rodham's class hardly felt like Virginia Water – it may as well have been Art School. The rooms had a self-contained atmosphere – quite unlike the rest of the establishment. It smelt of oil paint – and the hours vanished in silent absorption with colour. Then I'd take off for 'The Nostril' café in Farnham to talk with Steve before returning home. On this occasion—surprisingly—Jack was there. He and Steve were in deep discussion – and they looked somewhat solemn.

"I wonder what's going to happen with Savage Cabbage when you buggers go off to College?" Jack asked Steve as I approached their table.

"Well . . . we won't be able to keep up the gigs will we?" Steve replied.

"No . . . " I replied sitting down with a glass of ginger beer *". . . but – there'll be holidays. No reason we can't at least play a couple of gigs this Christmas and Easter next year."*

"How'll that work though?" Jack asked *" . . . 'cause Ron . . . seems to want to avoid the bloody subject altogether."*

I tended to go along with the atmosphere of denial. We had a good situation with gigs – and, as I didn't like the idea of discussing the end before the end was well in sight, I didn't mention the future.

"Yeah . . . I've noticed that . . . " Steve mused *"I suppose we've been having too much of a good run to think about the fact that time's running out – for where we've been taking it I mean."*

"We could hit the road in the Summers though . . . " I suggested. *"We'd get Kooks Kleek—and other places then—and Dave says the Marquee Club's definitely possible."*

Steve brightened at that idea *"Right . . . and there'll still be the pub gigs at Christmas and Easter – as you said."*

Jack nodded violently *"Too right Mr Arbuthnot."*

"There doesn't have to be a rule about how a band operates" Steve opined *"We've had a lot of really good experience and now we're going to develop our skills so that we can really be something. I mean it's been really useful to have had a taste of being out there—on stage—before we take music studies further. I mean, by the time we finish Vic'll be professional on bass and you'll be . . . vying with Ginger Baker?"*

"Steve's right" I agreed quickly in order to cover up the veiled wryness of Steve's allusion to Ginger Baker. *"We don't have to follow anybody's rules for how often we play. I mean – we don't have to keep our reputation up by playing every night. We have a reputation whatever happens – they'll remember who—we—are. I've got no doubt at all that there are a lot of people who'd be eager to hear us again after a break away from the circuit. We're* Savage Cabbage—*the*—Blues band."

"Exactly Mr Arbuthnot!" Jack excalimed *"I mean . . . we could really go for it any time . . . and . . . of course . . . some people do*—quit—*College . . . "*

Steve bristled invisibly. I knew him well enough to detect his unease. *"Yeah . . . but it doesn't have to be like that for everyone"* Steve said – mainly directing his comment to me. *"I mean, you wouldn't want that – would you?"*

"No" I replied emphatically – although I was sympathetic to Jack's feelings on the matter *"Not at all. I think we're going to learn valuable things at College. And . . . we want to be more than a small time gig band don't we?"*

Jack couldn't argue with that – but he looked as if he'd not heard what he wanted to hear.

"We want to make albums that'll amaze people" I continued *"I want to produce mythical paintings of Robert Johnson meeting Legba, riding his Terraplane, arriving in Chicago . . . There are endless things to learn about at Art School – and we'll need that for the grand 'Robert Johnson Project'."*

Steve nodded – relieved that I wasn't considering Savage Cabbage going professional immediately rather than following our planned course.

"We'll find a way to make it work" he replied *"We've got a really interesting situation."*

Jack wasn't sure. *"Well yeah—you—do. You 'n Ron'll go to Music College and—Mister Arbuthnot here—will go to Art School. He'll be busy designing fantastic album sleeves while you 'n' Ron are playing bloody minuets or whatever. But what'll—I—be doing?"*

This was an embarrassing juncture. *"Well Jack . . . "* I ventured *" . . . college isn't something that came up suddenly or anything. It's where we've been aiming all along – you've known that since we all met up."*

"Yeah . . . " Jack admitted *" . . . I'm not really blaming you – it's just that it seemed a long way off back then – and now it's 6 bloody months away. My parents have got some idea about a career at Midland Bank or whatever – and that'll drive me bananas . . . Trouble is – I don't have any other ideas. My girlfriend Cynthia thinks it's a bloody dream come true or something 'cause her father's the bloody manager of the Farnham branch"* Pause *"Can you imagine it! Working in a bloody bank is bad enough – but having your girlfriend's frigging father breathing down your neck's going to make it a prison. I'd be catching crap in every direction – there'd be no bloody escape."*

"That sounds about as vile as a thing could be" I groaned *"I'd rather be in the Army kitchens than work in a bank."*

"*Well . . .*" Steve offered " *. . . you'd be earning money . . . and . . . you've always wanted to build yourself a Ginger Baker percussion arrangement. They don't exactly give those away do they? Two bass drums would be a lot of fun . . .*"

Jack accepted the situation and recognised that he'd no one to blame but himself for his lack of plans. "*Yeah, true enough . . . but it's not an—*exciting*—future is it – not 'til you three are back in circulation again.*"

"*I have no idea . . .*" Steve offered diplomatically " *. . . but it's not as if we're leaving the planet is it. We'll still be meeting up – and, as Vic said, you can build up your gear and practise. Your parents are bound to loosen up once you're working. I mean, they can't complain about what you buy when—*you're*—the one buying it. You can get the amplification Ron's always on about – and . . . well there's all kind of things you can do.*"

"*Right Jack*" I continued from where Steve left off "*I'll be in Farnham for a year—*at least*—and we can play the pubs as a duo – you can scale down the drums and I'll play lap slide. I could get the* DEBIL *mic'd up.*"

Jack smiled at that idea. "*Hadn't thought of that. Maybe I'd even get used to your . . . what did Ron call it?*"

We all laughed. "*Rubato*" Steve replied.

My private thoughts on the matter were not exactly ebullient regarding playing as a duo with Jack – but I felt I owed him loyalty. "*You could try jug and washboard too*" I suggested. "*We'd be like a jug band.*" Then I had to explain what a jug band was.

"*Washboard eh . . .*" Jack muttered "*that's hardly glamorous.*"

"*It's as glamorous as you make it . . .*" I said " *. . . and jug bands are an important part of Blues.*"

Jack was silent for a moment – so Steve chimed in *"He's right, jug bands are pretty wild. You heard of Ian Anderson's Country Blues Band?"*

"Yeah, they play some wild stuff" I agreed *"You heard 'Stereo Death Breakdown'?"*

"It's a great album . . . " Steve continued *" . . . and the washboard on that is fierce."*

Jack looked vaguely mollified and repeated *"Washboard eh . . . and maybe . . . high-hat?"*

"Sure" I replied *"and anything else you want to add – there's no limit apart from what you can carry in that car of yours."*

"Right . . . that could work. Not enough room for the whole kit, but I could take the cymbals . . . "

"Certainly Jack . . . " I laughed *" . . . just don't drown me out. The* DEBIL*'s not exactly loud y'know."*

Jack had a car – but the car was just another bar in the prison cell his parents had built. The car made him even more obliged to them as far as we could see. The car was a Ford Anglia. Ron called it a Fraud Anglican. It was an estate [2] model and Jack was happy about the idea that he could pile equipment into it.

"There'll be room for your bass amp and PA in my car – so we should still be able to kick up a storm."

Jack had to leave at that point – but I was glad something had been resolved for him before he left. He turned to wave goodbye at the door of 'The Nostril' and he seemed to look happier than he'd done when I first saw him ensconced with Steve.

---

2 Station wagon in the USA.

"*I'm not sure*—where—*Jack's going*" Steve remarked once Jack was out of earshot "*Whenever I've asked him about it he's been edgy.*"

I had similar concerns "*Yes . . . Jack doesn't have a feeling for Art or English . . . so I wonder what he's going to do . . . in terms of the creative field I mean.*"

Of the four of us – Jack was the least interested in higher education.

"*I've got the impression he wants out*" Steve confided "*He mainly wants to earn money so he can escape from his parents.*"

"*Seems so . . . he's talked that way to me too. Jack gets by on pocket money doesn't he?*"

"*Yeah . . .*" Steve shrugged " *. . . but there seems to be a generous amount of it.*"

"*That's the problem though – isn't it*" I pointed out – feeling somewhat exasperated "*Because of that, his parents have got him chained down.*"

Steve shook his head "*Yeah – but it's not*—just—*the money is it. I mean*—my—*parents don't do that. I get pocket money – but they don't use that to force things on me. My parents are human beings, not white-collar suburban Neanderthals.*"

I thought that was as plain as day "*Yeah . . . I know your parents are really decent – and you have a good relationship with them. I suppose I'm just talking from my own experience – the way things have been with me. I needed to make my own money to stand up for myself – but you and Ron haven't had to do that have you.*"

"*No . . . but you're right about Jack*" Steve agreed.

He sat back in his chair and gazed into the strange ceiling and the papier-mâché stalactites that hung from it.

"He'd do better to get some independence – but . . . I don't think he's that keen on working for money on top of the time he spends on his school work. He feels as if he struggles to keep his head above water at the best of times when it comes to examinations."

One face Jack displayed was the wish to escape any way he could. The other face was fearful of parental disapproval. He was tormented and obviously embarrassed by the fact that he couldn't stand up to his parents. His embarrassment was heightened with me around – because he knew all about my 'hair confrontation' with my father. He was in awe of that episode. He tried to write it off to the fact that I was in a different social bracket—where such anomalies occurred—but he knew I'd made my stand nonetheless. His parents were hyper-cognisant that I'd somehow crept out from amongst the morass of the lumpen proletariat and—according to Steve—took every opportunity to impugn my character. The working classes were criminal by nature—as far as they were concerned—and I was not to be trusted.

"Jack made the mistake . . . " Steve confided *" . . . of citing you as a free spirit on one rare occasion when he contested their views"* Pause *"They apparently hit the roof."*

"I can imagine . . . " I yawned *"I s'ppose that just resulted in peaking their loathing for me to an unprecedented height."*

"Got it in one. They'd be best of pals with the Dales."

"I don't think so Steve . . . I don't think the Dales would warm to them much more than to me. The Hackmans are not exactly cultured are they . . . I mean – if you asked them if they liked Brahms they'd probably tell you they'd never tried one."

"Know what you mean" Steve guffawed. *"They think that discussing investments is the pinnacle of refinement."*

We both felt sorry for Jack. All I knew was that as the months of the last year of school dwindled – Jack became increasingly opaque and introverted. The 'jolly japing Jack' I'd known the year before was in severe decline. There was a weight on his shoulders that he'd never discuss. I made the mistake of pressing him once – in the vain hope that I might be able to help him. He just glared at me and said that certain things were private. Maybe it was Cynthia. We never quite knew the lay of the land where she was concerned, in the early days of his discontent.

I never saw Cynthia – so for all I knew she could have been a figment of his imagination. I mentioned this notion to Steve – but he vouched for her existence. He'd met Cynthia on several occasions at Jack's home.

"What's she like?" I asked.

"Better not to know" Steve replied.

That just made me more curious. *"Really?"* Pause *"I don't think you can just leave it there . . . think you'd better spill the beans Steve."*

"She sulks . . . " replied Steve taking a deep breath *" . . . I call her the incredible sulk."* [3]

"Clever . . . " I laughed *"That sounds hideous. If there's one thing I can't stand it's sulking. There was a 'frowning Fiona' once and I didn't last more than a week with her"* Pause *"What else?"*

"She gives him instructions all the time. Thinks his drumming's a waste of time – and sucks up to his parents with that idea."

"Ouch" I yelped in horror *"That's intolerable – why doesn't he get out?"*

---

3 An allusion to 'The Incredible Hulk' series released by Marvel Comics in 1962.

"*Don't think he can*" Steve opined.

"*What d'you mean? All he needs to do is say 'goodbye' . . .*"

"*You'd think so . . .*" Steve replied "*but . . . I think he's nervous about ever finding another girlfriend or something. You know how it is. He's worried about looking like a gnome.*" Steve noticed my look of confusion. "*Ah . . . that drawing you made of him last year . . . well . . . I think it looked . . . too much like him*" Pause "*Don't you remember? He said you'd made him look like a sodding gnome . . . and Ron said you'd got him spot on with that. I'm afraid Jack took that to heart because it's how he sees himself anyway*" Pause "*So . . . he has this idea that the number of girls who want to date a gnome must be limited.*"

"*Right . . . that's not a brilliant self-image to have is it . . . ?*"
I pondered "*You know — I didn't deliberately make him look like a gnome . . . I just copied the photograph he gave me*" Pause "*Y'know . . . he'd look a lot—less—like a gnome if he let his hair grow out.*"

"*True*" Steve shrugged. "*Cynthia likes it though — and . . . anyhow . . . she thinks he should be concentrating on a career. To be fair, he's not done that yet — and . . . it doesn't look as if his grades are going to get him into university. He doesn't really know what he wants to do. She thinks university's a bad idea and that he'd be better off getting on the promotion ladder in some company and . . . his parents agree with her.*"

"*This . . .*" I groaned "*. . . is getting worse and worse. Why is university a bad idea? You'd think that with their point of view they'd want Jack to go to university . . .*"

"*No . . . not at all*" Steve responded dismissively. "*His parents aren't university educated — all they're concerned with is money. They think money's the answer to everything — but then the same goes for Cynthia's parents. They're as brain dead as Jack's parents. I've met them at Jack's — they're like a pair of warthogs.*"

"*Anyhow*" Steve continued "*the main thing is that Jack's parents think Cynthia's the bee's knees. I'd agree with them as far as an insect's legs are concerned*" Steve laughed – but his laugh petered out "*. . . and . . . they've got him pretty much married. It's hideous.*"

"*You're right Steve . . . it would've been better not to have known.*" I felt deeply sorry for Jack and it put a crimp in the rest of the day – or at least whenever I remembered what Steve had said.

"*So . . .*" I asked "*. . . is she intelligent, witty, or alarmingly attractive?*"

"*No, no, and no. She's not stupid – but she's as dull as . . . well . . . she doesn't comprehend Monty Python. She finds it irritating. She likes Benny Hill and circus-clown slapstick. As to being attractive . . . it's hard to say. I think Jack would make a better looking girl.*" Steve was welcome at Jack's house—unlike me—and so he had witnessed the situation first hand.

"*That sounds . . . gruesome . . . I mean . . . why?*"

"*I really don't know . . . apart from the gnome thing*" Steve replied "*and it's not as if I can ask him why he goes out with a girl who looks like a water buffalo, laughs like a hyena, and prattles like a parrot*" Pause "*Maybe that's the best a gnome can hope for . . . ?*" Pause "*I mean – if you think you look like a gnome . . .*"

"*Y'know Steve—I'm almost curious to see this wonder—maybe Jack likes her . . . robust personality . . .*"

"*Yeah, well . . . she's not exactly robust . . .*" Steve demurred "*. . . she has headaches a lot – and she's kind of physically temperamental.*"

"*You mean she's a hypochondriac?*"

"*I s'pose so. She's complaining of something or other more often than not – but . . . Jack's mother's a hypochondriac, so they get on well.*"

I got the feeling that we'd be looking for another percussionist at some point in the future – and that made me feel sad.

I wanted to help Jack. I wanted to show him that he wasn't tied to Cynthia if he didn't want to be. His parents didn't have to call all the shots forever.

"Thing is . . . " said Steve *" . . . Jack's father's a little bit like your father – but so's his mother. Jack never gets a break – he's got two overbearing rigid parents and they've got the money to keep Jack in line. You never had that – but Jack's trapped by it. Jack's never had to earn money with paper rounds and weekend work. He doesn't even work a few weeks of the Summer holidays . . . so . . . his parents have him by the short and curlies."*

That seemed like a nightmare scenario. Steve could see me looking a little stunned. *"And . . ."* he continued *"since you had that big fight about hair – your father doesn't even try to change you any more. You're in a better position than—all—of us . . . in some ways."*

As Steve continued, the subject become grimmer sentence by sentence. It seemed there was no way out for Jack. It was as if we were watching him mount the steps of the gallows. Cynthia's parents lived in the same avenue. They were good friends of the Hackmans. They played Bridge together every Friday night. The fathers played golf together – and probably engaged in all manner of similarly grotesque activities.

They're arranging paper doilies for a tepid afternoon tea / With malformed middle aged monsters mainlining verdigris / And golf engulfs all consciousness like a miniature Sherman tank / As they nail their eyelids in unison just to close their ranks / There's nothing left for me to say – about their prim lobotomies / They can continue interjecting – it don't mean that much to me. Larkin/Bruce/Schubert—Savage Cabbage—It Don't Mean that Much to Me—Savoy Green—1970

I started seeing how lucky I was. My father had his problems— sure—but he'd backed down in the end. He now seemed relatively reasonable.

We were polite—even cordial from time to time—and I was free to do as I pleased. I was free to keep the hours I kept without let or hindrance. I was quiet when I crept through the front door in the early hours – and I was always up for breakfast in the morning. Being up for breakfast and eating like a fiend seemed to be a sure sign—as far as he was concerned—that I'd not taken to drugs. Even with my father's disciplinary excesses, I'd always had my mother to make sure the situation never crushed me – so I was fortunate. Even Steve's and Ron's parents muttered occasionally about their ever-lengthening hair and increasingly bizarre sartorial sense – but I was free. Free. What a word *that* is!

There's a bunker at the end of the garden where bombs can't find you I'm told / You could live out your life in that shelter and come out again when you're old / But you can keep that museum of morals along with your Regency chair / 'cause I'm tired of living on the entrails to the footnotes in Vanity Fair. / I prefer being where there's a smile in the air I can do just like I please / 'cause they can't tie me down—I won't stick around—I'm just a thread in the breeze.

Larkin/Bruce/Schubert—Savage Cabbage—Just a Thread in the Breeze—Savoy Green—1970

Freedom was priceless – and I had it. Of course, I didn't have the time that the others had – but my money was my own. No one had bought or sold me. I owed nothing to anyone – apart from the affection I offered naturally.

Oh, freedom—Oh, freedom—Oh, freedom over me / And before I'd be a slave – I'll be buried in my grave / Oh, freedom Traditional—Spiritual

I even took to buying my father the odd tie – simply because I could. This seemed to please my mother immensely. So, all was well with the world – apart from the absence of Lindie Dale and the harrowing horror of Jack's home life.

It was hard for me to contemplate Jack without a deep gnawing despondency about his future as a percussionist.

"Is there—nothing—we can do? I asked Steve.

"I've made a few comments but it seems to make Jack feel worse."

Jack seemed to prefer denial. When he was with us he seemed to rise out of the gloom that was stealing over him – and when he played his drums the old radiance returned. I wondered who those drum skins *were* – when he thrashed them as he did. I mentioned this to Steve – and he thought I was on to something.

Ron and Steve had brief liaisons with ladies every now and then – but they never lasted. They tended to burn out on account of the time that was spent with music and playing gigs. Ron and Steve thought that ladies would turn up at some point. There were bound to be ladies who were as enthusiastic as they were about Blues – and then there'd be no problem. There were always enough ladies in the audience and although no one was throwing themselves at us – we all had the sense that this kind of thing might occur. I was still pining for Lindie Dale and so I was a rarefied and remote being as far as romance was concerned. Until I forgot Lindie I was immune to attraction.

Night jostles her stars raining sand and cotton / It is scorching but sighing silence weaves the glories of summer / Signals of minute heated crimes are everywhere / People overthrow thrones – great lights in the West and in the East / Tender rainbows at noon – and now all the bells answer / Noon is waiting, deaf like a great animal rousing its limbs from all four corners / As it advances its claws are the shadows and light beams of the sky falling on our heads / Wind is expected and today will be blue like a flag.
Philippe Soupault—Gold Medal—translated by the author and Lindie Dale

I'd turned Lindie into some fantastical figmental fairy who flitted in and out of my thoughts incessantly. *Sighing silence had woven the glories of summer* into the charmed Autumn in 1968. *Night had jostled her stars* – but now, a year later, it *rained sand and cotton* on a romance that once had been. It was not exactly a painful situation – because I'd become accustomed to it. The sensations were as familiar as the motorcycle ride to school. Green traffic light eyes and sunset hair. I could have plunged into a vat of lovelorn romantic drivel about it – but the idea of writing '*Each night I ask the stars up above – Why must I be a teenager in love?*' [4] was about as nauseating as eating nine entire packets of Jaffa Cakes. [5] I was content to be incurable.

"*You could do better mate!*" Jack said "*She's a bean-pole.*"

I knew that Jack meant well – so I thanked him for his opinion and quoted Bob Dylan "*Give me a string bean – I'm a hungry man.*" I found I could always quote song lyrics – even from songs I didn't know that well. I think I must have only heard that line once and it attached its tentacles to my conceptual infrastructure.

Well, I rung the fallout shelter bell / And I leaned my head and I gave a yell, / "Give me a string bean, I'm a hungry man!" / A shotgun fired and away I ran.
Bob Dylan—Talking World War III Blues—The Freewheeling Bob Dylan—1963

How does a person forget? Or rather – how does *an odd boy* forget? It's not exactly a matter of choice is it? Or is it? Maybe it is.

---

4 Doc Pomus/Mort Shuman—Teenager in Love—originally recorded by Dion and the Belmonts—1959
5 Jaffa Cakes are rather nauseating biscuit-like cakes made of three layers: a circular sponge cake base, a middle layer of orange-flavoured jelly, and a coating of chocolate covering the top.

I could decide not to dwell on Lindie intellectually—that worked —but the visceral texture of unrequited love endured under my rib cage like a dense metamorphic pebble. The pebble was impregnated with maundering memory – wordless yet sensationally eloquent. The trick was probably to have got hold of the pebble and thrown it into the sea. *'Break, break, break on thy cold grey stones, O sea!'* Maybe that thought ran through Tennyson's mind when he wrote those words . . . *'And that my tongue could utter the thoughts that arise in me.'* The trouble was that this pebble always seemed too valuable to throw away. It was the third stone from the sun. It had evolved an atmosphere. It was an extremely small planet – and on that planet I felt the inspiration to write poetry and lyrics. So . . . it was not terrible – and I was always available for band rehearsals.

Break, break, break, / At the foot of thy crags, O Sea! / But the tender grace of a day that is dead / Will never come back to me.

Alfred Lord Tennyson—Break, Break, Break—1834

At band rehearsals and gigs I was free of spontaneous images of Lindie – so I knew that I wasn't irredeemably strangulated by unrequited love.

Ron's father had a pretty fine tape deck. It was an EMI Green machine.[6] It was not quite clear to anyone why he possessed such a thing as he never seemed to use it. Ron thought that his father just enjoyed technical devices. It was some kind of hobby along with private band radio communication. He used to have chats with people in different parts of the world which seemed an interesting pursuit. I thought you could probably learn far more about what was going on in the world that way than listening to the news.

---

6 A BTR four track of BBC broadcast quality.

Ron's father was happy for us to use the tape machine and so we took it off to Weyflood Village Hall in order to spend a day recording all our songs. It was a marvellous day. We'd taken the equipment to the hall the night before as the place could be locked – and we wanted an early start.

Jack had been in a bad state the night before – vaguely on the verge of tears and as tight lipped as a pair of pincers. He had that look we all recognised as *'Don't meet my gaze. Don't look at me. Don't ask me anything. Don't speak to me.'*

That was relatively easy as setting up took time and effort. Once the hall was set up for the next day Jack went home. I went to the Running River Pub with Ron and Steve and we wondered what sort of a recording session we were going to have with Jack looking as if he'd been diagnosed with a terminal illness. We all knew it was a combination of Cynthia and parental pressure – so there was no need for speculation. We decided to leave the subject alone and hope for the best – and strangely enough 'the best' was what we got. Jack turned up the next day still looking brittle but—prior to recording—he attacked his drums in a startling manner – and started laughing. At first the laughter was fairly normal – but it proceeded to get louder and crazier 'til he was screaming uncontrollably and punishing his drums in the most violent manner. We stood and stared at him, not knowing what to make of it. I realised that something needed to happen – so I nodded at Steve and Ron and we launched into an extended jam. Jack eventually stopped screaming and his rhythms began to sound as if he was starting to relate to the rhythm the rest of us were playing. Something had obviously happened to Jack in more ways than one. He made a breakthrough with percussion at the end of the improvised havoc – we'd never heard him play so well.

Jack grinned at us *"Fierce! Bloody fierce! You're all bloody fantastic. Bloody brilliant. Thanks for being my friends – in spite of everything. I still don't want to talk about it – but I've made my mind up about something extremely important. It's all gonna be fine. I'll tell you about it next week when things have settled."*

We told Jack that we'd never heard him play as well. We'd not seen him as cheerful in months. We ran through the songs one by one and it was surprisingly easy. There were only two songs we had to re-record – but mainly because Ron and I weren't happy with the vocal delivery. Steve and Jack thought it was fine – but Ron knew how well I could sing at my best and somehow I was missing something on two of the songs due to the acoustics of the hall. We started moving the speaker cabinets around to see if we could improve the sound. Then we had to move armchairs here and there for an hour before we were satisfied with the way the vocals sounded. Eventually we got the right degree of punch. It seemed that we really needed a studio if we were to sound as good as we could sound.

Ron was going to get copies made of the tape for us all – but didn't know how long it would take. I wanted to send the tape off to a record company at some point but thought I'd have to research a little. I thought we'd also have to record our covers of old Blues numbers and that was arranged for the following month.

Something's in the air tonight – there's something on the wind / Whatever it is – it's a mystery door that will not let you in. / Rip-tide dog contingents are barking at your heels / Concealing recriminations that they seem to feel / I can't see you at all right now 'cause fate has blocked the view / And it's the 19th time since midnight, it's looked like déjà vu.
Larkin/Bruce/Schubert—Savage Cabbage—Déjà Vu—Savoy Green—1970

The following week Jack told us he'd bid goodbye to Cynthia. He was in bad odour with his parents over it. *"I told them it was totally unreasonable to be told I should have feelings I didn't have. I told them I didn't love Cynthia. I'd never loved Cynthia. They'd foisted her on me – and I just went along with it all."*

It was of course impossible not to ask a question – and Ron was the one to ask it *"So . . . why did you go along with it?"*

"Well . . . " Jack looked a little embarrassed *"I had no girlfriend at the time . . . and—to be honest—I . . . hadn't really had a girlfriend before . . . not really in the way you'd say you had a girlfriend anyway."* Jack went silent for some moments and we waited. It was not usual for Jack to open up like this and so we were all intent on giving him as much space as he needed. *"We'd moved from Wiltshire and . . . well . . . I didn't know anyone apart from Steve – who made friends with me almost straight away"* Pause *"So . . . Cynthia was good company at first . . . and it was good to feel that I was alright and had a girlfriend and all that . . . "* Pause *" . . . but then she started acting as if she owned me or something. It was creepy – and my parents just made it worse by inviting her round—all—the—bloody—time as if it was—my—idea. I tried telling them that she sulked when things didn't go how she wanted them to go – but they just made me feel as if she had good reason to be unhappy with me. They told me any girl would get fed up with my obsession with music. I tried telling them that her sulking wasn't just about band practices. It was about anything I liked that she didn't like – but they'd take her side on everything. They said it was quite reasonable for her not to want to watch Monty Python with me because Monty Python was 'ridiculous nonsense'. I was supposed to be grateful that she was such a good example or some such thing."*

"Sounds as if you were railroaded" Ron commented shaking his head in dismay.

"Too right bwana[7] *. . . "* Pause *"Then . . . she starts talking about getting engaged as if it was the next bloody step."*

"My God!" Ron yelped *"They really—were—planning to sell you down river."* [8]

"Yeah . . . maybe that's my qualification to be a Blues drummer . . . "

"Good you can see it that way Jack" Steve smiled – mainly to lighten the atmosphere.

"My parents agreed with her—of course—and started talking as if I'd made some sort of promise or something. The whole sodding thing was bloody ridiculous and I told them I'd never made any kind of promise about anything. I said 'I'm only 18 *– and making plans for the rest of my life is out of the question.' I told them it was too early to be making choices like that."*

"What did they say to that?" I asked

"You may well ask Mr Arbuthnot . . . they got devious and backtracked" Pause *"They said I was being extreme and that they were talking about the future. They weren't talking about next week or next year."*

Ron beetled his brows *"So how long—were—they giving you?"*

"Well . . . " Jack sighed *"They got cagey about that. They just said 'There's no harm in talking about the future.' They said I should see it from her point of view. If I couldn't talk about the future then she was right to think I wasn't reliable – and we should stop seeing each other. So I said 'Fine by me!'"*

---

7 East African meaning 'master' – used as a respectful form of address corresponding to 'sir'. Swahili from the Arabic 'abuna' meaning 'father'. Jack often addressed Ron as 'bwana'—especially when he wanted to agree passionately—but the other band members never enquired about it.

8 Selling someone down river originated as a phrase in Mississippi. Slaves who caused trouble were sold into the far harsher conditions on plantations in the lower reaches of the Mississippi river.

"*It*—is—*unacceptable*" he continued "*I'm not accepting it.*' It was a —really—*bad scene. They backed off in the end though. I told them I couldn't imagine being married to her . . . in fact it was*—the last thing in the world—*I wanted.*"

"*And then? What did they say to that?*" Ron asked almost white with repressed rage on Jack's behalf.

"*Then . . . they came on me with something else. They told me how embarrassing that would be for them – having to face her parents and having to be shamed that I'd led their daughter on!*"

"*Led their daughter on!?*" Ron shouted.

"*That's what they said. I could*—not—*bloody believe it! I told them I'd never led her on about anything and it was them who was pushing it all the time. They set the whole sodding thing up and they pushed it every inch of the way!*"

"*So what did they say to that then?*" Ron responded.

"*They couldn't really argue with that, could they . . . so they faffed around trying to cover it over. They told me it was what they thought I wanted and that they'd obviously made a mistake.*"

"*That was bloody big of them*" Ron sneered.

"*Not really . . .* " Jack sighed " *. . . that was yesterday . . .* " Pause "*When all my troubles seemed so far away . . .* " Jack laughed almost hysterically " *. . . but now it looks as if they're here to stay – or something like that.*"

"*Never known you to quote lyrics before Jack* " I smiled

"*First time for everything Mr Arbuthnot*" Pause "*So today . . . it's obvious they've been talking it over together and working out a new plan of attack . . .* " Pause " *. . . this morning—over bloody breakfast—they decide to think of it as some kind of quarrel we'd had – and that after a while we'll patch it up.*"

Jack was silent for a moment and then continued "*I told them that it was nothing like that at all. I said we'd had plenty of disagreements and they were always the same – her wanting me to be how she wanted me to be. But—of course—how she wants me to be is how they want me to be – so she's in the right and I'm wrong*" Pause "*Then I lost my rag and shouted at them.*"

"*What did you say?*" Steve enquired.

"*I said 'Why don't you just get rid of me and get the son you want!'*" Pause "*Then . . . I walked out without waiting for an answer – but my mother followed me out and said they didn't mean it to sound as it sounded and that I shouldn't feel whatever it was I was feeling . . .*" Pause "*I shouldn't have accepted that . . . but I did*" Pause "*Well . . . my mother looked really upset and it would have been – well . . . I couldn't just leave it like that.*"

I felt like saying '*I would have left it—just—like that*' but somehow it didn't feel appropriate.

"*And then?*" Ron asked.

"*I went out to think it through and to avoid Cynthia if she came round*" Pause "*Then, this evening . . . before I came over here, they had another talk about it with me.*"

"*And!?*" Ron almost snapped.

"*Now . . . they're trying to turn it round. I think they've been talking to Cynthia or her parents or something. Cynthia blames it all on you three of course . . . well not so much you—Steve—it's more you and Ron*" Jack laughed slightly dementedly "*My parents say you're both depraved louts – 'specially you, Mr Arbuthnot . . .*"

"*Especially me? What have—I—ever done?*"

There was that word again: depraved. My father had called Blues a 'depraved row'.

My main sins were that my parents were low-budget – and that I rode a motorcycle. We didn't live in a detached eight bedroom house. Nor did Steve – but his father was a Police Superintendent and Steve went to Grammar School. Still, what did I care?

"Jack's parents are banal bourgeois bigots!" Ron cackled *"Politically slightly right of Attila the Hun! So I can't see that their opinion of you was going to cause you any loss of sleep Frank."*

"True Ron . . . but still . . . I'm not keen on my name being manipulated as part of the planned suppression of Jack."

"So . . . " Steve enquired *" . . . where's it been left?"*

"It's been left with my parents thinking that—after a while—all will be well. So . . . " he let out a long sigh *" . . . I've probably got some heavy discussions coming up over the next months, 'til they finally realise I'm deadly serious about not wanting to buy an engagement ring – even if they pay for the bloody thing!"* Jack laughed a harrowing ghoulish laugh at that point.

It seemed that Jack expressing his intention to us was helpful in terms of feeling sure he'd maintain it. Still – we were just glad that Jack was able to smile again. We had a gig coming up playing warm-up for Love Sculpture at a school in Camberley. Ron and Steve were slightly concerned about how Jack's situation and resulting mood would affect the gig – but decided that he had enough courage to brave it out with his parents.

I was less sure. I tended to see Jack as living on the edge. I thought he could flip either way at any point but said nothing of this to Ron or Steve. I saw Jack as a financial prisoner – and therefore vulnerable to pressure 'til he left school and got a job. Until that point I'd expect traumatic vacillations.

I just hoped they wouldn't wreck any gigs – or drive Jack over the edge. I'd heard the word suicide when I was 7. It was something I couldn't rule out in Jack's case – and that troubled me greatly.

Your complicated dream's stripped down to the bone, / Your mantelpiece magician's on the 'phone, / Your temperamental orchestra is on the run / And they'll no longer play for anyone, / The verbs have changed in every line you knew / It's the 19th time it's looked like déjà vu.
Larkin/Bruce/Schubert—Savage Cabbage—Déjà Vu—Savoy Green—1970

I started keeping a careful eye on Jack – but after a while it seemed unnecessary. He returned to being the bright spark we'd known before – replete with scatological rejoinders and fantasies of the glorious future. His percussion continued to improve – and the rest of us decided he must have passed the hundred thousand mark listening to Ginger Baker's drum solo 'Toad'. Jack still had a long way to go – but then so did I.

I was a staunch supporter of Jack's efforts, whenever Ron wondered ever-so-slightly discontentedly about Jack's progress. *"He'll get there Ron. You always tell me I'll get there – and he's working like crazy."*

Ron shrugged *"Yeah . . . I suppose so – but you can't compare like that. You're a vocalist harp player who's adding bass – and Jack's a drummer who's not invested in amplification yet."*

This was always a sticking point with me *"Yes—Jack's not the most brilliant drummer—but Jack's a friend and he's trying hard. He's got his parents to deal with – and he's just got through that nightmare with Cynthia. He's got to take it slowly – he'll get amped-up at some point . . . when he can, y'know."*

Ron conceded that Jack's situation wasn't the most conducive and accepted that friendship was worth more than skill – but only where skill was being developed.

"He's a good bloke—I know that—and I suppose I get too impatient with him." Ron could always be won round.

"Right – and as he gets older, his parents'll fade out of the picture – you wait" I added *"It'll all be fine in the end – and we've got a shoal of gigs coming up."*

We had. We were looking ahead to Guildford University. Then we had our second gig at Eel Pie Island. Some time later there was the promise of Southampton University, Canterbury, Farnham, and Rochester Schools of Art. We—*were*—flying, and Jack seemed to be flying with us.

9

all my love's in vain

I followed her to the station with a suitcase in my hand, / Well it's hard to tell it's hard to tell, when all your love's in vain.

Robert Johnson—All My Love's in Vain—1935

Yuletide loomed: a chasm of gloom replete with a television set. I was in some other galaxy at the time however – and had no need to anticipate the annual Christmas Day and Boxing Day [1] penitentiary. I was riding high—centre stage—and learning the trade. I've always enjoyed the lead-up to the festive season—the coloured lights and revelry—but rarely *the season itself*, 'til more recent decades. The Winter bank holidays were often grim affairs and everyone I knew seemed to be ensconced with parents. Mistletoe hung thick everywhere I looked. I loved the colour of the plant – but the message it carried mocked my lovelorn state. This would be the second Yuletide I'd spend without Lindie – and that seemed to carry a message of permanence that I found irksome. The holiday season is not a wonderful time for unrequited love—or for being separated from a GIBSON EB3—but 'til that ghastly festive hiatus, I lived on stage. The stage was the perfect place. It was challenging – but I had no concerns there other than vocals—howling on harp— and playing bass to the best of my ability.

---

1 The Feast of Stephen – the day after Christmas Day, known as Boxing Day in Britain.

The last gig before the apocalypse of apathy was to be a 6th form dance – but that was three weeks away. It was for 16- to 18-year-olds so we had no great objection to being booked as the warm up act – we'd just create sufficient thunder to make them wonder why they hadn't booked us as the main act. Word had been getting round and we *were* getting more gigs as the main act.

"Maybe one day we'll be on before Hendrix! Think of that!" said Jack.

Yes – we all thought of that. That would be it.

"That would swing the deal forever. He'd hear us and then . . . " Jack had that insane look – as if he was about to . . . *fire all of his guns and explode into space.*[2]

"Then what?" said Ron—chewing through an apple as ever.

Jack looked puzzled – so Ron elaborated *"He'd hear us – then what? What would happen then? He might just walk away thinking we were a brilliant band but never say a word to anyone."*

Steve shook his head *"C'mon Ron . . . you—*know—*that's not how it is. Jack's right. We're as good as it gets – especially with Cream off the scene. No one's playing real Blues with a lead anywhere near as good as you play. Hendrix of all people would recognise that – you're out on your own in this country."*

I backed Steve *"You're also—*highly—*individual. No one can call—*you—*imitative – of anyone. You're completely out on your own. Everyone else over here imitates Eric Clapton, Peter Green, or Jeff Beck as best they can – and you're ahead of all of them. I don't know about the USA – but from what I've heard – some have got speed like Johnny Winter – but they don't match you with improvisation or breadth of style."*

---

2 *Fire all of your guns at once / And explode into space* Mars Bonfire—Born to be Wild—Steppenwolf—1968

Ron couldn't exactly argue with Steve as far as music theory went – and he couldn't argue with me in terms of my history of listening. He always said '*Frank's got the ear.*'

"*But it's still a daydream at this point – we've still got to take the world by storm . . . and that might never happen*" he concluded.

"*Well yes . . .*" I said "*. . . but a bat can look at a bedroom.*"

"*Yeah and a cat can look at a king*" Ron laughed "*We can do that alright.*"

"*You're definitely the most intriguing guitarist on the scene . . .*" Steve pointed out "*That goes without argument . . . and, I'd like to hear—you—play with Jack Bruce and Ginger Baker. Now—that—would be an ear-opener. I mean – Eric Clapton was brilliant with Cream – but if he had the Avant-Garde Jazz-cum-Classical in his Blues improvisations that you have . . . that would seal the deal forever.*"

"*It's not just—me—any more – you've been doing the same thing for a while now – and even old Frank here*" Ron chuckled "*sometimes does surprising things on bass—up the bloody neck—when he's—not—supposed to.*"

Steve turned to me with a grin and it was evident he was pleased on my behalf that Ron had noticed my getting ideas above my station in some of the long improvisations.

"*Y'know though . . . maybe Eric Clapton was the dynamic that kept their Blues numbers—as—Blues . . .*" Ron said returning to the question of Cream "*If—he'd—brought Jazz into the mix as well . . . they might've lost something crucial – to what gave Cream their sound. Just think about it – how would Spoonful have sounded if Clapton had gone off into Jazz scales?*"

I wondered about this – because I tended to take Steve's point.

I didn't say anything because I didn't want to hurt Jack's feelings – but it occurred to me that Jack's percussion was far enough away from Ginger Baker to allow the rest of us to go out on a limb. I mentioned it to Steve later and he thought I had a good point in two ways; first the point itself – and second, that I didn't mention it. We didn't really need Jack to vie with Ginger Baker – or to amplify his bass drum.

"*So . . .* " I said " *. . . what is it about—us—and the way we sound? What makes sure that—we—remain rooted in Blues – I mean, when you and Steve go out on a limb?*"

"*Well . . .* " Ron grinned " *. . . that's our—secret—isn't it.*"

That was a mysterious comment mischievously delivered – and we all looked at Ron to continue. Steve and I confided to each other—with a slight shift in facial expression—that we had the same shrewd idea of what was coming next.

The pause eventually got too long. "*So what's our secret then Ron*" Jack blurted out " *. . . don't keep us all in suspense—if we've got some bloody secret I'd like to know what it is, just in case anyone ever asks me —y'know—like Chris Welch from the bloody Melody Maker or something.*"

Jack could be a complete unwitting comedian sometimes – and he had no idea why we were all in tears of laughter.

"*Our secret*" Ron replied "*is that—we—are—all—rooted . . . in Blues. We don't—have—ideas of ever moving away. It's our central core. We have our Acid Rock numbers—thanks to Frank—but they're additions to our Blues set. They're there to show we're versatile and creative – that we're real musicians, not just pentatonic high-speed noodlers*" Pause "*And . . .* " Ron looked around slowly 'til he alighted on Jack.

"*And what?*" asked Jack in a slightly irritated tone – which made Ron keel over laughing.

"We have our—major—Blues weapon!"

"Right Ron . . . " Jack responded with some exasperation *"Bloody sure I know what—that—is."*

"Come on Jack" Ron roared with mirth *"Use y'bloody noddle mate! How could we—ever—be—anything—else but a Blues band with old Frank here? Think about it. He's—never—going to sing anything else, is he? And even when he does – it ends up as Blues"* Pause in which Jack still looked confused *"Think about it. Everything he sings that —isn't—Blues turns into Blues. I mean – look what he did to Feeling Groovy!"* [3]

Understanding suddenly dawned in Jack's face *"Right . . . I said he could make Feeling Groovy sound like the devil's national—bloody— anthem. So Mister Arbuthnot's – the major weapon eh . . . How does it feel to be . . . "*

I cut Jack short *" . . . one of the beautiful people? Now that I know who I am, what do you want me to be?"* [4]

Jack shook his head *"Any—chance—he gets, he does that – he probably dreams in bloody lyrics."*

"That's an astute observation" I informed Jack – and Ron sputtered his apple across the room.

These conversations were always a welter of mirth – but it was true, there was no way I'd ever be anything other than a Bluesman. These evenings were always over too soon – try as I would to protract them.

---

3 Simon and Garfunkel—The 59th Street Bridge Song (Feelin' Groovy)—Parsley, Sage, Rosemary and Thyme—1966
4 *How does it feel to be /One of the beautiful people? / Now that you know who you are / What do you want to be* Lennon/McCartney—Baby You're a Rich Man—Magical Mystery Tour—1967

I was the only one who didn't have to be at school for the first lessons of the morning. Virginia Water school didn't mind the 6th formers arriving late if they had no early lessons and all mine were in the afternoons.

School had become a lightweight obligation. I only had English and Art as subjects – so there was plenty of time to complete the necessary essays at school rather than in the evenings. Steve, Ron, and Jack didn't have it as easy – but then again, they didn't have to work every weekend. I would have liked to have spent more time with the lads—especially with Steve and Ron—but the idea of not being financially independent was anathema to me. I had thoughts about a MARSHALL amplifier for the EB0 or the EB3. Ron's bass amplifier wasn't powerful enough and nor was the one I'd inherit from Steve's Uncle Stan. I wanted 100 watts for the bass and 200 watts for PA so that my vocals could fill larger halls.

With English and Art as my only subjects, I'd segued into a quasi-Art School environment without realising it. I spent most of my time in the Art Department and started widening my interests there. There was a large ceramic studio and although I had no great bent toward sculpture I thought it a good idea to explore what the school had to offer. I enjoyed working with clay and made a number of strange objects which my brother Græham still has sitting around his home.

Sometimes I'd sit in the 6th form common room completing my English essay or chatting with Beowulf who often brought his guitar to school. I can't remember Beowulf's given name—or that of his friend Grendel—but Beowulf suited him so well that I never enquired. Cream and Jimi Hendrix played alternately in the common room, so even when I wasn't on stage or in band rehearsals – I was surrounded by *the sound*.

There were other albums occasionally on the turntable such as:
Aynsley Dunbar Retaliation, Chicken Shack, Canned Heat,
Butterfield Blues Band, Taste, Duster Bennet, Allman Brothers,
Savoy Brown, and Johnny Winter. I heard a great deal of music
at school and the variety was astonishing. I didn't like
everything I heard but I regarded the hearing as an education.
I tried to listen seriously to everything and Beowulf always
brought in something weird—like Clark Hutchinson—in which
the vocalist screams his way in a maniacal manner through
psychotic distended Blues-rants about anything and everything.
Extremely strange and yet exciting because it was like nothing
else I'd ever heard. I was not drawn to emulate that style but I
was glad that someone was taking flight in that direction.
Beowulf wrote the most extraordinarily deranged poetry –
linguistics from the other side of somewhere:

*You give me the hump like a Bactrian camel – Bactrian camel under dead
alkaline bacterial batteries / Under Alka-Seltzer assault tanks of fish
battery in friar truck try a fuck fuselage / Battered truck-stop stuck under
Alcatraz bagatelle bathyscaphe seesaw sideline screaming headlong down /
Headlong down under the bestial belly of all worlds bragging buttocks /
Barrage of bourgeois buttocks jet stream garage – barrage buttocks into
rivers – sound of tomorrow killing time / Killing time to electric drill
strumpets doing time and sliding still on stilts / Killing buttocks of time—
killing kitchen clock dinner grills—roasted ships in league belching tempest
too late to forget / Groaning gowns and clowns still stamping tiny feet—in
ears—in sands with bag legged brothel creeper shoes / Trooping the colour of
cosmetics girls in the wheelbarrow crossfire foxfire flash harry trumpet /
Cosmetics girls in the wheelbarrow kicking legs in crotchless fishnet spaniel
euthanasia / Cosmetics girls in the tweedle-dum tweedle-dee dispenser /
Wheelbarrow sparrow—cows to pigs diving like lepers with arrows in
default seismic underwear consortium / Wheelbarrow cosmetics girls rivets
cash register pig sleeping bag on every road and contraceptive balaclava /*

Wheelbarrow ministers in parliamentary session coughing blood like sodden
tea bags / Bystanders strangle their windows hovering in daytime
nightmares hoovering train-scape fugitive pillows / On the dawn line lawn
of delays and nightshade catapult burning forever in garter belt lavatory
cistern jumping sideways / And cardigan mole molesting mole-sters of Last
Noël / Nightshade catapult burning forever and cardigan manhole /
Nightshade catapult burning forever and cardigan motorway disaster /
Breast pocket watches as breasts watch breasts on the crest of magnesium
sulphide / But you can't take it back—no!—the sea of cosmetic girl
dreams is not any staple-diet anyway-motorist cadaverous colon in knicker
elastic subterfuge / But you too—goose headed trilobite—in your infrared
drain that never shone like darkness ever again / Never shone like
darkness again / Never shone like darkness again.

Beowulf—One Lump Or Two—1970

Beowulf's poetry—*had*—to be heard. He'd shout it so loudly
that it would make you slightly dizzy – and, very few people
wanted to hear it. I thought he was brilliant. I wished I could
write in a similar way – but I could never reach that peak of
immaculate lunacy.

"But why would you want to get that loony?" asked Jack.

I had no immediate answer.

"Well . . . I feel Beowulf's in touch with . . . something. I admire the way
he throws words together – 'hoovering train-scape fugitive pillows' is . . . I
don't know what it is – but it's superb in . . . some way."

"Yeah . . . in some way – but in most ways it's crap" Jack scoffed.

"Well . . . it's easy to say that – but I could never start with a line like
'You give me the hump like a Bactrian camel' because it wouldn't be poetic
enough for my prim and prissy sensibilities about words – and yet here's
Beowulf saying what the hell he likes at a thousand watts."

"*Right*" Jack laughed "*I'll take the thousand watts – but he can keep the rest.*"

I kept that piece of poetry. I'd look at it from time to time. I wondered how I could say something in similar style – yet . . . without being derivative. I thought Beowulf could write lyrics – but he had no interest in rhyming or scanning. He basically just wanted to be screaming anything at the top of his lungs. He liked my poetry – but thought that I needed to express more anger in it. I told him that I didn't enjoy anger a great deal. I wasn't really subject to anger and when I got angry I simply turned into some sort of iceberg. It wasn't the shouting kind of anger – just some kind of chilly logic-driven factuality that I'd deliver as if I had the last word – and there was no doubt about it. I could almost count the number of times I'd got angry on the fingers of one hand and every time it had happened I'd regretted it. I said that my problem was that I could always see reasons why people were as they were and that tended to defuse any sense of rage that might have risen on a more regular basis.

Jack thought my lyrics were as strange as they needed to be. "*You don't want to start writing stuff that means nothing. That bloke just writes whatever comes into his head – anyone can do that.*"

Well yes . . . "*But do they?*" I asked "*That's a question worth asking.*"

Jack looked exasperated "*Well of course they don't – because it's a bloody waste of time writing a load of old bollocks. He just does it to look as if he's the most far out freak in the fucking universe anyway.*"

Well that was an interesting point. '*Is that all that Beowulf did?*' I wondered. Steve put it another way when I mentioned it to him. "*D'you think he's ever worked with poetry the way you had to work with that Mr Preece?*"

Good question. I asked Beowulf and he said that he hadn't.

"What's the point – that stuff's dead and gone."

I made no comment – but 'that stuff' was not dead and gone. That stuff was alive and well as far as I was concerned. If stuff could be 'dead and gone' then all anyone could ever do was write more 'stuff' that would be dead and gone some time later.

"I think that what you like about Beowulf's writing is that he occasionally throws out really amazing word combinations that you like – but I think it's an accident—just one lucky accident after another" Steve nodded sagely *"There are more lines that don't work than those that do. I think that you find it hard to write like that because you compose – and you take a lot of time with each line. The other thing is that all his poetry is the same. If you've read one you've read them all – because they're all crazy in the same way."*

I mused on this question as I took my leave to avail myself of the facilities. Steve passed me a sheet of paper when I returned *"I'd like you to read this poem."*

I took the sheet of paper and read it with interest. It seemed to be a Beowulf poem—or one that looked similar—but Steve had written it.

"Mmmm . . . now there's a thing and no mistake. When did you write this?"

Steve laughed *"Five minutes ago when you went to the loo."*

The poem was not quite as electric as Beowulf's – but it had many of the same features. I scanned it back and forth for quite a while. Eventually Steve said *"So I'm a poet too now – am I?"*

"Well yes . . . " I insisted *" . . . how could I say you're not? Everyone's a poet. Maybe it's not your major direction – but I'd say that you must have—some—talent, or you wouldn't even have—tried—to write this."*

"*There's no winning with you when it comes to this kind of thing is there?*" Steve shook his head in mock disbelief "*What puzzles me, is the fact that you're—so—critical of yourself and so uncritical of others.*"

I'd never looked at it like that – and pondered the idea briefly "*That's not entirely true Steve – there's plenty that I think is useless.*"

Steve accepted that was accurate "*. . . but you're never critical of anything avant garde or just plain weird.*"

I sat with that for a while – because Steve was never critical without good reason. "*You're right about that Steve . . . I think . . . I may have to take a look at that. I think I probably forgive any form of creativity as long as it's weird. There's just not enough that's weird – unless you live in London . . . I think I see it as . . . a matter of loyalty. 'Cosmetics girls in the tweedle-dum tweedle-dee dispenser' is—some kind of genius—but it isn't . . . in the end . . . what I want to write.*"

"*I'm relieved to hear it*" Steve chuckled.

Later Steve played me Captain Beefheart's 'Trout Mask Replica' album and it hit me right between the eyes.

"*So that's where Beowulf found his muse . . .* " I told Steve " *. . . still . . . it's impossible not to be influenced.*"

"*It's obvious – when you hear it. It's completely derivative*" Steve replied.

"*Still . . . Beowulf's out there doing it – and I can't damn him flying with his enthusiasm*" I demurred "*Maybe I'll just have to be influenced by— so many people—that my influences become some sort of sea.*"

"*Some sort of sea?*" Steve enquired with a bemused expression.

"*Yes . . . out of which unlikely and previously unknown fish leap.*"

"*That'll do it*" Steve chuckled.

The weeks rolled by – and the Friday night approached when we were to appear at the 6th form dance. We'd never played a regular school before and felt a little . . . peculiar about it. We strolled in trying to give the impression that we were as far removed from any association with the school as it was possible to be. Strangely enough – it wasn't difficult. No one looked at us as if we should be in the audience. The equipment had a lot to do with it. Everyone who knew anything knew a MARSHALL amplifier. They had the name MARSHALL in hand-script lettering on them – and we had four of them. We also had the 'name guitars' and word soon got round amongst all those who knew the equipment – that we were serious.

I mentioned this to Ron who grinned *"It's our introduction. That's—why—we never have to tell anyone who we are. We just set up and play – without a word. First they see the gear. Then they hear us. Then—you—say goodnight in that maniac style of yours – and we're gone. Then they tell everyone they know, that we're—it—and that's it. Simple."*

"But we're playing warm-up for Love Sculpture and that doesn't make us 'it' . . . that annoys me . . . " I muttered – intending only Ron to hear.

"They're not the main act though" Jack commented. *"They're just better known – and they're a bunch of poseurs especially that ponce* [5] *with the frilly shirt."* It didn't take much to make Jack fume about possible inequities in the local music scene.

Ron just grinned *"We'll see . . . "* and proceeded to make the final tuning adjustments to his guitar. As I watched Ron an image from the past crossed my mind of the boy who'd waited for Legba to come and tune his plastic guitar.

---

5 1960s British expression meaning an effete man.

The image was gone in a moment and I was back on stage again. Ron was staring at me with a puzzled look – aware that I'd vanished for a moment. I grinned at him and he grinned back. I'd tell Ron the story later – it'd make him laugh.

Steve had broken his spectacles that day. They were taped up, so he decided not to wear them on stage. Steve looked unfamiliar without his spectacles and the effect gave him a wonderfully deranged visage. He couldn't see much beyond his guitar and so he stared into the audience as if they were simply a light show. Something about that look made him seem utterly at ease and confident as he waited for Ron to lead in. Suddenly we launched into *Crossroads* – which was the one song we played completely differently from the way Cream played it. We played it as a slow Blues with passionate riffs between each phrase.

You can run, you can run, tell my friend boy Willie Brown, / That I got the crossroad blues this morning, Lord, baby I'm sinking down.

Robert Johnson—Crossroad Blues—1936

We sang the words as they were written by Robert Johnson. He was one of the only Bluesmen whose words I *never* changed. It was as if Robert Johnson's words were sacred somehow. I really did believe he'd been to the crossroads and that there was a hellhound on his trail. It's not that I didn't respect other composers – but there was something eerie about Robert Johnson that kept me from ringing the changes on his lyrics. I probably had a wordless sense – that singing Robert Johnson's lyrics somehow stood me at the crossroads. It was a preposterous notion—and one that only a 17 year old could've had—but there was a direct line between me and Robert Johnson when I sang. I just became what I thought he was – and the fact that I was a white boy from Surrey in the late 1960s missed me completely.

The notion of Legba kept flittering at the back of my mind. Had Legba really turned up for the 12 year old I used to be? Was that how I sang Blues? I thought he'd never showed – but here I was . . . being the Bluesman I'd always wished to be. Maybe that big black man just snuck up behind me and breathed on me or something. Maybe things weren't actually as obvious as the stories told. Maybe Legba was something beyond understanding or outside normal human reason. How was I to know? All I knew was that when I got on stage I'd become someone else. I recognised the person I became. He was as much 'me' as I was – but the space I inhabited also changed. Steve, Ron, and Jack changed too. They were living in that twilight world with me. Each was a professional musician – and each . . . had a hellhound on his trail.

After Crossroads, we hit *Hellhound On My Trail; Believe I'll Dust My Broom; Kind Hearted Woman Blues; 32-20 Blues; From Four 'til Late; Rambling On My Mind; When You Got A Good Friend; Come On In My Kitchen; Little Queen Of Spades; All My Love in Vain; Walking Blues; Sweet Home Chicago; and Travelling Riverside Blues* – an entire Robert Johnson set. That was Ron's idea. He thought it would show Love Sculpture who the Blues band really was.

We got two huge encores and finished with *Born Under a Bad Sign* and *Spoonful*. We often finished with Spoonful – tired but happy and still full of whatever it was that we had. If they'd encored all night we would have played all night – but finally it was over and we quit the stage with people still yelling "*More— more—more—more—more.*" I grinned as I left, thinking that it wouldn't be that long before people started painting 'Ron Larkin is God' on walls here and there.

Steve and Jack decided to get a reasonably early night – but Ron and I stayed on to hear Love Sculpture. We were keen to hear how much better the main act was than the support band. Ron and I just looked at each other in disbelief after we heard them.

"How d'you rate the lead?" Ron asked with the very slightest grin playing at the edges of his mouth.

"Well . . ." I replied *" . . . he's not slow – but he's not inventive."*

Ron looked thoughtful. *"Anything else?"* he enquired – attempting to look as non-committal as possible. I could tell—knowing Ron as I did—that he was not impressed by the guitarist. I wondered why Ron was asking me – when he was the best judge available on the subject.

I ventured some ideas *"Well . . . I think that he's not as adept as he sounds . . . he's got some sort of system . . . He picks a lot of notes in tight groups. Most of the riffs he plays are repetitive triplets. He moves up and down the neck playing those little patterns. I thought he was quite good at first – but he was immediately less interesting when I picked up on his method. I think . . . if he tried to play some of your riffs—not even your long riffs—he'd find it either difficult or impossible."*

Ron grinned and said *"You know . . . you're a far better vocalist too . . . and . . . I reckon you'll make a fine guitarist one day."*

High praise from Ron – but I never did. I play guitar – but I'm no guitarist; I just write insane lyrics.

Love Sculpture was a Rock band of the late '60s. Dave Edmunds, their lead guitarist and vocalist, went on to be quite famous – so our early comments on his style should be taken with a pinch of salt. Love Sculpture had a hit record in 1969 with their high-speed Rock revamping of Khachaturian's 'Sabre Dance'. It was enjoyable – but Ron and I, as Blues purists, were not excited about it.

We observed Dave Edmunds a day or two later sitting with his guitar in the café area of the Friar Tuck fish and chip shop in Frimley, Camberley. It was near the high school where we'd played the night before – and we'd come to pick up the amplifiers we'd left in the safekeeping of the school. We always intentionally 'spoonerised' [6] Friar Tuck – but, that fact notwithstanding, there was Dave Edmunds practising silent riffs. He didn't recognise us from the warm-up band who'd preceded him the night before – and we didn't draw attention to ourselves.

Ron leaned over and whispered "*You were right about the triplets.*" He laughed about my use of the term 'triplet' because I didn't know what it meant musically. I'd just coined the word to mean rapid three-note phrases. On the way back to his house Ron said "*I'll tell you about triplets [7] one day – it's really quite interesting because you throw them into the vocals quite often.*" But – I never got that particular music lesson.

When the train rolled up to the station, I looked her in the eye, / Well I was lonesome I felt so lonesome, and I could not help but cry
Robert Johnson—All My Love in Vain—1935

The Christmas of 1969 passed – and I found myself riding over to the Queen's Oak. I was in a free and easy frame of mind in spite of the fact that several weeks had passed without seeing Lindie. It was a Friday night. I came rolling in with a fair-sized grin—and then, suddenly, there she was—arm in arm with some grotesque military type. The haircut was unmistakable – but beyond that, he had an abbreviated nose, a weak chin, an outlandishly garish Crimplene cravat, and a pink nylon shirt.

---

6 A spoonerism is a verbal slip where the first letters of two words are accidentally exchanged.

7 A triplet requires a musician to fit three notes (or rests) into the time value of two notes (or rests).

218

He wore one of those ugly—ugly—*ugly* square-cut 'bum-freezer' jackets. It was pale brown—tending to mauve—and had *almost* as much style as a drain pipe. I noticed that his pale olive herringbone trousers were a little on the short side – exposing an unsightly extent of tartan sock. He boasted one of those klutzy thick chain-link bracelets with a plaque that had his name engraved on it. To cap it all he wore tasselled golf shoes.
I sensed that he probably had a medallion under his shirt as well – but I thought better of imagining anything further than the string vest that was visible through his shirt. I was aghast.

It don't look right but I may be wrong / I've got your number – so it won't take long, / I rode down your way – but wasn't by choice / Tried to woo you with my dark brown voice. / I cleaned up all neat like a street parakeet / Combed my charisma and buttoned my feet, / I hear you sighing in that flickering fan / So I'm playing my last card however I can.
The Author—Playing My Last Card—1968

Lindie was as elegant as ever—she would have looked elegant in a boiler suit [8]—and I wondered how she felt on the arm of such a sartorially challenged individual. She looked a little shocked to see me – and smiled rather wanly.

"*Hello Vic . . .* " Her voice was thin and reedy and sounded as if it was coming from along way off.

I could hardly speak – but managed "*Happy . . . New Year Lindie – I . . . yes . . . so . . . right . . . good to see you.*" Then I clammed up. I had no idea what to say or what to do next. Lindie froze up too – and although she opened her mouth to speak, nothing emerged.

---

8 Coveralls in the USA.

Pete—standing next to me—said *"Bloody hell Vic, you look like that corpse that falls through the doorway in 'Public Enemy Number One'*[9] *– what's up?"*

I turned to him—as if in a dream—and gave him a wide meaningless grin. *"Had a . . . sudden cramp . . . in my . . . foot Pete. I'm . . . fine now. In fact . . . I'm sitting on top of the world."*

By the time I'd turned back to see whether I could say anything more articulate to Lindie – she'd moved away. I felt a bizarre mixture of relief and misery. I sat down with Pete and sipped half-heartedly at my ginger beer.

Pete eyed me suspiciously *"If you don't mind me saying – you're wearing a bloody weird expression."*

I attempted to rearrange my facial muscles *"I'm just . . . well . . . I guess Lindie . . . "*

Pete looked sympathetic *"Right . . . yeah . . . that pox-ridden pillock*[10] *must be her new fella. Didn't know you still had hopes there. I s'pose she wasn't going to sit at home forever."*

It was a kindly intentioned statement – but it made little sense to me. *"There are . . . other things you can do apart from sit at home Pete – I mean . . . how could she . . . "* I ran into the wall of silence again.

Pete sat observing me with a look of slight anxiety – and so I started speaking again *" . . . we were translating French Surrealist poetry together at the end of last term – and now . . . here she is with . . . "* words failed me.

---

9 Public Enemy, 1931, starring James Cagney.
10 British term of abuse—now rare—with a similar meaning to: pitiful fool, poltroon, or schlemiel.

They didn't fail Pete " . . . *with an utter fucking prat* [11] *dressed like an inmate from the asylum.*"

That was about the shape of it as far as I could see. *"So why would she do that? Is she going to have conversations about music and . . ."*

Pete nodded his head sagely at me and said *"Y'know . . . I don't know how to say this . . . but people always show you the side of themselves they want you to see – and you're the kind of maniac who always sees the best in people."* Pete could obviously see me turning a whiter shade of pale and decided to say something optimistic. *"Still . . . this could just be some bloody lame prune her parents lumbered her with. I mean he's obviously some sodding squady her bloody father knows. She'll get shot of him before long – I mean who'd want to be with that cretin."*

That made some sense. It made me feel better – but it was an unintentionally laid trap and I stuck my foot firmly between its jaws. Hope had returned. *"Maybe you're right . . . Lindie didn't look . . . well – she seemed upset."*

"I should think she would!" Pete laughed. *"You'd have to be brain dead not to be upset being seen with a creep like that."*

Pete was trying his best to cheer me up and I succumbed – but out of a sense of obligation. I was *not* looking forward to Stormy Monday and I knew that Tuesday would probably be worse.[12] I would have to face Lindie at Virginia Water. What would we say to each other? I would be cheery as usual—I knew that—and I intended to avoid all sense that I was not swimming with the current.

---

11 British term of abuse. Originally a singular 'buttock' – later an insignificant person or dolt.
12 An allusion to 'Call it Stormy Monday (But Tuesday Is Just as Bad)' by T-Bone Walker—Stormy Monday—1947.

I wasn't going to lay a 'tears of a clown number' [13] on her.
I'd just grin mildly—say hello—and see what happened next.
I spent the weekend washing pans for the Army as usual and the
evenings with the lads talking about what new Blues numbers we
might add to our set. We decided to work through all the
Robert Johnson numbers – as that seemed to be an extremely
serious repertoire.

"That could be an album one day y'know" Ron speculated.

"A triple album" I added *"with paintings of Robert Johnson based on
those two known photographs. I'd like to paint him driving his
Terraplane."*

Steve grinned broadly at that *"I—like—that idea."*

Ron chuckled *"I sometimes forget that you paint as well as sing and
write lyrics – but before we get that far, I think we'd have to work on each
one of 'em to get just the right feel. There'll be a way to play each one of
those songs as electric Blues numbers – and getting it right will take a lot of
time—a lot of time—and . . . of course, no record company would bring
out a triple album no matter how good it was."*

I said what they could have predicted I'd say *"There has to be a
first time."*

Ron grinned *"Yeah . . . but seriously – I don't think that's the way to
do it. I'd wanna be more adventurous than a triple album."* I raised the
stakes to a quadruple album – but that wasn't the way that Ron's
mind had been turning.

"No . . . There's 29 songs, right?" Right *"So if they're going to be good
long numbers with real class instrumentals that means four or five songs an
album – and that means six albums."*

---

13 An allusion to 'Tears of a Clown' lyrics by Smokey Robinson—Smokey Robinson & the
Miracles—Make it Happen—1967.

"*But!*" Ron exclaimed cutting in before I'd had time to speak "*we'd bring 'em out—one—at a time. That way people'd be waiting for the next album – and, we'd have time to work each song into a classic. We wouldn't have to compromise on—anything—and we'd only bring them out—when—we'd got 'em totally right.*"

My eyes widened "*Blimey Ron . . . that—really is—the way to do it! No one would—ever—be able to do it again! It'd be like the—complete—adjectival works of Shakespeare – but Blues!*" Steve and Jack weren't used to Ron going off on flights of fancy like this – but they agreed. It was a genius idea.

"*Yeah . . . we'll have to work on that at Music College*" Steve followed "*but . . . even then . . . it'd take quite some doing to bring—that—off . . .*"

"*But*—bollocks! *We can do it!*" Ron cackled "*No more 'Mister Caution' from me! I've seen the light! By the time we're out of College Jack'll be going great guns. He'll get down'n'do his homework – I c'n hear it already. His 'Bugger-off Cynthia Boogie' was a real tour de force – and I can see where he's going now. I've even got to like him going heavy on the cymbals. And—you'n Frank—you'll be playing bloody counterpoint with each other by then—as well as Steve does with me now—and, y'know what else!? I've been thinking 'bout taking up violin at College because I think there's a place for electric violin or viola in Blues. Whatcyha think of that then?*"

"*Jesus Ron!*" Jack yelled "*We're gonna blow people's—bloody—brains out!*" We all fell about laughing.

"*Y'see . . .*" Ron went on "*I've got it all worked out. Adding electric violin and piano would get us the variety we'd need without using some sleazy horn section. I've been working at piano – and . . . I'm probably better than my sister now—especially with boogie.*"

Then Ron turned to me *"And—as Frank knows—I've been working on Otis Spann riffs on guitar"* Pause *"Well . . . I've been working guitar riffs out on piano too – and it's really quite interesting."*

"Right" I enthused *"That—*would*—be the works. Although . . . you on guitar or violin—and piano—would require laying down tracks in a studio. . . "*

"Right Frank – there'd be no point in going for live albums with this" Ron replied *"Y'see I'd want to use 12 string acoustic too in some parts – and a* NATIONAL; *if I could ever get hold of one. In a studio the 12 string'd be as loud as the* TELECASTER *and I could weave 'em in and out of each other 'cause we'd need to ring the changes – like double-tracking you on harp Frank."*

What a thought. Ron had really put his mind to this idea. It—*was*—utterly brilliant. We all sat back and went into some kind of trance – as if we could all see the completed project. I was thinking of album sleeves and how I'd develop the theme over six album covers. It was a vast majestic vision.

Whilst I was musing on album sleeves Steve had been thinking along other lines – and finally came out with his conjecture. *"I think Cream really—*had*—something with Crossroads. Even though we're not totally enthusiastic about what they did with that song, they—*did *—make it their own. The way we play it . . . sounds . . . too much like the original. That's good in one way – but it's not become an electric Blues number yet."*

"I've been thinking along those lines for a while . . . " Ron nodded *" . . . but I haven't come up with a fresh approach that works."*

"Trouble is . . . " I commented *" . . . that Cream's Crossroads is— there—smirking at us . . . just daring us to change it. It's got that nice little seven note riff that—*everyone*—knows – and you can just feel the audience being disappointed that we don't play—*that*—adjectival riff."*

"There's no getting round it" Ron observed *"We'll have to come up with our own riff – and it'll have to be even better."* That was a tall order – but Jack and I felt Ron and Steve could do it if they battered at it for long enough. So that was how we spent that Sunday: Jack attacking bongos whilst Ron and Steve improvised on acoustic guitars in every direction. I sat and listened intently, occasionally yelling out *"That's good – that's close."* Every time I picked up on a motif Ron would notate it – then I'd follow the riff on harp. By the end of Sunday evening – we had our own Crossroads.

I went to the crossroad, babe, I looked east and west, / Lord, I didn't have no sweet woman, ooh well, babe, in my distress

Robert Johnson—Crossroad Blues—1937

The procedure was wonderfully creative and *almost* took my mind off Lindie. She was absent for periods – but any lull that occurred opened the door through which she walked back into my mind – arm in arm with that sartorial horror of a soldier.

Monday arrived. I parked the pixie chariot at Virginia Water and strode across the car park. At one point I exclaimed *"This—is—not—happening!"* almost as if the words might change something.

Beowulf overheard *"That's more like it! A little anger! Good line! That's—just—what you need!"*

That was bizarre *"I'll be working on it 'wulf"* I replied and grinned at him in what was probably a deranged manner. I was going to have to work on the artificial grinning business.

I opened a door and started walking down the corridor. Lindie came drifting at me—like the mirage of magnificence she was—and I grinned on cue.

"Can I talk to you outside?" she asked.

I nodded my assent with some kind of piercing dread. At first I was too self-obsessed to notice she was weeping. Snow was falling and the flurries of flakes made it difficult to focus. *"It's . . . it's—not—like you think. I wouldn't—do—a thing like that to you."* Everything suddenly turned back-to-front.

"Lindie, what's wrong?" I asked putting my hand on her shoulder. Lindie looked bewildered and slightly crazed.

"What's wrong!" she shook her head almost violently *"My parents are wrong! I'm wrong! Everything's wrong but you! But we can't be together and . . . I'm—so—miserable! You weren't supposed to—be— there that night! I wouldn't have had you be there for anything! Not for anything! But it just happened . . . and . . . I was almost sick when I saw how sad and shocked you looked. Sidney's just the son of a friend of my father. My parents just landed me with him for the evening . . . They told me they thought I'd like the company. I think they have ideas about it – but they're not my ideas. It wasn't my idea to go out with him – and I'm —not—going out with him – I just went out that evening."*

I was massively relieved – and wondered what would happen next.

"I expected you to be angry . . . " Lindie almost whispered *" . . . and that you wouldn't want to talk to me again."*

Now there was a concept. It took me a moment to gather some words together. *"How could I be angry with you? I'm sad we're not together as we were – but not as sad as I was now you've said what you've said. I'd like us to be together – but I don't know when that can be . . . it might take a year or . . . "*

Lindie looked at the ground and made awkward movements with her feet.

"My parents . . . " she commenced *" . . . are still the same . . . but I —did—talk to them about what happened and how horrible they were to you. I've never shouted at my parents before . . . I told them you'd been polite to them and that you kept being polite no matter how rude they were."*

Lindie was silent for a moment and I just stood there – dazed and confused.

"Once they'd calmed down enough" she continued *" . . . they admitted that they'd been rude to you. They told me they were sorry for that. They said they thought you were much older than you are. They thought there was something strange about you just appearing in the last two years at Virginia Water. My father had the insane idea that you'd been in a Borstal[14] or something. He actually phoned Mr Ironsides and found out he was wrong – and that you were my age and . . . my father even admitted to feeling foolish . . . "*

It was a long story – but we both had a free period and so I sat and listened. Lindie's parents had relented about her being my friend at school. They'd admitted that I was a well-spoken intelligent fellow and that their reaction was simply based on my appearance. Her father admitted that describing my mother as 'a German' was unworthy of him and that they should have shown me proper hospitality even though they disapproved of my appearance. This was all looking promising 'til the blow fell.

"The thing is . . . " she almost whispered *" . . . that although my parents are very old fashioned . . . I—can—always talk to them . . . and they do have some . . . well . . . they're just worried about me and what will happen in the future."*

---

14 British 'Borstals' are prisons for youths under 23. They are educational facilities intended for reforming the teenage petty criminals. A good description of life in a Borstal can be found in 'Two's Up!' by Kris Gray—memoires of a Borstal Boy—2011.

I listened to Lindie's account of her parent's reasoning and realised they'd marshalled their points in such a way as to give the jury no choice about the verdict.

"If Savage Cabbage failed . . . we'd have no financial future – because Art School can't guarantee that. If Savage Cabbage succeeded we'd have no future either – because you'd be travelling all over the world. I'd either be left behind – or . . . I'd have to tag along."

I waited to see where the reasoning would go next.

"I thought about it – and . . . it's all just too . . . frightening. I'm afraid of that life . . . and I know it. It's weak of me – but . . . I don't think I'm the kind of person who could live like that."

What was I to say to that? I couldn't give any kind of guarantee that Savage Cabbage would be an album-based band or whatever.

"They accepted that you didn't take drugs . . . but . . . they said it's well known that the music scene is a drug scene. They said . . . that there was no guarantee that you wouldn't . . . 'succumb to peer pressure' . . . I suppose it's happened to others – hasn't it?"

"Well . . . " I answered – extremely slowly *"Yes . . . I suppose it has – but you know my point of view . . . and you know that I don't change my mind about ideas I hold strongly . . . "*

Lindie nodded her agreement *"Yes – I know that. That's what I told them. I told them you'd be going to Art School too and that Savage Cabbage wasn't the only thing in your life. But . . . they said your chances with Art as a career were slim and even if you worked hard there was no guarantee of anything. And . . . well . . . they said this wasn't the basis for raising a family."*

Then came the final blow.

"I know you well enough to know you wouldn't change your mind about drugs – because you don't change your mind about things. You don't compromise yourself . . . and maybe that's the thing that makes it impossible – because I wouldn't want you to compromise or to change anything."

She still loved me and was miserable in being parted from me – but she couldn't face a life that might have no security. Her parents had said that there was no point in continuing a relationship if it couldn't lead to marriage. It was unfair to me as well. What a thought. Unfair to *me*. The Dales had really got this thing wrapped up. They'd covered every angle. What was I to say? There was nothing to say in favour of *the odd boy*. There was nothing even to suggest. I felt stunned.

"We'll always be friends though" she offered—and I accepted—with no sense of what the words meant.

"The future's still the future though . . . " I ventured tentatively with the words clawing at my throat " *. . . and no one can tell what'll happen. I'm not going to walk away from you as if finding someone else was the next thing on the horizon."*

"I feel the same . . . " Lindie replied " *. . . but . . . the end of Virginia Water will probably mean different directions for us."*

Lindie was eminently sensible. She'd looked the thing square in the face – whereas I was still in serious denial about the ultimate fact of it all. There could be no *ultimate* facts about the directions taken by human beings and the future *had to be* open-ended. Philosophically, I was right. Realistically, I was somewhat in error.

I was eager to change the subject and to continue the friendship we'd had – but Lindie was too desolate to speak. My failure to be desolate was merely my refusal to accept the inevitable.

We sat together in silence holding hands as if we were waiting for the executioner. It was our turn next and the guillotine was standing somewhere just round the corner. The minute hand of the school clock eventually sent Lindie to her French lesson. I retired to the 6th form common room to play 'Oh Death' on the DEBIL.

Death—Oh Death—see what the Lord a-done, / And I know—Lordy I know—my time ain't long. Charley Patton/Bertha Lee—Oh Death—1934—Jo Ann Kelly/Tony TS McPhee—Gasoline—1970

Pete came in out of the snow and grinned at me *"Saw you and Lindie out there – how goes it mate?"*

I had no idea what to say or where to start *"Are you up for a long story?"*

"Is it a good story?" he asked.

"It's a bloody—bloody—bloody awful story – worst bloody story I ever heard . . ." I was not used to swearing and had no idea how to be creative with it.

"S'pose I better hear it anyway . . . may as well know the worst."

I gave Pete the horrible details and he sat staring at me 'til I'd I finished. *"Right . . . the . . . bastards . . . The bloody evil bastards . . . They really stitched you up didn't they . . . The y covered—every—fucking—angle."*

"That's what they did" I stated in a flat nondescript manner. *"Sometimes Pete . . . "* I'd started speaking but couldn't get the words out. I was suddenly fighting back tears. I didn't know what I was going to say – but something welled up and swept over me from head to toe.

"You'll get over it mate. It's bad – but you'll get over it—and there's plenty of fierce birds out there."

'*Fierce birds . . .* ' those words pulled me back together again. They were just too funny. '*Fierce birds . . .* ' I could see them in my mind's eye: eagles and falcons – their fell swoops on unwary prey . . . I never did call ladies 'birds' but Pete meant extremely well with his words of consolation.

I nodded "*Yes . . . that's true . . . and . . . you're right—I'll get over it sooner or later—but in the meantime . . .* "

In the meantime what? I had no idea.

"*Art School's gonna be great! You just wait. It'll be fantastic there – and you won't even think about any of this! Fuck that bastard Brigadier! Fuck his whingeing wife! Fuck 'em all!*"

What a concept. I always was literal – so Pete's expletives actually proved helpful in changing my mood. "*Yes . . . you're right . . . There probably—will—be a time when I won't think of any of this . . .* " then, silently, I added ' *. . . next century.*'

Pete wandered off to his next class and I picked up the DEBIL. I slid the chromium tube up the strings and it howled on my behalf.

When the train it left the station, there was two lights on behind, / When the train it left the station, there was two lights on behind, / Well the blue light was my blues and the red light was my mind, / All my love's in vain / All my love's in vain. Robert Johnson—All My Love in Vain—1935

10

starry dynamo in the machinery of night

*The carpetbagger stands there bragging 'bout his shares / He's running
with the hounds and chasing with the hares / He's displaying his evasions
here for everyone / As if his sly collusions weren't undone / I'm not gonna
wait to see the whole thing through / 'cause it's the 19th time it's looked
like déjà vu.*

Larkin/Bruce/Schubert—Savage Cabbage—Déjà Vu—Savoy Green—1970

The lads often talked about other bands – and sometimes word
would get back about the way we were viewed. Malcolm
Collinwood—lead player with *Measure for Measure*—considered
Ron unexciting. This didn't worry Ron.

"What's 'unexciting' s'posed to mean?" he asked almost rhetorically.

"It means that Malcolm Collingwood's musically ignorant . . . " I laughed
*" . . . and . . . not—*that*—bright."*

This flipped Ron's irritation into hilarity *"Well—*yeah*—we all
know that – but what's 'unexciting' mean to him?"*

"Psychoanalysing Neanderthals is outside my experience" I replied –
which had Ron in tears. After a while Ron resumed his line of
enquiry – so I proceeded to elaborate *"People think it's exciting
when guitarists riff high up the neck – but I think that's musically
juvenile"* Pause *"If you find eunuchs exciting . . . "* I chuckled
" . . . then you're a bit of a let down."

Ron had that face that wasn't sure what I was saying—so I went into detail *"If your idea of excitement is a castrato, then a tenor isn't that interesting – let alone a baritone. He probably finds my voice unexciting too."*

"So it's—where—I play on the neck that's unexciting?" I nodded my assent *"The great . . . steaming . . . pillock . . . "*

"Exactly" I emphasised *"Y'know . . . when my brother was 12 he'd always be turning up the treble on the record player. He grew out of it by the time he was 15 – Malcolm Collingwood's just never grown out of it."*

"That's an interesting point of view . . . " Ron replied *"I wouldn't have thought of it being to do with maturity or anything like that."*

"Well . . . I can't say for certain – but most people think that high frequency twittering is the closest thing to an orgasm. It may be lack of maturity . . . or it might just be cultural primitivism . . . "

"Lack of sophistication?" Ron suggested.

"Yeah—my father's the same—he likes to hear people hit high notes, as if it were some kind of accomplishment. It's nothing to do with voice quality. It's got more in common with all-in-wrestling—and enjoying seeing people being turned upside down and thrown out of the ring. It's all to do with primitive spectacle. That's why I'm not interested in people playing guitars behind their backs or destroying instruments or any of that stuff. To me . . . the high end of the neck is where you go to impress people – it's like Gazzer on his long-scale bass – squeezing his adjectival lemon high on the **G** *string."* [1]

"Like limbo dancing in reverse . . . " Ron jeered *" . . . not how—low—can—you—go? It's how—high—can—you—go? What—is—wrong—with these bloody people?"*

---

1 The G string is the highest pitched string in on a 4 string bass guitar.

"*Popular culture I think . . . There's always some tenor Opera singer who's the latest to be called 'The King of the High* **Cs**' *– as if being able to sing high notes is glamorous.*"

Ron nodded "*Yeah what about an 'Emperor of the Deep Effing* **E***'?*"

That had me convulsed. I wasn't used to Ron playing with language in that way "*You keep on like that Ron and you'll be a song writer before I make a bass player. Anyhow, I'm certain it's a primitive level of appreciation. Besides which, fast playing high up the neck is easier because the frets are closer together – so it doesn't really represent dexterity either.*"

Ron mentioned the popularity of screamers in Rock. "*Led Zeppelin had gone in for it as well since they left Blues for Rock* " he sneered.

"*I wonder if my vocal range is a handicap? I mean – I can't scream can I . . .* "

"*I'll break y'bloody nose if you ever start screaming*" Ron reassured me "*Screamers are for teenage audiences*" Pause "*Thing is . . . most people have lousy speakers. If your speaker can't handle bass – then you get a muddy effect. That's why people go for the treble end. Most people hear Pop through radios and the music has to carry. If anyone produced bass-biased Pop – it wouldn't work on the tiny speakers in most radios.*"

That was a revelation. Everything—when you scratched the surface—was locked into commercial concerns. It went back in history too. Even Mozart had suffered the dictates of Moloch. There were always those who held the purse strings and those who had to follow the popular lead in order to put food on the table. In 1782 Mozart wrote and conducted an opera 'Die Entführung Aus Dem Serail', which exceeded—by far— the conventional limits of tradition with its elaborately extended librettos.

This elicited Austria's Emperor Joseph II's well-known banality *"Too many notes my dear Mozart."* Mozart was naturally bewildered by the Emperor's remark – as there were the exact number of notes required by genius – but as Bob Dylan put it *'Money doesn't talk, it swears.'*

To push fake morals, insult, and stare / While money doesn't talk, it swears / Obscenity, who really cares / Propaganda, all is phoney.
Bob Dylan—It's Alright Ma (I'm only Bleeding)—Bringing it All Back Home—1965

The other opinion about our band was that Steve was too elaborate on bass. His playing got in the way of the lead.

"That's what some people used to say about Jack Bruce though" said Ron *"Some people—including Ginger Baker—said he was 'too busy' on bass – that he overplayed."*

That was bewildering *"Right 'Too many notes my dear Bruce.' How the hell can you overplay?"*

Ron set out to inform me. I could tell I was in for information because he made a certain shift in his chair *"Well – it's all a question of how you see the rôle of bass. Most people see bass as a rhythm instrument rather than a melody instrument. From this point of view bass is supposed to work hand-in-hand with percussion – and play at a lower volume than lead. Having the bassist play lead is fine if you've got a great percussionist like Ginger Baker – but . . . Our Jack [2] needs some help from the bass. His percussion can't stand alone without bass supplying rhythm as well. Of course, that's where—you—come in."*

---

2 Jack Hackman was often referred to as 'Our Jack' in order to distinguish him from 'Their Jack' – i.e. Jack Bruce.

Ron gave a fiendish grin *"That's—*your*—rôle now. I thought it was crazy at first – but the 'two bass line-up' makes total sense with Steve playing six string bass as a second lead instrument.*[3] *It's a genius move – as I've told you before. Don't know why no one else has thought of it. Don't know why I didn't believe it would work earlier – especially as you've wanted to play bass since you first heard one. How long ago—*was*—that?"*

I knew exactly *"Since I was 12."*

Ron looked as if he was undergoing slight self-recrimination and so I interrupted as he was on the edge of speaking *"I'm playing bass now – so I'm as happy as it's possible to be without Lindie Dale."*

Ron grinned *"I'll sell you that* EB3 *just as soon as I get something arranged about getting a* GIBSON ES355. *I just need to know how much money I need."*

Why wait—I thought *"Ron – just tell me the price and I'll hand over the readies. It might take me a couple of weeks – but I needn't keep you waiting. I've got things I could sell."*

Ron considered for a moment *"I'd rather wait. For one thing I don't want to charge you too much. In fact, I'd rather just give it to you – but I need to discuss things with my parents. They're sometimes touchy about me buying and selling. Anyhow I want to give you the best deal I can – so don't sell anything yet."*

The moment had come. The instrument was mine—to all intents and purposes—and I immediately shelved several plans and trips to London to buy albums. Albums could wait.

---

3 Steven Myatt—in his Jack Bruce biography entitled 'Jack'—quotes Bob Brunning *(of Brunning Sunflower Blues Band)* as saying that Cream ' . . . *might have benefited from a fourth member . . . playing conventional, 'invisible' bass alongside Ginger, disappearing into the rhythm, and allowing Eric and Jack to alternate lead and rhythm guitar down in front of the stage.'* Chapter 10, page 138.

*A tailor sews a seamstress out on the ballroom floor / While I'm chasing
down the daylight to contravene the law, / There's an orchestra of jugglers
– they're playing dice with fate, / The show's begun and it won't be long
before the floodgates break.*
Larkin/Bruce/Schubert—Savage Cabbage—Before the Floodgates Break—Savoy Green—1970

After thanking Ron effusively for his wise decision – I returned
to pondering "*Our Jack's never been heavy on bass drum—he's a big
cymbals enthusiast—so I suppose I must fill in for the bass drum.*"

"*Especially because his bass drum isn't amplified . . .* " Ron nodded
" *. . . you can hardly hear it . . . course Ginger Baker had two bass drums
– and provided more than enough rhythm for Jack Bruce to be inventive.
Our Jack produces a bloody deluge of treble because his unamplified bass
drum can't compete with the volume level of the band. Jack's going to need
to do something about that at some point though . . . because even with you
on bass he's too tinselly.*"

"*Yes—that's true—but . . . I think that might be a little unfair. Y'know
me – I've never been that keen on heavy percussion and I think Jack's got
quite an exciting sound – I've not heard anyone else work the cymbals quite
so much—not even Ringo—and I think that's something that makes him
stand out.*"

"*Yeah alright . . .* " Ron agreed " *. . . but I'd like to get a little more
guts from him nonetheless . . . That means money of course, and that'll put
his parent's knickers in a twist.*"

Jack's never getting amplification was fine by me. I thought the
volume of his drumming was right where it should be. I've
never enjoyed loud percussion – no matter how fine. Steve
thought as I did – that percussion shouldn't be intrusive. I felt
that Ron was probably right though. In the final analysis, Ron
was *always* right.

The Larkin's Steinway grand stood in the music room where
Ron kept his guitars. A music room – I was awestruck when I
first entered that environment in 1967. Fortunately I'd been
brought up to be unusually polite and so his parents liked me.
I was 'tranquil' and I seemed to be a peaceful influence on Ron.
He never got agitated when I was around. He never got irate
about anything I did or said. That hadn't been the case with
other friends – so I came as some sort of minor miracle of
composure. I was welcome any time. Ron had been sitting at
the piano during our discussion. He launched into a piece from
Bach's 'Well Tempered Clavier' and I sat back and listened
with delight.

"Y'know . . . " I said *" . . . if that was played on two saxophones . . .
tenor and bass . . . I bet most people would think it was avant-garde Jazz."*

Ron chuckled *"You should be going to Music College . . . If it wasn't
for the fact that you missed the boat with music lessons . . . you could
have . . . "* Ron noticed my expression and changed tack
*"Yeah . . . well . . . you're going to Art School and you're the man who's
going to paint amazing album sleeves – like that portrait of Hendrix."*

"Yeah Ron . . . " I grinned in response *" . . . there'll be time to learn
more music along the way – and you can show me anything I need to
know."*

Ron started playing another piece from Bach's 'Well Tempered
Clavier' and I listened in complete contentment. Then Ron
threw some changes on the piece – and it slowly and almost
imperceptibly turned into Blues – but with guitar riffs instead of
the more familiar rolling boogie. This is what Ron had told me
he was working on and I lay back in the copious armchair
allowing myself to be thoroughly drenched by the beauty of
Ron's improvisation.

The Larkin's music room felt like some kind of home and their support of Ron's musical endeavours was a symbol of the perfection that life should be. Everyone should have the opportunity to learn music and everyone should have the opportunity to see that life is more than it's mainly presented as being.

The only thing that raised concern in Ron's parents was his being 'on the road' with the band as often as we were. The number of gigs had been escalating and I started detecting some sense of caution being expressed. In answer to an oblique question from Mrs Larkin, I assured her that I remained committed to going to Art School for the next four years and that Steve was going to Music College. I told her that I didn't know what Jack had in mind. She seemed somehow mollified by that – but I wondered about the nature of her concern. I concluded that it must have something to do with school homework – but that was not a satisfactory answer being that Ron's lowest marks were over 80%. I mentioned it to Ron, as I was slightly disconcerted by his mother's enquiry – tentative though it was.

"*Yeah—well—she's always worried about me getting enough sleep. She's big on sleep. She'd just rather we didn't do the Sunday night gigs – and I've more-or-less gone along with that.*" Ron looked to me for some kind of approval.

"*It's not unreasonable – I know that you three need to be up for School*" I said with a friendly shrug. What couldn't be helped couldn't be helped.

"*So you don't mind?*" Ron asked – in a grateful manner that seemed slightly unusual.

"Well of course I—mind—Ron. I'd play gigs every night of the week if I could – but I don't resent it. I'd really—not—want to upset your parents. I'd like everything to roll on in the best way for all of us – and that's not possible if your parents get irate. I mean – look at Jack's parents and what I have to put up with there. They won't even have me in the house and they're obnoxious when I phone."

Ron appreciated my candour *and* my diplomacy.

"Thanks a lot" he replied *"I know that gigs mean a lot to you – especially . . . well . . . with how it went with Lindie—gigs must take your mind off . . . "* Ron came to an abrupt halt as if he'd said too much.

"Yeah . . . well . . . that's true Ron – and . . . it's good of you to think about it like that . . . but life goes on. I'll have to get over Lindie before I get to Art School. I want that to be a fresh start. I want to arrive there feeling . . . lively and ready to roll. You and Steve'll be at Music College and gigs'll stop completely for a while anyway."

Ron smiled reassuringly *"We—will—get the occasional gig in the College holidays you know. I'll have a car soon and we can visit. We'll all need to keep practising and maybe there'll be the odd gig in Leeds and certainly London."*

Ron was obviously concerned about me and—for a moment—I found it almost unbearably touching. *"It'll be fine Ron—it'll all be fine—we've got a good future. I don't know about Jack though . . . "*

Ron made a gesture of mild exasperation. *"Yeah . . . Jack . . . I don't know—what—to make of Jack sometimes. He has—no—idea where he's going or what he's going to do with his life. He thinks that Savage Cabbage is his 'superstar exit' from his poxy parents and Synthetic Cynthia – and that's a problem as far as Savage Cabbage goes. He wants to quit everything else and escape – but the rest of us are taking our time in order to build something better than a teenage band . . . but . . . "*

241

Ron shook his head wearily " . . . *if Jack can't get out—that—way he'll probably go back to Cynthia.*" I wrinkled my forehead. Ron noticed "*Yeah she's still a possibility y'know.*"

"*No . . . I thought he—*made—*his decision*" I exclaimed.

"*Right Frank—well yeah—if you'd made the decision it would've been made . . . but Jack . . . *" Pause "*I know he made his stand – but I don't think it'd take much for all that to collapse. He's not like us. He's a good bloke and I like him – but he's weak. He wouldn't opt for sleeping under a hedge or anything – like you told y'father.*" Ron chuckled "*That still makes me laugh.*"

"*You really think he'd go back to Cynthia after—*all—*he said?*" I was incredulous.

"*I think he would. All it would take would be some sort of calamity and he'd run for cover.*"

I found this intriguing "*I thought—I—was supposed to be the philosopher.*"

"*Well you are – it's just that you don't see faults in other people unless they're hitting you with a cricket bat. I mean – you'd have run off with that Swiss au pair girl if she'd asked you, wouldn't you?*"

"*Yeah . . . I have to admit that I could've done . . . but for the fact that it wouldn't have got me to Art School – and that would have been stupid – and of course there were you, Steve and Jack.*" There'd have been no way I'd have walked out on Savage Cabbage.

"*Point is . . . it wouldn't have been—*fear—*that held you back.*"

"*No . . . it wouldn't have been fear . . . I'd never let—*that—*stand in my way. Once you do that you're dead.*"

When you got no more assurance than a great big hunk of lead / If you don't respond to romance, Jack, you're dead.

Jordan Louis—Jack You're Dead—1947

Ron made his usual 'didn't I tell you so' gesture "*You see – that's the difference. You're not desperate like Jack . . . but you*—will—*dive in at the deep end if it's what you want. That's why*—you're—*the philosopher. You can make those decisions about life and live with them*—without—*getting enraged. Like that*—bastard—*Brigadier Dale . . . I'd have bought a machine gun or stuck a landmine in his nice gravel drive.*"

"*So anyway . . .* " I said with exasperation "*What*—about—*Jack? What*—can—*we do to help him?*"

Ron shrugged "*I've no idea. We can't live his life for him – and with Steve and me gone there's not much you can do on your own. There'll be no cosy evenings for you round at the happy Hackmans.*"

I cracked my knuckles one by one as if it would summon up some bright idea. "*I suppose . . . he'll stay around here. He's not bound for university anywhere.*" Jack wasn't dim by any means – but he wasn't academic. He wasn't inspired either. "*Nothing at school interests him . . . and somehow*—like me—*he missed the boat with music.*"

Ron shook his head to suggest otherwise "*Steve told me he could've taken music. Jack can be a bone idle sod sometimes. He had the opportunity to catch up with extra classes and if he'd done that he could have taken music all the way through like Steve and I did.*" I hadn't known that so exactly before . . . "*Yeah*—I mean would you've taken that option?*"

It wasn't even a question "*Absolutely. I offered to sit in with the 1ˢᵗ years and take every music class going.*"

Ron grimaced in frustration "*Yeah, like I said*—that's—*the difference between you and Jack.*"

"*Jack's worked extremely hard on drumming over the last year.*"

243

"*Yeah . . .*" Ron agreed " *. . . Jack can do it when he puts his mind to it – but the end of the Summer term's his jump-off-point to nowhere as far as I can see.*"

I had some slightly more hopeful feeling and ventured "*We'll probably meet up at the Art School and get some sessions in. I'll be getting the* GIBSON *EB0 soon and—as soon as you're ready to sell—the EB3. Maybe there'll be some other musicians and we can jam—but I don't know what'll happen when I leave for wherever. I don't fancy staying in Farnham and taking my Art degree there. I'd rather try Leeds Art School or the RCA in London as you're going to the RCM.[4] The RCA would be great—it'll be easy to play Kooks Kleek and The Marquee Club. We've got the contacts now – and maybe we could play as a duo from time to time.*"

"*Yeah . . . sounds like a good idea*" Ron replied – not exactly convinced.

I still didn't answer the question that hung over Jack "*I wouldn't like Jack to just fall away or something. I like Jack—and I can see him turning into a great percussionist—but he's . . .* "

Ron finished the sentence for me " *. . . he's lost. He hasn't got a clue what he wants to do. I think he'd jump for the band as a profession if it wasn't for us three going to College. I think he'll just get a job somewhere —marry Cynthia—and sit at home watching the sodding television.*"

"*That's what worries me . . .* " I said grimly " *. . . and—that's—what I want to avoid.*"

Ron wrinkled his nose "*It wouldn't surprise me if we were looking for a drummer by the time we leave College.*"

---

4 RCM is the 'Royal College of Music' and the RCA is the 'Royal College of Art'.

That was a horrible thought – and, although I agreed with the factuality of Ron's view, I decided internally to do anything in my power to save Jack from himself.

Ron picked up his 12 string F<small>RAMUS</small> and starting picking out ideas for lead riffs that would work with Willie Dixon's 'That Same Thing'. It wasn't long before Ron had something quite clever worked out and I pulled out a few harps to see which would work best. I settled on slant [5] with my **A** harp and it worked well. We played the song through and we both liked the way it sounded.

"Harp's perfect with that song" Ron commented.

"We'll have to play it for Steve so he can work on the bass riff."

Ron laughed *"That's more your field now isn't it?"*

I must have looked confused because Ron raised his voice *"Go on then – plug in the* EB3 *and see what you can do."*

I reached over—took the G<small>IBSON</small> EB3 from its stand—and plugged it into the amplifier. *"Start here and move up to here . . . right . . . then come down – something like that."*

Ron gave some vague indications as to frets by pointing. He knew I had no idea of where an **A**^{b} or a **C**$^{\#}$ might be located. I knew how to tune strings but it was all vague from there on. I just played by ear. Ron just kept playing the melody line and I fiddled around 'til something seemed to work.

"Y'know—Frank—I think you've already got a style. You're slow and awkward on new material—don't take this wrong, you just need to learn music—but you're definitely interesting . . . and quite different from Steve."

---

5 Slant harp is used predominantly in Blues where the harp plays a second higher than the key in which the song is set. Cross harp is where the harp plays a fourth higher.

"There's a touch of Jazz in how you play when you're confident of the bass line" Ron continued *"It's your timing – it's really quite distinctive . . . you leave . . . rests where I wouldn't expect rests . . . and . . . it takes a lot to do something I don't expect."*

We talked the morning away. It wasn't often I had a free Saturday morning – but I'd been on sick leave from the Army Kitchen with a scalded arm. The doctor had kindly given me a month off and I was making the most of it.

Ron seemed especially pleased I'd called 'round – as there was some notion that Steve and I had been friends since the Jurassic period. I got the feeling that Ron was enjoying the sense that our friendship had grown into something that stood on its own. For my part I valued Ron as highly as I valued Steve. They were a remarkable pair and each played a crucial rôle in my life. They each brought me on in different ways – and I was increasingly aware that our time together was running out and so I wanted to spend as much time with them as I could. I'd ride over to Steve's in the afternoons and we'd all get together in the evenings.

On my third free weekend Mr Larkin commented on the weight of our equipment—the amplifiers had grown in size—and said something about being careful when we lifted them. He'd directed this at Ron – but I said *"I do most of the lifting with Steve— it only takes two—and we enjoy it anyway."*

Ron's father smiled blandly *"Steve—is—quite a strong lad . . . and you look as if you could do more than your fair share. You're both considerably stronger than . . . "* the inconclusive sentence ended abruptly. I noticed Ron's expression harden. Mr Larkin also noticed his son's expression and continued unconvincingly *" . . . stronger than most. It must be a tough life for those who have to make their living . . . that way."*

246

I agreed – but my agreement was met with a slightly peculiar non-response. It was as if something had happened – but I had no idea what it was. There was some connection with Ron and lifting and I wondered if Ron was prone to a bad back. He'd never mentioned it – so I was perplexed. Steve and I often joked with Ron about his fingers when we took charge of the carrying.

"Can't have you damaging those fingers – they're our ticket to glory . . . " I thought my comment would be well received by Mr Larkin – but he nodded peremptorily and said he'd leave us to our music.

Ron was evidently highly annoyed with his father. *"Tough life— right—like being a fucking merchant banker's a doddle. Getting bloody ulcers is 'having an easy life' right? Music's not an easy life – but show me an easy life and I'll show you a gibbering jelly fish."*

It seemed necessary to defuse Ron so I added *" . . . or a three-toed sloth in carpet slippers perhaps?"* But Ron didn't laugh. He acknowledged what I'd said was amusing—with a nod of his head and an attempted smile—but he was clearly still irritated.

"Merchant banking . . . " he muttered *"I'd be more likely to die of sheer excitement."* Ron was too irate to eat his apple and just rolled it from hand to hand like a grenade.

"I wouldn't argue with that Ron. Trying to count my change is as much as I can do – merchant banking would kill me in a matter of days. Gigs— are—hard work though – and will be 'til we stop being our own roadies."

It would've been glorious to have walked off stage at the end of an evening without packing our gear. Sometimes enthusiasts would help – but you had to keep an eye on them to make sure their enthusiasm didn't extend to walking off with equipment. I was just glad I had a strong back.

Some people say a man's made out of mud / But a poor man's made out of muscle and blood / Muscle and blood, skin and bone, / A mind that's weak and a back that's strong.
Merle Travis—Sixteen Tons—1946—performed by Tennessee Ernie Ford—1955

I told Steve about the unsettling encounter with Mr Larkin and the unlikely comment Mrs Larkin made the week before. Steve scratched his head with both hands in the way he had just before he launched into a problematic subject.

"I think . . . " he commenced after due consideration *" . . . that Ron's parents worry about him – but I don't know why. It's not the drug scene or anything like that – but there's something that makes them edgy."*

"D'you ever pick up on any worry from your parents about gigs and lifting heavy amps?"

"No not at all. They're happy I get some exercise." Steve was inclined to put on weight. *"Humping amps is a bit like weight lifting. My father even said he'd get me some weights so that I'd have a bit more muscle for lifting."*

The thing that foxed us both was the fact that Ron's parents seemed strangely protective of him. Ron, although thin, was wiry – even though he never played sport. For mysterious reasons he'd opted out of sport completely at school. He'd used the time for music practise and we wondered how he'd swung such a good deal. Steve had tried to get a similar situation at Farnham Grammar – but it had not been permitted.

"It's probably because he goes to a private school" suggested Steve *"I suppose if your parents are paying – you get to pick and choose."*
That made sense – but most parents thought sport was a fine thing for a young lad. There was no sense to be made of it and asking Ron was not a good idea. It was a subject that rubbed him the wrong way.

Ron's parents eventually came to realise that I was serious about the band as my ultimate career. Ron must have let something slip in terms of my being at Art School and designing our album sleeves – and I came to be seen as a fly in the ointment. Ron's parents became disgruntled with the fact that I received music lessons from their son. They paid for Ron's music lessons and there was no reason why my parents shouldn't pay for mine. Well . . . there was a reason – they couldn't afford it. Ron told his parents he wanted to give me lessons—I hadn't asked him for them—he'd volunteered. They backed off a little at that – but gave him grave warnings about the Rock'n'Roll industry. It was high risk, high voltage, high stress, and illegal highs that ended in death. I wasn't banned from visiting but the Larkins were no longer as warm and welcoming. I no longer called round unexpectedly.

Ron's parents started making noises about Music College at this point – and the suggestion of going to the LSE [6] and joining his father in merchant banking was posited as the preferable choice. This incensed Ron to the point that his parents backed off. Ron wasn't openly angry with his parents—but they could tell when his pressure gauges swung into the red—and took it as the point to back off. I'd seen it myself on two occasions and wondered at the strangeness of it. It was as if his anger held some peculiar power over them. They accepted his preference for RCM over the LSE and Ron's tight lipped fury abated. On the occasions I'd witnessed tension – I'd stared out of the window, pretending I wasn't there. I'd waited for Ron to suggest retiring to the music room – and followed on as if I were invisible.

---

6 London School of Economics.

"It's all arranged anyhow!" snapped Ron *"They can't go changing everything round now. I'm going to the* RCM *and that's the end of it!"*

It seemed that Ron had to restate his case to me privately as a matter of honour – as an acknowledgement that the future was going to be as he'd determined it. I'd just nodded – hyper-aware of parental ears in the adjoining room.

There were plenty of things that made Ron angry. He got quite angry with the organisers at Eel Pie Island. It was our 3rd gig there and Ron was not happy with the publicity and the financial deal. I had to talk him down from a high pitch of annoyance.

"We—know—*the deal now "* I told Ron *"Next time we'll make sure the arrangement's watertight in advance. We're learning the ropes – and we were bound to get cheated from time to time."*

That calmed Ron down. It calmed Steve and Jack too.

On the way home Jack chuckled *"I think you're the shrink of the band. We'd sometimes be ripping people's heads off if you didn't cool us down."*

Steve and Ron laughed about that for a straight ten minutes and we all felt better for it.

The gig—in spite of the organisational problems—went extremely well, and in the end management promised a better deal when we played again. We'd warmed up for Rory Gallagher and Taste and the crowd were entirely with us. We'd all worried about coming on before another Blues band – because sometimes the warm up band is ignored.

Before we went on however, Rory Gallagher caught sight of Ron on stage silently riffing on his TELECASTER and asked him if he'd like to plug into a big amplifier. Ron thanked him and took advantage of the offer.

Then Rory Gallagher uncased his Stratocaster and suggested they play together. He obviously had a duel in mind.[7] It was pyrotechnic – and the audience were spellbound by it. I'd never heard Ron play wild, crazy, and all-out-fast before. People were still arriving—as the show hadn't commenced—but the atmosphere was charged. The two guitar heroes came to a natural conclusion—laughed maniacally—and congratulated each other.

A few people had told us afterward that it was a great evening. They'd not expected two main acts. *"That's what I like to hear!"* Jack exclaimed with delight *"We're really rolling now – by next year . . ."*

Ron never let him finish *"By next year what? By next year I'll be at College and so will Frank and Steve. Don't get me wrong Jack—this has been fantastic—and you're really coming on. You were good tonight and there's not really so much difference between you and the drummer in Taste. But we don't want to charge at this and get into a mess."*

I could see Jack twitching slightly and thought I'd better say something *"Really—Ron's right—there's no rush about this. I really don't believe there's anyone better out there – not as far as British bands go. Three years or so is going to let us break onto the scene with some extremely solid material. Ron and I have been working on some Willie Dixon songs and we've worked out a fierce riff to 'That Same Thing'. I'd like to be able to do that with his whole repertoire – but that'll take time. Just imagine following the six album set of Robert Johnson songs with all Willie Dixon's slow numbers."*

Steve hooted wildly *"We'd go down in history for that."*

---

7 Rory Gallagher liked to stage duels with his own band members at that time.

Ron grinned wolfishly *"Right – but that's a monumental task. To do that with—every—song and make each one a seminal work would take a few bloody years. You wouldn't want to rush a thing like that – and y'know . . . I'm not even sure it's possible. That's like painting 60 steaming Mona Lisas in a row."*

Jack shook his head in disbelief *"This is the man who just won the guitar duel with Rory Gallagher. It's written—mate—it's written. It's going to happen. There's no stopping us."*

Jack was highly excited and Ron was highly wary. *"Jack . . . I'm gonna tell you something. I didn't—win—anything. We just had some fun on stage. Rory Gallagher just had to work a littler harder than he expected. He's a—very—good player. It wasn't a question of anyone winning or losing – we both called it quits and had a good laugh."*
But Jack wouldn't have it that Ron wasn't the victor.

"Ron's right . . . " I declared in a determined manner *"Ron wasn't the victor – I'm the only 'Victor' round here."*

Even Jack thought the quip worthy of a laugh – and it terminated the subject of who won the duel. Ron nodded at me extremely slightly to indicate that he was grateful that I'd managed to change the subject. We all seemed to have our rôles within the band – and one of my rôles was to keep everyone from exploding when situations were exploitative or mistakes were made. They came to rely on me for that – and I had no idea how I'd gotten myself into that situation. It wasn't that I couldn't get irritated – but I never let it take me over.

It began to get tricky as more rumbling noises were emanating from Ron's parents. *"Teenage fun is one thing – but this is another"* Ron's father had opined. It was time to ease up – especially as examinations were fast approaching.

Jack told Steve and me "*I'm completely bloody flummoxed. Why—exactly—are Ron's parents worried about the exams? He gets A grades all the time for everything and it's hardly going to make any difference if he puts in more hours. How much higher can you get anyway? 'A' to the power of bloody 16?*" This remark had us in tears.

"*You may laugh*" Jack continued "*but my bloody grades are abysmal in English and I'm going to have to work like a maniac in every subject. It sometimes pisses me off the way Ron just sails through.*"

It wasn't useful to feel resentful. "*Yeah Jack – but you have to remember, that's part of why he's such a brilliant guitarist*" I shrugged "*I wish I was bright as well – but . . .*"

Fortunately that made Jack laugh "*You're not bloody stupid Mr Arbuthnot. It's just that you refuse to do—*anything—*you don't want to do.*" I couldn't argue with that. "*It's all well and good being a bloody anarchist if you're going to Art School – but where am I going?*" Steve and I exchanged a glance. Jack turned to Steve and added "*You're going to Music College and—*you—*get good grades without too much bloody effort.*"

Steve pointed out that he was a year older than us – which accounted for his apparent ease of study. I was finding this school grades business a little tiresome but thought it churlish to yawn. I decided to pull out my harp instead and blow some slow, quiet, mournful Blues. Jack and Steve stopped talking and sat listening 'til I'd sucked my final deep warbling note.

"*Thing is . . .*" I said "*. . . none of us have completely easy situations. Steve and Ron had several ladies walk out on them because of the band – and . . . well . . . you know about my situation . . . 'she gone and left me, she's gone to stay – well she's gone, but I don't worry, because . . . '*I'm sitting here with you fellows—and—an unfinished glass of Beaujolais.*"

It didn't take much to change Jack's mood – and we thankfully left the subject of school grades behind. We didn't quite know it as clearly as we should have done – but we were *all* sitting on top of the world. Life was not perfect – but some parts of it were ferociously good. Being on stage was a side step into eternity for each of us. Whatever was happening outside those pools of perfection couldn't intrude. It felt as if we occupied the lofty heights of Cream at those times. *". . . and in some sense . . ."* I said with reference to being like Cream *" . . . what's the difference?"*

Jack put on his let me explain face *" Big venues, big money, albums, American tours—and—groupies."*

Yes . . . that—*was*—a big difference. *"I'll take the venues, money, albums, and American tours – but I'll refer the groupies to you Jack. They wouldn't interest me – unless they were good conversationalists."*

Jack shook his head *"It'd take your mind off Lindie."* The room went quiet for moment and I looked Jack in the eye and replied *"No Jack . . . it—would—not."*

Jack recognised that this was the end of the subject – and that he'd overstepped the mark with me. It took a lot to vex me but Jack managed it from time to time. I realised that he was feeling uncomfortable so I said *"But . . . making albums . . . now that would be a thing. Being in a studio and being able to record 'backwards guitar' with bass as well as lead – that would absorb my interest for months at a time."*

Steve's face brightened noticeably *"Albums . . . that would be really fantastic – and the technology's exploding. By the time we're finished with College it'll be astonishing and we'll be able to develop ideas at College that'll set us up for that. We'll be the Beatles, Cream, Bob Dylan, and Jimi Hendrix rolled into one. We'll be able to orchestrate – like Frank's idea about contrabassoons and . . . "*

The conversation rolled from that point into increasingly giddier heights where sounds knew no limits. If Ron had been there he would have added a sense of realism – but as he wasn't we all pushed the boat out as far as we could take it. It never stopped being exhilarating – and there was something utterly obvious about the fact that we were the happening thing and that stardom was assured at some point. The only regrettable aspect of this was that Lindie knew I was bound for stardom – and it was that very direction which made me an impossible option.

"Stardom's quite a prospect isn't it" Steve stated almost rhetorically.

"Yeah . . . and there seems to be an unstoppable quality to it" I replied.

"So . . . " Steve began on a different note *"Would you give up stardom for Lindie Dale?"*

"Can't honestly say – can I? It was never on the cards" Pause *"She said she couldn't live with herself if I gave up something so important – because I might come to regret it"* Pause *"She also said you, Ron and Jack depended on me . . . and I couldn't walk out on you for her sake. And . . . that's true – I couldn't"* I was perilously close – either to swearing violently or bursting into tears – but I did neither *"This—is—the —thing—about—life that—I—find insane!"* Pause *"There was nothing I could say when she said that."*

"Yeah . . . " Steve sighed.

"I had this vision you see . . . " I continued *" . . . of something that'd work for everyone."*

"Yeah—well—it's possible to ruin good situations y'know."

"I know . . . but I thought that if you weren't selfish and always acted in a kind generous way . . . what could go wrong?" I sighed *"Well now I know, 'cause the whole situation with Lindie went about as wrong as anything can go."*

If today was Christmas Eve and tomorrow was Christmas Day, / All I would need is my little sweet rider, Just to pass the time away, / To pass the time away. Robert Johnson—Hellhound On My Trail—1937

"Maybe Percy Gordon was right – and I—am—*an imbecile"*
I chuckled mirthlessly.

"No Vic . . . life—is—*just as simple as you feel it*—should—*be. It's just that things go wrong sometimes . . . and there's no fixing them"*
Steve replied.

"I might've considered a haircut . . . " I moaned. Steve nodded, grimacing in expectation of what was coming. " . . . *it's what my father would've recommended – and . . . he'd have been right."* Steve waited quietly as I continued *"Could've got some spectacles without blue lenses – wouldn't have cost a fortune."*

Steve decided it was time to curtail me *"Y'know, it's pointless to whip yourself. If you want whipping I'd be happy – I've got a length of garden hose that would do the job a treat."* [8]

That was funny enough to make me laugh. Steve knew how to derail my maudlin maundering. He'd done that on previous occasions when I'd bent his ear on the subject of Lindie.

"Yeah . . . you're right . . . my mother would still have been 'a German'. My father would still be a wartime Major – and I'd still be working class."

These wretched ideas had been chasing each other's tails through my head for days – and, sitting there with Steve, I realised that nothing would have made any difference.

"It's—as it is—*isn't it . . . and there's*—nothing—nothing—*that could've been any different."*

---

8 British expression meaning 'perform the task exceptionally well'.

Steve agreed emphatically *"Right! Anyway . . . you can't turn yourself upside down and inside out to suit her parents' prejudices – especially when the changes would've been so bloody impossible. You know . . . my parents are fairly conservative in a lot of ways – but they like you. They always—have—liked you."*

That made me laugh again – because a thought crossed my mind *"Well sure Steve—I appreciate that—but maybe that's because I don't want to marry you."*

We both roared with laughter. Steve said he was glad I had a sense of humour.

"I should've—known—Brigadier Dale would sooner let his daughter marry an adjectival mercenary than take up with me. Anyway . . . the alternative to laughing is—extremely—dreary. Life's too short for that."

And I'm so glad, and I am glad, I am glad, I'm glad / I don't know what to do, don't know what to do, I don't know what to do, / I'm tired of weeping, tired of moaning, tired of groaning for you.
Nehemiah Curtis 'Skip' James—I'm So Glad—1931

There were many things I didn't know – that I *should* have known. Ron's parents obviously knew about his medical condition – but I didn't know. I should have known that Ron's parents were simply looking after him as best they could. It seemed obvious later that Ron knew about his condition. There were so many clues—in hindsight—that pointed to the fact that Ron knew his parents had his health as their primary concern when they chivvied him about the band and staying up too late.

It seemed insane in retrospect that all this was hidden from his friends – but maybe that was the way that Ron wanted it. Ron was a force of nature and although he evidently loved and respected his parents – there were definite sticking points with him. We were similar in that respect. That's why we understood each other so well. We could both be adamant.

Ron remained insistent about Music College. Steve and I both knew that Ron's parents weren't over the moon about the RCM. They'd acquiesced only because he'd be near his elder brother.

It was a time of such promise and success for Ron – but the tension with his parents about the band and Music College must have placed him under enormous pressure. I saw signs that all was not well – but I'd seen Ron looking haggard before. I knew these things passed. I thought that all would be well when the dust settled – but fate overtook him.

Ron died of a heart attack before he reached his 18th year. It wasn't long after our Wrecclesham gig. That's the last picture I have of Ron. It's imprinted in my mind. We'd finished the gig with 'Spoonful'. I'd thrown out my usual lines to the audience and when I'd spun—gesturing at Ron—to call out *'Lightning Ron Larkin, the*—main—*man, on lead guitar!'* Ron grinned at me. He nodded—and narrowed his left eye in *that way that he had*— indicating with a gesture of his forefinger that my performance on rhythm bass was now met with his approbation. I had arrived at last. It still seems like yesterday. Like an hour ago. A millisecond million watt halogen bulb—like the sun— impressed his expression into my visual memory. I'd finally made it—right there at the end—and Savage Cabbage never played again.

I saw the best minds of my generation destroyed by madness . . .
angelheaded hipsters burning for the ancient heavenly connection to the
starry dynamo in the machinery of night.
Author's abridgement—from Howl—Allen Ginsberg—1959

Something staggering had occurred. Steve and I knew it. Savage Cabbage had been an enormous possibility – but Ron's death was the final curtain call. We couldn't play without him.

The idea of finding another lead guitarist wasn't even discussed. We knew it was over. I saw Steve as much as before – but Jack dropped out of contact. When Steve and I met we'd talk about Ron – but we never said anything about what we'd do next or where we'd go in terms of a band. We were too desolate to talk about the future in those terms. There was no point in generating ideas. Any thought of speaking about a band without Ron would have seemed like a betrayal of friendship and a betrayal of what he was as a musician. Ron was irreplaceable. Life would have to take care of itself. Time would have to pass.

We weren't invited to Ron's funeral. We didn't know at that time that you didn't have to be invited to funerals. We never knew when the funeral was held or what the exact circumstances of his death were – beyond the fact that he'd had a heart attack at home. I was stunned—utterly wretched—for . . . how long? I cannot remember.

Steve died a month later – at the age of 19. He was a year and nine months older than me – Ron nine months younger.

He blew his mind out in a car, he didn't notice that the lights had changed.
Lennon/McCartney—A Day in the Life—Sgt. Pepper's Lonely Hearts Club Band—1967

Some musical heroes and heroines of *the lost time* fell by the wayside through insane full-flight experimentation – some through simple physiological mishaps and accidents. Steve Bruce took out three street lights before his car came to rest upside down with flames guttering through the windows. The news filtered through in dribs and drabs. His father was in the car. No one knew who was driving. It was a multiple collision. It may have been one or two lamp posts – my memory of those details are vague.

I phoned my brother Græham in 2008 – and he confirmed *"Three lamp posts – it's so strange that I remember that . . . "* Said he had no idea where the information came from – it was just sitting there unattended in the back of his mind.

I rode to Steve's funeral – wondering if I'd have an accident on the way. It would be poetic. *"Third time lucky"* I sighed as I kick-started the pixie chariot. The thought of being the third victim of circumstances didn't worry me. I'd either live or die. It was all the same to me on that day.

Steve's mother had contacted me because she liked me. I expected to say comforting things to her – but I burst into tears. She comforted me instead – in spite of the fact that her husband and younger son had died. I thought I was adult and possessed of self control – but I felt like a child. The world had fallen apart around me. Nothing made sense. I found myself trying to find some kind of reason – even though I knew that the universe was entirely irrational. I tried to convince myself it was alright that life was senseless – but that resulted in my cerebral cortex hunkering down into a contracted block of ice. I peered out of bloodshot crevices at the apparent normality of existence. I was no longer a Blues hero – or any other kind of goddamn hero. There was no way I could sing about this—not yet at least—not for some time to come.

It would have been good to have played some Blues – but I couldn't have carried it off. The funeral was probably just one of those everyday funerals where the vicar says ' . . . *and now to the father—and to the son—and into the hole 'e goes.'* That is how I always heard it when my relatives died. I used to wonder at the pragmatism of it.

There were funerals throughout my childhood because my father was old enough to be my grandfather. It wasn't 'Four Weddings and a Funeral', it was more like 'forty funerals and no wedding'. Songs like 'Death Letter Blues' and 'Oh Death' seemed fairly normal to me.

Early one morning he'll come a creeping in the room, / And I know—Lord I know—my time ain't long. Charley Patton/Bertha Lee—Oh Death—1934—Jo Ann Kelly/Tony TS McPhee—Gasoline—1970

I have no memory of the funeral other than a blur of words. It was over seconds after it began. Then we were back at the Bruce household. Mark was in *foreign parts* – meeting a man from the motor trade. The relatives didn't know me. I sat in a chair in silence. No one approached me. I had no desire to be approached.

Much later it occurred to me that I'd not taken the 1959 GIBSON EB0 home with me. His mother hadn't thought of it. It was the last thing on her mind and I never asked. She had too much on her plate to think of guitars – and the birthday present that was to have been. There were relatives with whom to converse and an endless list of grim duties.

I saw the MARTIN sitting in the living room where Steve had left it. He must have been playing it shortly before his death as there was some sheet music propped up against it. I'd played it quite often at Steve's house. It wasn't that I desired it. It would have been a reminder – but like most guitars it had six strings missing. Cut a hole in the front and fill it with ferrotype diaphragms? No . . . that would've been a crime. I looked at it fondly. Maybe it was just as well.

Some years after the funeral, it occurred to me that I'd have liked to have had that MARTIN as a reminder of the songs we'd sung together and the ideas we'd had. We'd had so many conversations about music. We'd grown up with musical possibilities. We saw too much potential to enumerate it all or find avenues for it all.

Things in those days were either profoundly important or 'cheesecake visionary' – but whichever, you just picked up on a message and ran with it. You ran with it because *everyone who was anyone* was running with some message or some mission. Everyone was going somewhere with a glowing purpose. Everyone seemed to know what that *message* was, even though none of us knew *what it meant – beyond what it appeared to be*. It was illusion. Often serious illusion: illusion lived with integrity; illusion lived in desperation; illusion sandwich; illusion for breakfast, lunch, and dinner. Rolling and tumbling through vignettes of verve, vitality, and vainglorious vagaries. We'd been standing at the edge of the future and it looked overwhelmingly brilliant. We had poetry, music, and art all swirling around us. We had too many ideas and too little time to codify it all.

Now people I'm gonna tell you, as near as I can, / About the death of Leroy Carr, well he was my closest friend.
Amos Easton—Death of Leroy Carr—1935

Jack Hackman got engaged to Cynthia. I heard it through the grapevine: sold his drums—got a job at Midland Bank—and disappeared into the corporate world. Didn't hear of him again 'til years later – because his parents prohibited my calling, or even telephoning. He never answered letters. He mustn't have wanted to meet up with me anywhere else. Maybe telling me that he was back with Cynthia was too much to endure, in view of previous discussions.

I saw him briefly in the Nostril Cafe—early September '75—but our conversation was surreal. We were from two different solar systems. Jack had married Cynthia – but the marriage lasted little over a year. I listened to his story – and . . . it was what I would have expected. What he did after that ephemeral meeting, I never really knew. A friend of Lindie wrote to me— in 1988—that Jack was rumoured to be remarried – and that his son was a drummer. Happy thought indeed. I hoped it was true.

The auditorium is silent this Winter – there's a sign saying gone to the war / There's a cast iron journal of numbers that's bolted and chained to the floor / There's a limousine waiting for Christmas in a library dripping with sweat / I might take a look—but it ain't in my book—and I ain't going there yet. / There'll be endless skies of such beauty once you throw away all of the keys / So they can't tie me down—I won't stick around— I'm just a thread in the breeze

Larkin/Bruce/Schubert—Savage Cabbage—Just a Thread in the Breeze—Savoy Green—1970

In January 2005—whilst researching for '*an odd boy*'—I heard Jack had died in a hang-gliding accident back in 1990. There's a bolt. It keeps a hang-glider together. Hang-gliders call it 'The Jesus Bolt' – because when you lose that bolt . . . '*Jesus!*' is considered to be your last spoken word. I was sad to hear that news. The final link was lost.

Time to leave.

part three

july 1970 — september 1970

chapters one — six: living on solid air

John Martyn OBE

11th of September 1948 — 29th of January 2009

You've been living on solid air — you've been missing your sleep and you've been moving through solid air. / You've been walking on solid air; you've been taking your time — you've been walking on solid air. / You've been painting it blue — you've been living on solid air. / You've been seeing it through — and you've been living on solid air. / I know you, I love you; I'll be your friend, I could follow you—anywhere—even through solid air.
Solid Air—John Martyn—Solid Air—1973

"Very few people are trying to reach the heart these days . . . I feel strongly that there's a great dearth of the heart everywhere right now."
John Martyn—New Musical Express—1973

"On the 18th of September 2008 I received a letter about chapter 6 of Part III of an odd boy, which conveyed the words '. . . deeply touched by what you wrote . . . ' Then—on the 29th of January 2009—I received news that John Martyn had died in his home in Ireland. I will remember him as one of the most talented musicians and composers of the two centuries in which I have lived. He should have known far wider appreciation and recognition. There was no one like him."

The author

"John Martyn was so far ahead of everything else it was inconceivable."

Eric Clapton

Albums: *London Conversation—1968 / Road to Ruin—1968 / The Tumbler—1968 / Stormbringer—1970 / Bless the Weather—1971 / Solid Air—1973 / Inside Out—1973 / Sunday's Child—1974 / Live at Leeds—1976 / One World—1976 / Grace & Danger—1980 / Glorious Fool—1981 / Electric—1982 / Well Kept Secret—1982 / Philentropy—1983 / Sapphire—1984 / Piece by Piece—1986 / Apprentice—1990 / Cooltide—1991 / No Little Boy—1992 / The Church with One Bell—1998 / Glasgow Walker—2002*

1

march 1970 – early july 1970

the blenkinsopps

Who sank all night in submarine light of Bickford's floated out and sat . . . / Listening to the crack of doom on the hydrogen jukebox, / Who talked continuously seventy hours from park to pad to bar to Bellevue to museum to the Brooklyn Bridge, / A lost battalion of platonic conversationalists jumping down the stoops off fire escapes off windowsills off Empire State out of the moon . . . Abridged from Howl—Alan Ginsberg—1956

We have to slip back in time now . . . to a point before Ron and Steve returned to the sky. Hell, why not? I spent a few years wishing I was back before that terrible ante mortem vitæ pars.[1] It's not possible to describe my interview at Farnham Art School without stepping out of time.

So let's roll the clock back to March 1970 and take a vector that will lead into the world of Art – and the artists who took *the dark out of the nighttime and painted the daytime black.*[2]

Painting and drawing were a parallel track to Savage Cabbage. So this is a series of vignettes which describes my sitting in earshot of Allen Ginsberg's Jazz generation of Art students in Farnham '. . . *listening to the crack of doom on the hydrogen jukebox . . .*'

---

1 Ante mortem vitæ pars – before the death of the life of the party.
2 Bob Dylan—She Belongs to Me—Bringing it All Back Home—1965

Farnham Art School was founded by Lieutenant Colonel John Luard[3] in 1866. One hundred and four years later in March 1970—just prior to my Art School interview—I sat in the little café in West Street opposite that marvellous building. I looked out of the café window at the drizzling rain. Cars squelched by occasionally sending up a fine spray of oily water.

I don't dislike drizzle – but its effect on cardboard can leave something to be desired. My folio—already damp—was propped against the radiator and seemed to be drying nicely. Life was just about to change gear.

This was the café where the Beatniks sat and drank weak English coffee for hours – discussing poetry and Jazz. At the age of 10 I'd cycle into Farnham of a Saturday morning—before going to spend time with Steve—just to listen to Beatnik Art student conversation. On Saturday mornings Steve went for guitar and music tuition – so I needed to arrive after he returned home.

I told Steve—on one such afternoon—that the Beatniks *had a way of talking*; a language that wasn't like anything else I'd ever heard. It was so—weird—that I almost didn't understand it . . . but it was marvellous to listen to them. They sometimes called people *cretins* or *philistines*.[4] Steve had laughed when I'd said that and asked me why Beatniks described people in that way. I'd thought about it for a moment and replied that the Beatniks seemed to say such things about people who didn't like John Coltrane or Miles Davis.

---

3 Lieutenant Colonel John Luard [1790 – 1875] 10th Regiment / 16th Lancers / 4th Dragoons 1809, served at the battles of Waterloo and Bhurtpore. He wrote a History of the Dress of the British Soldier published in 1852.
4 Cretin: a fool; a person afflicted with cretinism – a mental handicap due to a congenital lack of thyroid hormone. Philistine: an uneducated person indifferent or hostile to culture.

The Beatniks seemed to be messianic in some way. I'd asked Steve whether he'd ever heard of John Coltrane or Miles Davis. He hadn't but said he'd ask his father. Mr Bruce was happy—as ever—to inform us. It wasn't his kind of Jazz – but he said that they were very talented musicians. I had thought that would be the case.

I'd looked up the word cretin in the dictionary. My discovery made me laugh and I told Steve that I thought someone had to have a goitre to be a cretin. Steve had laughed and told me that he didn't think it was compulsory. I'd been convulsed by that comment and it had been several minutes before he could get any sense out of me. I'd asked Steve whether his father had any records of John Coltrane or Miles Davis we could listen to – but no. Steve had already asked. His father had merely heard them at someone's house before the family moved to Farnham.

I often wondered what kind of Jazz it was – because the reverence was palpable when those names were mentioned. Their names had the same immortal feel to me as the names Jack Bruce or Jimi Hendrix would later. I have only to hear the name 'Jack Bruce' and I hear 'Spoonful' or 'Born Under a Bad Sign'. I hear his supernatural bass – the riffs that ran all over the neck. The Beatniks would speak about John Coltrane and Miles Davis in that way. It would be a long time before I heard their music – but their ghosts haunted the café: wild grinning ghosts who blew saxophone and trumpet as direct messages from infinity.

The conveyor belts have broken and the escalator's stuck / The Black Mariah's broken down the police are out of luck / And their uniforms are dreaming jazz – those echoes make you spin / 'cause the hour's nearing midnight and the owls are on the wing.
Larkin/Bruce/Schubert—Savage Cabbage—The Owls are on the Wing—Savoy Green—1970

The Beatniks in Farnham formed the pre-psychedelic wave—the pre-Blues wave—and it was clear to me that I wanted to grow up to be *one of those people*.

I wanted to be sitting in that café talking about Blues. The coffee was terrible – but the Beatniks were amazing. They were so different from anybody else I'd ever seen. I wondered where they'd come from to be like that . . . ? What must their families have been like . . . ?

What was it about the Art School that made it a coven for these witches and warlocks of Jazz? It didn't really matter that they were talking about Ornette Coleman and Archie Shepp – Lawrence Ferlinghetti and Allen Ginsberg. They could have been talking about Bach and Boccherini, Milton and Blake – it wouldn't have mattered. It was the *way* they talked of these Artists. No one talked in that way anywhere else. It was the deep-rooted fervour and zeal with which they spoke.

There's nothing intrinsically more exhilarating about Jazz or Beat Poetry than anything else – it's just the excitement and enthusiasm of the individual playing the Jazz or reciting the Beat Poetry and how that proliferates within interlocking circles of *like minds*. I was looking at a vivid living culture – a cultured generation. I was peeking in on a great secret. The café proprietor and staff were clearly unaware of the great secret. They weren't listening to it at all. That's what made it a secret. I was the only outsider who was in on it – and that made it an irreplaceable part of the week: my Saturday morning on another planet.

*The station's closed for the Halloween there's something in the air /
They've got signs that flicker off and on to welcome Baudelaire / But
nobody seems to notice that the time has come to sing / And the hour's
nearing midnight and the owls are on the wing.* Larkin/Bruce/Schubert—Savage
Cabbage—The Owls are on the Wing—Savoy Green—1970

I am sure now that if I'd been brought up in circles where
people were excited about Baroque music and British poets – I'd
have dived headlong into that instead, or *as well as*. The Beatniks
were simply there as a statement of culture that was missing
elsewhere in 1960's semi-suburban Surrey. It was a sorry Surrey
with no sari. A Surrey with a 'short back and sides' rather than a
Surrey with a fringe on the top.

*All the world will fly in a flurry – when I take you out in the surrey, when
I take you out in the surrey with the fringe on top.*
Rodgers and Hammerstein—Oklahoma—1955

My application to Farnham Art School had been made back in
January. My interview rolled into view in March like a cerulean
billiard ball coming at me—across fields of green baize—in
some palatial frontier saloon.

I pulled the pocket-watch out of my waistcoat and looked at the
time. It was still far too early – but I crossed the road to meet
my fate. My art folio was a cumbersome affair made at school.
It was sturdy enough – but it was made of heavy card and
weighed enough to make it quite a burden. I would have liked to
have afforded a proper folio – but I'd blown my money on Blues
albums and a new MARSHALL amplifier for vocals. Not the most
sensible move as Savage Cabbage had only a few months left to
play before Steve and Ron went to Music College – but I wanted
more volume.

I'd buy a proper folio for my degree course interview the following year – it was no problem. The string that kept the folio together cut into my fingers as I crossed the road – but what was a little pain when a person owned a 200 watt MARSHALL MAJOR amplifier?

It was strange entering the main Art School. It was a beautiful old building. Strangely no one seemed to notice me. I'd thought I'd be questioned as to my business – but no. I asked a passing student—with seriously long hair—where the interviews were taking place but he had no idea. He was helpful though and suggested I ascend the stairs to where the offices were. They'd be able to tell me up there. *"Yeah—good luck man— really!"* he called after me. That was a good start. I lumbered up the narrow wooden stairs and was glad to get to the top. From there it was simple. I was directed to a room where I could wait.

There were a few other people my age: each with a folder, each with a fine head of hair. I looked around at the clothing and costumes: buckskin elf-trousers and fringed boots; Afghan embroidered sheepskin coat and knee-high moccasins; tattered Mod Union-Jacket [5] patched with different colours of satin; and, a sea of patched and faded Levis. Miss Rodham had advised me to wear my suit . . . and so—apart from my US polo boots—I felt about as suitably dressed as a ballerina down a coal mine.

I eased off the tie—slid it into my pocket—and felt immediately better. My high collared white satin shirt collar—released from the confines of my waistcoat—completed the transformation.

---

5 A jacket made from one or more Union Jacks – the British national flag. These—although relatively rare—were Mod attire of the mid 1960s.

Names were called and gradually the occupants of the room changed: purple suede trousers and aged plimsolls with multicoloured laces; Afghani dress and white lace-up boots; red regimental jacket emblazoned with pins and badges; huge knitted emerald green dress tied with a broad leather belt that looked vaguely Indian; floor-length chamois leather skirt and beadwork bolero top.

My friend Pete Bridgewater—and Mary Riddell, a lady in my art class at Virginia Water—weren't there. They'd been given other days and times. I wondered why. It would have been fun to have gone together. No one seemed to know anyone. We were all isolated individuals and no one seemed up for conversation – although smiles were often exchanged.

As I'd arrived early it wasn't long before I was an old-timer in the waiting room and I started grinning at each new person who entered. *"Hello – where you from?"* I tried.

"Somewhere else man" a bearded fellow with Shakespearean pointed shoes answered.

"What a coincidence!" I beamed *"That's where I've just come from."*

"Hey . . . you're right—there—*man, didn't know what to expect from a suit."*

"Yeah . . . right . . . wasn't my idea." I felt like saying that I liked my Uncle Charles' Edwardian suit . . . in certain situations—especially school—but decided it would be better to remain comprehensible as a prospective Art student.

"I'm from Alton man—bit remote—but there's some good music happening there" he replied.

We fell to talking about the music scene in the pubs around that area and that led inexorably to talking about Blues and Savage Cabbage.

"Yeah, like—really man—heard of Savage Cabbage. Ever play Alton?"

"Once – a few years back. We mainly play Art Schools now – but we might be up for another pub gig this Summer. I like pub gigs – lot of atmosphere."

We were deep in conversation about Blues when the room filled. Several people arrived at once: Levi jacket and patched puce satin trousers; dilapidated leather greatcoat with an unlikely assortment of buttons; brocade Nehru jacket with paisley shirt —*and*—trousers; and, a floor-length fur coat with sheepskin mini-skirt, woollen tights and Moon boots.[6] Then my name was called. I jumped forward quite briskly—still spellbound by the wonder of it all—with my folder under my arm. I wished my friend from Alton good luck and entered the inner sanctum.

John Morris and Ken Brampton awaited me in a room that smelled of oil paint. All Foundation Course interviews were conducted by John Morris and a random lecturer – but I wasn't aware at the time that I'd have little contact with Ken Brampton from that point on.

It was a strange – but exhilarating experience. In some sense real life was about to commence.

John Morris had a Vandyke beard – but I liked him nonetheless. He emanated a sense of severity – but there was nothing tricky about him. He looked as if I could trust him. Ken Brampton seemed the friendlier of the two at first—but apart from having a fabulous walrus moustache—I didn't warm to him. The two men asked confrontative questions – questions I didn't expect.

---

6 Moon Boots were huge long-haired furry après-ski boots first made in 1970 by Tecnica of Giavera del Montello, Italy. They were unusual in having no evident right or left foot.

Miss Rodham—the art teacher at Virginia Water—told us the interview would be *different*. It wouldn't be like talking to school teachers. We'd be spoken to as adults. We'd be expected to reply as adults – and that might be a little intimidating. She was right – but that was good news to me.

We were the small group of reckless individuals who'd decided to pursue *further education*[7] in a direction that probably doomed us to unemployment. That was the line taken by our school – and probably every other school for that matter. We were all given serious advice *not* to take this step – but only three of us ignored it—Pete, Mary, and *the odd boy*—the rest unwisely chose to take art at Teacher Training College instead. I say 'unwisely' because the Education Department—governed by Moloch—had decided that Britain was short of teachers. It therefore established far too many Teacher Training Colleges. Parents thought this was a safer option – and so, many prospective art students were convinced to take a course which proved imprudent in hindsight.[8]

There's black ice at the cross roads and three degrees of frost / And they skid in all directions to prove that they're not lost / But that makes little sense to me when the show might just begin / 'cause the hour's nearing midnight and the owls are on the wing. Larkin/Bruce/Schubert—Savage Cabbage— The Owls are on the Wing—Savoy Green—1970

Ken Brampton wanted to know who I was *"What interests us, is whether you're—actually—an artist . . . or whether you think Art School is a 'cushy number'. Are you serious – or are you along for the ride because you've got nowhere else to go?"*

---

7 British term for all full-time education beyond the age of 18.
8 By the end of the 1970s there was a glut of teachers and 'Teacher Training' art teachers found it difficult to find employment.

I met their gaze "*I think you'll find that I'm one of the most serious people you'll ever meet.*"

Ken wasn't impressed "*How long did you rehearse that?*"

"*About as long as you rehearsed the question*" I surprised myself by the speed at which I came back at him.

Then, two things happened at once. John laughed out loud and Ken attempted to say "*We're not here to play games*" but John's laughter drowned him out.

"*Alright—very funny—I think we've established that we're all serious here. Now let's look at your folio.*"

I smiled and opened my folio. They flipped through it fairly quickly obviously entirely unimpressed. I felt suddenly slightly anxious.

"*You will have to learn how to draw from life rather than copy photographs*" John commented. Ken agreed. Both observed me dispassionately.

"*Yes. I've not had the opportunity to do that yet.*"

"*There—are—classes open to the public every Saturday at Farnham Art School in painting and life drawing. Didn't you know about them? Or were you taken up with other interests?*" Ken enquired – with a penetrating look in his eye.

I gave an entirely lame reply "*I didn't know about them . . .*"

"*Most parents . . .*" stated Ken in an authoritarian tone "*. . . whose children show—serious—interest in drawing and painting seem to find out about the classes. It doesn't take a great deal of research. There's information in every public library.*"

"*It's reasonably well known . . .*" John added "*. . . that you can't rely on art departments in the average school to build a folio for Art School.*"

"Oh . . ." Pregnant pause " . . . *well . . . my father never encouraged me too much with art . . . he doesn't take it seriously – in terms of employment, I mean. So . . . I don't think he'd have thought about art classes. He was more concerned about my poor Maths results . . .* "

"*So your parents don't approve of your application?*"

"*They're fine about it – or at least they are now. I'm more-or-less independent . . . and it's what I want to do. My father doesn't try to influence what I do any more. My mother's—always—been happy for me to pursue art though. It's a pity I didn't know about the art classes because I would have liked to have gone – but then . . . I've worked weekends since I was* 14 *which—would—have made it difficult unless there'd been evening classes.*"

Both John and Ken looked a little taken aback by that. "*You've worked—every—weekend since you were* 14*?*"

"*More-or-less . . . yes*" I started babbling in some vain attempt to make my case look reasonable "*You see . . . my parents never had that much money – so they couldn't have run to art classes in any case. I'm not complaining or anything – it just that . . . well . . .* " I ran out of steam.

"*That answers it as far as I'm concerned*" John cut in with a sympathetic smile. "*You're obviously a worker . . . I can see that by this painting. I don't personally—like—this kind of thing – but it represents considerable effort*" Pause "*How long did it take you to paint this?*"

It was a Surrealist oil painting—on photographic linen—of Jimi Hendrix taken from a poster. He was standing in our back garden – with my mother and father in the background drinking cups of tea at the garden table. My brother Græham was cleaning his bicycle by the side. Jimi Hendrix was in black and white and the garden was painted in colour.

"I really couldn't say exactly . . . It was painted over a period of about a month or maybe longer. I worked on it at home and—as I said—I work every weekend so I only had evenings."

"We presume that weekend work would come to an end – were you to be accepted here?"

"Yes—certainly—I've got a holiday job lined up for July and August – but after that I won't have to find extra money. I've looked into the grant situation and that's all taken care of . . . if I'm accepted."

John nodded gravely *"So . . . why's Jimi Hendrix portrayed in monochrome? Did you take the image from a black and white photograph?"*

"No. It was from a colour photograph – but I wanted him to look like something from a dream or vision. You see . . . he's not really in the garden – he just lives in my mind and I wanted to show that. It could have been the other way round too because sometimes he seems more real than my parents' garden."

John smiled *"I like the painting better for hearing the explanation – but as we pointed out, you will need to work from life when you're here. How d'you feel about that? It will be a change. Sometimes when people have a developed style they're not keen on changing."*

"I'm looking forward to developing my skills in whatever way possible. I want to be . . . as good as I can become."

"What . . . " John asked *" . . . do you want from Art School in that regard?"*

"Just being here . . . and . . . learning whatever I can." There was no reply – so I continued *"I want to be in Art School – I've always wanted to come to Art School – it's where I feel I belong . . . this is where I want to be. That might sound a bit simple-minded – but . . . "*

John looked at me benevolently and Ken said *"Well at least you're honest."*

"Where do you want it to lead you – what sort of future do you have in mind?" John asked.

"I have no fixed idea at the moment. I rather thought that something would suggest itself through the experience of being here. I am open to possibilities and want to explore as much as I'm able. I was told that Foundation introduced you to everything you can do at Art School – and that sounds just what I want at this point. I like working hard at anything I love doing."

That seemed to hit the right note with John *"Can you give us some examples of the kind of things you love?"*

"Blues." It was out of my mouth before I had time to calculate. I described making the DEBIL – and Ken—having asked for precise details of how the DEBIL was made—was impressed at last. *"You should have brought it to the interview – it would have given us a broader sense of your skills."*

"I'll bring it to show you when I come to the Art School in September – or sooner if you like."

"So it's a foregone conclusion that you've been accepted?" Ken grinned – but this time in a kindly fashion.

That stopped me. I had no quick reply . . . *"If I'm not accepted this year . . . I'll have to apply again next year – but I'm hoping it won't have to go that way."* There was no response to that – so I blathered on *"I write songs. I've written poetry since I was a child. I like the way that word and image can be combined on record sleeves – although I don't think I want to take my interest into graphics too much."*

John asked *"Have you ever combined word and image?"*

"Yes – for the school magazine. I helped produce it and it contained three pieces of my illustrated poetry. I designed the cover too. They're in the large envelope at the back of my folio."

Ken pulled the magazines from the envelope *"My God . . . these things are as*—hideous—*as they've always been – but then you won't have had any choice about the typography and format."*

"I did try to suggest a change – but I was told that the cover had to remain in the traditional form." I directed them to the section where my work was to be found and they read the poetry. I was surprised. I'd expected them simply to peruse the imagery and layout.

"You have a way with words" John commented *"You never thought to take English at university?"*

"No . . . I've always wanted to come to Art School – and . . . I don't really want to get into more analysis. It almost ruined A Level English Literature for me. I would have liked to have taken A Level English Language – but the subject wasn't available."

John Morris nodded and sat back in his chair *"I think you can take it as read that you have been accepted. There's no need to wait for the letter – just make the best use of your remaining time at school in the Art department. Do you have any questions?"*

"Nothing as yet . . . but . . . is there a musical society or anything of the kind at the Art School?"

"Yes – there's a Folk and Poetry Club . . . " Ken replied *" . . . and I'm sure Blues would be welcome."*

The barber's shop is up for sale the clippers jammed with rust / There's no one in the beauty shop that anyone can trust / There's a hurricane feigning lethargy and six other deadly sins / 'cause the hour's nearing midnight and the owls are on the wing. Larkin/Bruce/Schubert—Savage Cabbage—The Owls are on the Wing—Savoy Green—1970

The situation at Virginia Water became amorphous. The status of *the leavers* was obvious to all. Those who'd turned 18 went to the pub in the lunch hour – and even those who hadn't. The teachers—realising they had no control over us—became quite relaxed, even friendly. The atmosphere became free and easy – but in a slightly eerie way.

I stopped wearing the remotest semblance of school uniform. After being accepted at Farnham Art School I turned up in my Bluesman outfit. No one said a word – not even the main uniform enforcer, Mr Havilland.

Mr Blenkinsopp—the history teacher—grinned at me occasionally, noticing my appearance. I never studied with him but he was always around. He had a kindly expression but seemed a little like an adult school boy in his appearance and hair style. He didn't understand Blues lyrics – or so I thought. Maybe—being a school teacher—he was simply a consummate diplomat on the subject. We had an informal concert at School toward the end of my time. I went on stage with the DEBIL over my knees and performed a Blues set. Those in the first year 6th hadn't heard my 'John The Revelator' performance the year before and had never seen the DEBIL. There was great curiosity about it and I agreed to show it to those who were interested afterwards.

I took the stage and placed myself on the chair. I stared into the assembly of familiar faces and looked around. Some of the audience looked awkward – as if they'd got the impression I was nervous. They looked a little uncomfortable at my silence. I'd just lapsed into a day dream—*listening to the crack of doom on the hydrogen jukebox*—and as soon as I noticed people looking expectant I said.

"Savage Cabbage people—if you've heard of them—I'm all that's left. So I'd like to dedicate my performance this evening to Ron Larkin, lead guitar —Steve Bruce, lead bass—and Jack Hackman percussion. Ron Larkin died of a heart attack and Steve Bruce died in a car accident."

I made no mention of Jack. *"Best musicians I've ever heard . . . best friends I ever had."*

Shocked susurrations emanated from the crowd as I paused *"But hey people!"* I shouted *"that's the*—history—*of Blues. So – who was I with Savage Cabbage anyway? Why I was Farquhar Arbuthnot: vocals, harp, rhythm bass, and Master-in-Lunacy.*[9] *But now . . . "* I slid the chromium tube up the strings *"I'm . . . Frank Schubert! Delta Blues dilettante and Cro-Magnon Man of Chicago chicanery! Second cousin of Donald Duck—associate of Jesse James—and close personal friend of Genghis Khan. Let it rrrrrroll!"*

I caught Mr Blenkinsopp in peripheral vision, grinning broadly. I felt relieved. I'd never launched forth like—*that*—at school before. The uncomfortable faces had dissolved into amused amazement. I belted out 'Death Letter Blues' the Son House[10] number, followed by a few Robert Johnson numbers. I sang some pretty lurid lines too. I thought nobody would know what I was singing.

Lord I'm going to Chicago, believe I need my ham bone boiled / You know them mean St. Louis women – they done let my ham bone spoil.
WC Handy—St Louis Blues—1914

---

9 The position of Master in Lunacy was established by the Commissioners in Lunacy Act 1842.

10 Eddie James 'Son' House Jr. [1902 – 1988] was a friend of Robert Johnson and Charlie Patton. He was an important influence on Robert Johnson and later on Muddy Waters. He was born in Riverton, near Clarksdale, Mississippi.

Mr Blenkinsopp—the archetypal suburban school teacher—sat there tapping his foot as if he was at a Mississippi juke joint. Mr Blenkinsopp could have passed as a chartered accountant any day of the week – but here he was looking as if he was having the time of his life listening to me and my maniacal music-machine. It turned out that he had a severe penchant for Blues and Jazz. How was I to have known?

He came up to me afterwards *"Well Victor—or should I say Frank —that was an inspired performance. I did wonder if I would ever hear you sing and play again after your remarkable rendition of Son House's 'John the Revelator' in the first year."*

"I'm very happy you liked my performance, Mr Blenkinsopp."

"I did—indeed—but I must say I—am—saddened to hear of the death of your friends . . . that must be a terrible blow . . . terrible loss."

"I . . . " I began *" . . . yes."*

Mr Blenkinsopp noticed my eyes had suddenly grown misty and changed the subject. I'd been fine on stage—although sad—but sympathy always precipitated tears.

"And you played in a band? A Blues band?"

"Yes—but it was Chicago Blues, not Delta—so we were an electric band."

"So you will probably be a fan of Muddy Waters and Howling Wolf then?" Mr Blenkinsopp ventured.

"Yes!" I replied gleefully *"Particularly Muddy Waters."*

"You probably know that he is connected back to Son House, Willie Brown, and Robert Johnson. I notice that you favour Robert Johnson."

"I do – Savage Cabbage used to play quite a few of his numbers."

"In Chicago style?"

"More-or-less, yes. We were reworking them . . . we had an idea of taking each one – and developing it so that it wasn't just an electrified version of the original. We wanted to make each song a Chicago-style masterpiece and I think that Ron and Steve would have done that."

"You say nothing of—yourself—in this process though?"

"Well . . . there—is—a reason for that" Pause *"I did work with Ron and Steve – but they were so far ahead of me with music that – well Ron in particular . . . I think . . . was a genius"* Pause *"Yes definitely, he—was —a genius. He could play anything – and Steve was almost the same."*

"Such a waste—such a waste—I am truly sorry. You seem to handle your instrument well however – and you can certainly sing."

I smiled *"Yes. I'm not shy about my voice. I don't have quite the sound I'd like – but I keep working at it."*

"Your friends must have respected you as a singer."

"Yes . . . they did. They even said some kind things about my rhythm bass playing." Mr Blenkinsopp asked—so I explained—about the idea of rhythm bass.

"And you never thought to take music at school?"

"I thought about it a lot – but it wasn't possible. There was no music at my last school and by the time I got here it was too late to start . . . you see . . . Mr Ironsides said it wouldn't work to join all the classes from 1ˢᵗ year to 5ᵗʰ year in order to the take an O Level."

"Mmmm . . . " Mr Blenkinsopp mused *"well now . . . that is a pity."* I detected some trace of concern in his voice as if something needn't have been the case.

"And . . . evening classes?" he continued.

"We're not that well off . . . " I replied *" . . . and my father wasn't keen on my taking art—or—music further. He doesn't see it as leading to employment."*

"I see—I see—well . . . But you're bound for Art School now I hear. Miss Rodham told me when I asked after you."

Mr Blenkinsopp had asked after me? Why had he asked after me? I was never in his class. Mr Blenkinsopp noticed my expression *"Ah yes. Well . . . I was wondering about you . . . I have been wondering about you since I first heard you play. It occurred to me that—once you were finished with school—I'd enjoy chatting with you about Blues. It's not something that works well when you're in a position of authority – but now we can speak on equal terms."*

That was a new idea. Did teachers *do* that? Obviously they did. This was a new world to me and I got the eerie felling that Mr Love had returned from beyond the grave. *"That would be marvellous. I've not really been able to talk much about Blues with anyone who knows anything since my friends died. I mean I can tell people about Blues – but there's no one to tell me anything any more. And conversations don't really go very far when the person you're talking to hasn't heard a quarter of the names you're mentioning. I mean, I don't know anyone who'd link Muddy Waters with Son House and Willie Brown. That's – music to my ears."*

He was pleased. He asked about Jack and what had happened to him.

"Jack . . . well . . . his parents never liked me . . . and, they never liked Jack being a band member anyway. I never see him now . . . and well . . . who knows, maybe he'll drop me a line sometime. I've written a few cards – but he's not replied. I think of him as having died of suburban values . . . He sold his drums . . . "

Mr Blenkinsopp could see he'd touched another tricky subject and swiftly changed tack. We had a truly fine conversation and he examined the DEBIL extremely closely. *"Remarkable— remarkable—how did you come to make this ingenious instrument?"*

I explained – and those who'd wanted a closer look at the DEBIL sat round listening to the tale. Mr Blenkinsopp knew Blues as well as I did – or maybe better. Names tripped off his tongue as easily as they'd have done with Ron – but he knew more about the earlier part of the 20ᵗʰ century and even the 19ᵗʰ century. He was a history teacher after all.

I found out later that it was Mr Blenkinsopp who'd stood up for me after my performance of 'John the Revelator' in the school assembly. He knew all about Son House and the Style 'O' NATIONAL RESOPHONIC guitar he played. I am always amazed at just what goes on in the background. It was sad in retrospect that we'd not got to know each other earlier. I'd severely misjudged the man—but it was still an ambivalent situation. I had no idea if he really knew what the 'jelly-roll' meant in Jelly Roll Morton. Did he know that Blind Lemon Jefferson was not actually completely blind? Blind Lemon's vision may have been seriously impaired from birth – but the lemon in question was not a citrus fruit, as indicated by his song:

Mmm—mmm—black snake crawling in my room—y'know some pretty mama, better come get this black snake soon.
Blind Lemon Jefferson—Black Snake Moan—1926

Mr Blenkinsopp said that I'd have to pay him a visit and listen to some of his collection – I took him up on his offer half a dozen times before Art School commenced. I needed some distance on the fact that Steve and Ron had died – and evenings with Mr and Mrs Blenkinsopp served extremely well to that end.

I started out calling them Mr and Mrs Blenkinsopp – but on our first dinner they became Michæl and Sandra. *"We're not at Virginia Water any more you know "* Michæl laughed *"so none of this Mr and Mrs Blenkinsopp – we're Michæl and Sandra."*

"Thank you—that's really good—and I'm Frank, Frank Schubert."

"Yes . . . I was meaning to ask you about that Frank – is there a story behind that . . . and that other name you used on stage – I didn't quite catch it?"

"Farquhar Arbuthnot . . . that was a joke really – that was my stage name with Savage Cabbage because they thought that Victor Simmerson didn't make it as a Blues name."

"Fine Yorkshire name though – but I suppose you're right, it is a little remote from Mississippi or Chicago. What were the others called?"

"Steve Bruce, Ron Larkin and Jack Hackman."

"I see . . . yes . . . there's a certain punch to those names . . . but, tell me about Schubert? How does that fit in with Blues?"

"It doesn't really . . . it's my mother's maiden name. My grandmother was the niece of Franz Schubert."

"Sandra!" Michæl called *"Guess who's come to dinner!"* [11]

Sandra hurried through from the kitchen and Michæl announced *"The great grand nephew of Franz Schubert no less!"* That really broke the ice – and suddenly they really *were* Michæl and Sandra.

We were on good terms and a lively conversation was had about music of every kind. Although not greatly enthusiastic about Cream—from what they'd heard—they could accept that they'd been a highly talented band. When I told them that our music was quite similar to Cream – they paid great attention to my explanation as to the way they merged Blues with aspects of avant-garde Jazz. They asked me to bring an album next time I came and they'd listen more closely.

---

11 Michæl Blenkinsopp is referring to 'Guess Who's Coming to Dinner' released in 1967 starring Spencer Tracy, Sidney Poitier and Katharine Hepburn—produced and directed by Stanley Kramer—written by William Rose. The movie deals with the issue of interracial marriage.

It took me the ten miles home before my delight began to wear thin. Steve and Ron grew in my mind. It was talking about Cream that had triggered me. I was still floating in a personal thundercloud—crazed with the lightning of loss—with Steve and Ron flickering in the melancholic miasma.

I could weep at the drop of a hat – even though life was full-tilt with gigs to play. There were also ladies to admire, in order to distract myself from the fact that Lindie Dale was lost to me – barring an unlikely turnaround of events and concepts.

Michæl and Sandra had some interesting books – and put me onto all kinds of fascinating leads. They had a great wealth of knowledge concerning Blues and Jazz. I was not so interested in the Trad Jazz because it seemed to have gained a lot of fancy trimming and frills at the expense of raw power – but I listened as attentively as they listened to Cream – and therefore enjoyed what I heard. One idea that Michæl mentioned—that I took up immediately—was a set of books by Stephan Grossman. One was entitled 'Delta Blues' and the other 'Country Blues'. They were fascinating.

I wanted to find more material of that nature because I was keen to learn something of Lead Belly's style on 12 string. It struck me that playing slide on 12 string would be an innovation. I'd not come across anyone who played 12 string slide . . . but I'd need a custom converted NATIONAL RESOPHONIC guitar for that – and that sounded like the world's most enormous pipe dream.

The second time I visited Michael and Sandra Blenkinsopp, I was treated to an evening of Lead Belly. Huddie William Ledbetter had a strong clear voice. It was he—and Jo Ann Kelly —who inspired me to play 12 string. Lead Belly's 12 string sounded like an orchestra – and I could see that it would suit the way I played.

"The topics covered in Lead Belly's [12] *repertoire are impressive"* Mr Blenkinsopp informed me *" . . . racism, cowboys, cattle droving, prison, work, sailors, President Roosevelt, Adolph Hitler, and Howard Hughes."*

I was going to have to investigate Lead Belly further.

"Do you know the origin of his name?" I asked.

"Ah yes . . . Lead Belly got his nickname whilst in prison – as a play on Ledbetter and his toughness. One prisoner tried to cut off his head with a knife – but he grabbed the knife and almost killed his assailant. He then used the nickname for his recording work."

"Didn't he once come to Europe?"

"Yes—that's right—in 1949. *He began his first European tour, but fell ill and died later that year in New York City. Lead Belly had a huge repertoire including quite famous songs like: House of the Rising Sun and Midnight Special."* [13]

These would be great songs to sing in Farnham. I still carried an insubstantial un-worded notion in my mind that my father was really Son House and that I'd been mislaid somehow and my folks in Louisiana were wondering what had happened to me.

I had a half-sister who lived in America—Monica from Santa Monica—but the idea that I'd ever be able to go to such a place seemed remote in the extreme. She was not interested in Blues. She agreed with my father *"Blues is disreputable, unmusical, and played by criminals."*

---

12 Many sources give his name as 'Leadbelly' – but Huddie William Ledbetter always used 'Lead Belly'. 'Lead Belly' is what appears on his gravestone – and is the spelling used by the 'Lead Belly Foundation'.

13 Michæl Blenkinsopp also mentioned: Where Did You Sleep Last Night, Ain't It a Shame, Leaving Blues, and When the Whip Comes Down.

Michæl shook his head at that idea "*Blues lyrics abound with snapping pistols in people faces, drinking, and promiscuity – but this is a culture which had to survive within an extremely repressive society in terms of racism. And—of course—I can enjoy a novel set during the Napoleonic wars without being an advocate of warfare. It's a question of images as . . . abstract emotional vignettes.*"

Well I feel like snapping my pistol in your face, / Some lonesome graveyard gonna be your resting place. Muddy Waters—Can't Be Satisfied—1959

"*So . . .* " Michæl opined "*Take Muddy Waters for example . . . this is domestic violence and contemplated murder – but it is also a word painting, in which the words have a charge. The 'emotional power' of the lyrics need have no connection with the action described. The 'emotional power' has a meaning of its own which is quite distinct from the desire to commit homicide. The same thing is true with humour. One can laugh at a joke on the subject of death without subscribing to the idea that the death of a person is a laughing matter.*"

"*Right . . . and laughing at a joke about death wouldn't mean that you'd crack jokes at a funeral.*"

"*Exactly. It's a question of context.*"

The evenings I spent with Michæl and Sandra Blenkinsopp were fascinating. it occurred to me that it was tragic that—as a history teacher—he could not offer an examination course on 'The History of Blues'.

"*Yes—I would like that—but there is no possibility of such a course being offered. Maybe in the future perhaps – when some educational changes have been instituted.*"

As I sat in the front parlour—sipping a glass of wine—Sandra said "*A little known fact about Blues is that the 'mean spirited cheating partner' who is so badly in need of punitive measures – actually stands in for the boss of the plantation. When someone sings 'I asked her for water, she gave me gasoline' – the 'she' in question is probably the 'he' who exploits the singer.*"

"*Now—that—is an eye opener*" I said.

"*Yes . . . If you don't understand the Jim Crow*[14] *environment of the South you'd be led to assume that terrible relationships were the norm amongst Blues performers.*"

"*The truth is . . .*" Michael observed "*that singing a song about snapping a pistol in the boss' face might lead to a lynching. Although . . . I wouldn't imagine you would need to obscure Brigadier Dale in a Blues of your own.*"

I almost spilt my wine. How on earth had Sandra Blenkinsopp come to learn about him? Seeing I was slightly aghast, she explained "*The school—large as it is—is a tiny village and very little escapes the notice of teachers – especially if they care about their charges. Michæl came to hear about . . . well your separation from Linda Dale . . . that must have been very difficult for you.*"

"*Yes . . .*" I sighed "*Suppose a Bluesman has to expect Jim Crow*" Pause "*and Brigadier Dale's as close as it gets in Surrey.*"

"*Most unfortunate—most—unfortunate*" Michæl exclaimed "*Deeply to be regretted in this day and age.*"

---

14 Jim Crow – derogatory term for an African American. The 'Jim Crow laws' were state and or local laws in the USA between 1876 and 1965 which enforced de jure segregation in public places such as military services, schools, public transport, restaurants, and lavatory facilities. The Jim Crow laws were finally overruled by the 1964 Civil Rights Act and the 1965 Voting Rights Act.

"*Brigadier Dale was in contact with the Headmaster* . . . " Sandra commented shaking her head as if still in disbelief " . . . *demanding to know who you were and whether you were the age you claimed to be.*"

"*Full of hot air and rhetoric*" Michæl added with fervour "*Utter windbag of a man!*" Pause "*Of course . . . some things*—are— *confidential information – and, he found he was unable to bully the Headmaster. Mr Ironsides was able to reassure the pompous despot without informing him of anything he had no business to know.*"

"*A foul . . . most objectionable . . . self-opinionated . . . high-handed . . . !*" Sandra exploded " *He seems to think everyone else is a junior rank in the Army. You would do better to have a barracuda as a father-in-law.*"

So . . . it was common knowledge amongst the teachers – and, unbeknownst to me, Michæl Blenkinsopp had more-or-less been my fairy godmother. He'd watched over me. He'd stood up for my out-of-kilter uniform – and who knows what else.

Wonders—*never*—cease.

2

goodbye frank schubert

I'd been 18 for a month. Officially an adult. The *final* end of my school years stared me in the face. The face of the future— which peered at me—had baleful eyes that betokened nothing. It was a ga-ga ghoul – ominous but impotent. The future was an empty space rather than the open horizon of unlimited potential. I ought to have been excited by the prospect of leaving school but I wasn't – I was still *listening to the crack of doom on the hydrogen jukebox*. Lindie's 18th birthday lay a month away and I knew there'd be no change in her circumstances. She'd have her birthday and the right to vote – but I knew I'd be the most pitiful kind of dolt to hold out any hope of radical change. Brigadier Dale was still who he was and so was his wife – and, unless the Dales changed fairly radically, I'd have to bid Lindie a final farewell and head out into the void.

I felt odd about that juncture—or disjuncture—or whatever it would turn out to be. I was gleeful, to a certain extent—*naturally* —but I was still living in the shadow of the deaths of Steve and Ron. The big divide at the end of Virginia Water felt a little like death, when it should have felt like liberation. I felt as if I was suddenly unprepared to move away from what I'd known. Maybe so much had fallen apart that school started to look like a friendly supportive environment.

But I knew that my short-lived episode with Michæl and Sandra Blenkinsopp was not exactly *what school was*. They'd had to wait 'til I was no longer a 'school boy' before they could be open with me. But . . . what if I could have had another year of drifting at school, playing Blues at impromptu school concerts and having dinner with the Blenkinsopps – *that* would have been an attractive proposition. There was Michæl and Sandra's Blues collection – and, their impressive library. Maybe the school would think again about music lessons . . . It would be a great advantage to be able to spend a year learning music by sitting in on the classes available. Ron had been dumbfounded by the fact that the school wouldn't allow me to sit in on classes with the youngsters. I wished I'd pushed harder – but at the time the verdict seemed pretty final. I still knew people in the lower 6th and got on with them well – better in fact than the people in my own year. Somehow they'd got used to me being there – as they'd entered the 6th form with me as an established part of the school. To those in my year—apart from the Blues cognoscenti —I'd never quite stopped being the new boy. Although the others were friendly, they were never quite as open to me as those in the year below; especially the girls. For the first time in my life, I wished I could slip back a year in age.

These thoughts wafted through my mind – but even as they did, I knew it was ridiculous to be daydreaming in such a manner. I didn't take speculations any further – but I wished I could rearrange life in some way that made the sequence of events a little more comprehensible. Things had happened that *should not* have happened. Steve and Ron had died. They should not have died. Lindie Dale had abandoned me—albeit regretfully—on the basis that I was about to embark on an abominably hazardous life. A hazardous life . . . was that what I really wanted? I was no longer sure.

Was I a romantic fool who had no notion what he was doing?
Yes – but what was the alternative? Study Maths and become a
chartered accountant? No. So—romantic fool or otherwise—I
was heading in a direction I'd already taken. There was no
changing course without having a brain and heart transplant.
I remembered the night in 1964 when I'd sat naked at the
crossroads waiting for Legba with a detestable plastic guitar.
I saw 12 year olds at school and wondered how on earth I'd
done what I'd done. They looked so young and so incapable of
acts of such outlandish folly. Then two years later I was having
a passionate liaison with someone almost twice my age. I'd
heard that people often saw their lives flash before their eyes
moments before death. It occurred to me that I was about to
die—not literally—but circumstantially and symbolically. I was
just going to implode or something and end up at Brookwood [1]
like Mr Love.

*Did you ever wake up to find – a day that broke up your mind, /
Destroyed your notion of circular time – It's just that demon life has got you
in its sway.* Jagger/Richards—Rolling Stones—Sway—Sticky Fingers—1971

There were no definite venues where I could meet anyone I used
to know – and even those I used to know were not exactly close
friends. Pete Bridgewater and Greg Ford were occupied with
manifold means and devices. They had other fish to fry.
I didn't even have a skillet. I'd see Pete when I got to Art
School. I'd see Greg as and when. In the interim I felt as if I'd
woken up in the film set of an existentialist movie – in a period
when the actors were on location somewhere else. I was
wandering like the witless witness in the wardrobe department
of woeful weariness.

---

1 The local mental hospital – now they are called psychiatric hospitals.

Every meeting had to be arranged individually – apart from ad hoc meetings at the pub. It seemed strange – school had been a fact of life for so long, that the end felt vacuous. However the last days—after the examinations were over—were also a delightfully nebulous time. There was nothing to do but play guitar, listen to music, and talk with friends. They'd disappear from time to time for interviews. School was enjoyable at that point – even though some people drifted away. There was no point in being there after the examinations were over but I attended right up 'til the last day. I turned up at school later than usual – and often went off earlier, to the homes of various friends. I realised that there were people I'd miss – even though I did not know them so well. There was a sense in which just having these people around as part of a tableau was important to how I manifested. Who was I without them? That was simple to answer. I was the same person I'd been every school holiday [2] – but now the holiday was permanent. Surprisingly the girls vanished first. I'd not expected that. It took me a while to learn that Lindie Dale had left school for good and ever. In the end it was her friends Susan Wilcox, Sarah Bradley, and Daphne Morgan who told me.

"Lindie just couldn't bear to say goodbye to you" Daphne said sheepishly *"Said it was just too painful for her and . . . she thought you'd . . . understand."*

"Yeah . . . right. Of course . . . " I lied *". . . of course . . . I understand completely."* I understood nothing at all – but there was no point saying that. The look on my face must have conveyed my devastation because they put their arms around me. Sarah cried, which startled me into a sense of necessary equipoise.

---

2 Recess in the USA

"Yeah . . . Lindie was right" I continued *"There's just no changing some situations . . . and . . . "* Pause *"Lindie made the right decision."* I said nothing of what Michæl and Sandra Blenkinsopp had said. It was privileged information.

"You really think so . . . ?" Sarah asked.

"Yeah . . . " I smiled through vaguely gritted teeth *"or rather . . . no. It depends how you look at it. I'd have liked to have said goodbye – but . . . maybe . . . I'm too much of a fool for my own good. I think she made the right decision."* I said it partly to make them feel better about having had to tell me and partially because I could see that it was true – intellectually at least. What they *hadn't* told me was that *Sidney the soldierman* had become a regular visitor to the Dale household. He was a Sandhurst Military Academy officer cadet and Brigadier Dale had taken him under his wing. His parents lived in York – so Sidney sometimes spent his shorter furloughs with the Dales. This was information that Susan, Sarah, and Daphne felt I didn't need to know. Looking back they were right. It would have made me crazy. I would have had to have visited Brigadier Dale and told him what I thought about his master plan. *'Brigadier Dale'* I might have said *'I hope you and your wife never come to regret manipulating your daughter. I hope you never feel ashamed. I hope you never feel guilty that she just might have had a better life with me.'* But I never got to make that speech.

I took Susan, Sarah, and Daphne out for a drink that evening and I managed to enjoy myself far more than I'd expected. It was as if they were the guardian angels of my peace of mind. They remained at school for two weeks longer and we went up to London to visit the Art Galleries. They took me out for a meal and we had a wonderful evening and talked incessantly.

I enjoyed being with three ladies and felt somehow immensely privileged that they wanted to spend time with me. We talked about the exhibitions we'd seen and the paintings we liked the most.

"*I really liked that John Martin painting* . . . " Sarah said with glee " *. . . brilliant textures and colours.*"

"*Right! 'Satan on the Burning Lake' . . .*" I replied "*I—love—those mezzotints.*"

"*They're kind of . . . creepy though* . . . " Pause "*Gave me the impression he'd*—been—*to hell and*—seen—*that.*"

"*I've never understood all that 'hell thing'* . . . " Susan mused " *. . . and 'the devil' . . . and all that.*"

"*No . . . well . . . It is strange*" I replied "*If I really think about it – it's kind of unhealthy for there to be a personification of evil*" Pause "*and it gets mixed up—y'know—with other ideas like anarchism and freedom . . . and then that starts making the devil look like some sort of intriguing rebel. I know the whole story about Lucifer rebelling against God – but I think it's unfortunate that anarchism gets tied in with evil. I think you can be a kindly rebel – a rebel without a sub-clause.*"

"*Lindie always said you were clever with language*" Daphne laughed.

"*Yeah – I'm the saint of clauses y'know.*" They fell about laughing at the Santa Claus reference and I continued "*Apparently William Blake thought that Satan was really the hero of Milton's 'Paradise Lost' and that Milton wasn't exactly opposed to the Devil.*"

"*Really—that's wild—I never knew stuff like that was going on in those circles*" Susan exclaimed "*What else d'you know about all that?*"

"*Not much . . . I'd have liked to have read more – but there's only so much you can read in a day. I'd like to have a whole army of bodies who'd read all the books I want to read – but . . . without that possibility I'm stuck with making choices. I know that John Martin was creating these mezzotints after the French Revolution – so he was reacting to 'the reign of terror' – y'know the guillotine and all that horror of people accusing each other of having been aristocrats. Not that I'm in favour of aristocrats in particular – but there has to be a better way to change the world than viciousness and murder*" Pause "*The interesting thing about John Martin though, was that most artists of that period left the hard work of abrading and burnishing the copper plate to professional engravers – but*—he—*did it*—all—*himself. He worked directly on copper plate without preliminary sketches – so he was wrestling with the materials – and kind of got inside them.*"

"*Yes . . . I know what you mean*" Daphne remarked "*There's a whole world in there when you stand and stare into them. It's like they're almost three dimensional.*"

"*Indeed . . . yes . . .*" I replied "*It's amazing. People really don't understand*—how—*he did what he did, now – and no one can reproduce it. It's like he went somewhere no one had ever gone before . . .*"

We passed the rest of the evening roaming through all manner of subjects and finally caught the train home. I'd left the pixie chariot outside Sarah's house and so walked home with her.

"*Y'know . . . I think Lindie's going to miss you*" Pause "*She used to tell us what amazing conversations you had*" Pause "*I don't think she's going to find it that easy to find anyone else to talk to in the same way.*"

I was glad it was dark and my face therefore relatively invisible "*Yeah . . . well . . .*" Pause "*. . . but then . . . I also knew two fellows who could talk about anything.*"

"*Steve and Ron?*"

"Yes. They were pretty widely read – especially Steve. We'd talk about all kinds of things – so there must be other fellows out there who have a vocabulary beyond foop-baw" [3] Pause *"I'm hoping to meet them at Art School."*

"Wish I was going to Art School . . . My parents want me to go to teacher training college though . . . "

I didn't know what to say in reply to that – because it sounded like a continuation of school to me. We'd been on a visit to one of those places and it seemed horribly institutional. The lecturers dressed like school teachers and there was no sense of freedom. The students all looked as if they'd been manufactured at the Department of Protracted Normality.

"Pity – it would have been fun to have gone to Art School with you." I mounted the pixie chariot and purred off into the night thinking that there were a few too many things in life that were a pity.

The Art studio at school was still open and I spent most of my time there working on a large piece I'd begun. Susan, Sarah, and Daphne occasionally came up to see me in the studio. They were always interested in looking at my paintings. My final piece was an oil painting.

"Where—is—that?" asked Daphne.

"It's the lane behind my home. It's lined with trees and that willow tree there was at the end of Mr Love's garden." I explained about Mr Love. *"I invented Mr Love as I remember him. I had to look up pictures of Evelyn Waugh – because Mr Love dressed in that Edwardian style."*

---

3 Football.

"*He sounds a wonderful old man*" commented Sarah "*He must have been very important to you . . . that you're painting him now – after all these years.*"

"*Yeah . . . He's very important to me. Mister Love started it all off, you see. He probably had no idea where I'd take it all . . . But then neither do I . . . at the moment.*"

"*So . . . is that you with him in the painting?*" Susan enquired

"*Yes – I inserted myself – but, as I was at the time.*"

"*It does look a little bit like you . . .*" Susan mused.

"*It's based on a photograph of me from that time.*"

"*. . . but you didn't have long hair back then did you?*"

"*No . . .*" I replied with a grin "*. . . it's not about realism exactly – it's about the world I would have wanted . . .*" I felt my throat lock in as I made that statement and had to force myself into a frame of mind where tears would not result. "*It's a . . . kind of hybrid image – emotional archæology and wishful thinking. If I had a picture of Lindie as a young girl I'd have put her in the deckchair next to me.*"

"*Yes . . .*" Susan smiled wanly "*she should have been there.*"

"*The deckchairs look kind of pre-war . . .*" Sarah observed – noticing that Susan looked a little tearful "*And where did you find the picture for that old record player?*"

"*The deckchairs belong to my parents and they're pretty old*" I replied "*The gramophone's from an advertisement in an old National Geographic.*"

They were intrigued and I continued explaining the elements of the painting. A NATIONAL TRICONE was propped up against the willow tree. "*In order to paint it I had to study the effects of light on flat chromium surfaces. Those were hard to find . . . so I used a mirror as the model which made the TRICONE look like part of the garden.*"

"*It looks a little like the* DEBIL *– but it seems to have a lot of strings . . .*" Sarah observed.

"*Yes . . . it's a* 12 *string* NATIONAL. *That guitar doesn't exist yet – but the act of painting it is the key to making it happen. I'd want to have one made one day.*"

"*Can you just—*have—*guitars made for you then?*" Daphne asked.

"*Certainly . . . yeah*" I replied "*Those who—make it—professionally in music can be innovative with instruments. I heard Eric Clapton created a hybrid by having a luthier fit a* STRATOCASTER *neck to his* TELECASTER" Pause "*So I know a* 12 *string* NATIONAL TRICONE *is possible. It's just a question of what it would cost . . . People are busy out there in the music world – ringing the changes in all kinds of ways. I mean Pete Townsend and Jimi Hendrix talked with* MARSHALL *about the amplifiers they wanted and the* MARSHALL STACK *came out of that.*"

"*You've managed to find out a lot about all this haven't you . . . *"

"*I suppose I have. It was going to be my life I suppose – and it seemed important to know as much as I could about everything connected with electric Blues.*"

"*I've always liked the way electric guitars look . . . *" Sarah commented "*. . . but I never thought playing an electric guitar was a possibility for a girl.*"

"*What?*" I was almost speechless "*There's no law against it – apart from parents that is. Y'know—*one day—*something's got to be done about parents. I mean they do need to enforce some discipline – but some of them really get beyond themselves. The world should be wide open for anyone to do anything – I mean, women can join the Army – so what's wrong with giving it hell on a* TELECASTER?"

"*You're going to be an interesting father one day*" Sarah laughed.

"*Well . . . given the opportunity.*" The three girls shrieked with laughter and Daphne tried to say something but was unable to articulate it for her fit of the giggles. I didn't want the subject to drift back to Lindie again so I said "*I heard the rumour that there was a solid-state electric resophonic guitar in the late '40s – early '50s, but I've never been able to find information or picture references anywhere. If there had been I would've put one of those in the painting.*"

"*Thought bass was your instrument*" Daphne commented.

"*Yeah . . . it was . . . and I'd like to think that an electric resophonic bass would be possible.*[4] *There're so many possibilities . . . and I've been busy finding a way into the heart of it all.*"

These ideas whirred and whirled around as I sat and painted. I was like some Palæolithic cave painter in Lascaux – but I wasn't painting the buffalo I wanted to catch, I was painting the instrument I wanted to play. The scene of my painting was seen through a lattice work of willow branches so that our forms were dissected and intersected by the tree. I was working from photographs. There was no way to work on that at home and so I stayed with the painting 'til the end. I signed it Frank Schubert – then left it there. Goodbye.

I found a note on the floor, it almost sent me off in a trance, / She said it's nothing that you done, I'm just leaving in advance.
Memphis Slim—Empty room Blues—1941

And then Susan, Sarah, and Daphne departed. I waved them goodbye. We'd stay in touch. We wrote to each other fairly frequently for some years—'til husbands arrived and children appeared—but we never lost contact.

---

4 NATIONAL RESOPHONIC GUITARS made a prototype Resolectric bass in 1998 but decided not to market it.

I sometimes wondered about them and how life would have been if I'd become close to one of them – but I'd known them through Lindie and it was as if they existed as an indivisible trio. Lindie was still burnt into my mind and it wasn't really possible to see anyone else clearly. That would have to wait.

Many things were mysterious in the Summer before I started Art School. It was as if the Summer had no intention of ending. Time usually flies – but as the days passed, the starting date in mid-September failed to draw any closer. A heavy foot had settled on the brake of reality. Maybe it was the ghost of Einstein showing me that time was relative. I had a photograph of Einstein on my bedroom wall. I liked his face and wondered what it would have been like to have met him. He was a genius – just as Ron had been a genius. I wasn't a genius—I knew that —but I also knew that I had some kind of connection with genius. I wondered whether I could ever amount to anything on my own – or whether I'd have to meet another Ron or another Steve. Would such people want to know me if I met them? That was a question and whilst I was pondering, Jeremy Franklyn almost walked into me.

Jeremy Franklyn was a lad from the past. He'd been a year ahead of me at Netherfield. He'd got married and now lived in a flat up from Aldershot Railway station. He commissioned a painting from me when he saw slides of my work on 'darkness' from Virginia Water School. He had a slide projector and we spent an evening looking at slides of Albania where he'd visited relatives with his parents. I brought slides of my art projects. I painted images of what things looked like under extremely dim lighting. The idea was that you had to look at the images in partial blackout conditions. They were painted in vivid colours so that they'd look like colours appeared in semi-darkness.

We spent a while meeting up with each other. I liked his wife – but she was rather quiet. She seemed to want him to take charge of the conversation. I felt unsettled by that. I was used to ladies having their own voices – and having opinions. I was always uncomfortable when ladies subordinated themselves in this way – or became submissive whether they liked it or not.

Jeremy was eventually disappointed in me for various reasons. I didn't want to join him on a group trip to Morocco. He was arranging it with a group of friends – and I didn't respond well to having persistent pressure exerted in that direction. 'No' meant 'no' and—stammer notwithstanding—I tended not to be too pleased if that wasn't clearly understood. He'd made it sound like some mystical great adventure – but it sounded to me as if he and the others were keen to smoke the local produce. I'd only met one of the 'others' and he seemed laconic and vague.

Lying in a den in Bombay with a slack jaw, and not much to say, / I said to the man, "Are you trying to tempt me / Because I come from the land of plenty?" Hay Strykert Sinclair—Men At Work—Down Under—Business as Usual—1982

Hanging out in some dismal dive with deranged denizens of the demimonde seemed infinitely dreary to me – but then camel rides seemed tiresome to him.

"They have camels in Morocco – you know."

"Yeah . . . ? Maybe – dunno – not my scene."

"In Morocco you can go off into the Sahara on camels across the Atlas Mountains . . ." I was interested in the possibilities of camels. *"I've heard there are fig groves there."*

"Yeah . . . well . . . I'm not that interested in . . . boys' adventure stuff . . . or . . . tourism."

"Well I'm not interested in lying around in Morocco—or Marrakesh or wherever—with a bunch of taciturn hippies hell bent on unconsciousness."

"Your loss man . . . It's an inner quest – and y'know . . . it'd . . . help you."

"No—thank you—Jeremy, I don't need help."

"Like really man . . . Y'need to look inside yourself."

"Yeah well . . . I've done that . . . I had an x-ray when I was 11 and it wasn't that interesting."

Jeremy shook his head as if I was dense and proceeded to explain what 'looking within' meant.

"I was trying to make a joke Jeremy."

Jeremy looked at me in an odd way *"You've never seen the truth have you – I can hear, by what you're saying man."*

"I've seen all I want to see Jeremy. I see colours and hear sounds every day – and if there's more to see, I'll see it by looking longer. I don't need to dope myself to do that."

"It opens doors man . . . and you don't know what that is 'til they open. Then you see it all . . . and you see yourself . . . as you are . . . and then you stop chasing everything as if there was 'somewhere' or 'something' to get."

*"Give it a rest Jeremy. Give me an adjectival camel—*any—*day of the week."* Jeremy shrugged and shook his head as if I was missing the best opportunity that life afforded. *"Anyhow—camels or no— I'm preparing to go to Art School – and I'm booked at a few venues, so you'll have to count me out."*

Before we drifted in different directions however – he decided that I should go and see a fellow in Aldershot *"Stuart's a meditation master."*

"A meditation master in Aldershot – that's a turn up for the books."

" . . . and . . . " Jeremy smiled ingratiatingly *" . . . he's not as far away as Morocco. You should meet him – he'd have things to say that you'd find useful."*

"Sounds interesting . . . I'm always open to learning something." Tibet was always somewhere at the back of my mind. Magic, mystery, spirituality, and Eastern religions were woven into most conversations in those days and there always seemed something to learn. *"I've got nothing else booked up on Thursday evening – so yes, I'll come and meet him. He's open to being visited is he?"*

"Yeah . . . well, he would be . . . wouldn't he . . . His . . . is a life of service."

"Not a military man by any chance?"

"No . . . " said Jeremy – obviously irked by my lack of seriousness. *"C'm'on . . . man . . . that's not what I meant by service . . . Not—everyone—in Aldershot's a soldier. I think you—know —that."*

"Yeah Jeremy, I know that . . . I'm just over-reacting y'know . . . to your loathing of camels."

Jeremy nodded. He accepted that he'd been high handed with his boy's adventure comment *"I guess it could be cool riding off into the wilderness and getting high on the altitude. Atlas mountains yeah . . . yeah. Maybe another time."* He then informed me that Stuart was the grandson of Aleister Crowley [5] – or some such thing. It could have been that he was the great grandson, grand nephew – or maybe the whole thing was crazy.

---

5 Aleister Crowley—Edward Alexander Crowley [1875 – 1947]—was an English occultist and writer.

"Who's Aleister Crowley?"

"Aleister Crowley? Well . . . he was the leading magician in the Golden Dawn and Ordo Templi Orientis. He wrote 'The Book of the Law' . . ."

"That doesn't really mean much to me . . . I'm afraid. I've never read that kind of material."

"They called him 'The Wickedest Man in the World' because he was . . . y'know, totally free . . . of the chains we all wear. That's why we need to look inside."

"What's 'wicked' about being free?"

"That's just how ignorant people saw him man."

"Yeah there've probably been people who saw me as 'wicked' . . . Brigadier Dale and his wife amongst others . . . "

Jeremy shot me a quizzical glance – and so I gave him a potted history.

"Right . . . so you understand what I mean then" Pause *"So . . . Crowley yeah . . . he's a brilliant chess player, painter, and poet – as well as being an astrologer and mathematician . . . "*

"Impressive" I replied wondering where the discussion was leading.

"He had no limits y'know . . . " said Jeremy knowingly *"He was a profound experimenter with psychotropics – and bisexual too."*

"I suppose I've got my limits then" I stated as blandly as I could.

"Y'really—don't—want any fucking limits man."

"You'd be up for having your arms and legs amputated then?"

"C'm'on man – that's extreme – I'm not talking about . . . there's nothing anyone can answer to that and it just avoids the point."

"*No . . . it's just not what you want to hear. I think everyone's entitled to the limits they choose – it's just that they have to choose them and know why they've chosen them. The limits I've chosen leave me free to explore the world in a way that I find . . . stimulating. I explore the sense fields – I look out rather than looking in. It's just a different approach. You've got yours and I've got mine – I'm not trying to convince you of anything.*"

Jeremy looked slightly confounded for the first time in our conversation "*Yeah . . . right . . . well, that doesn't sound like the normal trap that everyone's in.*"

I inferred that I was still seen as being in some kind of trap "*So now—you—understand what—I—mean.*"

"*Yeah . . . whatever you like I s'pose*" Jeremy responded languidly "*But . . . y'really should read up on Crowley man. Y'know—and this is really some story—he was invited to preside over this public discussion on occultism in San Francisco . . . earlier part of the Century—right—and there were some pretty powerful types there . . .* " Jeremy confided in conspiratorial tone "*He was so disgusted by the low level of intelligence of the—so-called—magicians, that he climbed onto the table—dropped his trousers—and bared his arse at them. Then—right—he shat on the table and left! Can—you—believe that!*" The tale is apocryphal for all I know – but that's what Jeremy Franklyn told me.

"*Yeah . . . I can believe that . . .* " I laughed "*. . . but what's so fascinating about public bowel movements?*"

"*Well . . . up to—you—man*" he laughed "*Anyhow . . . it's worth thinking about – but . . . Stuart's more into Zen.*"

"*So he'll keep his trousers on?*"

Jeremy didn't laugh. He just stared at me in a way I found slightly disconcerting.

"Yeah . . . more than likely – but . . . you'll need to take this seriously or there'll be no point going. Stuart's . . . well . . . he's got a brilliant mind— utterly—utterly brilliant. He's totally amazing. He's got such depth of insight – he knows everything about everything and everyone. There's nothing he can't see. There's probably no one like him in England."

"Well . . . I'm interested in almost anything unusual. I can't say I really understand why it's a good idea that I go and see Stuart – but I'm open to whatever comes my way."

It was all settled and a time was arranged. It was mysterious – but it had an edge of which I felt ever-so-slightly wary. I was somehow suspicious that it was connected to the Morocco trip – and that more pressure might be put to bear on me about making the trip. I put it down to paranoia and decided to go along with it. Jeremy seemed to think it was a fantastic opportunity. I had no great interest in Zen in particular – but I was always open to learning something about anything strange.

Jeremy wore an expression which seemed to betray that he had something in mind – something he wasn't making clear. It occurred to me that he was being withheld about some aspect of what was to follow. Still . . . I was up for any kind of inexplicable adventure. I let him have his mystery.

The streets are full of normal people all dressed in velvet cloaks / And I'm looking on expectantly trying to figure out the joke / There's a looking glass in every door and a quote in every sling / 'cause the hour's nearing midnight and the owls are on the wing.
Larkin/Bruce/Schubert—Savage Cabbage—The Owls are on the Wing—Savoy Green—1970

We arrived at the house on the appointed evening and were let in by a gaunt young man dressed in black. It may have been some kind of Zen costume for all I knew.

I wondered momentarily if he was wearing makeup – but decided that I was mistaken. The fellow uttered a word in a language I didn't know. I wondered whether it was some sort of Zen greeting. I offered a cheery hello and received a sneer in return. I obviously didn't know the right language – but that didn't bother me. Let them have their code language.

Stuart wasn't immediately available so we went into the garden. There were some monkeys in a cage that extended the full length of the garden. I was delighted to see them – but I made an error of judgment—or so it was deemed—by smiling at the monkeys. The monkeys reacted to my smile by screaming and rushing at me. They shook the cage in an infuriated manner – and I was pulled away from the cage. *"You should never smile at monkeys. They take the sight of teeth as a sign of aggression"* Jeremy explained. I had the feeling I was being lightly reprimanded. I should have *known* this simple fact about monkeys. Why should I know about monkeys? I decided to make no comment.

After a while I was told that I should go upstairs to see Stuart. He had agreed to give me an interview. Interview? What interview? I was encouraged to go up because *this was how things happened here.* This was not what I'd anticipated. I thought I'd meet Stuart as you'd usually meet a person. I didn't want an interview—I hadn't asked for one—but *in for a penny in for a pound.* What had I got to lose . . . ?

I knocked on the door and was summoned inside. A stocky middle-aged man was sitting in a large chair. He had a pensive air that appeared studied. He had a Vandyke beard which I spontaneously designated as a 'monkey beard'. The room was dim apart from the summer evening sun streaming through the window onto the seat where I was to sit. It made him a little hard to see.

There were shelves lined with books – and photographic portraits on the walls of ugly people who seemed to be doing their best to look as if they were *something out of the ordinary*. They looked as if they were from the turn of the century.

I introduced myself – but he countered my introduction by saying "*I—know—who you are.*"

"*Right . . . Jeremy will have told you . . . but . . . there appears to have been a mistake*" I stammered slightly "*I'm sorry but I haven't requested an interview and I'd not like to waste your time. They just said I should come up here and I didn't want to be rude.*"

He looked at me sternly "*I am not in the habit of making mistakes.*"

"*I didn't mean your mistake—I meant Jeremy—but anyway . . . what's this interview about?*"

He looked at me intently "*Do you—know—what—you are doing . . . and why?*"

"*Mostly.*"

"*And why are you so sure?*"

"*Why not?*" What was this nonsense? "*But . . . why are you in doubt about how sure I am – you've never met me before.*"

"*Why do you need to be defensive?*"

What the hell was that supposed to mean? "*Well . . . I suppose it comes out of your asking me strange questions. I didn't expect to have to answer things like this . . . but*—if I can ask you a question—*why d'you need to question me? What's this all about?*"

"*This—as you know very well—is merely further defensiveness . . . further evasion . . . Why the pretence?*"

I became angry at this point, or the closest I get to 'angry' – which looks something like a stalagmite.

Whenever I turned into a stalagmite, the stammer would vanish. *"Look, I don't know why I'm here apart from the fact that Jeremy wanted to introduce me. I didn't come expecting an interview or whatever this is supposed to be. I thought we were just going to meet . . . like people meet."*

He smiled in a quirky manner and said *"Now we—both—know—that—is not true."*

This was absurd. *"I really don't know—what—you're talking about; or what you want from me. This whole thing's ridiculous. Who the hell—are you—to be questioning me? Is this some sort of Zen thing – because if it is I'm not interested in Zen."*

"Why do you need to contest me? You will gain nothing from this childish bravado." The encounter was getting more outlandish by the minute.

"I'm not contesting you, or whatever—that's—supposed to mean. I'm just answering your bizarre questions – even though I don't understand why you're asking them. I don't know what this warped meeting's about. Jeremy just suggested I should meet you—because you're supposed to be interesting or something—and I just went along with the idea."

I was exceedingly irritated at this point and had grown incredibly wary.

"You just went along with the idea did you? Really . . . Why do you expect anyone to take you seriously when you don't know what you're doing or why your life is not in your own hands?"

That was his first relatively sane question – so I made the mistake of answering in a personal manner *"I know exactly what I'm doing. I know enough to know that life's as much in my hands as it can be – at the moment. It's wreckage—in parts—but that's not a problem that time's not going to fix."*

"I don't expect life to make a lot of sense at the moment" I continued *"because my two best friends have died less than two months ago. My band's dissolved. I lost the girl I loved because her fascist parents didn't approve of me. I'm trying to make it on my own as a performer. I'm struggling with a new guitar style. I'm about to start Art School in eight weeks. And so, yes, I—am—feeling at a loose end I suppose, or I wouldn't be here talking to you now. I had nothing planned this evening that's all – and being at a loose end is—*strictly—*temporary."*

He eyed me maliciously. I started feeling that I shouldn't have revealed anything about myself to *Mister Monkey Beard.*

*"So . . . you feel this is a—*temporary—*hiatus?"*

"Yes – that's exactly what it is."

"Really . . . really . . . I think you're completely lost – and you always have been."

I liked this situation less and less *"No – you'd like me to—believe— that I'm lost for some reason – but I don't buy it. You can think what you like about me – I don't need your approval."*

He allowed an uncomfortable silence *"I am stating a fact. You will not help yourself by hiding from it. You should feel free to admit that you feel lost. You would find it so much simpler to be honest."*

"The only thing I feel at the moment is that it wasn't one of my best decisions coming here. I don't like this situation—I don't like you—and you have no right to force this interview on me, when I've told you I didn't come here for an interview."

Silence again. *"You would find it a relief to be honest about yourself. How long do you think you can go on living a lie?"*

I left a silence this time because fear and anger were oscillating. Satan oscillate my metallic sonatas. That's a palindrome – but it portrays something about me at that age – when I was pushed.

"*Lies are obviously more familiar to you than they are to me – and the only relief I need is relief from your adjectival self importance. Who—*do—*you —think you are?*"

"*You—know—who I am.*"

"*Yes. You're supposed to be some sort of Zen teacher – but I don't see what any of this has to do with Buddhism.*"

"*I don't know what young Jeremy has said . . . but Zen is simply a method I employ – one of many methods. What concerns me is this 'sadness' you're feeling about the death of friends. This isn't just about their deaths. This isn't new to you is it? And the loss of a girlfriend is a common experience at your age. It's not a tragedy. The tragedy . . . is that you've been sad all your life. I think you're on the edge of tears aren't you.*"

"*Actually no – I'm just wondering when you're going to drop your trousers and shit on the table. Jeremy mentioned that as a possibility.*" Horror— I'd gone too far—*why* had I said that? I knew why. I'd hit the point where anger had overcome any sense of self-preservation. It was an icy statement delivered with slow cold deliberation.

Silence. He leaned forward staring at me. Anxiety cut in. Where would this end up? Where might the course of events be leading. I wondered whether it was actually possible just to get up and leave – or whether that would not prove simple. There were enough people in the house to forcibly detain me – *if* he were to give the word. Was *that* on the cards? He was waiting for me to speak – employing silence as a means of coercing me into blurting. He *was* succeeding in making me uncomfortable by glowering at me with unblinking eyes – but I decided I wasn't going to be intimidated. It was a cheap trick he'd developed. Two could play at that game. I just sat there and stared him out.

No – I wasn't *that* brave. It was a ploy that occurred spontaneously. The light from the window was striking my spectacles, causing reflections that obscured his eyes. I appeared to be looking directly into his eyes – but I was not meeting his gaze.

Down in Louisiana back in the big bayou, there are paths that you don't cross – places you don't go.
Kent 'Omar' Dyles—Omar and the Howlers—Mystery Walk—1996

His gaze had been a little too much for me and my adventitious spectacle shield worked wonders. After sitting like this for what felt like an hour—but was probably a few minutes—he said "*Go.*"

For some reason I didn't feel like being ordered about by *Mr Monkey Beard* so I remained where I was.

"*I said go—leave—now.*"

"*Heard you the first time*" I replied "*My father's more threatening than you. You're pathetic.*"

All lies of course, I—*was*—intimidated. I got up as slowly as I could to show that I was not anxious. I moved toward the door.

"*Your life is wasted. You will experience nothing but misery and purposelessness*" he intoned ponderously as I walked through the door. "*You failed the test.*"

I didn't turn round – but at the head of the stairs I answered "*There—wasn't—any test.*"

I took another step down the stairs "*Didn't—want—any test.*"

Took another step down the stairs "*Didn't—ask—for any test.*"

And another step "*Didn't—take—any test.*"

He said something then – but I was at the foot of the stairs and didn't make out the words.

You see that woman, who walks the street, / You see the policeman, out on his beat, / But when the law get ready – you got to move.

McDowell/Davis—Rolling Stones—You Gotta Move—Sticky Fingers—1971 [6]

I opened the front door and walked out. Some sounds of agitation jittered in my wake like a party of fractious baboons – but I couldn't make out what was being said. I realised then, that I was nervous. Home was close. I walked quickly – but took an indirect route that couldn't be followed by car. I took a narrow lane – and cut through a garden to get back to another road. I put some complex distance behind me. It was probably needless – but I had an extremely nasty feeling about *Mr Monkey Beard.*

Oh he's a grill monkey, he don't get no peace, / His woman done left him now 'cause he's all covered in grease.

Michæl Radford—Stale Urine—Grill Monkey Blues—Egon Is Watching You—1993

He was sinister from way back. Although I'd stood my ground, I was aware that I'd got way out of my depth. I wondered what Jeremy's part in it was – and what was going on in that house. It felt unhealthy . . . almost disgusting – but I couldn't work out how revulsion had arisen. I'd been unnerved certainly – but why was I also nauseated? Maybe it was just the way that fear can sometimes make people vomit. I decided I was not keen on discussing the matter with Jeremy Franklyn – or meeting up with him again. I felt I'd been manipulated and was not pleased with myself for having gone along with it. I should have known something was wrong with meeting this so-called Zen teacher. I should have been wary after Jeremy's superior attitude with regard to camels – and his insinuation that I was a mere tourist.

---

6 Originally by Mississippi Fred McDowell—Fred's Worried Life Blues—1964

I wondered what *he* was and what his relationship was to
Mr Monkey Beard. Maybe they all defæcated on tables to pass
the time. I came to no conclusion. Perhaps it was better not
to know.

It made me wonder about men and why many of them tended to
be enamoured of power at the expense of others. That's
generally why I've preferred the company of ladies. I'd had
good male friends – but they were dead. Soon after that Jeremy
took off for Morocco and so I never got to find out what that
weird meeting with *Mr Monkey Beard* was supposed to mean.
I felt the adult world approaching and encroaching in ways that
demanded rapid maturation on my part. I couldn't wander the
face of the Earth being sensitive and falling prey to every card-
carrying egomaniac who inveigled me into his schemes.
I needed to develop a little healthy cynicism . . .
Time to move on.

*The carnival's out on mainstreet in honour of the squire / They're waving
banners in the road but they can't see the fire / Some girls in diamond
dresses started calling "Let us in." / 'cause the hour's nearing midnight
and the owls are on the wing.* Larkin/Bruce/Schubert—Savage Cabbage—The Owls
are on the Wing—Savoy Green—1970

3

july 1970 – august 1970

johnny's in the basement mixing up the medicine

The didacts got collated – stapled backwards in a file / On a concrete barge to Cairo pulled by crocodiles, / They thought they were all quite clever to make their way to town / But they got caught in their hotel room with their defences down.

Larkin/Bruce/Schubert—Savage Cabbage—See What's Going Down—Savoy Green—1970

With Blues, you never know—in any absolute sense—who sang anything first. Jo Ann Kelly attributed 'Louisiana Blues' to Muddy Waters but Ma Rainey sang 'Louisiana Hoo Doo Blues' in 1925 as: *Going to the Louisiana bottom to get me a hoodoo hand – gotta stop all of these women from taking way my man.* Hattie Hart sang 'Spider's Nest Blues' in 1930 as: *I'm going to New Orleans to get this mojo fixed of mine – I am having trouble, trouble; I can't keep from crying.* Lightning Hopkins sang 'Mojo Hand' in 1960 as: *I'm going to Louisiana, and get me a mojo hand – I'm gonna fix my woman so she can't have no other man.* There were many others – almost year by year since 1925. In 1970, I sang 'West Street Blues' at the Farnham Art School Folk and Poetry evening as: *I'm going down along by West Street, ain't got me no mojo hand – but I'll show any-a-you real fine ladies – that I'm a jelly roll making man.*

When I sang solo I always localised Blues: songs like 'Bush Hotel Blues' – referring to being thrown out for being long-haired and colourful. Closest I ever got to colour prejudice. 'Guilford By-pass Blues' told the story of a motorcycle breakdown in inclement weather. Blues lyrics seemed to be general property. Blues musicians just rang the changes and added their own slant. Blues melodies were general property too. The only feature of Blues which is actually individual, is the individual who sings and plays Blues. You either have the gift or you don't. I don't know that I had the gift – but I didn't have 'pink voice' and, I sure-as-hell meant it.

Got a letter this morning, how you reckon it read? Said, / 'Hurry— hurry—gal you love is dead.' / Grabbed up my suitcase—took off down the road, / But when I got there she laid out, on that cooling board.
Son House—Death Letter Blues—1937

I somehow seemed to feel that the Blues musicians I'd known since the age of eight knew me as well as I knew them. They'd been with me so long that they existed almost as friends. Some children have imaginary friends – but I lived in an imaginary juke joint.

I'd read Voltaire, Rousseau . . . visionaries, revolutionaries . . . it was like I knew those guys, like they'd been living in my backyard.
Bob Dylan—Chronicles: Volume One—chapter two—The Lost Land

BB King, Bessie Smith, Big Bill Broonzy, Big Mama Thornton, Blind Lemon Jefferson, Buddy Guy, Howling Wolf, Ida Cox, John Lee Hooker, Lightning Hopkins, Memphis Minnie, Mississippi John Hurt, Muddy Waters, Robert Johnson, Son House, Willie Brown, and Willie Dixon . . . *it was like I knew those people, they'd been living down my back lane with Mr Love.*

I learned about the lives of Blues musicians mainly from album sleeves. There were no books as far as I knew. In *the lost time* you had to go to London to get Blues albums – and *the going* was like a pilgrimage. There was a Jazz music shop in London—*Dobell's*—that imported Blues albums from the USA. Entering that shop was like entering a cathedral, except that the choristers were sometimes professional musicians. For all I know I could have rubbed shoulders with Jack Bruce and Eric Clapton – I might not have recognised them at that time. I'd have recognised Jimi Hendrix – but no one of his description ever walked in. The albums in the Blues section had come from somewhere else. They'd come from the place where Blues musicians lived – and it may as well have been another planet. There was boogie-woogie piano, Delta Blues, Texas Blues, Louisiana Blues, Chicago Blues – everything and more. I could only buy a half a dozen albums at a time – because that was all I could run to on what I earned. I'd work all weekend at the Army kitchen – and once a month I'd go to London and buy Blues albums. There was a guitar shop near Dobell's where I bought nothing at all – but occasionally played a few instruments they had in stock. There was a DOBRO once—wooden with a copper cover plate—the like of which I've not seen since. There was a SIMKA – a NATIONAL copy that sounded like a metal suitcase from hell. Both had two drawbacks: they were 6 string guitars and they were more expensive than even dreams would allow. I still longed for that GIBSON EB0 but it was emotionally implausible to enquire about it after the death of Steve and his father. Moloch was grinning in my face.

There's one thing to bear in mind – a true friend is hard to find. / Don't you mind people grinning in your face.

Traditional—Son House—Don't You Mind People Grinning in Your Face—1989

I'd have to wait 'til such time as I could obtain real money – but even so, what was I going to do as a solitary bass player? Why was I even having such an idea? I kept catching myself in denial about the fact that Steve and Ron were dead – and having to wake up to the reality of my loss.

I continued to work for the Army in Aldershot when I left school – and before I started at Farnham Art School. I worked at Cavans Road Army Married Quarters Removals. I humped [1] furniture and rode round in removal trucks. It was an easy job with plenty of relaxed sitting-around. There were a few older students there – but none from Art School. They were mostly on Summer holiday from universities around the country. One was a guitarist called Jasper Stanwell – an English literature student about to begin his final year. He was a singer / songwriter and he'd taken three years out roaming Europe with his guitar. He was already 25 years old and had an air of having been an adult for a century. I'd never met anyone under 40 with quite such self-sufficiency or confidence. He was a wild card too – a rabid intellectual epicurean who went at life full tilt. He was a political anarchist and massively well read. He quoted more than any human being I'd ever met. He seemed to have read two thirds of the available literature in the English Language. I thought I was reasonably well read – but in comparison with Jasper, I was some kind of lower primate.

Jasper and I talked a lot about music too because he knew a great deal on the subject – and from an improbable variety of angles. When he talked music he talked history, geography, politics, sociology, and philosophy.

---

1 In British vernacular 'humping' furniture pertains to furniture removal.

Every subject we explored was an education and I started feeling as if I should be taking notes. He knew about legends: Greek, Roman, Norse, Germanic, Celtic, Arthurian – and a whole ream of fascinating details concerning Sumerian, Babylonian, and Egyptian myth. He'd read the works of Claude Lévi-Strauss [2] and almost fell out of his chair laughing when I said I only knew of his trousers. I'd never heard of any *other* Levi Strauss. Jasper could always allude to some remote historical fact—pointing out the origin of a word—and go on to tie it in with the European Enlightenment and World War II. He reminded me of a participant in Herman Hesse's Glass Bead Game.

Jasper was a modern Folk style enthusiast and sounded a little like Al Stewart in his playing style – but Al Stewart in overdrive after downing three pints of rocket fuel. I liked his fancy finger picking and flat picking styles. He was delicate and precise – but had immense slam. He almost tore the strings off the guitar when he played and I wondered how many strings he got through in a week.

"Yeah" he laughed *"I break strings quite often – but I'd break 'em more often if I used the light-gauge fairy-set you use."*

He wrote fine lyrics – which made me realise I had a long way to go with lyrics. He had that way of mixing ordinary and strange, that I was struggling so desperately to find.

---

2   Claude Lévi-Strauss [1908 – 2009] was a French anthropologist and ethnologist – regarded as 'the father of modern anthropology'. He posited that . . . the 'savage' mind' has the same structures as the 'civilized mind' and that human characteristics are the same everywhere. This observation saw its culmination in 'Tristes Tropiques' a seminal work which placed him as a central figure in the structuralist school of thought. Structuralism is the search for underlying patterns of thought in human life. His writings influenced sociology and philosophy.

I could write well enough within Blues idiom – but he told complex stories in his songs. They weren't Folk-misery numbers – but arcane adventures that employed Rock & Roll symbolism and language entwined with strange imagery from Mervyn Peake. Fantastic convolutions in which people were being eaten by owls and sailing canoes through windows. I *loved* that stuff and wanted to try my hand at it – but it needed far more skill than I had. I needed to learn a great number of chords. Jasper showed me twenty or thirty strange chords: minor and major sevenths; fourths, fifths, ninths, elevenths, and thirteenths; suspended and diminished; flattened, sharpened, and augmented chords. Wild chords up beyond the 9th fret. I made notes. I was determined to learn these chords. He showed me how to play 'Like a Rolling Stone' starting in E and travelling up the neck in a series of E and stretched E shapes.

"*Fierce!*" I exclaimed "*Never seen*—anything—*like that before. I thought that chords up the neck were all barré chords. It's an adjectival miracle!*" Suddenly I could play up the neck – the place all the *real* musicians played.

He showed me an **A**m like a **D**7th shape up at the 9th and 10th frets on the 2nd 3rd and 4th strings. I was amazed at how the chord sounded. It had all the power of the bass strings played open – but with the æthereal sound of the high notes chiming like the sun piercing thunderclouds. You could move between the two forms of **A**m and they'd sound like an orchestra. Jasper also showed me a fantastic series of weird chords to accompany the Lennon/McCartney song 'Dear Prudence'. It was simple – yet eerily melodic. I'd never known about this approach. Ron had taught me a great deal – but he seemed to come from somewhere else – an approach that was far more mainstream in terms of how to learn chords. Jasper's approach—like Jasper— was anarchic.

I'd walked into my own music academy and I was being paid to be there. Johnny was *in the basement mixing up the medicine* [3] – and he was concocting a *strange brew*. [4] These chords were some kind of otherworldly alchemy – a far cry from the 'teach-yourself books' with which I'd previously encumbered myself.

"This doesn't mean you won't have to get to grips with barré chords though – so don't get—too—excited about it."

I have always remained grateful to Jasper for opening up the neck of the guitar for me.

Fortunately work at Cavans Road only proved to be an occasional interruption to guitar sessions with Jasper. He was a great fan of Bob Dylan and made me realise that I should have paid Bob Dylan far more attention than I had.

"If you want to write songs – you'd better listen carefully to Dylan. He's a master of the combined Folk-Blues-Rock idiom. No one's anywhere near him. Y'see – he's gone beyond genres – he's become his own genre."

"I can see that . . . wonder how I missed it? I really liked the Dylan songs I heard back in '66" Pause *"Somehow I didn't investigate him . . . I really should've done."*

"You didn't hang onto the albums then?"

"Never owned them" I replied shaking my head *"Belonged to my girlfriend Anelie – and when she went back to Switzerland . . . they went with her."*

"Not—of their own accord—I'd imagine" Jasper quipped.

---

3 Subterranean Homesick Blues—Bob Dylan—Bringing it all Back Home—1965
4 Eric Clapton/Gail Collins/Felix Pappalardi—Cream—Strange Brew—Disraeli Gears—1967

"*No – but I'd have liked to have witnessed that . . .* " I chuckled "*Anelie was a great fan of Dylan. We often spent evenings talking about his lyrics. She found them hard to understand – and I tried to unravel his language as far as I could.*"

"*How—*old*—are you?*" Jasper enquired.

"*Just turned* 18."

Jasper looked quizzical "*Hard to imagine two—*14 year-olds*— having that kind of conversation. Sounds rather intellectually advanced . . . I would have thought.*" It was evident that Jasper suspected exaggeration on my part.

"*Really?*" I knotted my eyebrows "*Well . . . I never actually—*liked *—being a child that much – and my friend Steve was almost 2 years older than me. He was—*extremely*—bright. Big reader too – so I suppose that had an influence*" Pause "*Well . . . I suppose I—*should*—also add that. . . only—*one*—of us was 14 . . . Anelie was 22.*"

Jasper roared with laughter "*You—*are*—a fucking rare one, and—* no*—mistake. Not that I care – but I suppose it didn't occur to either of you that unless your arrangement was platonic, that's strictly illegal?*"

"*Funnily enough, we never discussed that . . . Someone did tell me sometime later – but I don't think it would've made any big difference to me at the time. You see . . . as long as it was alright with Anelie . . . it was alright with me. I mean – I didn't make that law did I? I don't see why I should have to abide by laws other people make—*if*—they're not harming anyone. Just because you're born in a country with certain laws doesn't mean that you naturally agree with them all or accept them does it?*"

"*Natural Anarchist thinker too – good for you!*" Pause "*But bloody hell – don't some people just have—*all*—the luck! There were no—* intellectually stimulating*—au pairs when I was that age – I had to wait 'til I was 17 before I saw a pair of anything.*" Jasper was in full swing.

"*So . . . anyway – joking apart, tell me about how you*—unravelled— *Dylan for her then?*" he laughed "*while unravelling each other – no doubt. That's a total gas.*"

"*Well . . . yes . . .*" I dissembled in order to change the tone of the conversation "*I encouraged her to relate to Dylan . . . as she related to surrealist paintings. Anelie loved Surrealism – she introduced me to the work of some amazing painters: Max Ernst, Magritte, Salvador Dalí . . .*"

"*Very surprised you didn't follow up on Dylan then – he's a Surrealist if there*—ever—*was one. Just look at 'Hey Mister Tambourine Man' – I'd have thought that was*—right—*up your street.*"

"*Right*—*it is, should've done*—*because I*—definitely—*found Dylan intriguing. However . . . psychedelic Blues was exploding at the time and . . . I got . . . a little distracted. Then . . . when Anelie went back to Switzerland . . . somehow I didn't have the heart to invest in replacing those albums – and then . . . Savage Cabbage . . .*" I suddenly choked up.

"*Yeah . . . that makes sense. Tragic waste, that . . . Anyway – on to the next blast of grapeshot eh. No one gets out of here alive. Can't let the past stand in the way of the future.*"

That made some sort of sense – but emotionally it was incomprehensible. "*Yes . . . true enough . . .*"

"*So . . . go out and buy some fucking Dylan albums – and take a look at Leonard Cohen while you're at it. You've got some catching up to do.*"

I had indeed. There was just so much out there. So many wonderful creative personalities peppering infinity with their perfect gestures of Art.

I wished I could jump into the TARDIS [5] and take three years out at the 'Jasper School of Life' and come back in time for the first day of term at Farnham Art School. I'd heard of Leonard Cohen. He'd written that amazing song 'Suzanne' with its eerie melody and oblique concatenation of words. His voice was a trifle dreary to my ear – but I was certain he meant every word he sang. Jasper loaned me a Leonard Cohen album—and some Dylan albums—and I spent the next Saturday listening and jotting down words. It was remarkable that there were two people who could pen songs of such stature. Each had a unique style – even though there was some sort of basic genetic structure. It was something to do with the interleaving of the ordinary and extraordinary – and, with some kind of referencing system that relied on the semantics of Black American perception.

Commuters chew their papers on the train lines going East / I'd ask them what the time was but they'd tell me it had ceased / Then they'd lecture me with maladies and shoot me through with tape / But I'd somersault twice backward and accomplish my escape. Larkin/Bruce/Schubert—Savage Cabbage— See What's Going Down—Savoy Green—1970

Apart from Mr Preece—and the Misses Rodham and Elphinstone—Cavans Road was more of an education than the last seven years of school. Jasper talked almost incessantly – and he had a good listener in me. I was like a giant sponge for new ideas. I just kept asking questions and he kept on answering – in vans, lorries, trucks, staircases, warehouses – even whilst hauling wardrobes through windows on ropes. This was how school *should* have been.

---

5 TARDIS: Time And Relative Dimensions In Space – the name of the time machine-spacecraft of Dr Who in the BBC science fiction television programme of the same name which ran from the 1963 – 1989 and was relaunched in 2005.

I learnt so much from Jasper that it's hard to itemise it. It was a flow of information that wove in and out of political opinions and strange philosophical meanderings. As Jasper was an anarchist – I trusted his point of view. He didn't think that socialism was the answer any more than anything else.

"Socialism's the lesser of the evils . . . but it merely offers temporary help to people who've been socially deprived . . . " Jasper shook his head in exasperation *" . . . then the politicians institutionalise their reforms – and manipulate them as new instruments of repression. No one will be free as long as they give over their responsibility to governments."*

"You're preaching to the converted" I responded. *"I just never knew I was an anarchist."*

Jasper grinned *"Just as well . . . who knows what other trouble you'd have got into – quite apart from Little Miss Emmental."*

Come writers and critics who prophesise with your pen, and keep your eyes wide, the chance won't come again . . . and don't speak too soon, for the wheel's still in spin, and there's no telling who that it's naming.
Bob Dylan—The Times They Are a-Changing—1961

I'd thought that I knew who that *wheel's spin* had named – but it had just disbanded in spite of its world-class lead guitarist and its unique line-up with two bass guitars. These had been no safeguard against death – and I was left staring into the vacuum of no one's eyes. There was no deal[6] on offer either – simply the sense fields and any creative connection that turned up. I was fascinated by the fact that I had senses and that those senses were windows on the sense fields.

---

6 You said you'd never compromise – with the mystery tramp, but now you realise / He's ain't selling any alibis – as you stare into the vacuum of his eyes / And he says: *"Do you want to make a deal?"* Bob Dylan—Like a Rolling Stone—Highway 61 Revisited—1965

The Arts were the key to being alive – and I felt that being alive was far more fascinating than most people imagined. When I looked around me, I saw people using their senses as if they were 'safety measures' – mere sensing devices to ensure that they didn't fall over or walk in front of cars. At best people took to bird spotting – but then it was more a matter of collecting information or seeing something rare. It occurred to me that there is nothing special about something just because it's rare. That's Moloch's idea. If it's rare or unique you can charge big money for it. Moloch, of course, is illiterate. Moloch encourages the notion that *some things* can be 'very unique' and therefore very expensive however worthless they may be.

Mister Dali's romancing lobsters to pass the time of day / An' I'm conjuring with the windows – just trying to get away, / But high tide's at the wrong time and mercury's falling fast / Taking the road to uncertainty 'cause I know that nothing lasts.

Larkin/Bruce/Schubert—Savage Cabbage—See What's Going Down—Savoy Green—1970

If you're looking for something amazing – just take a look at a garden snail. They're astonishing.

Everything is special—*in simply being*—and the senses are the passport to that *world of specialness*. The world of vision, sound, tactility, fragrance, taste, and ideation are simply too much for one life. They overflow *as far as the senses can detect*.

Everything is infinitely crammed with potential. You could spend an entire life researching a subject and never get remotely near the end of the explorations. There's wealth unimaginable – right in front of your nose, at every turn. One thing leads into another, and another, and another – lured on by the shine on the passing moment.

The Lone Ranger and Disraeli were conversing with the moon / Trying to fix a chaperon for the girls out in the dunes, / Their wires had crossed them sideways and the hour was getting late / Before they lost their bearings and discovered their mistake.

Larkin/Bruce/Schubert—Savage Cabbage—See What's Going Down—Savoy Green—1970

Fascination flourished in the fibre of the phenomenal world – wherever I looked, listened or read. Bob Dylan's words were fascinating.

"He's obviously looked into this thing" I observed *"He—sings—Art doesn't he . . . I really wish I could find a way of writing songs like that— or even starting to write that kind of material—but whenever I try, my lyrics end up stilted and overworked."*

"Yeah . . . " Jasper replied – because he'd seen examples of my lyrics *"Dylan's radically concise at one moment and profoundly florid in the next – but without any form of disjuncture. I wouldn't lose heart though – there are plenty of good phrases in your lyrics. You've obviously got a feel for language – it's just that you haven't quite got into the idiom yet. You've got to cross the divide between poetry and lyric writing. You have to remember that—melody carries the meaning – so the lyrics don't have to be too heavy-handed in terms of colour. If lyrics get too gaudy they turn into some sort of bloody—garish—tie-dyed grandad vest."* [7]

"Yeah . . . that's—always—the problem. Y'see . . . I read a line like 'She's well acquainted with the touch of a velvet hand like a lizard on a window pane' [8] *and I want to write something like that . . . but then— somehow—I just can't find 'Mother Superior jump the gun' . . . "* Pause *" . . . and then . . . I get stuck."*

---

7 British vernacular for a long sleeved undershirt with a buttoned placket opening. They were popular in hippie culture where they were hand dyed in vivid colours.
8 Lennon/McCartney—The Beatles—Happiness is a Warm Gun—Double White Album— 1968

Jasper pondered in silence for a moment or two letting his eyes run over one of my songs. He made some nascent explanatory gesture with his hand *"Yeah . . . right – I can see that you're heading in the right direction. You—know—what you want . . . and so all you have to do is keep battling with it. Take Dylan's line 'Johnny's in the basement mixing up the medicine, I'm on the pavement thinking about the government.' There's so much in those lines – but it's the—economy—that makes it work."*

"Right . . . " I replied with monumental slowness *"And—of course —you can't interpret it beyond what it seems to mean in the moment."*

"Thought you interpreted Dylan for your Swiss amorata?" Jasper laughed.

"Yeah . . . but I had no personal interest in interpretation. Analysis and interpretation were what I most disliked about studying English at School. It wasn't good enough to say what I liked about word usage – I had to explain what the adjectival poet was saying. How the hell did I know what Yeats was saying? Maybe Yeats didn't know what he was saying. If Yeats knew what he was saying why didn't he write it down in plain English!?"

"Hey! You've really got some—feelings—on this subject!" Jasper cackled – evidently delighted that I'd deviated from my mild mannered mode.

"Yeah . . . " I laughed *"As far as I'm concerned poetry isn't just some sort of code language for something else that clever literary people can unravel. That'd make poetry little different from crossword puzzles – or like working out messages like 'Paul is dead' if you staple the Sgt. Pepper album sleeve to the ceiling and stand on one leg with your eyes closed – sniffing the edge of the album."*

"Yeah . . . your right . . . it—is—cretinous. That stuff annoys me as well. It's the pabulum of the nouveau puerile" Jasper had a way with words ' *. . . pabulum of the nouveau puerile.'* That was genius.

"Right . . . " I chuckled *" . . . maybe if you read the last line of Yeats' poem 'Death' backwards it'll tell you something else you don't want to know: Death created, has man – bone the to death knows he."*

"Actually . . . " Jasper mused *" . . . that—is—quite interesting if you flip the words 'to' and 'the' – maybe there's a future in this: Death created, has man – bone to the death knows he."*

Nor dread nor hope attend / A dying animal; / A man awaits his end / Dreading and hoping all; / Many times he died, / Many times rose again. / A great man in his pride / Confronting murderous men / Casts derision upon / Supersession of breath; / He knows death to the bone / Man has created death. William Butler Yeats—Death—The Winding Stair—1929

Then the truck pulled in and we climbed into the back. We had to empty some rooms of all furniture and appurtenances in the married quarters. The trucks always had ample sacking to protect furniture and so the rides were always comfortable. We sat back and continued our conversation.

"So—you see—when I read poetry" I said *"I'm reading paintings. When I'm listening to music, I'm listening to paintings. And . . . it's like that when I write poetry too – but with songs . . . "*

"Yeah . . . songs are about life y'see. Sounds like you've already had a lot of life go down . . . seems to have gone down all around you – but you haven't found a way to paint it yet. It's a different style of painting too. You're used to painting like Turner or something – and the lyrics you're trying to write are more like . . . Picasso."

"Mmmm . . . thing is . . . I really don't like Picasso that much – or any of the Cubists."

"*Well maybe not Picasso then—you know more about painting than I do —but someone who handles the grittier end of things. Maybe . . . *" Jasper opined "*when you've got enough Blues under your belt.*"

"*Yes . . . but when will that be?*"

"*When you've learnt the*—fucking—*barré chords*" Jasper quipped – and I slapped my fingers on another attempted **B**m on Jasper's guitar. Was I—*ever*—going to be able to do that? With Ron and Steve dead I had to get inventive with Blues on my own. I had to learn to write Blues lyrics like some kind of Englishman – even though that had little appeal to me.

Mr Brown and Queen Victoria were playing hide the eel, / When the carbon dated telegram came to tell them what to feel, / They pulled out the old projector and taught it how to play / But it hid its eyes in folding maps and looked the other way.
Larkin/Bruce/Schubert—Savage Cabbage—See What's Going Down—Savoy Green—1970

We both took our guitars to work to practise in the idle time – but when Jasper first saw the DEBIL he told me it was a joke. "*It's a remarkably well crafted joke – but a joke nonetheless. No one'll take you seriously playing an abomination like that.*"

"*Well . . . *" I replied with a grin "*That depends on what I—do— with the* DEBIL. *Some of the old Blues players used beat-out wrecks y'know. Passion's the main deal with Blues. I'm not a fancy player in any case.*"

"*Yeah—well—if you don't mind me saying, that's kind of obvious . . . *"

"*Right Jasper . . . *" I replied with a frustrated expression "*But I make no adjectival—secret—of that fact.*"

He nodded "*Let's hear what you do then.*"

I played 'Come on in my Kitchen' and when I'd finished he grinned "*Well . . . maybe you—*can—*get away with using that bizarre contraption.*" He paused a moment and continued "*You've got twice the volume you need with your voice—and you're a far better singer than I am—so maybe people won't notice that piece of tarted-up wreckage you play.*" Then he laughed "*You completely drown it out in—*any—*case.*"

Jasper was middle-class so he was full of words like 'bizarre contraption' and 'abomination'. I knew what he meant – but at that time it did not come naturally for me to throw words like that around. I employed unusual words in poetry but I had never learned to talk in that way. It seemed like some special skill that middle-class people had. They probably took classes in it – and it always impressed me. I loved language and thought that everyone should be able to increase their vocabulary. My father had an enormous vocabulary but didn't tend to use it too much in deference to my mother. Her English grammar was sound but she never ventured too far into major polysyllabics. My father used to learn a new word every week and use it in conversation. He was a great autodidact and that's something I picked up from him. It was a shame he never really came to stumble on that fact. I had a broader vocabulary than anyone I knew – and it was all down to him. The problem was – that it didn't seem to be *the done thing* to use it. People would look at you as if you were trying to prove something if you used unusual phrases such as 'atypical formulations'.

I thought long and hard about Jasper's comment on the DEBIL and decided that he was right in various respects. I'd have to buy a regular guitar. What I really wanted was a NATIONAL – but they were out of my league financially – so I settled for a brand new 12 string EKO, a jumbo-sized guitar.

Jasper had recommended the EKO as being extremely good value. EKO guitars were finely made – they had an expensive sound and low action. I was pleased with it – but knew I'd have my work cut out to sound believable on it.

Jasper looked incredulous when I showed him the 12 string: "*Why in—*hell*—did you get a* 12 *string if you want to play Blues?*"

"*I like the sound*" I answered with a broad grin "*After the built-in orchestra of tintinnabulating tin-foil-toads I had inside the* DEBIL, *a* 6 *string sounds—*extremely*—thin and weedy to my ears. Besides which, it's what—*Lead Belly*—played . . . and I've heard Jo Ann Kelly on* 12 *string too – so I know Blues can sound superb on a* 12 *string.*"

Jasper shrugged his shoulders in mock despair "*Yeah alright – I've heard of Lead Belly. Didn't know he'd played* 12 *string though – but who's Jo Ann Kelly?*"

"*English woman—terrific voice—you'd mistake her for a black American performer. She's brilliant.*"

"*Alright—that's two and one's English—but that still doesn't make it the instrument of choice. So beside Lead Belly – who else of the originals played* 12 *string?*" he asked – not expecting me to have an answer.

"*Blind Willie McTell, Blind Boy Fuller . . . and Blind Blake*" I responded – and then after a pause I continued "*Also Mississippi John Hurt, and of course Reverend Gary Davis.*"

Jasper grinned broadly "*Stone-the-crows, but you've done you're bloody research.*"

"*No . . . it's not really—*my*—research. Most of this comes from Mr Love, a splendid old gent I used to know . . . he'd been to the States and collected Blues. Then Ron—the lead player in Savage Cabbage—he knew a lot. He had a* FRAMUS 12 *string and knew some of the history too— whoops, I left out Memphis Minnie—and then there was Barbecue Bob and his brother – but I can't remember his name.*"

336

Jasper burst out laughing – but in a delighted kind of way
"You're one of a kind – but maybe you'll make it because of that. Never knew there were so many 12 string players . . . and now there's you: Voluble Vic Alpenhorn" Jasper added with reference to my Swiss liaison.

"I might have been tempted to use that" I laughed *"if I wasn't using Frank Schubert. But y'know—about 12 strings—there's a prejudice against them that no one's willing to define. Some say it's the jangle. Some say they're hard to tune, harder to play, you can't fingerpick them, or they're slow or whatever else."*

"Yeah" Jasper laughed *"I'd agree to—all—of that."*

"So I'm going to start saying standard guitars have 6 strings missing."

"I think you should do that!" Jasper responded laughing at my intensity *"World needs some different fucking opinions."*

"Right—glad you agree—and the Eko*'s got some fine boom to it. I enjoy playing it – even though . . . it could use some resonators."*

Jasper shook his head in amused disbelief *"Put resonators in a bloody 12 string and you—could not—sing over it!"* he cackled *"Well . . . maybe—you—could"* Pause *"Did you take singing lessons to get that bloody loud?"*

"No" I grinned *"Never had a music lesson either – not since I left primary school at any rate. All I know I learnt from friends. I just sing all the time – sing whenever I can. Always—have—sung. My mother used to like me to sing Christmas carols – and I enjoy singing almost anything. I think it was Big Bill Broonzy started me off . . . had his example when I was 8 – and that showed me how it was supposed to be. So . . . I just copied him."*

"Remarkable . . . you did well . . . Can't say that practising ever helped me get any more volume though. But what about diminuendo?" Jasper asked *"Can you soften your voice as well as tumble the walls of Jericho?"*

337

"*Sure*" I sang 'Oh Death' and made it plaintive.

"*Alright—I'll buy that—but what about Opera?*" he laughed.

"*I'm not . . . that well educated in terms of Opera – but I'll give you a verse of Schiller's 'Ode to Joy' from Beethoven's 9th Choral Symphony.*"

Jasper nodded "*That'll be a blast—go-ahead—hit me with it.*"

I burst into song "*Freude, schoener Götterfunken, Tochter aus Elysium, Wir betreten feuertrunken, Himmlische, dein Heiligtum.*" [9]

"*In bloody German too . . . think you've got a profession there*" Jasper chuckled "*If I could sing like you, I'd have a record deal on my hands.*"

Frank Schubert betreten feuertrunken . . . Enter Frank Schubert – drunk with fire. Schiller shimmered and shimmied: *Seid umschlungen, Millionen!* To be embraced, millions! *Diesen Kuss der ganzen Welt!* Kissed by the entire world! Well, not quite – I'd have settled for making albums and entering into cooperative ventures with those I admired. *Freude trinken alle Wesen* – all creatures drink joy at the bosoms of nature. Yes indeed! That's what I'd wish.

"*You're going to need to*—master—*guitar though*" Jasper added "*A singer-songwriter's gotta be able to lay down a good accompaniment. No good thinking you can do a John Lee Hooker. That works for those old Black guys – but it won't wash for the likes of you and me. You've really got to get those fingers nimble.*"

"*Yes . . . I am . . . what an idea though . . . that was Ron's forté – and . . . I'm strictly pianissimo unless I'm playing the* DEBIL.*"

"*Well . . . at the moment – but you definitely*—don't—*want to be a three chord wonder.*"

---

9 Schiller—Ode to Joy—An Die Freude—1785

"*No . . . but I congratulate myself*" I replied hopefully "*that—thanks to you—I've passed beyond that at least . . .*"

"*Yeah . . . somewhat . . . but there are players out there who really*—are —*masters.*"

"*I take your drift Jasper. I'm knuckling down. I really am.*"

"*Still . . .*" he laughed "*Don't go getting too good – don't want you stealing my show.*"

I'd go home after work at Cavans Road and practise the chords Jasper had taught me. I kept a note book to draw the chord shapes so that I wouldn't lose track of them. I knew these chords weren't easy to find because most of them were not in the chord books. Jasper told me that it wasn't really possible to list every chord variation in a book without it being too cumbersome and expensive to market.

"*How do you learn these chords?*" I asked Jasper.

"*Same way you're learning them. I learned them from Roland Meyers – really fine guitarist. He was seeing my sister at one time. My sister didn't like him much – so he used guitar lessons as a way of keeping his foot in the door.*"

I loved this stuff. It was an oral tradition – and I wondered how far it went back and how many people knew these off-the-wall chords. One day Jasper told me he'd show me some chords that sounded better on 12 string – but it was toward the end of my time at Cavans Road – and so the lessons in 12 string chords didn't progress as far as I would have liked.

"Chords sound different on a 12 string" Jasper told me *"Fingerings that sound discordant on a 6 string can sound great on a 12 string because of the way that the strings vibrate. They sympathise with each other and you get a mellowing effect due to the strings having this tendency to fall in line with each other harmonically. The more strings on an instrument, the more that effect is noticeable. It works that way with a string harp."*

This was fascinating and got me wondering about an 18 string guitar. There was a South American 18 string guitar but I'd never heard of anyone who played one. Jasper rolled his eyes at that idea.

"I'd learn to play your 12 string before you get too carried away with ideas like that. You need a guitar built like a piano to take the strain of that and the neck would be awfully fucking wide."

"Yes . . . that's true – but I have an idea for the future of building some kind of SUPER DEBIL *– like why stop at 18? You could have a 9 string guitar with tripled strings – a 27 string behemoth."*

"Where—did—you come from? You're totally incorrigible – never heard such outlandish Byzantine whimsies." The idea seemed to tickle Jasper, who tended to see me as his little brother. I was—after all—a brother-in-arms as an anarchist, so he put my whimsies down to youthful exuberance. *"If I'd not seen that* DEBIL *of yours I'd say you lived in cloud cuckoo land* [10] *– but . . . you do seem to have the determination to manufacture your daydreams in the real world. I have to admire that. Don't think I'd have had the patience to make a brute like that."*

---

10 'Cloud cuckoo land' is a British expression applied to someone who is deluded or lives in a fantasy world.

"Well . . . It's a question of necessity being the mother of invention. If you haven't got a thousand to buy a NATIONAL—*and you want one—you just have to do whatever you can. That's the way I live life Jasper. I have to do —or make—what's in my mind. If I didn't do that—whatever work it took—life wouldn't be worth living."*

Jasper laughed *"You're gonna have to look out for that passion of yours, it could well kill you one day – but I can't argue against it either. Just get to grips with music and there'll be no stopping you."*

Jasper—although hard wired with opinions—was always supportive and ready to teach me anything about music I wanted to know. Like all things however – our sojourn together at Cavans Road came to an end. He left at the end of July to go back to university. He'd earned as much as he needed to earn – but I had some weeks still to run. I needed a flying start at Art College and didn't want any short fall in finances to crimp my style.

I bade Jasper farewell and he grinned *"See you at the Farnham Folk and Blues Festival. Just make sure you put in the practise – I've staked my reputation on the fact that you're good."*

I grinned like a jet-propelled lemming *"Then that's just what I'll be."*

Harald Hardrada's bought his ticket for the bridge at Stamford Zoo / But no one saw him coming in, 'though he was right on cue, / So he threw them all a party and drank them with delight / While you and me rolled out of town to decorate the night.

Larkin/Bruce/Schubert—Savage Cabbage—See What's Going Down—Savoy Green—1970

4

august 1970

derailed gears

Virginia Water School seemed distant and remote. I never rode
in that direction again apart from a few evenings with Michæl
and Sandra Blenkinsopp, and as I traversed those familiar miles
of road, the Stones song 'Last Time' ran though my mind.
Michæl and Sandra Blenkinsopp were leaving Surrey—a Head of
Department post in history had become vacant in some splendid
establishment in Cumbria—and they were relocating. There was
a suddenness to it that unsettled me. *"Life just keeps ending—*
every—bloody—five—*minutes"* I growled under my breath as I
puttered to a halt outside the Blenkinsopp's semi-detached
house in Lobelia Crescent. I'd been expecting to continue going
to Michæl and Sandra's for dinner from time to time when I was
at Farnham Art School – but it was yet another derailed future.

*"We're very sorry indeed not to be able to continue these delightful evenings
with you Frank"* said Sandra.

"It's unfortunate . . . " continued Michæl *" . . . that these career
opportunities have to be seized upon at the expense of the rest of one's
life . . . We shall miss our conversations with you – and we're sorry that it
comes at such a time. We've been happy here in Surrey – but I would have
to wait another 15 years for promotion at Virginia Water."*

I told Michæl and Sandra it was kind of them to be concerned and that I'd really appreciated our evenings. And then there I was riding back to Farnham – and it really was the last time I took that road. It was a curious thing. Michæl and Sandra were going to disappear from my life almost as suddenly as they'd appeared. In one way it was sad—I would miss them—but in another it occurred to me that life was like this. The way I saw it was that you could either grieve the departures or you could celebrate the appearances. There'd always be new appearances and maybe they'd always be timely. Michæl and Sandra appeared just in time to cushion my fall when Lindie left without saying goodbye. Susan, Sarah, and Daphne had been there too – and now I was on the road again.

I missed Jasper Stanwell after he left – but he'd inspired me to forge ahead with music and to forge ahead with my life. He'd made it seem entirely possible *"With some solid practise behind you – you could still become a Bluesman. You've really got it in you and I can see you really taking off one day. You've got plenty of time too. I sometimes wish I was your age again."*

Those words had a vapour trail like a jet æroplane – stretching across the sky of my imagination. *I could still become a Bluesman.* I would build up the calluses on my fingers with assiduous determination. The barré chord was my objective. If I could master barré chords the Art of song-writing would open up to me. I'd write testimonies to eternity. I knew that they were waiting to flow from my pen – that fabulous old marbled green Pelikan German fountain pen my grandmother had left me.

Farnham Art School also seemed far off, if only by virtue of its intangibility. It lay waiting like some mystery-land just over the horizon of *what life had been.* I was about to become a real artist and to live a miraculous life for four years at least.

I'd observed Art students in their natural habitat – just being who they were. I'd experienced Art School at a distance at my interview and I'd been on a visit with Miss Rodham before that. It was a school without externally imposed discipline – where everyone took personal responsibility for the creative impulse.

Every time I thought about it I felt highly excited – a sensation that had been absent in the last weeks of school. Apart from Pete, there'd been no one there I knew – and I was determined not to latch on to him as some sort of security blanket. I'd need to make new friends. I'd need to explore on my own. I felt as if I was living a life strangely independent of past and future. In some ways that was valuable as it allowed me time to experience myself as a vacuum in terms of whom I'd been and who I might become. I also appreciated the nebulous quality of living outside time. It enabled me to postpone the final point at which I'd have to come to terms with the fact that Steve and Ron were gone – and that Lindie was a dream which never came true. I settled into the pattern of a working week – and weekends on which I'd practise the Blues numbers in my slowly developing repertoire.

Most weekends there'd be a spot for me to play at some pub in the area – mostly the Queen's Oak. Dave was a stout fellow and —although I was not Savage Cabbage—he was happy to give me spots.

"Y'should get another—band—mate. This country Blues lark's alright —and y'do it well—but it's not exactly goin' to set anyone on fire is it?"

"No Dave—it's probably not—but where am I going to find a band like the one I had?"

"*Yeah mate—tough one—see the problem . . . young Ron was a good'n –
fucking brilliant to tell the truth . . . Bloody bad luck t'say the least of it.
Them boys was—all—good. Steve was pretty nimble – nimblest bloody
bass I—ever—heard. Like you were—fucking professional—never—
seen—that before with lads of your age*" Pause "*So . . . what about Jack
– what's 'e doing then? You two could put out some feelers eh?*"

"*Jack . . . well . . . Jack's sold his drums and gone to work at Midland
Bank.*"

"*What!? 'es done—fucking—what!?*" Dave nearly shouted and I
repeated my statement. "*Bloody Nora . . . the little prat . . . Can't
believe it mate. Boy's a bloody idiot. You lads 'ad it made—y'know; 'ad
it—made.*"

"*Yeah . . . think you're right . . . We had it made. Anyhow . . . if you
ever hear of anyone looking for a vocalist – I'm up for grabs.*"

"*Right . . .*" he nodded "*but you played bass too didn't yer. Someone's
bound to want a bass player with a voice like yours.*"

"*Yeah Dave . . .*" I sighed "*if I—was—a bass player—but I was only
rhythm bass y'know and rudimentary at that..*"

"*What's rhythm bass when it's at home then?*"

"*It's a simple and—terminally—unexciting backing line that disappears
whenever I start to sing. So I need a—lead—bass like Steve's to cover for
me when I sing. Y'see . . . singing and playing bass at the same time is
extremely difficult. There are very few people who do that. I only know of
Jack Bruce and Paul McCartney – oh and Willie Dixon.*"

"*Right—right—never knew that . . .*" Pause "*So what'll yer do with yer
bass now?*"

"*Never was—my—bass . . . It was Ron's . . . I was going to buy it –
but . . .*"

"*Yeah right . . . bloody shame . . .*"

"I mean . . . if I—had—that bass I'd work at it . . . and see if I could make it as a vocalist bass player – but that'd take a few years. Steve's a —very—hard act to follow" Pause *"In fact . . . I don't think I'll ever be as good as he was."*

"Never say—never—son, never say never. Y'know . . . where there's a will there's a way—eh?"

"Can't argue with that Dave—just trying to be realistic—anyhow . . . if you—do—hear of anyone who wants a Blues vocalist and harp player – I'm always around. Has to be Blues though – I'm not really that much of a Rock singer."

"I'll do that mate—I'll do that—I'll get back to yer if I hear anything on the grapevine . . . but—in the meantime—yer always welcome to take the odd spot here. Can't promise more than once every month or so though – y'know 'ow it goes. The kids want excitement."

Yes. I knew how it went – and it was no big problem. There was Art School and I didn't really want too much exposure before I'd improved my chording skills. The barré chord was still a monstrous stretch and I wondered how anyone ever managed to play them as easily as they seemed to do. With me it was always a two stage operation: the barré – and then fractions of a second later, the chord.

The next thing I knew I was booked for the Cordwainer's Arms – Dave had given them a call. Rough and slightly aggressive as he'd seemed at first, Dave was a good fellow – a genuinely kind man. It occurred to me that Dave's brash exterior was a shield against the world. He was touchingly grieved by the loss of Ron and Steve and also by the disappearance of Savage Cabbage. He did think that Blues was on the wane – but he also thought that we had something that went beyond that fashion.

"Y'play—bloody—good music lads . . . bloody good music, and there's—always—a demand for that – whatever it's called. It's all R&B anyway, it's just the names that come and go."

Although this new solo gig venue was good news, a certain dread stole over me. Gazzer Mitchell frequented The Cordwainer's Arms. The possibility of bumping into him didn't exactly fill me with joy. I'd not seen hide nor hair of Gazzer for six months – and wasn't keen to run into him. I don't know why I was so concerned about meeting him. There was no absolute contention between us. Yes, he'd tried to poach Ron from Savage Cabbage – but unless he'd turned grave-robber, there was little chance of that. Then it struck me that I might be apprehensive about some comment he might pass – about Savage Cabbage, Ron, or Steve. If he said anything snide . . . I—*might*—just have to break his nose on Ron's behalf . . . just for old time's sake. It's not that I'd developed a violent disposition all of a sudden – but it wouldn't have been out of character for me to have done something like that. There'd have been some oblique concept such as owing it to Ron. It would have been stupid but I'd never been afraid of looking stupid. It occurred to me that Ron must have come within a fraction of an inch of breaking Gazzer's nose on various occasions. If Gazzer showed up and said anything—*anything at all*—I'd have to . . . well, I just hoped he wouldn't be there.

I turned up on the night with my two ridiculously large guitar cases strapped to the sissy bars of the Pixie Chariot. I was to perform most of my set on the DEBIL – with one number on 12 string EKO: 'Sitting on Top of the World'. One number on the 12 string EKO hardly seemed to justify bringing the guitar to the gig – but I had to start using it publicly at some point. I'd got that number down reasonably well – but it was still a strum rather than flat picking.

I sang a few unaccompanied numbers embellished by harp. They were a sure way of getting everyone foot stomping and hand clapping – and that—*always*—created a good atmosphere. Gazzer Mitchell was nowhere to be seen as I opened up the cases and took my seat with the DEBIL across my knees. I felt a surge of relief and concomitant confidence. I'd used the DEBIL a few times with Savage Cabbage – as an intermission piece. It'd been Ron's idea – he thought it important that I kept my hand in as an instrumentalist. The crowd always seemed interested and were polite enough to look happy and applaud – but I could always tell they were eager to have Savage Cabbage back again.

It was good—albeit slightly desolate—to be sitting there as a remnant of Savage Cabbage. As I tuned up it occurred to me that that's where Ron and Steve would want me to be. I never tuned the DEBIL with a pitch pipe – I just took it up from the bass string. It was only ever in tune with itself. It suited my voice to drop the bass string to **C** and enabled me to use heavy gauge strings. That was Jasper's idea and it worked well.

As I sat there—vaguely mesmerised by the misty yellow glow on the surface of the DEBIL—I realised that I'd lapsed into some sort of non-conceptual reverie. When I looked up, the audience were sat there looking at me expectantly. I grinned at them, relieved that Gazzer was nowhere to be seen. *"Goooood—evening—madams, monsieurs, mes enfants, mad hatters, caterpillars, dormice, and Alice; where—ever—you are. Glad to—be—here. Right people, my first number's . . . well – I think you'll see."* I launched immediately into 'Death Letter Blues' by Son House.

Got a letter this morning—said—how do you reckon it read? / **Red—
yeller**—lord—**green'n'blue!** / *Said 'Hurry, hurry—gal you—you
love is dead.'* / *Grabbed up my suitcase—yeah—took off—down the
road* / *When I got there she's laying—laying on that cooling board.*
Eddie James 'Son' House—Death Letter Blues—with additional colours interjected by the
author.

Time for a number with harp. *"Next song people . . . is a big
responsibility. Sometimes . . . the—key—in life is knowing who to blame
– and so I'd like to tell you people – It's Nobody's Fault but Mine!"*
Laughter *"Lot of people have sung this song – but no one knows who
wrote it. Everyone adds a change here and there y'know—adds a walrus or
a nine-legged octopus—so if you know this number, don't be too surprised."*
I let out a howl on the **G** harp.

Ron and Steve they taught me how to play, / *Said Ron and Steve they
taught me how to play,* / *Well If I don't play and my song ain't sung –
ain't nobody's fault but mine.* Author's parody—Nobody's Fault but Mine—1970

I ran through 'Sitting on Top of the World', 'John the
Revelator', 'Born Under a Bad Sign', 'Hoochie Coochie Man'
and several others. I finished my set with 'In My Time of Dying'
as an encore – and was feeling happy about my performance.
I was mightily relieved—when my set ended—that Gazzer was
not to be seen. What—*had*—I been worried about? Well . . . it
would have been a little perturbing to have seen him sitting there
with his professionally smug expression – the one that was
designed to humiliate anyone who wasn't damn sure of
themselves. I was feeling damn sure of myself that evening and
so I wondered what it would have been like to have had that
tested. I packed up my guitars and chatted a while with a few
people who were interested in my lap-slide style – and the
strange guitar on which I played it.

"*You*—really—*built that yourself?*" I was asked. He had a sketchy moustache and wild yet slightly timid eyes. He made me feel like *the ancient of days.*

"*Not quite . . .*" I replied "*It's more a case of having re-built it. It started out as a cheap nylon strung piece of rubbish that I picked up second hand. Cost me three pound ten from a junk shop.*[1] *The neck was as bowed as hell – but that works fine for slide.*"

The young man looked at it marvelling. I wondered how old he was – 15 . . . I guessed. A—*little*—young to be in a pub [2] – but then I'd been too young for all kinds of adventures . . . I told him about the ferrotype diaphragms and he hung on every word.

"*Where d'yer—get—things like that?*"

"*Army Surplus Store, Aldershot.*"

"*Yeah!?*" he said excitedly "*I'd like to try this—I really would—it's amazing! How much did—they—set you back?*"

"*Half a crown . . . as far as I remember . . . Well . . . under ten bob anyway.*"[3]

"*I'll go over there tomorrow and 'ave a look. Did they 'ave a lot of 'em?*"

"*They had a whole bunch – but they were glad to be rid of them too – so I don't imagine they'll be re-stocking. There may be other Army Surplus Stores though – you'll have to look around.*"

His name was Nigel Walton and he asked me how long I'd been playing and how I got started "*So where d'yer learn this style?*"

---

1 £3 and 10 shillings, £3.50 in decimalised currency.
2 18 was the legal age for being in a pub – but in Britain at that time 16 was considered acceptable even by parents.
3 Half a crown was two shillings and six pence, the equivalent of 12½p. Ten bob was 10 shillings – 50p.

"Copied Mike Cooper. He's got an album out called 'Oh Really!?' – you should get it if you want to pick up this style. He's the only one in Britain playing lap slide as far as I know – and he's far better than I am. He'll be playing at the Queen's Oak next week. You should really go see him."

Nigel nodded enthusiastically *"What's Mike Cooper play?"*

"Real NATIONALS *for a start"* I laughed *"He's got two vintage models – a* TRICONE *and a* STYLE *'O'. They're beautiful and they sound like . . . well – you'd have to hear them. They sound nothing like this creature"* I said indicating the DEBIL *"They're really loud and crystal clear – every string's like a bell."*

"Yeah . . . well . . . I bet they cost an arm and a leg too."

"You'd be right. I've seen them for close-on £700 in London."

"But this . . . " he replied *" . . . you can't buy—anywhere—and it's something I could make!"*

"Good luck – it's a lot of work though" I replied and gave him the details of construction he wanted. He asked one question after another and I kept answering. He got to hear the whole Savage Cabbage saga. It was an odd sensation. I was looking at a mirror image of myself with Jasper Stanwell. Strange to have that situation reversed – but somehow it felt like the sanction of providence. I wasn't any big deal – but I was someone with a violently loud voice and one helluva strange instrument.

"Howd'yer get that—surface—on it though?" he asked – slightly mesmerised by the way it glowed.

"Car enamel. I just kept spraying it and rubbing it down every few coats. Must be about 60 coats on it. Kills the sound stone dead of course – and, unless the ferrotype diaphragms cut in, it sounds like a potted pig."

Strangely this admission did nothing to lessen Nigel's fascination with the DEBIL. Finally the young man walked away saying that he'd like to try it out himself. *"You should definitely do that"* I replied *"But do it with a 12 string – that's what I'd do if I was starting over with the project. A 12 string would have a truss rod and you could use heavier gauge strings"* Pause *"And maybe don't paint it silver—or if you do—don't turn it into a car."*

Eventually I moved toward the bar to relieve my thirst with a glass of ginger beer. I never did like English beer and red wine was sour and too expensive in pubs. I'd just paid for my pint and turned round to find a chair – when Gazzer Mitchell came into focus. Gazzer was poker-faced and looked as if he was going to be trouble. This was a bad dream. My brain went into hyperdrive trying to figure out a way to avoid this meeting – but *that* line of conjecture took less than a second before it evaporated.

"Gazzer—good to see you—didn't know you were here" I laughed artificially *"Lucky for you . . . you missed my set."*

Gazzer gave a sheepish grin—quite unlike him—and pushed out the chair next to him with his foot. *'Niiiiice Western boots . . . '* I thought. I could use a pair of those. They were lizard—or some kind or reptile—and I wondered how much a pair of boots like that would cost. They'd be just the thing to wear when playing lap-slide – because the audience would get a good view of them. Gazzer interrupted me in my high speed conjecture.

"Didn't miss it—heard your set. Came to hear you . . . You were good."

Was this Gazzer? *"Thanks . . . Gazzer. Glad you enjoyed it."* I was vaguely flummoxed. What could compliments from Gazzer betoken?

"Didn't know you played that style."

Yes—this *was* Gazzer—but I couldn't quite understand the situation. There was no angle, no sarcasm, no insult, no ironic witticism. *"Yeah . . . played Delta before Savage Cabbage . . . actually . . . it goes back a long way with me. I've just gone back to it because . . . "* and there I was stopped in my tracks with a lump in my throat. Damnation – *why* did that *always* have to happen?

Gazzer cast his eyes down for a moment *"Yeah . . . sorry . . . real sorry to hear 'bout Ron. He was . . . he was the fucking best. Really was man . . . Best there—ever—was. Better than Clapton. Better than Hendrix too."*

I was still having difficulties aligning this apparition with Gazzer Mitchell *"Probably only—us two—would say that – but . . . yes . . . you're right. Don't think we'll see another Ron Larkin this side of Armageddon."*

Gazzer nodded. He seemed genuinely moved. *"Would've liked to have heard him use wah-wah pedal though. Jeeeeez – can you—imagine—that, man?"*

"Yes . . . often did imagine it. He could've gone to the moon on that" I agreed. *"Ron never did like effects though. He liked Hendrix—who didn't—but said that Steve and I were weird enough without him joining in. Y'know – Steve and I liked to use effects on our Acid Rock numbers."*

Gazzer smiled wanly *"Yeah, you had some really—far out—numbers man. You fellas took weird right out the fucking window. So how—is—Steve? You blokes planning anything?"*

Gazzer noticed my throat lock in on itself. I was silent for a while waiting to speak without bursting into tears.

"Well . . . y'know . . . Steve died in a car crash . . . couple of months back."

Gazzer let out a string of heavy handed expletives that caused the barman to scowl. He wiped a tear from his eye – so I let my own lachrymosity be as it was.

"*Yeah . . .* " that was all I could say. We sat there in silence for a while. There was nothing to say that seemed of any immediate significance.

Eventually Gazzer said "*Sorry 'bout that . . . move I made man . . . y'know, when I tried to get Ron into Freighttrain – that . . . that wasn't cool.*"

"*It's fine—no worries.*"

"*Just wanted to say it . . . y'know . . . felt it was right to tell you.*"

"*Yeah—thanks Gazzer—don't blame you for that . . . You have to make moves like that. Plenty of people do it. If he'd been playing in your band I might have done the same.*"

"*Good of you to see it that way.*"

It was. I knew that – but I would always rather be friendly than not, so I decided to make a friendly enquiry "*So . . . anyway . . . what's Freighttrain doing now?*"

Gazzer shrugged "*De—railed—man . . . Derailed Gears*" [4] he quipped. Humorous comment – but not something you could laugh about. I smiled—exceedingly slightly—just to let Gazzer know the pun had not passed me by.

"*It's all over . . . like—history—man . . . and . . . I'm, well . . . I'm fucking history too.*"

"*Sorry—really—sorry to hear that. What the hell happened?*" I suddenly felt genuinely sorry for Gazzer.

---

4 'Derailed Gears' – word play on Cream's 'Disraeli Gears', itself a play on a mishearing of derailleur gears.

"*Jim, man . . . busted for smack*"[5] he whispered "*Knew he*—used—
the stuff man . . . but that—mad—mad—*bastard had enough to plaster
a fucking wall*" Pause "*He's been done for possession*—and—*dealing.
Pigs said there was too much for 'personal use'* – so he—had—*to be
dealing.*"

Well *even I* knew Jim Sutton made money dealing. I was
surprised that Gazzer wasn't aware of it – but said nothing to
that effect. "*I'm really sorry to hear this. What's going to happen?*"

"*Well . . .*" he took a deep breath "*he'll be inside for 3 years.*"

That felt like some kind of hammer. "3 **years**!" I yelped feeling
vaguely stunned. The very idea of *prison* sent a shiver down my
spine. I knew these things happened – but this was a horror
story. "*. . . 3 . . . years . . .*" I repeated in a long drawn out sigh.
I couldn't conceive of being in prison for 3 years. It felt like a
life-sentence. I sat there staring like a startled frog. This was the
real world and it was homing in at terminal velocity. There was
a song I sang—a number about being on Parchman Farm [6]—but
the reality of exactly what that was never hit me. *My* Parchman
Farm—like so many things—had been a fairy story; a fantasy
like having been raised as a poor Black boy in Mississippi.

"*Yeah man – but he was lucky it wasn't more*" Gazzer's voice roused
me from my self-absorbed state of dread.

"*More!*" I almost squeaked.

"*Well*——yeah——*man . . . It would have been 10 – if it hadn't been
so bloody obvious he was a*—major—*user . . . and then there was no
money around . . . so the pigs couldn't pin the*—big—*number on him.*"

---

5 Heroin.

6 Parchman Farm—Mississippi State Penitentiary—built in 1901, is the oldest prison in
Mississippi. A fair few Blues numbers have been written about it and several Blues musicians
were imprisoned there, including Bukka White and Son House.

This was all way out of my league. I knew nothing of porcine penal philosophy or the ins and outs of their procedures in relation to narcotics. The only policeman I ever knew was Mr Bruce – and he was entirely affable. I kept 'the police' and 'Mr Bruce' in separate compartments – and when I was with Steve I was careful not to regurgitate any hippie anti-police rhetoric.

With some trepidation, I asked " . . . *and Ed?*"

"*Ed? Jesus man . . . Ed's—out—of—his—head. Fucking pigs busted him—same time—man. He got off lightly though. Just a fine—large bloody fine man—but still . . . and, well . . . he's out of it. Up shit-creek man – without a paddle. The whole—fucking—thing's a god-awful bloody mess.*" Gazzer was obviously highly disturbed by the whole thing – and I could understand why.

"*And you . . . Gazzer?*"

He shrugged "*Wasn't there . . . by the time the stinking pigs arrived at my parents' I'd got shot of—everything—I mean everything—man. Like I was clean. I mean Jesus – I only ever did devil's dandruff[7] anyway. Never fucking touched anything else – I'm not stupid.*"

"*I'm relieved. I'm relieved you're in the clear.*"

Gazzer smiled in a forlorn way – touched by my concern "*Yeah man – clear as you can be in a fucking fog.*"

I was almost reeling with the news. I started feeling as if I was in the middle of the mess along with Gazzer. It was almost as if the police were about to descend on me as well "*This is all . . . well . . . it's the worst thing I've heard for . . . a while . . . I'm so sorry . . .*"

---

7 Cocaine.

Gazzer drained his beer *"Y'know man . . . I wanna say . . . "* he coughed with emotion and what seemed to be bronchitis *"I'm real sorry I used to give you all that crap about your short scale – your EB3. I just get full of myself man – 'specially when I've had a few lines y'know. I'm kind of surprised you'd talk to me after all that."*

Well yes – it surprised me too. *"Under the bridge Gazzer. All gone."* He looked at me as if he failed to understand *"It's the past. Gone somewhere or other . . . I mean, it seems a long time ago now with . . . everything else that's happened. Y'know . . . with Steve and Ron gone – it kind of puts things into perspective . . . and everything else— y'know—seems pretty trivial"* Pause *"Well . . . apart from the bust that is. That must have been hell . . . "* Pause *" . . . but . . . this, is—*now —*and—*this—*is where we are"* Pause *"Y'know Gazzer – I've—never —really gone in for hanging onto stuff I'd rather forget; so really, don't worry about it."*

*"Yeah man—*too right—*and . . . here we are . . . *here—*we—*fucking —are. *Good to see yer man."* Gazzer looked cheered by what I'd said and continued *"Y'know . . . never—meant—anything by it man. Kind of expected you to throw it back at me – same way . . . but you never did . . . and I never really figured that out. It was . . . kinda strange . . . doesn't matter anyhow – everyone's entitled to be how they are – but . . . you never got pissed off. That's amazing – and like, well, thanks for that."*

"Nothing to thank. It's just not my style Gazzer – I don't get angry about anything, unless it's pretty serious" I grinned *"I'm . . . kind of . . . eccentric in that way."*

"Really man" he laughed *"Like really."* And that seemed to draw the curtains on the past for both of us in a way that seemed kindly.

"You see Gazzer . . . one of the problems I've always had with the average —male—of the species, is this 'locking horns' business. Seems to me that a lot of men ridicule each other as some sort of social sport – and if you don't join in they either don't know what to make of you – or they think you're docile. Either way it tends to be a drag."

Gazzer nodded *"Right . . . never thought of it like that man. So . . . you just—never—join in?"*

"Well sometimes it's occurred to me that I could . . . just to smooth social relations or whatever – but then I'd have to have lived inside that game y'know . . . and the adjectival—rules—of the game are that you leave— no—weaknesses on view – and . . . a weakness can be—anything—that's not in line with whatever the general Nazi regulations happen to be."

Gazzer looked a little confused *"Like?"*

"Well . . . like wearing a cravat when it isn't Christmas Day – that's the working-class rule. Like being observed enjoying anything a little too much – that's the middle-class rule. Like being caught liking the wrong album – that's the hippie rule. Like ironing your Levis, starching your shirt, or doing—anything—that's not hip. Like doing or saying—anything— out of the ordinary with whatever group it happens to be. Do that – and some mighty male 'riduculant' swoops down on you from the lofty heights of professional ennui with some adjectival acerbic rejoinder. Then—you— have to come back at him—at the speed of light—*and say 'Yeah! But did yer know yer flies* [8] *are undone!' or whatever drivel."*

"Right yeah . . . " he nodded slowly and thoughtfully *"See it—see it —sounds a drag"* Pause *" Really—y'know—when y'say it like that man . . . total bummer"* Pause *"You make it, kind of clear really . . . yeah. And . . . actually . . . yeah, it's not really cool at all to lay trips like that on people."*

---

8 British mis-usage of the period i.e. *" . . . yer fly is undone! "*

"Glad you see my point of view Gazzer. I've always felt the whole thing's insane – and the idea of learning the tricks of the trade just to be accepted is almost like having your nose amputated so that nose-less people won't laugh at you in the street." Gazzer almost choked at that point. *"That's why I generally prefer the company of women."*

"Now yer talking!" Gazzer beamed *"Women—man—women! I fucking—love—women!"* Pause *"Trouble is . . . m'girl friend left me."* He shook his head, staring at his feet while he collected himself *" . . . over this scene with the pigs . . . and the bust and all . . . it was, like, too much for her – and her parents went spare, like—*ape-shit—*when they heard about it"* Pause *" . . . heard the same thing happened t'you a while back."*

"Yeah . . . it did" I inwardly groaned. I'd had enough of this story – but I thought I may as well empathise. *"Yeah Lindie's father's a Brigadier with a bunch of medals – y'know: 'Call Me God' / 'Kindly Call Me God' / 'God Calls Me God'*[9] *. . . he had one or the other – or all three."*

*"Hell man – you really do pick'em . . . There's no winning with those guys. Guys like that'd put you in gaol for pissing in a public—*lavatory *—man."*

"Yeah . . . he phoned the school" I explained *"Thought I'd been in Borstal and wanted me castrated as a public service or whatever"* Pause *"The marinaded goitre interrogated me in his front room y'know. He was indescribably rude. I'd really never come across—that—before . . . I mean I've met a few common-or-garden Tory bigots – but this one made Goebbels look like St Francis of Assisi."*

---

9 British military honours: Most Distinguished Order of St Michæl and St George: CMG (Companion) KCMG (Knight Commander) GCMG (Knight Grand Cross).

"*Right . . .* " he nodded "*I know how*—just—*how that is. Felicia was forbidden ever to see me again—anywhere—no matter what.*"

We clinked glasses and drank to our fate. Gazzer had regained a sense of humour and we talked for quite a while about the music scene. He asked after Jack.

"*Well . . .* " I replied "*Jack's gone to earth* [10] *hasn't he. Seen neither hide-nor-hair of him for months.*"

Gazzer looked shocked "*So the Jackrabbit's done a runner*—whoa! —*that's . . . that's . . . well . . . I dunno know what to*—say—*man.*"

I let out a deep sigh "*Yeah—vanished—down the benighted bunny-hole. Parents won't take phone calls – and . . . Jack hasn't been in contact since Ron died. Didn't contact Steve either – just left the pox-ridden planet. Gone to work at Midland Bank or some other branch of hell. It's . . .*"

"*Insane*" Gazzer stated vehemently "*Really man . . . that makes*— no—*sense at all . . . I mean*—why—*would he*—*do*—*that? You gotta be Mister Sodding Straight from way back to work in a place like that.*"

"*Yeah . . . I s'pose so – or you've got to be something or other.*"

"*Yeah man – but it's a*—leper—*colony.*"

"*It's something alright . . .* " I replied "*I think he probably just got frightened. Jack never was—heroic—exactly . . . and his parents always did make most of the rules. I did tell him that I'd play a duo with him when Steve and Ron left for College. That—was—the plan. He'd have been on washboard and any lightweight percussion gear he could get into his Fraud Anglican.* [11] *That—could—have been fun.*"

---

10 Gone to earth is a fox hunting reference common in Britain.
11 British nick name for the Ford Anglia automobile.

"*Man he was lucky to be with Savage Cabbage—at—all. I don't be—* lieve—*it! He shoulda stuck with—*you—*man! God*——*damn*—— *loser . . . fucking*——*pygmy*——*halfwit . . . I mean—*why—*would he walk out on a—*friend—*like that!?*"

"*Short of money maybe . . . but I don't think he saw it as walking out on me. I think he probably just collapsed under the weight of it all . . . his parents . . . Cynthia . . .*"

"*Cynthia man . . . Jeeeee—sus Christ . . . saw him with—her—once . . .* " Gazzer winced "*Closest thing to the Hound of the Bloody Baskervilles I—ever—saw.*"

"*Never saw her Gazzer – but I heard reports from Steve. Seems you two'd be in agreement . . .*"

"*And him with that—poodle—haircut! Jesus, man – can you believe it! Can you be—fucking—lieve it!*"

"*I mainly tried not to believe it Gazzer . . .* " I grinned "*Jack's haircut or his girlfriend*" Pause "*It could have gone another way . . . but . . . I think he just got too frightened.*"

"*You looking to form another band then?*"

"No . . . " Pause " *. . . well . . . might join one – if I could—*find—*a Blues band. They seem to be a bit thin on the ground though. No one wants a vocalist either – unless they play an instrument and harp doesn't seem to count much anymore. I was only ever rhythm bass with Savage Cabbage in any case.*"

Gazzer started at that and exclaimed "*Oh come—on—man! You were getting it down – you were getting it down! Heard you over at the Compton in January! You were right there man – right there!*"

I thanked him for his kind opinion "*Well . . . I—have—improved . . . that's true – but I still find it extremely difficult to sing and play bass at the same time – especially Born Under a Bad Sign.*"

Gazzer agreed "*Yeah man—that's—a tough act . . . gets better with time though. Wouldn't let that hold you back.*"

Too right—I wasn't going to let it hold me back—but I had to be realistic. I wasn't going to tell people I was a bass player 'til the time when I could play along with anything – and sing at the same time. I was feeling a little concerned that Gazzer might want to team up with me to form another two bass line up – so I decided to sidestep him by asking him about his plans "*So . . . what d'you have lined up then? Got any plans?*"

"*None to speak of man. Gotta spend some time on the wagon. Got too blasted man – outta control y'know.*" He intimated that his parents had grounded him financially. "*M'father . . .*" he said with some embarrassment " *. . . insisted—I look for 'regular employment' y'know . . .*" Pause " *. . . or go to college or whatever – right? Well— fuck—that . . .*" Pause " *. . . or anyway . . . the alternative's that I'm outta the house. Can you be—lieve—that man? Can you—fucking— believe that!?*"

I could well believe that "*Grim . . .*" Pause " *. . . I was almost on the streets once – but the situation turned around. Maybe your father'll calm down given time.*"

"*Yeah—really—when fucking hell freezes over.*"

"*Got anything in mind?*" I enquired.

"*Naaaaah . . .*" Pause " *. . . nothing. Got the Summer though, before the—axe—falls . . . so . . . I s'pose something'll turn up. Something maybe . . . maybe something . . .*" Gazzer trailed into silence.

His parents had been humiliated by the midnight police raid on their house – their house being ransacked for narcotics. There were neighbours staring from behind lace curtains and it was social suicide for people like his parents.

I needed no convincing. Gazzer was what my father worried about in terms of the direction in which he'd seen me moving. Suddenly I had an insight into my father that made me reassess his attitudes. I'd buy my father that record of Handel's Oratorios he'd mentioned . . .

Gazzer's mother and father had played all their major upper middle class parental cards – and he was reeling. I could see the situation – and it was ghastly. I was glad no one held the purse strings in my life. The Army kitchens weren't heaven – but they gave me an income.

"You guys had it right with dope and all that head-shit" Gazzer commented *"Used to think you weren't hip—like you weren't up to it —or some kinda bloody bollocks like that – but . . . "* he exclaimed a series of almost silent expletives with a harrowed expression *" . . . kept you outta—this—bloody mess hasn't it . . . "*

"Yeah . . . it has . . . but y'know – I just wasn't that interested." Gazzer looked incredulous – so I continued *"If I'd fancied it . . . I wouldn't have thought too much about the law either. It wasn't about being law-abiding or anything like that. Always been an anarchist you see. It's got more to do with being an Artist."*

Gazzer looked unconvinced *"Art? I thought most artists did— something—or other?"*

"Maybe they did – but this one doesn't. Y'see . . . I was just born psychedelic. Always—have—seen and heard weirdness – but I need my wits about me to record it and remember it all. That's how I write lyrics. That's why I'm always making notes."

"Yeah man – noticed you doing that. You always done that?"

"Always. I'm always seeing things and getting ideas from all over the place. It's kind of never-ending."

"Shit! You must have a lot of—songs—man!"

"100 or more . . . but they're not all finished – and they're not all good. They're mainly . . . well just works in progress and . . . they need to be perfect before I do anything with them. I want to write as well as Dylan – but that's not something that happens without a lot of work."

"The songs you were singing tonight though – some of those I'd never heard before."

"Oh those – they're all old Blues standards. I've just written my own words and thrown some changes on them. Blues lyrics are . . . well I can write those without too much effort. The thing that's difficult is branching out into the thing Dylan does or that Cream did with 'White Room' and 'Sunshine of your Love'."

"Yeah, good songs man – good songs . . . " Gazzer noticed that my glass of ginger beer was empty *"What're you drinking?"*

"Ginger beer."

"Right—good idea man—like John Mayall—right?" [12] I looked confused so he continued *"I mean—none of you—in Savage Cabbage touched alcohol either?"*

"No . . . Gazzer" I laughed *"We drank alright. It's just that I'm thirsty – otherwise I'd have a glass of red wine."* [13]

Jack did more than *touch* alcohol – but I didn't mention that. We weren't puritanical – we just wanted to stay alive and make sure we performed optimally.

"Don't drink beer?"

"No. Never touch the stuff. Never did like beer – wouldn't boil a dead giraffe's eyelids in the stuff."

---

12 John Mayall of John Mayall's Bluesbreakers was known to be abstemious and intolerant of drunkenness in his bands.

13 The author had been introduced to red wine by Anelie Mandelbaum.

"*You're a riot man!*" Gazzer laughed "*A far-out riot.*" He went off to the bar and came back with drinks: a foaming pint of something brown and ghastly – and a delicious pint of ginger beer. I thanked him and took a protracted draft. Performing was always thirsty work.

Gazzer's laughter was temporary – and his mood of nervous agitation returned "*Y'know I wake up with the jitters man . . . it's a fucking police state! The pigs can just drag you away man – in the middle of the fucking night! You can be in some stinking cell for days. It's gonna take a while to get through this . . . and make some decisions. I just don't know what I'm gonna do next.*"

I suddenly felt bad about my sidestepping the possibility of discussing musical collaboration with him. He was clearly nowhere near thinking in such terms.

"*You still playing?*"

"*Naaaaah . . . what's the point. What'd I be playing anyhow?*"

"*I know you're not asking for advice or anything – but I think you do need to keep playing. That's what I've done – and it seems to keep demented pterodactyls from roosting in my hair.*"

"*Might work for you—playing Delta—but I only know Rock'n'Roll*" Gazzer smiled wanly "*What'd I do on my own with bass?*"

"*Well . . . an instrument's an instrument. You can just play. I used to play Steve's EB0 and Ron's EB3 whenever I got the opportunity. I'd play anything that was lying around – I even tinkle on piano if there's one available.*"

"*Didn't know the EB3 you played on stage wasn't your guitar.*"

He asked—so I told him—how I'd missed both Steve and Ron's instruments by a matter of days.

"*Bummer man! Total*—fucking—*bummer!*" The bartender eyed Gazzer and I was wondering when we were going to get thrown out. There was only so much swearing that a pub would tolerate and Gazzer had been throwing expletives around with remarkable generosity. "*I'd be*—totally—*bloody pissed off if I was you. That's real bad luck man—real bad luck—you deserve something man for all the work you did with those blokes. I mean, you*—were—*the bloody front-man f'crying out loud!*"

"*Yeah . . . well . . . I was*" Pause "*I was something or other – until the cold front came in . . .*" Pause "*. . . and . . . as to bad luck . . . it was some kind of luck alright*" Pause "*If it wasn't for bad luck—if it wasn't for real bad luck—I wouldn't have no luck at all*" I sang without much credibility "*Actually . . .*" I added after pause for consideration "*I don't know so much about that . . . I've had my share of good luck.*"

"*Like losing Ron and Steve and both those guitars – not to mention everything else?*"

"*Yeah . . . maybe . . . I don't know . . . that's about as bad as it gets – but maybe the bass guitars would've tied me down or something. Y'see . . . I'm going to Art School at the end of September anyway and my two acoustics will be all I need for a while.*"

Gazzer nodded and a curious expression crossed his face "*Yeah man . . . like, what*—was—*that thing you were playing?*" he asked "*That fierce looking silver guitar you played over your knees? What*—is —*that? It's not a* STEEL NATIONAL [14] *is it?*"

"*No*" I replied "*It's a* DEBIL." and explained how it came to be.

Gazzer shook his head in bewildered amazement "*I'm gonna look out for*—you—*over the years . . . you're gonna*—go—*somewhere man.*"

---

14 NATIONALS were commonly known as 'STEEL NATIONALS' in Britain at that time.

That was true enough.

I went somewhere.

Then I went somewhere else.

Be that as it may, I never saw Gazzer again after that night.

William Tell's arranged his arrows to get his laundry done / He's taken the examinations to buy apples for his son, / His gold encrusted parrot has gone down on its knees / To pray to Marlene Dietrich "Won't you take me if you please." / Just open up your eyes now — see what's going down, / You'll never get away from here with your head stuck in the ground.
Larkin/Bruce/Schubert—Savage Cabbage—See What's Going Down—Savoy Green—1970

5

slide-of-hand

Looking through time writhing wild on the hill / Looking through signs tinting night as she will / Di'mond design lady swirling curls in the clouds / And it's a long way back to where I was – before I started out.
Larkin/Bruce/Schubert—Savage Cabbage—Before I Started Out—Savoy Green—1970

Jasper Stanwell was as true as his word. Got me a spot at the Farnham Folk and Blues Festival. When I rang the organisers, they'd already heard about me. Jasper had obviously painted a picture that only just resembled me. I was '*The new-boy of Delta Blues: Frank—slide-of-hand—Schubert! Destined to set light to the night!*' Jasper had a way with words. It made me laugh out loud when I got off the telephone – but I was also extremely touched that Jasper had gone out on a limb for me in that way. I was going to have to be as good as I could be. Well . . . I was practising every day and I couldn't do any more. I could still only manage one successful number on the EKO – but that got better all the time. I had a few other numbers on that guitar – but they needed a lot of work. My main instruments were still the DEBIL and harp.

This was the venue at which I'd heard Mike Cooper a few years before. It was going to be eerie being on stage there – when I'd been a wide-eyed spectator a few years back. Mike Cooper wasn't there on this occasion. Nor was Jo Ann Kelly. I was both disappointed and relieved.

I would have liked to have heard them live and maybe to have conversed with them – but I was not yet up to sharing a stage with either of them. How soon would that be – or would it be ever at all? They were still both *a million miles away, and at the same time . . . right there in my picture frame.*[1] How close did you have to be? That was always the mystery.

I was setting my gear up on stage—I was first on—when a folkie asked me, with a self-congratulatory sneer *"I presume you have an ignition key for that thing."*

He meant my guitar—the DEBIL—and he was making a joke about my guitar looking like a car – being that it was lustrous with silver-flake car paint: guitars were made of wood *not* metal.

"Ignition key" I replied *"Yes I do –* **A** *and* **E** *mainly . . ."* I smiled *" . . . but I also use* **G.***"*

He stared at me, confused by my reply *"What's that supposed to mean?"*

*"Sorry I was a little cryptic. The ignition—*keys*—I use are open tunings – in the keys of* **A**, **E** *and* **G.***"*

"You'd be better off putting wheels on it" he shook his head derisively.

"Thank you" I smiled at him, deliberately misunderstanding the nature of his remark *"I'd never thought of that. It'd make it a lot easier to carry 'round – it weighs 20 pounds."*

He walked away with another comment and I felt a little sad that he couldn't have allowed the situation to become humorous.

---

1 *'cause I'm a million miles away, and at the same time, I'm right here in your picture frame.*
Jimi Hendrix—Voodoo Chile—Electric Ladyland—1968

The Farnham folkies viewed NATIONALS with derision. They saw them as another version of an electric guitar – which of course had nothing to do with Folk music even though Delta Blues developed into Chicago Blues and was played by the very same Black Folk. Why did people have to roam the Earth trying to get one over on others? Why couldn't we just be friendly? Just because someone's not playing *my* favourite music doesn't impel me to make snide remarks about it. I decided that I'd remain friendly to folkies *whatever* they said. Strangely, folkies always seemed to like it when I sang unaccompanied – so I decided to include one of those numbers in my set.

I opened up the other guitar case – containing the EKO. It was a beat-up old hard case that I'd picked up second hand. I'd fixed the damage and sealed the rough edges. I'd stencilled Savage Cabbage on the lid of the case—for old time's sake—in a musty cabbage green. I'd also applied wire wool to the name to give a sense that it had been there for a while. I'd refurbished the inside of the case with green baize that my father had found on an old billiard table that was being re-covered in some Army venue in Aldershot. I'd mentioned that I wanted to re-line the guitar case and my father—practical as ever—turned up with the green baize one evening after work. My father knew about glue and all manner of things connected with furnishing – so I took his advice and he seemed glad that I was open to following his direction to the letter. I wanted to make a fine job of the case and I knew he was the one to facilitate that. He'd had a couple of old leather trunks in the attic that had seen better days and he said we could probably make a guitar case if we used both of them. They were beyond repair as suitcases and so it seemed a good idea. He had an awl and showed me how to use it – wetting the leather to soften it before stitching.

371

It took quite a while and a lot of hard work – but in the end I had a hard case for the DEBIL made of thin plywood and covered with leather. It was lined with several layers of army blanket and was horribly heavy—especially with the DEBIL inside it—but I liked the monstrousness of it. I used both suitcase handles on the case and all the brass hinges. Once the thing was oiled and polished it looked like something you'd strap on to play in some remote hill station in the British Raj. Life had become unbelievably easy with my father and looking back it seemed almost beyond belief that it had to be so difficult before the great hair battle of '68. And there I was two years later with hair streaming down my back.

I stood for my first number. *"Know I'm standing people – but I'm also sitting, as you'll see. This is a song . . . "* Pause *" . . . that's been played by The Mississippi Sheiks. It's been played by Howling Wolf. It's rumoured that it's also been played by Lightning Ferret Corpuscle and the Diesel Fitters"* Applause and laughter *"I used to know a fellow—a diesel fitter y'know—used to buy—all—his wife's undergarments. That's right people! He'd rummage through the knickers, saying 'dee's'll fit'er— dee's'll fit'er—dee's'll fit'er—but—deeeees—won't!' I imagine you don't need to know that"* Laughter and cat-calls *"However . . . was that a wolf-whistle I heard? Didn't know wolfs—could—whistle. But— hey—people here's my Wolf song! How———ling!"* Then I hit them with 'Sitting on Top of the World'. I played the EKO as if it were an electric guitar smashing the lightweight plectrum on the strings with the full weight of my thumb behind it – and damping to silence for the occasional phrase. I wanted to make sure that my solitary finger-chorded song was as monumentally savage as those I was going to play on the DEBIL.

I could see some eyes fixing on the silver body of the DEBIL standing next to me – and heard someone shout something out in the audience. I couldn't make out what it was but it sounded positive so I grinned at them all and adjusted the microphones so that both were pointed at the DEBIL. They'd both get my voice anyway – and I wanted to make sure that the DEBIL was heard. One of the sound-people indicated that one microphone was for vocals *"The guitar needs it more than me"* I called to him in the loudest whisper I could manage. Unfortunately—or fortunately which ever way you look at it—my comment rang out across the crowd. I decided that the best way to avoid embarrassment was to compound the crime *"Didn't mean to whisper people. I was talking 'bout the microphone—y'see—and . . . what I said was 'The guitar needs it more than me!' I can get loud y'know"* I laughed *"Been told that"* Pause *"Some—man—told me y'know . . . people tell you things"* Pause *" Think he was a zooooo-ologist"* Applause and laughter *"Had that kind of hairstyle—y'know—kind of . . . slicked back with Brylcreem"*[2] I laughed and began to sing the Brylcreem advertising jingle:

Bryl—creem, a little dab'll—do—ya, / Use more, only if you dare / But watch out, the gals will all pur—sue—ya, / They'll love to put their fingers through your hair.

"Never used it myself" Pause *"Anyhow . . . this zoologist—right—he had these—long—thin—sideburns"* Pause *"Gold tooth in front, matador's cape, and a—tricorn—hat"* Applause *"Had a chim—pan —zeeeee too, right up his sleeve – and a wombat wallet, would you believe."* The crowd hooted and applauded. They were on my side.

---

2 Brylcreem: men's hair product that appeared in 1928 made by County Chemicals, Birmingham, England – an emulsified blend of water, calcium hydroxide, dimethyl oxazolidine, magnesium sulfate, stearic acid, and mineral oil stabilised with beeswax.

"Y'ever hear of a man called Son House?" Applause – with some yells
of 'yes' and 'no' *"Well—I—ain't him, I'm Frank Schubert—late of
Savage Cabbage—but . . . "* Pause *"This is—his—song: Death—
Letter—Blues!"*

Ron always liked the way I threw lunatic language at a crowd.
Since I started playing solo—whenever I got loony on stage—I
seemed to *feel* his presence . . . off to my left . . . grinning . . .
somewhere in the empty space of death. The man who'd made
the ignition key remark was in the audience and I wondered if
I'd catch his eye. After a while I did – and I grinned at him. He
was good enough to grin back. I hoped he'd think more kindly
of Blues afterwards. 'Death Letter Blues' got substantial
applause and I felt it would be good to give them an
unaccompanied song – just to show them my range. I sang 'In
My Time of Dying' because I knew Bob Dylan had covered that
and the Folkies would know it. It was a risk – but I hoped
they'd find my rendition acceptable. Sure enough they did –
even though I rang the changes on the lyrics.

*Meet me mamma—meet me—meet me in the middle of the fair / If these
strings should fail me babe – wontcha feed me with a Plymouth pear* [3]
In My Time of Dying [4]—Traditional—with changes by Frank Schubert

Then out came the harp and I finished with 'Traintime'. That
kicked up a storm. As it was my first gig at the Farnham Folk
and Blues festival I was on early and only allowed four numbers.

---

3 The Plymouth pear is found in Europe – particularly France, Portugal, and Spain. In
Britain it is found only in Plymouth, Devon and Truro, Cornwall.
4 Originally: *Meet me Jesus, meet me, meet me in the middle of the air / And if these wings should fail me
lord – wontcha meet me with another pair.*

I could have gone on longer because the audience was with me – but decided that I was better sticking to the agreement. Better also, to come out on top than risk a poor finale. *"Frank Schubert people—thanking you—all—very much indeed! Laying you low with festive frogspawn – all the way from Jupiter's sulphur mines!"* [5] Applause *"Yeah—alright—thank you! Just in time too! Just in time to pelt you with hard boiled lobsters! Wildebeest vol-au-vents! Aaaaaaaaand . . . wish you an—extremely—good night!"* Applause—more applause —yet more applause. Someone—I guessed him to be the organiser—suddenly emerged out of my peripheral vision. I was off stage just about to begin buckling the straps on a guitar case. The man was gesticulating frantically and mouthing words I couldn't comprehend. *(I've never been any use with sign language or lip reading.)* Finally, I twigged. He was giving me the determined go-ahead to play an encore.

"Looks as if I haven't done yet" I boomed out as I walked in front of the microphone *"Seems like yer gonna have-t' hear s'mo' . . . Blues."* I pulled the DEBIL out of its case. *"This thing . . . "* I said, beginning to change the tuning to open **G** *"Is called . . . the DEBIL"* Pause *"It's called the DEBIL . . . because—**that**—is what it is. So . . . why . . . would—I—want to call it anything else?"* Applause and unintelligible yells *" . . . and so . . . here I am again with that—same —thing"* Pause *"Not that 'same thing' Muddy Waters talked about – although I'd like nothing better than that same thing right now"* Applause and whistles *"Some joker . . . Yeah—I said—some joker, called it 'the gerbil' . . . 'cause—y'know—it squeaks like a skewbald zebra on a frying pan!"* Pause *"I call it . . . the DEBIL . . . 'cause it—sounds"* Pause "LIKE—THE—DEVIL!" I finally had the thing in tune *"Son House, people! John the Revelator!"*

---

5 *Well my arrows are made of desire, from far away as Jupiter's sulphur mines.* Jimi Hendrix—Quote from Voodoo Chile—Electric Ladyland—1968

Riotous yelling that drowned the introductory chromium tube slide phases – so I repeated them 'til the DEBIL could make itself heard. Then I plunged into that number with such unprecedented violence that they had to lower the volume on the microphones a little. By the time I was through, I'd broken two strings and walked off the stage to uncontained whooping and clapping. The organiser came straight up to me *"Next year son! Want you back! Alright!? Next year alright!?"*

I nodded.

"Next time we'll give you a proper set and you'll be on the programme with the big knobs. Can you make it next year—same place—'bout the same sort of time?"

"It's possible" I smiled *"Never can tell . . . give me the exact dates and I'll check."* I was somehow sounding like Ron. He'd never sound excited when he was approached. He was always the epitome of cool – and suddenly there I was doing more-or-less the same.

"So Frank, Frank Schubert. Where d'yer—get—a moniker like that eh?"

"My grandmother. Her maiden name was Schubert" I replied.

"No—relation—I suppose?" he enquired *"To mister bloody—big-name—Schubert I mean?"*

"My grandmother was Clara Schubert – Franz Schubert's niece."

"Gaaaaaw—Blimey" he cackled *"Not trying to—extract the urine* [6]*— by any chance?"* I shook my head in denial. *"Really? Not trying to 'ave me on?"* I shook my head again *"Straight up?"*

"Straight up – but . . . I'm not Frank, I just anglicised 'Franz' and added my mother's maiden name . . . "

---

6 1960s British slang variant of 'take the piss' meaning to 'make a fool' of someone.

"*So what—*were*—yer then – before that, I mean?*"

"*Before—in Savage Cabbage—I was Farquhar Arbuthnot . . .* "

"*Fucker what?*" he laughed

"*Farquhar Arbuthnot*" I replied "*It was a bit of a . . . joke . . . y'know – it's an archaic name . . .* "

"*Yeah and yer better off without it too.*"

"*So . . . my given name's Vic—Victor Simmerson*" Pause "*But that's not a—*great*—name for a Bluesman is it.*"

"*That's the truth mate – that's the truth alright*" he grinned.

"*I never really liked Farquhar Arbuthnot that much – so when Savage Cabbage dissolved I changed to Frank Schubert.*"

"*Good f'you Frankie-boy*" he laughed "*Frankie—bloody— Schubert . . . if that don't beat all. Unusual, yeah . . . but it's got—*class *—I'll give yer that*" Pause "*So anyway Frank, name's 'arry – 'arry Blandon. And these . . . are . . . 3 numbers for yer Frankie-boy . . .* " he scrawled on a scrap of paper " *. . . where—you—can get hold of—* me. *Try to make it—after—*10.00 *and—*before—3.00." I took it and slipped it into my waistcoat pocket.

"*You give—*quite*—a talk in, dontcha Frank*" Harry grinned. "*Can't say it didn't—worry—me at first. Thought y'd lost yer marbles . . .* " he chuckled " *. . . but the crowd loved it*" Pause "*Y'know they really go for that zany stuff—when—it works. Makes you look like you're a high-flyer—if yer can pull it off—and you worked that crowd just bootiful mate – just plain bootiful.*"

"*Well . . . it's fun and I enjoy it.*"

"*Yeah – but it works mate – that's the main bloody thing. And y'know —why—it works mate?*" Pause "*Well I'll—tell—yer. It works 'cause —Bob Dylan—talks like that. 'eard him! 'eard 'im m'self! Back in . . . '66. 'course—too—off-beat for Brits back then. But—now— mate—now—it works a bloody charm. Like a—*bloody—*charm*" Pause "*Don't suppose you ever—saw—Dylan on stage did yer?*"

"*No*" I shook my head "*Would've liked to have done. I was only* 14 *in '66. Albums were as close as I got.*"

Harry eyed me curiously "*So . . . you're . . . eight—teen . . . you're saying?*"

"*And three months*" I chuckled.

"*Wouldn't have credited it—wouldn't have credited it—would've put you in your twenties . . . maybe it's the 'tache.*" [7]

"*Yeah—well—y'know . . . Harry . . . I've been in my—twenties—since I was* 14.*"

"*Love it—love it—you can just keep belting it out . . . so, 'owd'yer get started on—this—routine then?*" I told him about Mr Love, Mike Cooper, and Jo Ann Kelly. Then of course there were questions of how long and when and where – and gradually the whole story of Savage Cabbage tumbled out.

"*Well . . . you keep—goin'—Frank—you keep goin'—and I'll be seein' you. Just remember old 'arry Blandon when you hit the big time eh . . .*"

Harry walked off chuckling "*Frank Schubert . . . Frankie-boy— fuckin'—Schubert! Well I never did.*"

I put my guitars in safe-keeping in the room the Bush Hotel had allocated to Harry – and walked off to mingle with the crowd and hear the other performers.

---

7 1960s British slang for moustache.

I knew almost no one in the audience. No one from Netherfield School came to see me apart from a girl called Mary Williamson. Everyone else seemed to be elsewhere either preparing to leave for Universities or Teacher Training Colleges. Mary seemed genuinely delighted to see me on stage and almost astonished that I came to speak to her after my set – as if I was now one of the high and mighty.

*"I could hardly believe that was—*you*—up there"* Mary smiled sheepishly *"You sounded—well—like . . . you could be on TV."*

"Well . . . I've been playing publicly for two years now – so I tend to feel at home on stage. They were a really good audience too. It was a bit intimidating—once—back in '68 when I started. And . . . I suppose . . . it was like that again a little bit when I started playing solo. It was easy with Savage Cabbage because I knew I was with brilliant musicians."

"Well you sounded brilliant out there – and all that funny stuff you were saying. I couldn't understand any of it – but it made me laugh. It was making everyone laugh."

"I'm good at what I play – but I'm fairly limited at the moment. I just try to put on a good show. It's nothing special. The organiser was impressed by my crazy jive – but I've been working on that lunacy for long enough that it just tumbles out of my mouth."

"Well it all seemed really special to me and . . . you've . . . well you've become one of those special people . . . "

"Playing on stage doesn't make you special . . . " I sighed *" . . . this celebrity business is all 'here today – gone tomorrow'. They want to book me for next year – but I can't rely on that . . . "* Pause *" . . . and . . . y'know . . . it really doesn't make me special – being on stage. I just do what I do."*

"You can't pretend that's an ordinary everyday thing you do out there."

"Well . . . it's an ordinary everyday thing for me to play guitar and sing. The only difference is that there was an audience tonight."

"But that's the special bit – being able to do that in front of all those people" Pause *" . . . makes it a bit spooky talking to you I suppose."*

"Maybe people are special when they're performing – but when they're through with performing . . . they're the same as anyone else" I replied *"In any case . . . we were at school together. So it's not surprising that I should come over and say hello – or . . . that I should ask you out for a drink tomorrow."*

Mary's eyes widened a little. I had no clear idea why I'd made that proposition – but she seemed pleased I'd asked her.

"That would be . . . lovely . . . " Mary replied *". . . maybe I'll feel it's all a bit more . . . normal then."*

We fixed a time and I turned up on the pixie chariot and took her to the Queen's Oak. It was a fine evening for a ride through the country – I was puttering along at about 40 mph and Mary was enjoying the ride. *"How fast will this go?"* she asked.

"It'll touch a ton[8] *or slightly more . . . "* I replied *" . . . but I never take it there. At that speed the handlebars vibrate so much that I can't tell whether my hands are in contact. That isn't a pleasant feeling so I never take it over 90."* She said she'd like to see what that was like – and I said *"I'll take it up slowly and you can jab me in the ribs when you'd like me to pull back."* I took it up to 80mph when I found a good straight stretch. I felt no jab in the ribs but I decided to be cautious. I didn't want to scare her witless.

She was as white as a sheet when she dismounted *"I've never been so frightened in my life."*

---

8 100 mph

I apologised "*We only got up to 80 . . . you could've jabbed me in the ribs like I said . . . I'd have slowed down immediately.*"

"*I was too frightened to do anything and it just went out of my mind. I don't want to do that again going back.*"

I was happy to put her mind at rest on that score "*Even if you wanted to give it another try I wouldn't risk it at that time – the dew comes down and the road gets slippery. There are also police around looking for opportunities . . .*" I locked the chain round the back wheel "*Still . . .*" I grinned " *. . . you survived . . . might make a good story tomorrow.*" Mary was still too wide-eyed to speak so we headed for the pub door.

Seeking the trace of a face when it's sweeping away / Seeking the chimes of the spells and their vivid display / Wind soaring high and the sky's without doubt / And it's a long way back to where I was – before I started out. Larkin/Bruce/Schubert—Savage Cabbage—Before I Started Out—Savoy Green—1970

Mike Cooper was playing at the Queen's Oak—which is why I'd planned to go—and he'd brought both his NATIONALS and a regular guitar. I wanted to take at look at them both—close up —and he was most obliging. They were high Art—utterly unearthly—and I could understand absolutely why a person would have to have both. They were both dramatically beautiful in different ways. I loved the Art Deco look of the TRICONE – the weird way the triangular cover plate sat in the middle of the traditional guitar body shape. I could never imagine designing something as gawky or ungainly as that – and yet the design transcended itself. It had become a timeless icon that was simply not open to any form of improvement or critical comment. It was gorgeous in its functionality and simplicity which defied normal concepts of how shapes work together.

"*The* TRICONE *doesn't have the immediate punch or volume of the single resonator* STYLE O . . . " Mike Cooper explained " . . . *but it has a longer sustain and a mellower tone.*" He demonstrated the difference between the sounds.

"*Right . . . I can see why you'd need both . . . I can see that I'll*—have— *to have both at some time.*"

"*You need'em . . .* " he nodded "*You still play that crazy thing of yours?*"

"*The* DEBIL*?*"

"*Right, yeah . . . I remember. Well named*" Pause "*Quite a thing mind —don't get me wrong—I'm impressed with the work you put into it . . . but . . . it sounds . . .* "

"*Like . . .* " I interrupted " *. . . a cross between a tambourine, a tickertape machine, and a radio between stations?*"

"*Yeah . . .* " he chuckled "*. . . that sounds a pretty accurate description*" Pause "*So . . . why—if you know it sounds like hell—d'you go out there with it!?*"

"*Because I can't play anything near as well as you play and I have an extremely loud voice. People*—see—*the* DEBIL *more than they hear it – and I just put everything I've got into the vocals . . .* " Pause " *. . . but, y'know, you're hearing the* DEBIL *from the perspective of a man who owns two* NATIONALS *and so your take on it is going to be radically different from the average punter. Most people think that it's supposed to sound as it does.*"

"*Yeah . . . well . . . never thought of it that way . . .* " Pause "*Anyhow . . . it's seems to be a workable system for you . . . at least for now . . .* " Pause " *. . . heard Harry Blandon liked what you did in Farnham so I can't argue too much.*"

"I know what you mean though – I know I've got to get a NATIONAL *at some point before too long."*

"Yeah . . . a real resophonic guitar is what you need for lap-slide."

"Which would you recommend – if it had to be just one?"

"Probably . . . the TRICONE. *There are other models too—less well known —and there are* DOBROS *too, wooden bodied resonator guitars. That's a whole different sound. They don't have quite the bell sound that* NATIONALS *have – but they're good for other kinds of music. Country and Western players like them."*

Mary didn't seem wildly interested in the guitar discussion— which crimped me a little in terms of flooding Mike Cooper with questions—but that probably came as a relief to him. I changed tack in the conversation to open it out a little for Mary.

"I'm sorry not to have seen you when I played at the Folk and Blues Festival in Farnham" Pause *"I was there with Mary."* That was an attempt to insinuate her into the conversation.

"How'd you like the concert?" he asked – but Mary was monosyllabic.

"Yes."

He nodded to Mary and turned back to me *"I'd have liked to have heard you play – but I had another commitment . . . don't you find them a little provincial in that scene? Folk purists and whatever else?"*

"Yes—know what you mean—I've run into that but they seem to like my unaccompanied numbers."

Mary was fidgeting a little and looking uncomfortable so I moved on again to another topic hoping she'd be able to join in.

"I remembered that thing you said about the best Pop songs of the past being the Folk music of the future – and I've been looking at that in terms of Beatles songs."

"Surprised you remember."

"I've thought about it quite a lot – because I don't respect Pop – but find it hard to reconcile that with the fact that there are songs I like within the genre."

"Pop's the intention not the song" Mike Cooper pointed out – and of course I was immediately struck with that idea.

"It's the singer not the song . . . " I offered. Mike Cooper nodded and I cut in with a story *"I saw a movie about ten years back with that title. It was a Western about a conflict between a priest and a Mexican bandito. The priest arrives in a village and attempts to establish a congregation. The village is tyrannised by Dirk Bogarde—the bandito— who's prohibited religion – so when the priest begins to hold services, he retaliates by killing villagers in alphabetical order. The priest won't back down and the bandito calls a halt to the executions. He tells the priest he'll spare the villagers if he can answer his riddle. Is the truth in the singer or the song? The priest says it's the song – but the bandito says it's the singer. I forget how it all works out – but the bandito recognises that although he doesn't believe in religion he believes in the priest. It's the singer not the song."* [9]

Mike Cooper grinned a thoughtful grin *"Yeah . . . that's quite a tale . . . That was more-or-less what I was saying – just leave out the priest and the bandito."*

I thought that was quite an amusing response. We both laughed – but Mary looked bewildered and highly nervous. I left it at that and decided I'd have to look after Mary. She was obviously having a hard time.

I escorted her to a seat at that point and bought us both another drink. I had a ginger beer and she had a vodka and lime.

---

9 'The Singer Not the Song' was released in Britain in 1961.

"Celebrities make me nervous" Mary whispered *"You're alright because I know you – and although you're a performer it doesn't freeze me up. There's just something about those people that makes me feel stupid and dull. I can't think of anything to say. It was like that when Mr Pastry* [10] *came to the school and asked me what I'd had for Christmas."*

"Right . . . " I replied *" . . . I can understand that. I saw Mr Pastry at a garden fête—where Savage Cabbage had played a set—and he scared me witless. He had no lenses in his spectacles. Arrrrrgh!"* That made Mary laugh – which was a relief to me. I said I was sorry that I'd put her through it *"They're just human beings you know – they eat and sleep and . . . get colds too."* She agreed in principle – but said she was relieved to be out of the spotlight.

I told Mary the background to my exchange with Mike Cooper. He'd played an Everly Brothers number and made it sound just like a Folk song. *"It strikes me—aside from categories—that songs are just songs. There are labels like R'n'B, Rock'n'Roll, Rock, Acid Rock, Progressive Rock, and whatever else – but really . . . there are just songs."*

Mary was wide-eyed *"Yes . . . It's quite complicated isn't it. I wouldn't know where to start with it all . . . "*

"Well it's just that Pop is what you call a thing if the intention is Pop – and anything that looks like Pop could be a fine song—if—the intention was creative. As Mike Cooper said – Pop's not a style of music – it's an attitude and an intention . . . " Pause *" . . . so . . . to be classified as 'Pop' the attitude and intention have to prioritise profit making . . . via any assortment of crotchets that quaver* [11] *or that rise and fall by more than one note."*

---

10 Richard Lewis Hearne [1908 – 1979] was an English actor, comedian, and writer – the first actor described as a 'television star' due to being the first comic to star in his own programme 'Mr Pastry' in which he dressed in a black suit and bowler hat as an old man with glasses and a walrus moustache. He was famous for helping children's charities.
11 In the USA crotchets are quarter notes and quavers are eighth notes.

I'd hoped Mary would find the pun amusing, but the reference to currency-notes sailed by and she sat placidly – seemingly waiting for whatever happened next. Then Mike Cooper walked past having obtained a pint of beer. He'd overheard my last remark and said *"I think it's a pity musicians have to subjugate themselves to the music industry to make a living – and I feel sorry the general public's being conditioned into thinking they enjoy recycled trivia."*

"Right . . . " I replied *" . . . I've worked in factories where the nearest the management ever got to facing a strike was when the radio system broke down – and the work force lost* Radio 1 *"* [12] Pause *"Reminds me of soma – y'know 'A gramme is better than a damn . . . ' "* [13]

"You're a big fan of references . . . " he grinned *"Soma?"*

"Oh—right—yeah . . . Aldous Huxley—'Brave New World' . . . It was the drug that kept revolution at bay."

"Yeah . . . " he sighed *"We've got that alright."*

"Apart from your Everly Brothers number—and the occasional well written song—Pop's soma to most of the country as far as I can see."

He nodded agreement *"Yeah . . . soma formulated by the mainstream commercialist dictatorship."*

"Yeah" I laughed *"The regime that gives us sport, journalism, television, and soft pornography."*

"Well" he chuckled *"No one seems to be able to live without a constant dribble of it. It's what you find in most homes and work places as a background burble."*

---

12 The BBC pop station.
13 *A gramme is better than a damn . . . "* said Lenina mechanically from behind her hands. *"I wish I had my soma!"* Aldous Huxley—Brave New World—1932.

"*Yeah I've heard plenty of—that—in places I've worked – y'know, with presenters babbling half-heard inanities to fill the space.*"

"*Yeah . . . tell me about it . . .* " he laughed.

"*The problem seems to be . . .* " I continued "*That the Pop charts are the shop window and the record-buying public are exposed to what's on offer . . . so musicians—have—to display their wares in that window.*"

"*Not really . . . if you don't display your wares through that window . . .* " he replied " *. . . you have the Folk or Blues circuits and the small specialist labels.*"

"*True – but it's limited in terms of studio work. Studio time's expensive and creating what the Beatles created is impossible for anyone who's not famous.*"

"*Yeah—good point—but the problem about fame is that in order to become famous you have to serve your time.*"

"*Right – in the adjectival Pop factory producing processed packages designed for the high-street shop windows.*"

"*And the record companies own the shop windows . . .* " he replied with a resigned grin " *. . . so if you want to be heard you've very little choice unless you manage to blast through the corporate infrastructure – like Bob Dylan*" Pause "*The record companies also influence air time and never give space to anything other than fashion music. Money changes hands y'know.*"

"*Yeah . . . know what you mean*" I replied "*There's a lot of chicanery in the music industry. Vile term – music's not an industry. Music feeds the life of humanity.*"

"*Yeah—thanks for the tip mister philosopher—good luck with finding a* NATIONAL.*"*

Mike Cooper left at that point to set up – and I turned my attention to Mary *"Sorry about that—it kind of left you out—but I was a little stuck. It would've been impolite not to have talked."* Of course Mary could have said something – and I was sorry not to have conversed longer with Mike Cooper. I asked Mary what she was doing – just to change the subject. She had nothing much to say of herself apart from the fact that she'd got a job as a secretary at Crosby Doors in Farnham *"There's a really weird man there—Simon Prink—he keeps an onion in his pocket and he's always sniffing his hand."*

"His hand eh . . . must be his simian crease." [14] I offered by way of a jest.

Mary smiled—unsure as to what I meant—and continued *"We complained about it because we didn't know what he was doing at first . . . but his wife—who works in sales—told us it was an onion and he liked the smell of them—and that's why he always keeps one in his pocket."*

That had me almost weeping with laughter and Mary seemed pleased that she'd made a contribution to the conversation. *"That—is the weirdest story I've heard in a long time."*

"He does other weird things too" Mary continued – spurred on by her success *"He's always saying peculiar things that no one understands. Like this Summer, a wasp flew into the office – and he said 'Wasps are harmless – you just have to grab them by the sack.' It's so funny."*

"So . . . what did he mean by that?"

"No idea!" Mary laughed *"Then . . . d'you remember Oswald Osterley from school?"*

---

14 The simian crease is the single transverse crease which extends across the palm of the hand, created by the union of the two typical palm creases found in humans. A single crease in humans is sometimes symptomatic of genetic abnormality.

"*Yeah . . . fellow with the high-pitched voice? Father was a milkman?*"

"*That's the one. Anyway . . . now—whenever Simon's got difficulties with anything like the photocopy machine—Oswald calls out 'Grab it by the sack Simon!' It's a lot of laughs working there.*"

"*Right . . .*" I replied "*There's a lot of things in life that Simon needs to grab by the sack, as far as I can see.*"

Mary wasn't sure what to make of my last statement. I'd just intended to be amusing – but my sense of humour was a little to one side of Mary.

"*So . . . who is Mike Cooper – and how d'you know him?*" she asked.

"*Can't say that I—know—him exactly. I've met him twice and he's been kind enough to chat with me.*"

"*You looked as if you were friends.*"

"*No . . .*" I shook my head "*Not that I wouldn't like to be – but he's in another league from me.*"

"*I thought you said that no one was special off stage?*"

"*I did – and it's true. I really appreciate it, that Mike Cooper had the time to talk to me. I mean – when you're performing it's just not possible to talk to—everyone—who wants to talk to you. It wouldn't be realistic.*"

"*Yeah . . . I see that . . . I suppose. So why's he in another league then?*"

"*Well he's about ten years older than I am so he's had a much longer run at it – and he's a really fine guitarist whereas . . . I'm . . . ragged and rowdy. I've got a long way to go*"

I paused "*Y'see . . . Mike Cooper started as a singer and harp player—
like me—but then he was in The Blues Committee, with Paul Manning
and some others who played with some of the amazing American Blues
players like John Lee Hooker, Jimmy Reed, Son House, Mississippi Fred
McDowell, Bukka White, and Howling Wolf. He's played with Alexis
Korner's band Blues Incorporated too. That's a lot of experience – and I've
got nothing like that at all.*"

"*What about Savage Cabbage?*" Mary enquired.

"*Yes . . . that—would—count for a great deal—if—we were all still
together. We had no records though . . . We were just on the edge of all
that. Given another year I'm certain we would have swung something –
but . . .* Sailor V [15] *. . . So—as I said—we're in different leagues. And
that's not to mention the fact that he's played alongside Jo Ann Kelly,
Dave Kelly, Ian A. Anderson, and Tony McPhee . . .* " Pause " *. . . well
. . . I suppose Savage Cabbage played alongside Tony McPhee and the
Groundhogs . . . and, Rory Gallagher and Taste.*"

"*Sorry – but I haven't heard of any of those people.*"

"*They'd say the same about me.*"

"*That's a shame*" Mary offered "*It seems like this fame thing is really
quite a problem if you play music.*"

"*Yes . . . the 'fame machine' always sets out to control public taste so it can
be guaranteed to make a profit. Record companies and managers can be
ruthless and greedy . . .* " Pause " *. . . they're responsible for the fashions
in music – that force musicians to produce more of whatever style's popular.
Take electric Blues . . . that's no longer as popular as it was. At one time
the companies would record—anyone—who played Blues – just because
they'd tagged it as the hot selling music of the moment. Now it's changing
and the public are being—told—to buy something else.*"

---

15 C'est la vie

"It's a sad business" I concluded *"and the more I hear about it . . . the less I like it."*

"D'you have to stay in it then?"

"No . . . " Pause *" . . . I don't . . . "* Pause *"When I really think about it . . . it seems preferable to be low key and take charge of my own life. But y'know – I'm not really 'in it' anyway; I'm only on the edge of it. Sometimes it looks as if I'm about to be 'in it' and it starts getting really exciting – and then . . . the whole thing falls through."*

I'd talked for a while and gradually noticed that Mary was not exactly fascinated by the topic – so I asked her more about her life since she left school. She'd seemed very glad to see me – but that gladness evaporated by the time I'd expounded my ideas on music. Shortly after I returned to the table with further drinks I started feeling that our association was too bland to develop. It's not that I found *her* bland – it was more a question of experiencing our exchange as if we were talking through air that was full of milk or talcum powder. I couldn't fathom it. It wasn't that she wasn't friendly – she was. It was not that our conversation dried up—it was fine once I stopped theorising about music—but it felt as if she'd decided to have an evening with an old school friend who turned out to be a dangerous desperado brimming with perilous persuasions. I was also probably too weird – and talked too much about too many overlapping subjects. That was sometimes a problem. Weirdoes were fine for a fling – but not for the long term. The girls at Farnham Grammar went through a phase of having a 'pet freak'. I'd been a 'pet freak' but decided to retire from the position. Not that it was unpleasant – it was just emotionally nonsensical.

You say you've seen seven wonders and your bird is green / But you can't see me, you can't see me.

Lennon/McCartney—Beatles—And Your Bird Can Sing—Revolver—1966

I'd been some-kind-of 'toy boy' at the age of 14 with Anelie. Having been an amorous amanuensis to a 22 year old Swiss au pair girl had made a lot of sense – but being a pet freak was somewhat vapid. I think the Grammar School girl idea was that having a short relationship with a weirdo was an interesting life experience. I was not entirely happy with the idea of a relationship that was defined as short term from the outset.

Some folk rip and roar, some folk b'lieve in signs, / But if you want me, you got to take your time / Because I'm built for comfort, I ain't built for speed / But I got everything all the good girls need.
Willie Dixon/Howling Wolf—Built for Comfort—1969

Somehow Mary and I never met again. I called once but she was out. She never got back to me and time slipped sideways. There was still no telephone at home and so—barring letters or personal calls—I was inaccessible. Unless I was right there—as it were—I was on another planet.

Everyone was on the wing. You had to be—right there—or you were nowhere at all. Disconnection and discontinuity seemed normal. No one questioned anyone's disappearance or reappearance any more than dance partners would in a Pavane. The only difference was that the Pavane we danced had no end. There was no rhyme or reason to the song of our lives – and often, the songs didn't even scan. A person could lose contact with friends for no accountable reason, and years later a liaison would simply flitter in the margins of memory – a mirage and a sweet little mystery.

The time is flying fast and I don't care, to spend another night alone, / I want to see you but I don't know where, 'til then I'm walking on my own.
John Martyn—Sweet Little Mystery—Grace and Danger—1980

6

september 1970

john martyn

Some of us live like princes, some of us live like queens / Most of us live just like me — and we don't know what it means / To take our place in one world . . . / If you ain't got two words to say then I can't talk to you / No use crying, there's been no crime, I say it's just the way the wind blows / Just the name of the game, the way of the world
John Martyn—One World—One World—1977

Newquay is on the North Coast of Cornwall. It's not idyllic. It's not a lot of things. In the Summer of '70 it was a mainstream middle-management mediocre mercantile paradise. A holiday makers' town littered with smallish hotels and a few larger versions of the same. Then, there were the ticky-tacky giftie-shoppies, ice-cream parlours, and surfboard emporia that straddled several miles of coast. It was about as Cornish as the average ball bearing. Not the kind of place that would have attracted me. I'd have opted for the Lizard Peninsula — but *that* would have been a grave error at *that* precise point in time. It turned out that I was exactly where I should have been.

It was the family holiday. *Yet another way* of distancing myself from the deaths of Ron and Steve — and, from the terminal loss of Lindie Dale. Her brilliant green eyes *still* haunted my dreams.

I kept having to remind myself it was reasonable to feel sad
about my losses. Michæl and Sandra Blenkinsopp had told me
that a year was the 'standard minimum period' for grieving – and
that, even though I *should* try to enjoy myself, I shouldn't stifle
my emotions. I *should* talk to friends. Like whom? The friends
to whom I would have talked were ashes blowing in the wind.
Never mentioned it to my brother Græham because – well . . .
Græham had his own concerns. He *would* have listened – but
what would I have said? Who'd want to hear *that* goddamn tape
loop? *Tired of weeping, tired of groaning, tired of moaning for you.*[1]
Never mentioned it to my parents – because, well you just didn't
do that kind of thing at that time. I think my mother would
definitely have listened. She would have been kindness
personified – but I felt I had to be adult about it.

Grief was one thing – but being a lovelorn poet beyond the
school gates was *too* docile for words. Recognising the idiocy of
my self-imposed exile from the wider parameters of vibrancy I
suddenly found myself more spacious – and able to look around
me. I think that Steve, Ron—and even Jack—had cocooned me
somehow – or that I'd allowed that to happen. In all fairness
they were always cajoling me to move on – but as long as they
were around, I was able to pin secret hopes on Lindie. At the
time there was no sense in which I was dealing the cards, I was
just perusing the hand I'd been dealt. There were no hearts.
It was all spades – so life was going to look like Parchman Farm
for a while. There were no diamonds – but at least there were
no clubs, so the bastinado was not evidently poised to bludgeon
me into pork pâté.

---

1 Skip James—I'm So Glad—1932—Cream—Fresh Cream—1968

I thought it jolly decent of my parents to offer to take me on holiday – especially as I'd look *discreditable* to them in the hotel. I was pretty much a free individual by then – and lived more-or-less my own life. My mother and father were both keen for me to come – so I accepted graciously.

I took my new 12 string EKO with me. I decided I'd better sit on the beach every day and play 'til my fingers bled. I'd only had a short sojourn with Jasper Stanwell. He'd moved me on technically – but I still had a long way to go. I needed to get to grips with guitar chord-fingerings if I was ever to perform professionally. I'd been very well received at the pub gigs and particularly at the Farnham Folk and Blues Festival – but my repertoire wasn't extensive and it was still mainly played on the DEBIL with occasional harp numbers.

I hate to see evening sun go down. | 'cause it makes me think, I'm on my last go-round. Memphis Minnie—I Hate to See the Sun Go Down—1938

Græham was glad I'd decided to come on holiday and I was looking forward to spending some time with him. Græham was looking promising—his interests in music were developing—and he'd taken to asking me questions about life. He had a keen philosophical interest – although he wasn't artistic in any gargantuan sense. We'd have some fine conversations on holiday.

It was extremely good to have a brother at this point in time. We got along famously in Newquay – swimming and playing guitar on the beach. Græham had taken up guitar and was practising some rudimentaries – but I noticed fairly quickly that he had more natural aptitude than I had with chord fingering.

If he'd kept at it . . . in a year or two . . . we could have been a duo. He was working on 'Streets of London'[2] and seemed to be picking it up quite quickly. *"So—Græham—y'know . . . you can either play it like Ralph McTell—or—you could do—this—to it."*

Græham stared at me slightly bewildered. *"What—are—you doing there? With your plectrum I mean? What's the pattern . . . I can't really follow it at all . . . "*

Yes . . . what *was* the pattern? I went through a series of *" . . . up —up—up—down / down—up—down—up / down—down—down— up—down . . . "* before I realised that the rhythm kept changing all the time. *"Well Græham . . . it seems that the whole verse has a phrase-by-phrase rhythm . . . Mmmm . . . it seems to repeat it in each verse . . . well . . . almost . . . "*

"So there's no repeating pattern . . . ?"

"No . . . it seems to be about the stresses of the words . . . I'm also syncopating the thing so that it has more of a Blues sound to it."

"So . . . you're saying that you've only just worked out that you didn't know what you were doing?"

"Yeah . . . " I laughed *" . . . seems like it."*

"But how come you learned to play that way . . . when you didn't know what it was?"

That was an interesting question. *"Y'know . . . I just let my hand move and it happens. I s'pose my strumming must have got more complex since I first started . . . and now – this is what it's like. I found that I just don't like anything that drones on with equal note values and rigid structures. I like to change time signatures in a song."*

---

2 Ralph McTell—Streets of London—Spiral Staircase—1969

Græham laughed. *"Right . . . well . . . for the time being, I think I'll stick with the regular rhythm or I'll just get totally lost."*

"Yeah . . . that's probably a good idea . . . " I replied *" . . . 'til you can let rip with it."* I went off to take a plunge in the sea. I came back having cooled off and set to work on barré chord practice. I had no intention of performing in Newquay – so I'd left the DEBIL at home. If I'd had it with me Græham and I could have played together. I would have liked to have shown him some Blues.

As these things happen however, Græham pointed out that there was a Folk and Blues club in Newquay. It operated out of a church hall – and there was a performance on Saturday night. It was to be the last night of the holiday. I couldn't resist. I was a fish to the hook. I rang the number on the poster and asked about possible spots. I was told that the organiser was meeting someone at the church hall at lunchtime that day – and that if I showed up I could ask about it. I did just that.

Calling out rhymes in the lines that I knew all by heart / Calling the deal on the feeling that's falling apart / Waves crashing through – I can't hear myself shout / And it's a long way back to where I was – before I started out. Larkin/Bruce/Schubert—Savage Cabbage—Before I Started Out—Savoy Green—1970

I cased my guitar and walked up to the church hall. I sat down on a wall outside the venerable Victorian edifice looking out over the sea with my guitar case placed so as to give a good view of the name stencilled in distressed oxide-green: SAVAGE CABBAGE. I'd not sat there long before a friendly Glaswegian walked up and sat down on the wall with me.

We introduced ourselves. *"Frank Schubert"* I grinned, extending my hand.

He took it. "*John Martyn.*" The name meant nothing to me – but it was quickly apparent to me that he was a musician. Well, so was I – or so I had been when I had a band to back my vocals. '*A vocalist without a band—unless already famous—has as much chance of picking up a band as the Hunchback of Notre Dame has of getting a date.*' That's what I used to say from the Summer of '70 to the Summer of '72. We fell to talking. He noticed my guitar case—as intended—or rather, as it was intended for the organiser. "*Savage Cabbage eh – like the name. Thæt your band æs it?*"

"*Was . . .*" I said with a poor attempt at a grin "*Used to be my band . . . I was the vocalist.*" I told him about Steve, Ron and Jack. I didn't hold back in terms of what we had been or what we might have been. "*Played harp and rhythm bass too.*"

"*Rhythm bass—hey—thæt's bloudy intriguing æf I may say. S'what mækes a bass a rhythm bass?*"

"*Playing alongside a lead bass.*"

"*Ha! I—like—æt. Æt's fouking in—væn—tive. Næver hæerd-a-thæt before*" John Martyn commented "*Væry interesting. D'd-nay sound murky dæd æt?*"

"*No. That was a concern that Ron—the lead player—had at first . . . but we worked it out so that the two basses didn't really overlap.*" I went through the tuning arrangements and talked about how Steve had played slide on his 6 string Hagstrom. We talked a lot about bass and he talked of a friend called Danny Thompson who played double bass. I talked about the other instruments I played. Then I had to explain the DEBIL.

"*Yeah . . . næcæssity's the mother of fouking invæntion*" he laughed. "*I'd læke to sæ that thæng – it sounds a riot. You got it in yer case?*"

"*No—unfortunately not—that's the* Eko. *I wasn't expecting to perform y'see – I'm just here taking a break before Art School – and turned up on the off chance of a spot. I like to keep my hand in with performing whenever I can.*"

"*Ræet—goud louck t'yer . . . So whære did Savage Cabbage play thæn?*"

"*We played Eel Pie Island, Colonel Barefoot's Rock Garden three times. We'd been in contact with the Marquee Club and Kooks Kleek before we hit Death Row . . . we'd been all set to move out into wider audiences. Our gigs at Eel Pie Island were well received and our two bass line-up was starting to cause interest.*"

"*Yeah . . . I bæt—I just bæt.*"

"*Yeah 'cause Jack Bruce had raised a lot of peoples' expectations in terms of bass – and we were hoping not to disappoint those expectations.*"

"*Jack Bruce eh . . . hard act tæ follow.*"

"*Yes . . . but Steve Bruce was definitely in that league. I'd say he'd have been as good as Jack Bruce – if he'd had time to develop . . . but – his time ran out . . .*" Pause "*With Savage Cabbage—of course—he had me laying down the simple bass line – so the two of us were kind of comparable with Jack Bruce I suppose . . . well . . . on a good day . . . with a prevailing wind.*"

"*Wæth a prevæling wind hey . . .*" he laughed "*From which diræction?*"

"*From Ron. He was the prevailing wind from—all—directions . . . stupendous. No other word for it. He could play anything—anything at all—never heard his equal, with—any—Blues guitarist.*"

"*Hæ'd soume yeærs of expærience thæn . . .*"

"Yes and no. He was only 17 when he died – but he'd been playing piano since he was three and guitar since he was five. He was classically trained you see. He knew all these Jazz scales and weirdo Church Scales. He could play Bach on his bass – either straight or he could throw changes – y'know, make it sound like Blues or Jazz. He was a prodigy, I suppose. I saw him as being a little like Mozart or something. I was just lucky he was my friend and lucky that he settled on Blues as his major passion. Both he and Steve were going to Music College – and we were going to come out all guns blazing after they'd finished . . . and I was out of Art School."

John Martyn issued a silent expletive and shook his head *"I'm sorry—ræelly munn—tragic waste . . . "*

We sat in silence for a few moments – almost as people do at 11:00 every year for Armistice Day and then John Martyn asked *"Tell me aboout Eel Pie Island then. Hærd of it – but næver been thære."*

"It's kind of magical. It's got some history . . . There's been a pub on the Island since 1750 – and Charles Dickens took his tipple there."

"Ræally!? Hæ must hæve put back a few to write souma those weird tales of hæs."

"See what you mean" I laughed *"He summoned up some pretty strange characters. He might've danced there too 'cause the Grand Eel Pie Hotel had a sprung dance floor"* Pause *"Anyhow . . . in the '50s Arthur Chisnall launched a Trad Jazz night there. And in the '60s Mick Jagger played there when the Stones were being formed. That's when Eel Pie Island gained a reputation. Then came the Yardbirds, John Mayall, and the Who."*

"Quite a hive" John Martyn laughed.

"Yeah – there are two queen bees too!" I cackled glad to have an opportunity to crack a joke *"There are two old ladies who take a penny from everyone who crosses the bridge and say 'Thank you ducks.' They're a riot."*

"*Hilærious! Free-lance fouking tax offæcials. Last highway rorbbers æn Brætain perhaps.*"

"*Yeah – and everyone pays'em out of respect for their calling*" I laughed "*So . . . anyway . . . in '67 the hotel was closed by the police*" Pause "*But then some people made a squat out of it and opened it up again as Colonel Barefoot's Rock Garden.*[3] *It's a great venue. We liked it there – even though you had to be careful about getting paid properly.*"

"*Aye thæt happens . . . there's some bastards in this business I'll tell yer. S'who played there?*"

"*Rory Gallagher and Taste played there . . . good band—play some fine Blues—tempo's a little too fast for me – but that's just my take on it. Then there was Tony McPhee and the Groundhogs, Edgar Broughton Blues Band, and . . .*" I grinned "*. . . Savage Cabbage.*"

"*Aye—cracking name—cracking name. Would have liked tæ have hærd yer.*"

"*Yeah . . . I've always liked the idea of musicians getting to know each other and collaborating.*"

"*Did yer ever do thæt?*"

"*No it was all over before we really got started. We were on with Taste one time – and there's a story about that . . . not exactly collaboration but— anyway—before the concert Ron was on stage seeing to the amps when Rory Gallagher saw him there with his* TELECASTER *– and decided he'd size him up. They had one of those guitar duels that Rory Gallagher likes to have with his own band members – and they shook the place.*"

John Martyn grinned "*Who won?*"

---

3 In 1971 a demolition order was issued – and shortly after it burned down in mysterious circumstances.

"*No acknowledged winner . . .* " I replied with a shake of my head "*although . . . I wasn't in*—much—*doubt about it. They both laughed a lot copying each other's riffs – and . . . they just got faster and faster 'til they called it quits.*"

Ron told us afterwards that Rory Gallagher had made a few shortcuts in copying his riffs but that Rory Gallagher was definitively an excellent musician. I said nothing of this to John Martyn – it didn't feel right to be bragging about Ron. I left it there for what it was. "*Then . . . we were on with Tony McPhee and the Groundhogs. They're a great band – and I'm hoping they're going to keep Blues alive.*"

John Martyn was interested in where we'd played and so I gave a list of venues – the Art Schools, and the University circuits.

"*Were yer thinking of albums with Savage Cabbage?*" John Martyn asked.

"*Well . . . we were thinking . . . sure . . .* " Pause "*I've written twenty or so songs and we were going to use those on one half of the an album with our Blues numbers on the other.*"

"*If y'can write lyrics—munn—yer more-or-less made . . . if they're—gooud —lyrics thæt æs.*"

"*Well . . . they're—my—lyrics . . . and the band members liked them. I still feel they're too much like poetry and not enough like lyrics.*"

"*Thæt's nay prorblem munn!*" he grinned wildly "*Næver hæld Dylan back dæd it?*"

"*I don't think I'd be competing with him*" . . . I laughed " *. . . apart from the number of verses that is. I write a—long—song.*"

"Gooud fer you munn—but I think yer wrorng—Dylan bloudy needs people compæting wæth him. He's næ the only song writer on the bloudy planet – he's næ God y'know. Maybe you can give him a run for hæs fouking money!"

"Give Dylan a run for his money!?" I almost squawked.

"Sure – he's næ more than a munn fer all thæt."

"Aye" I quoted Robert Burns [4] because I loved the piece and recognised it in John Martyn's comment.

"What though on hamely fare we dine, / Wear hoddin grey, an' a' that; / Gi'e fools their silks, and knaves their wine; / A munn's a munn for a' that: / For a' that, and a' that, / Their tinsel show, an' a' that; / The honest munn, tho' e'er sæ poor, / Is king o' mæn for a' that."

John Martyn laughed loudly at that *"The accent is næ s'good fer Rabbie Burns – but ye know yer poet sure enough. So . . . Dylan may be brilliant – but there's næ ræson y'cannay be brilliant too – he's næ more than a munn fer all thæt."*

What a thought . . . but, who—*was*—this man? This was no late adolescent twaddle – this man was clearly giving it straight from the hip. He was speaking of Bob Dylan as another performer. I started to get an eerie feeling that I was way out of my depth – but our conversation was extremely lively and peppered with laughter, so I never felt intimidated.

"D'yer have æny tapes?"

"Yeah . . . we had tapes, plenty of tapes—and I'd been hoping to send them to a record company . . . but . . . without a band . . . "

---

4 Robert Burns [1759 – 1796] known as: Scotland's favourite son; the Ploughman Poet; Robden of Solway Firth; the Bard of Ayrshire; or simply, the Bard. Robert Burns—regarded as the national poet of Scotland—was also a lyricist.

"*Y'really—should—y'know.*"

"*Well . . . Ron's parents have them . . . and . . . that makes it a little tricky for me . . . it doesn't seem right to ask for them so soon after his death.*"

"*Fouking gæt'em munn! Go gæt'em afore they throw'em oout! Y'næver c'n tæll.*"

"*Really?*"

"*Yeah munn! Bloudy sure! Y'næver know – could be yer passport to fame and all the—good—stouff. Yer can't just kiss yer past goodbye like thæt. That's stouff's your's now m'friend. Take æt and do soumat wæth æt. Seriously munn, I'm telling yer. Do æt f'yer friends! Y'owe æt t'thære mæmory æf nouthing ælse.*"

John Martyn was obviously touched by the death of Steve and Ron. He sympathised with me and showed a surprisingly deep concern for my well being. He pivoted in my perception between being almost my age [5] to being 40 and fatherly. He was warm and natural – and struck me as a thoroughly kind and genuine person. He didn't have an axe to grind in relation to anything I said – and didn't put on the superior air that far lesser musicians sometimes gave themselves. He didn't press me with too many questions once I'd told him what happened to Ron and Steve – and seemed more concerned about what I was going to do with my future. "*Y'know, us people—us musicians—we need tæ stick together and support each other*" Pause "*Y'never know . . .*" he laughed "*. . . I might need y'hælp one day.*"

---

5 John Martin was born in 1948 and the author was born in 1952.

"And—although I'm sure you'll never need it—I'd be happy to give it. The only thing I have at the moment, apart from a few pub gigs, is an—in —on the Farnham Folk and Blues Festival. They seemed to like me there —want me back next year—the organiser enjoyed the lunatic stuff I say to the audience."

John Martyn grinned and nodded and I got the impression that he wouldn't be needing the contact I'd mentioned. Then the organiser—Andy Politter—suddenly appeared from the side of the church hall and our conversation came to an abrupt close. The organiser obviously thought nothing of interrupting a conversation by walking right into it. He had that ganzer macher [6] look about him. John Martyn nodded to indicate that he had to break off our conversation. He got up and chatted with the organiser. I tried to sit there in a nonchalant manner – looking out to sea as if I were not too concerned. When there appeared to be a break in the proceedings I piped up *"I'm . . . just passing through. I phoned earlier . . . They said I should meet you here – on the off chance of a spot y'know."*

"Who are you?" he asked.

Without missing a beat John Martyn replied *"Thæs æs—*Frank Schubert*—y'll have hærd of Savage Cabbage n'doubt—nice—*nice*— elæctric Blues band—but now hæ plays solo – Delta Blues y'know."*

And so there I was lined up for a spot. I had the eerie feeling that John Martyn was aware that I was more-or-less *Mister Nowhere Man.* [7] He was extending a helping hand to me – for no reason at all other than human goodness.

---

6 Yiddish: Mister Been-there'n'done-that.
7 Lennon/McCartney—Beatles—Nowhere Man—Rubber Soul—1975

I'd never really met anyone like this before in the field of professional music. John Martyn was a professional performer who saw me at the bottom of the ladder as a person to be helped rather than a person to be avoided for fear of being tainted by association. He evidently wanted to include me in his world when he said *"We're all in this together."* I'd spoken with a few musicians before and although one or two of them such as Mike Cooper had been kindly and open – no one had ever encouraged me *as much*, or seemed as disinterested in comparative status.

Maybe I wasn't doomed after all? Maybe I'd be able to form a band. Maybe I'd get to know John Martyn. I'd never heard his name before and had no sense of where to place him in the order of things. He said nothing to glamorise himself – but he had a presence and composure that was impressive.

Singing the notes of the ghosts in your tin violin / Singing the air everywhere in the shades of your skin / Rocks tumbling down and the mountain's been ploughed / And it's a long way back to where I was – before I started out.

Larkin/Bruce/Schubert—Savage Cabbage—Before I Started Out—Savoy Green—1970

"So, Frank . . . " queried Andy Politer *" . . . Schubert . . . ?"*

"Yes, Schubert – Frank Schubert."

"OK—fair enough, each-to-his-own—you'll be on first then, before our local Blues band . . . You'll be the combined warm-up for John Martyn. Three numbers suit you?"

"Suits me fine."

"Ten quid suit too?" he said with a slight sneer.

"Yeah . . . that'll work too—I enjoy playing—and I wasn't expecting a gig down here." That was intended to suggest that I usually played for more – but he didn't seem to pick up the message. He was hardly listening. I bid them adieu. John Martyn was to have lunch with the organiser. There was no sign of being included— for which I was grateful—so I strolled off in as little hurry as I could manage.

I suddenly realised that the **G** harp I'd thrown in my bag was blown.[8] I'd tried to play it on the beach and realised that one note was dead and another was on the way out. I had no rack[9] even if I *had* a harp. I rushed to the local music shop to buy a couple of harps – but the shop had closed at lunch time and wouldn't open again before Monday. What a grotesque situation . . . just me and the Eko. I practised for as much of the rest of the day as would not rip the calluses off my fingers.

I turned up early that night just to get the lay of the land. John Martyn was there ahead of me. He was sitting round the back behind the stage with his feet up on some old crates. He motioned me to sit down with him and pushed a chair over on which I could park myself. We sat together talking 'til I was due on stage. He had a two litre bottle of Italian red wine and was genteel in the extreme in his generosity.

"Apart from bass . . . " I said in answer to his question about my proposed set *" . . . I mainly play lap-slide – so this is going to be a little . . . well. I generally play one number on the 12 string—my best number —but I've not performed the others in public yet."*

---

8 A 'blown harp' has reeds that no longer function – due mainly to the excessive bending of notes.
9 A harp rack is a device worn around the neck that suspends the harp in front of the mouth – also sometimes referred to as a cage.

"*Always a first time for everything—dunnay worry—this æsnay London.*"

"*Yeah . . .* " I sighed "*I just wish I had a little ammunition . . . there are no harps to be had in Newquay.*"

"*Yer no telling me yer a fouking angel are yer?*" he laughed – deliberately misunderstanding my reference to harps "*Næver played harp m'sælf – can't be doing with a fouking cage on m'shoulders.*"

"*No . . . I don't like using a rack either. Can't be that expressive when you can't use your hands for muting and vibrato.*"

"*Thæt's why I've næver gone in f'r æt*" Pause "*So these songs then?*" he asked – harking back to the numbers of which I was not so confident.

"*They're workable – I'm just not quite as ferocious with them as I am with 'Sitting On Top of the World' and I like to be able to rip into a song as if I owned it.*"

"*Joust grin munn! Grin at the bouggers – and take næ hostages!*"

"*Good advice*" I laughed – and we chatted on merrily on all manner of musically allied topics. Our lively conversation took my mind off the fact that I was going to have to finger my guitar chords rather than play lap-slide. I was used to being on stage – but I was not used to the absence of my cherished length of chromium bath-rail.

Andy Polliter appeared and told me in a fairly perfunctory manner "*You're on.*" I bid John Martyn goodbye and told him I was looking forward to his set. "*Remæmber Frank – take næ fouking horstages!*"

I laughed and replied "*There'll be a sea of blood by the time you hit the stage.*"

I mounted the stage and strapped on the Eko. "*Good evening—ladies and gentlemen—manta rays and moray eels—and everything else on two legs. Goooood t'be here, and—*good*—to have eaten three hammerhead shark for lunch*" No response "*Had a little scampi on the side – y'know how it is . . .* " Still no response. That had never happened before. "*Lettuce, tomatoes, and cucumber too . . .* " I grinned at them "*Alright . . . Thank you—most obliged—helps to have a little . . . quiet, for tuning*" Pause " *. . . and for calming the pipistrelle bat in my waistcoat pocket.*" I'd already tuned – so I just detuned the bass string and tuned back up again. "*So without further ado . . . this is a song—never expected that did you—once covered by Howling Wolf*" Pause "*He put a—*big*—pie dish on it . . .* "

I was horribly and oppressively confronted with the fact that no-one was amused – whatever I said. The drivel I was gushing, was just that: drivel. When people had laughed at the Farnham Folk and Blues Festival – it was because I'd gushed Mister-Blues Hyper-drive Drivel – but here I missed the mark by a thousand miles. They failed even to stare at me in incomprehension. My talk-in was merely adolescent idiocy – and I felt like an idiot. This was going to be an extremely hard crowd to please.

I sang 'Sitting on Top of the World' to a moderately happy audience—they seemed to warm up a little when I started to sing – but received me only with less-than-average applause. It hadn't been the best possible decision to play my best number first. I should have finished on a roll of thunder. What was I going to do now with two less polished pieces? I'd try my level best – but I'd have to place too much concentration on guitar technique to really pour passion into the night. I gave them my version of the Blind Willie McTell song 'Death Room Blues'.

Early one morning, death walked into my room / Lord it took away both my friends, before the 6th of June.[10]

Another lukewarm pitter-patter. *"Thank you people—the frogs are coming later, I hear—just before I croak."* Some mirth shown by a few people at that so I went for it again. *"Y'know . . . only been to Newquay once before . . ."* Pause *" . . . found I wasn't there – and went home again. Life's like that sometimes."* I made some tuning adjustments *"Fish—everywhere—I looked though. Must've been that speech I gave – y'know . . . 'I had a Bream!'*[11] *right . . ."* One or two giggles – but otherwise relative silence and background buzz of audience members talking to each other *"Alright people – next song. Blind Willie McTell: Feel like a—*broke down engine mamma, *ain't got no—*driving—*wheel."* This time I whacked it with all I had. I had no alternative but to run with John Martyn's advice: *"Remæmber Frank – take næ fouking horstages!"* The sections of difficult chord changes I sang unaccompanied – as if it was intentional. I just slapped my hand on the strings to damp them and bellowed the line *'You all been down and lonesome, you know just how a—*poor—*man feels.'*

The applause was a little improved—but it was my last offering —and the last they'd ever hear of Frank Schubert. I was history. I wished I'd known a few people in the audience or that someone—*anyone*—would have started foot stomping or hand clapping in time to what I was playing. I'd never known such a staid crowd. I wished I'd sung at least *one* unaccompanied number—I could've stomped my own foot and kick-started the audience—but somehow anxiety washed that possibility right out of my mind.

---

10 *Early one morning, death walked into my room, Oh well it took my dear mother, early one morning soon.* Blind Willie McTell—Death Room Blues—1933
11 Reference to the speech given by Martin Luther King, Jr. " . . . I have a dream."

"*Goodnight people and thank you. I'll be playing Barabinsk*[12] *Russia tomorrow night! Hell of a town! Back in the* USSR *playing with my old comrade-in-arms Rasputin—and a pantheon of perfumed parrots—more than you've ever—*smelled*—in your life before. Didn't even know you could smelt a parrot . . . unless it was a cannon.*"[13] A minor titter followed that. I didn't wait to see if there was any need for an encore. There wasn't. I came off stage at the end of my turn with the applause dying away as I did.

Then the local band came on. The Bodmin Blues Band. They got applause simply for standing there. They made gestures of enjoyment that seemed designed to say '*Yeah—yeah—yeah, we're used to this—it's pleasant—but we don't need it.*' They were obviously on first name terms with half the audience and a lot of thumbs were being hoisted in token of greeting. They were brusquely confident with their *talk in.* They spoke of the tedium of tired out Blues clichés – and how " . . . *audiences must go to sleep half the time having to listen to 'Partially-sighted Citrus Whatever' fumbling his way through 'Well I woke up this morning . . .'* "

I hadn't even *sung*—that song[14] but the comment roused a few titters nonetheless. They then informed the audience "*So yeah friends . . . Got some—*very—*authentic pieces f'you tonight!*" Applause "*Rarely heard material – like really! Yeah! We been researching*" Applause "*and . . . we're going to perform 'em . . . probably for the—*first time—*right!*" Applause "*Yeah cool . . . really . . . Here we go.*"

---

12 Barabinsk – (Russian –Барабинск). Town in Novosibirsk Oblast – in the Baraba steppe, between the Irtysh and Ob Rivers.

13 The Parrot gun was invented by Robert Parrott, a graduate from West Point. In 1836 he became the superintendent of the West Point Foundry where he built the first Parrott rifled gun in 1860.

14 Robert Johnson—Walking Blues—1936

Then they played. I was sitting in the audience at this time and feeling about as happy as anyone could imagine under the circumstances. I was going to have to change my name or something. The Bodmin Blues Band were competent.
I couldn't deny that – but they weren't inspired. That their lead and bass weren't in the same class as Ron and Steve Bruce went without saying – but they were beyond me. I had no doubt however that I was a better vocalist. In fact, I was a *far* better vocalist. I wasn't shy about that conviction. The man on stage was a tenor but his tenor lacked tenor. His tenor was weedy and plaintive. There are tenors—like Steve Marriot—who don't need the lower register to be Black – but the Bodmin chappie's Blues was little more than kvetching. *'Going down the road feeling bad / Don't wanna feel this way.'* It was a repetitive whining dirge. I thought Woodie Guthrie—whoever *he* was—needed to go back to his daytime job. I later learnt that Woodie Guthrie was a fine performer and that the band got the words wrong anyway.

The words are quite similar but Woodie Guthrie sang *'I ain't a-gonna be treated this a-way'* rather than *'Don't wanna feel this way.'* It makes all the difference. And of course Woodie Guthrie *never* sang *'Going down the road feeling bad'* as horribly repetitively as the Bodmin chappie. A couple of dozen times in one song is a little much, even for those for whom patience is a virtue The warm-up band must have sung *that* line to death.

I only found out later that song is originally a Big Bill Broonzy song – but one that I'd not heard with Mr Love. Woody Guthrie wrote some different verses to it – but it's basically the same song. I made sure I heard both Woodie Guthrie and Big Bill Broonzy singing that song – and both were so far superior to the 'Cat-flap Men'—as I called them—that it made me laugh. *They weren't no backdoor men* – and I wasn't so bad after all.

Well . . . that's how I reconciled myself to the situation, once sufficient time had elapsed. Woodie Guthrie sang: '*Your a-two-dollar shoe hurts my feet, Your two-dollar shoe hurts my feet —Lord, Lord—And I ain't a-gonna be treated this way*' and Big Bill Broonzy sang '*These two-dollar shoes is killing my feet, baby, two-dollar shoes is killing my feet, right now – I ain't gonna be treated this way.*'

After their first couple of numbers I realised that they played every number at an unvarying 4:4 tempo. They never played a slow Blues and therefore were never called upon to play any extended riffs. Each song sounded more-or-less like the last – but the audience seemed happy enough. It was good-time dancehall Blues where no one's listening too much to the vocals and no one cares too much whether there's any real musicianship. I watched the lead player and vibrato was evidently not his forté. He played practically the same riffs in each number and was horribly repetitive. Of course I was comparing him with Ron – which was entirely unfair. I turned to the bassist and realised that I could have played most of the bass lines he performed. I also noticed that he never bent a string – and that was something I'd got the hang of almost immediately. I'd been slow to learn the bass lines – but I'd got the hang of bent notes and vibrato from the get-go. They had a fellow on keyboards and I had no idea how to evaluate that – apart from feeling that the keyboards made up for whatever was lacking in the lead and bass.

Hell hath no fury like a musician scorned – so I imagine they were probably better than I describe. I sat there in the audience wishing I'd brought the DEBIL rather than the new 12 string. If I'd had the DEBIL I could have roared and snarled – and no one would've dared say a thing.

*That second rate Blues band put me down, Yeah that cheap skate Blues
band done me down right now – I ain't gonna be treated this way.*
The Author's parody—2007

That's not a line I wrote at the time – but it's a line I should
have written. It would've made me feel better about myself.
I'd made myself look significantly less than mediocre – and it
was difficult to find much humour in the situation. On with
the show.

There was an intermission after the Bodmin Blues Band. I went
to sit outside on the wall to get some air – and get away from
the crowd. I had no desire to talk with anyone because I was
too absorbed with the horror of my tepid performance. I was
thinking of not returning – but that would have been an act of
rudeness to John Martyn who had been so kind and generous to
me. It would also be horribly inconsiderate to my brother
Græham who was keen to remain to the end of the evening.
I was deeply touched John Martyn's words and his genuine
conviviality. He must have known that I was not in his league—
or anywhere remotely close—purely by the things I failed to say
with regard to albums. Savage Cabbage *had* no albums. We had
some fine tapes. They'd been made on a high-end quality
machine – but when Ron and Steve died, access to those tapes
was lost. I could never quite face contacting Ron Larkin's
parents about the tapes.

*Staunching the blood of the wounds in the waves / Staunching the sun in
it's treble clef staves / Sub sonic bass in the canyon's rebound / And it's a
long way back to where I was – before I started out.*
Larkin/Bruce/Schubert—Savage Cabbage—Before I Started Out—Savoy Green—1970

When the second half of the concert looked as if it was about to commence, I went inside and waited. John Martyn appeared and the crowd gave him a huge round of applause. They obviously knew more about him than I did. It was as if Jimi Hendrix had walked on stage!

He had a table with some effects boxes and I looked on, intrigued as he fiddled. He had an ECHOPLEX. I'd heard of *that* contraption – but I'd never seen or heard one used. He turned to the audience after he twiddled the knobs to his satisfaction *"They call me 'Buttons McGegghy'*[15] *Ha—ha! Jus' gimme me a button . . . "* he laughed the final words and I never made sense of them. He concluded his adjustments before turning to the audience and announcing *"Soume people! Ha—ha! Soume people, I hear . . . are not—s'fond—of Blues clichés!"* He shook his head in mock disbelief and then roared *"But I louve a Blues cliché more thæn life itself!"* The crowd evidently loved this and welled up into laughter, whistles, and applause. *"So . . . I'm going to start out with a—gooud—old—number—y'll—all—know . . . only—tooooo— fouking—well!"*

I could hardly believe what I'd heard. I was on the verge of tears. He'd heard the whole put down on Frank Schubert and he was coming out on my side – all guns blasting. Then he launched into the Skip James number 'I'd Rather be the Devil' as if he'd got his wish and suddenly was Beelzebub growling from the depths of the endless inferno.

---

15 'McGeeggy' – John Martyn was born 'Iain David McGeachy' but the author was unaware of this at the time of writing – so the spelling has been left as it was remembered to reflect that.

Well, I laid down last night and I was trying to take my rest, / But my mind starts a-rambling like the wild geese in the West. Nehemiah Curtis 'Skip' James—I'd Rather be the Devil—1931—John Martyn—Solid Air—1973

When the ECHOPLEX kicked in my eyes widened. They continued to widen. I'd never heard sounds like that before – and *this* from an *acoustic guitar.*

He played those effects boxes with the most fantastic subtlety and light-fingered dexterity – but with a driving power that took no hostages. He'd been black-flagging [16] it since the day he was born! I'd thought that sounds like that were only possible in studios – and here he was procuring swelling waves of tone and swirling rhythms of tone, all sea-sprayed in a jet-stream of outlandishly lyrical riffs that chased each other like cirrus clouds around the moon and through my head. [17] That was his one Blues number of the evening and it tore the house down. If the Bodmin Blues Band members were in the audience they must have felt about as good as I felt when I left the stage. The applause was furious and in the middle of it John Martyn motioned me to stand. It took me a while to understand what was happening – but after a few more insistent gestures I stood up ... staring with bewilderment that was both bedevilled and beatific.

"Song's f'm'friend there! M'friend Frank Schubert! Big hand!"

Suddenly the hall erupted with applause – applause as loud as John Martyn has received when he first took the stage.

---

16 Black-flagging was a term used in the War Between the States to describe the Confederate Irregular who carried a black flag to show that they gave no quarter and expected no quarter – i.e. they took no prisoners or hostages.
17 'Bless the Weather' wasn't released until November 1971 – but John Martyn was playing music that would appear on that album.

It took me a while to understand what was happening. Even when I did understand, it made no obvious sense. It was closer to experiencing a situation as poetry, painting, or sculpture.

"He played some fine Blues f'ya earlier—real Delta Blues—big hand now!"

The Hall erupted again. I looked around and there they were – the audience for whom I'd been a big nothing a bare three quarters of an hour earlier. Fragmentary ideas flitted through my mind *'this applause is not for me; this is for Savage Cabbage; this is for how I was with Savage Cabbage; this is for how I was at the Farnham Blues Festival; and . . . how I will be in the mysterious future.'* Then suddenly I was jerked out of my reverie by John Martyn's voice

*"Ha—ha—yer-reet! Ha—ha! Up'n'coming Bluesman!—*Frrrrrank*—Schubert!—Big hand! Big hand!"*

John Martyn's voice trailed away into a slurred Glaswegian. The audience continued to applaud as John Martyn set up for his next number. I sat down having stood there for a thousand years—or milliseconds—washed in the electric tide of eternity; aflame with the heritage of Hoo-doo; caught in the Jetstream of the entire history of Blues.